Understanding Popular Music Culture

This extensively revised new edition of *Understanding Popular Music Culture* provides an accessible and comprehensive introduction to the production, distribution, consumption and meaning of popular music and examines the difficulties and debates which surround the analysis of popular culture and popular music.

Reflecting the continued expansion of popular music studies, the changing music industry and the impact of new technologies, Roy Shuker explores key subjects which shape our experience of music, including music production, musicians and stars, musical texts, musical media, audiences, fans and subcultures and music as political activism and ideology.

This heavily revised and updated third edition includes:

- new case studies on the iPod, downloading, and copyright;
- the impact of technologies, including on-line delivery and the debates over MP3 and Napster;
- new chapters on music genres, cover songs and the album canon as well as music retail, radio and the charts;
- case studies and lyrics of artists such as Robert Johnson, The Who, Fatboy Slim and the Spice Girls;
- a comprehensive discography, suggestions for further reading, listening and viewing and a directory of useful websites.

Roy Shuker is Associate Professor in Media Studies at Victoria University of Wellington, New Zealand. His previous publications include *Understanding Popular Music* (2nd edition, 2001) and *Popular Music: The Key Concepts* (2nd edition, 2005).

Understanding Popular Music Culture

Third edition

■ **Roy Shuker**

Routledge
Taylor & Francis Group

LONDON AND NEW YORK

First published 1994
by Routledge

Second edition published 2001
by Routledge

This edition published 2008
2 Park Square, Milton Park, Abingdon,
Oxon OX14 4RN

Reprinted 2009, 2010

Simultaneously published in the USA and Canada
by Routledge
270 Madison Ave, New York, NY 10016

*Routledge is an imprint of the Taylor & Francis
Group, an informa business*

© 1994, 2001, 2008 Roy Shuker

Typeset in Goudy by
HWA Text and Data Management,
Tunbridge Wells
Printed and bound in Great Britain by
CPI Antony Rowe, Chippenham, Wiltshire

British Library Cataloguing in Publication Data
A catalogue record for this book is available from
the British Library

Library of Congress Cataloging-in-Publication Data
Shuker, Roy.
Understanding popular music culture / Roy Shuker.
– 3rd ed.
   p. cm.
Rev. ed. of: Understanding popular music. 2nd ed.
2001.
Includes bibliographical references (p.),
discography (p.) and indexes.
Popular music–History and criticism. 2. Popular
culture–History–20th century. I. Shuker, Roy.
Understanding popular music. II. Title.
ML3470.S54 2007
781.64–dc22   2007012129

ISBN10: 0–415–41905–0 (hbk)
ISBN10: 0–415–41906–9 (pbk)

ISBN13: 978–0–415–41905–5 (hbk)
ISBN13: 978–0–415–41906–2 (pbk)

Contents

CONTENTS

Preface

This study is an extensively revised edition of *Understanding Popular Music* (second edition, 2001). Reflecting the continuing proliferation of publications in popular music studies, and significant shifts in the music industry, the earlier volume has been reorganized. A number of new chapters have been added, most others recast, and new examples provided of musical texts, genres, and performers. I have paid greater attention to the role of the Internet, the influence of which has been felt across music production, dissemination and mediation, and consumption. Each chapter ends with suggestions for further reading, and, where appropriate, listening, and viewing.

The change in title is to better indicate the broader nature of the field of study. Popular music *culture* locates the musical recording in the wider social field. It refers to the ways of making, disseminating, and consuming music; the economic and technological practices associated with these processes; and the sounds, images, and discourse (thinking, debating, and writing) created by these practices.

The impetus for the first edition of this study (Shuker, 1994) arose from what I then saw as a contradiction between the prominence of popular music as a cultural form and its relative neglect in media and cultural studies. By the second edition (2001), I noted the recognition of the economic and cultural prominence of popular music, and increased academic analysis of the form, with further writing consolidating established areas of inquiry and forging new insights. The consolidation and expansion of this literature has continued apace through the past five years (see 'Further reading', at the end of the Introduction).

Such work indicates the present vitality of popular music studies and the maturation of the field. The interrelationship of ritual, pleasure, and economics in popular music continues to create audiences, to fuel individual fantasy and pleasure, and to create musical icons and cultural myths. *Understanding Popular Music Culture* offers a contribution towards mapping this soundscape.

Acknowledgements

As in the earlier editions of this book, this heavily revised version has relied extensively on the work of many critics and 'colleagues at a distance', who have written extensively on cultural studies and popular music. Many of the 'best' ideas here are theirs; the errors of fact and argument – the bum notes – remain mine. To list them risks leaving out someone: a check of my text and references provides a roll call of sorts; my thanks to you all. I have benefited enormously from my membership of IASPM – the International Association for the Study of Popular Music– through its conferences, publications, e-mail discussions, and, above all, from the friendships and insights its members have provided me with.

For the provision of books and articles, material in press and unpublished papers, and recordings, my thanks to Keith Beattie, Shane Homan, Geoff Lealand, Michael Pickering, and Geoff Stahl. For helpful administrative and computer support: Jenny Finlay and Gregor Cameron. Thanks also to my students in various media studies and popular culture courses over recent years, who provided a critical initial sounding board for much of the material, and contributed many of the ideas and resources drawn on here; in particular, current graduate students Katherine C'Ailceta, Louise Bartle, Jasmyne Chung, Brannavan Gnanalingham, Nick Holm, Brooke Rae, and Giesela Visser. Thanks also to Jasmyne Chung for drawing the video of Nelly ('Tip Drill') to my attention, and contributing to the analysis of that section.

A particular debt of gratitude is due to Emma, my daughter and keen research assistant; my son Cameron, for greatly improving my acquaintance with digital music; and to Mary Jane, for undertaking the bibliography, and keeping me at the writing. For

ACKNOWLEDGEMENTS

their input and patience, my thanks to Routledge's Natalie Foster, Aileen Storry, and Charlotte Wood.

The following are reproduced with kind permission. While every effort has been made to trace copyright holders and obtain permission, this has not been possible in all cases. In the event of a copyright query, please contact the publishers. Any omissions brought to our attention will be remedied in future editions.

Black Eyes, Blue Tears
Words and music by Shania Twain and R.J. Lange
© 1997 Songs Of PolyGram International Incorporated, USA/Out Of Pocket Productions Limited, USA/Loon Echo Incorporated
Zomba Music Publishers Limited
Used by permission of Music Sales Limited. All Rights Reserved. International Copyright Secured

Born in the USA
Words and music by Bruce Springsteen
© 1984 Bruce Springsteen (ASCAP)
Used be permission of Music Sales Limited. International Copyright Secured. All Rights Reserved

Hell Hound On My Trail
Words and music by Robert Johnson
© (1978), 1990, 1991 MPCA King Of Spades (SESAC) and Claud L. Johnson
Administered by Music & Media International, Inc. International Copyright Secured. All Rights Reserved.

Love In Vain Blues
Words and music by Robert Johnson
© (1978), 1990, 1991 MPCA King Of Spades (SESAC) and Claud L. Johnson
Administered by Music & Media International, Inc. International Copyright Secured. All Rights Reserved

My Generation
Words and music by Peter Townshend
© 1965 (Renewed) Fabulous Music Ltd, London, England
TRO – Devon Music, Inc., New York, controls all publication rights for the USA and Canada.
Used by permission
© Fabulous Music Ltd Of Suite 2.07, Plaza 535 Kings Road, London SW10 0SZ

Introduction: 'What's Goin' On?'
Studying popular music culture

In July 2006, while I was working on this project, Bob Geldof visited New Zealand. The Live Aid founder and 'rock star', as the lead singer and main songwriter with Irish post-punk group the Boomtown Rats, then as a solo act, was widely reported when he described the country's foreign aid as 'shameful and pathetic'. Geldof's criticisms received prominent newspaper coverage, they were the subject of magazine cover stories, and he appeared on leading television and radio current affairs shows. He used these opportunities to explain the goals and progress of his Make Poverty History campaign, which is also supported by Bono. The surrounding public debate saw the Minister of Foreign Affairs and the Prime Minister both anxious to defend New Zealand's aid record, while welfare groups and letter writers rallied to support Geldof. To the public, Geldof is the rock star forever linked to Live Aid, who used his musical celebrity as a platform for social activism.

The episode indicates how popular music is part of the wider culture. During Geldof's visit, through the press, radio, television, and Internet, there were many further indications of such links. Reviews of Bob Dylan's new album *Modern Times* (Columbia, 2006), placed it among his best work, and alluded to his role as a key figure in the development of 'the rock canon'. The business press noted the increasing use of rappers to brand a range of consumer products; and the continued impact of digital delivery on the popular music industry. The implications for New Zealand press and radio, largely Australian owned, of changes in Australian media ownership laws to lift the limits on foreign companies owning shares in national media were widely debated. The death of Syd Barrett, Pink Floyd founder and long-time recluse, was viewed as 'cementing his place as rock's ultimate lost icon'. The final of *Rock Star Supernova*, a 'reality television' show to find a singer for a group formed by several ex-members of high profile bands, topped local ratings. The daily press included advertising and reviews for a variety of concerts and club gigs, newly released recordings, and the usual proliferation of advertisements for music retail: instruments, sound systems, including iPods, music DVDs and recordings.

This is part of the everyday discourse that surrounds popular music, and which provides a context for this study. Evident within these stories, reviews, and advertising, are notions of musical creativity and authorship, canonical texts, musical history, audiences, and music as a blend of entertainment, art, and commerce. Collectively, and alongside other such stories, they indicate the commercial and cultural significance of popular music. We are exposed to its ubiquitous global presence on a daily basis: through 'muzak' in shopping malls; on public transport and on the streets and parks though MP3 players and Walkmen; on MTV and mainstream television music shows; in film soundtracks and narratives; on the radio; through the music press; and 'live' in a variety of settings, from street buskers to clubs and stadium concerts. In cultural terms, popular music is of enormous importance in daily life, and for some is central to their social identities. In economic terms the products of the music industry make it a leading cultural industry, with income including not just the sales of recorded music, but also copyright revenue, tour profits, merchandising, sales of the music press, musical instruments, sound systems, and sheet music.

POPULAR MUSIC STUDIES

An 'archaeology' of popular music studies reveals a number of contributing approaches, which are historically situated and frequently in tension with each other. At issue have been questions of the nature and status of the musical text, and how we relate to and 'know' music. Engaging with these means addressing the relationship between the musical text, its authorship, production, and mediation, the nature of the listening experience and the social conditions under which these occur. The bulk of the associated writing has come out of musicology, sociology, and cultural and media studies, often exhibiting a tension around just where to primarily situate analysis. Depending on their theoretical and methodological allegiances, contributors variously privilege the musical text, its production and mediation, or its consumption. Generally speaking, two broad approaches (musicology and sociology), though still distinct, have increasingly converged. While popular musicology remains primarily an aesthetic discourse, focused on the music, it includes reference to the interaction of social factors; conversely, sociologically grounded studies, while emphasizing production and consumption, situate these processes in relation to the nature and authorship of specific musical texts and genres. (See the Notes for key contributions to this literature.)

While I refer to some basic aspects of musical analysis, and have included the analysis of song lyrics in considering recordings as texts, this is not a musicological study; I do not analyze music scores. My approach is situated rather in the general field of cultural and media studies, recognizing that the analysis of institutions, texts, discourses, readings, and audiences are best understood in their social, economic, and political context. I use the term 'popular music culture' to indicate this, and to signal my intention to integrate a range of topics into this introductory survey. Popular music culture refers to the ways of making, disseminating, and consuming music; the economic and technological practices associated with these processes; and the recordings, sounds, and images, and discourse (thinking, debating, and writing) created by these practices.

With some notable exceptions, academic analysis of popular music and its associated culture was initially slow to develop. During the 1970s and 1980s, even the increasingly popular field of media studies tended to concentrate its attention on the visual media, particularly television, and neglected popular music. In the 1990s, however, there was a veritable flood of material, as well as a marked increase in the number of courses either directly focusing on popular music, or on it as an aspect of popular culture within media and cultural studies. The new prominence of the field reflected the recognition of popular music as a global cultural phenomenon, associated with a multi-billion dollar industry, and a many faceted pop-youth culture reaching out into every aspect of style.

This emerging literary explosion took a number of forms and approached the topic from a range of perspectives. These included political economy, cultural studies, feminist studies, and media studies, this last with its own rich theoretical mix of film theory, semiotics, psychoanalysis, feminism, and social theory. As this list suggests, popular music studies is not a discipline, in the coherent sense that such a term implies, but is rather a field of study.

An indication of the scope of the field is given in volume one of the *Continuum Encyclopedia of Popular Music* (Shepherd *et al.*, 2003) which devotes a hundred pages to thirty entries on the approaches to it.

SETTING AGENDAS

As Horner and Swiss (1999: 7) observe, the different meanings given terms common to the vocabulary of popular music studies, including the very terms 'popular' and 'music', help shape the music and our experience of it. The meaning and utility of terms such as 'popular' and 'mass', especially in relation to 'culture' and 'media', are the subject of considerable discussion and debate. Similarly, 'popular music' and associated terms such as 'rock', 'rock 'n' roll', and 'pop', are used by musicians, fans, and academic analysts in a confusing variety of ways (see, for example, the discussion

3

of 'rock and roll' in Dettmar, 2006). It needs to be remembered that it is difficult to define phenomena which are social practices as well as economic products, and which are not static but constantly evolving. Indeed, precise definitions can be constraining; they should be regarded as frameworks for exploration and elaboration, rather than factual declarations to be defended. That aside, let me try to at least pin down the general nature of some of the concepts that are central to the analysis of popular music culture.

Popular media culture

'Popular' is a contested term. For some it means simply appealing to the people, whereas for others it means something much more grounded in or 'of' the people. The former usage generally refers to commercially produced forms of popular culture, while the latter is usually reserved for forms of 'folk' popular culture, associated with local community-based production and individual craftspeople. In relation to popular music, for example, this is the distinction often made between folk music, especially when acoustically based, and chart-oriented recordings, such as dance pop. Yet, as we shall see, such a clear-cut distinction has become increasingly untenable.

While popular culture is not all associated with the mass media, there is a reciprocal relationship between the two. The mass media involve large-scale production, by commercial industries, for a mass, albeit segmented, market. The term 'mass media' refers to print, aural, and visual communication on a large scale – the press, publishing, radio and television, film and video, the recording industry, telecommunications, and the Internet, to mention only the more obvious mediums of production and dissemination. Used as an adjective, 'popular' indicates that something – a person, a product, a practice, or a belief – is commonly liked or approved of by a large audience or the general public. Applied to the media, this means that particular television programmes, films, records, and books and magazines are widely consumed. Their popularity is indicated by ratings surveys, box office returns, and sales figures. To a degree, this definition of 'popularity' reifies popular cultural texts, reducing them to the status of objects to be brought and sold in the market place, and the social nature of their consumption must always be kept in mind.

That aside, this study equates the 'popular' with commercial, cultural forms of entertainment, and I regard markets as an inescapable feature of popular culture. Popularity is central to popular culture, as its various products and figures (stars, auteurs) attain general social acceptance and approval. In a sense, a circular argument holds here: the popular are mass, the mass are popular. Contemporary popular culture in the United States and Canada, the United Kingdom, and New Zealand – to mention only the national settings I am primarily concerned with in this study – forms the majority of mass media content, while the majority of popular culture is transmitted through the mass media.

Obviously, my use of the term 'culture' rejects the argument that anything popular cannot, by definition, be cultural. Although a high–low culture distinction is still very strongly evident in general public perceptions of 'culture', the traditionally claimed distinction between 'high' and 'low culture' has become blurred. High art has been increasingly commodified and commercialized, as with classical music's star system of conductors and soloists, while some forms of popular culture have become more 'respectable', receiving state funding and broader critical acceptance. Yet clear distinctions and cultural hierarchies remain widely held, not least within particular cultural forms, by those involved in their production and consumption.

My use of what is one of the most difficult words in the English language, is in a sociological rather than an aesthetic sense of culture. In an influential and widely cited discussion, Raymond Williams argues that contemporary usage of 'culture' falls into three possibilities, or some amalgam of these: 'a general process of intellectual, spiritual, and aesthetic development'; 'a particular way of life, whether of a people, period, or a group'; and 'the works and practices of intellectual and especially artistic activity' (Williams, 1983: 90). This can be seen as a useful, if overly expansive, definition. My interest here lies primarily between the second and third of these definitions; and in the relationship between them – the way particular social groups have used popular music within their lives. This is to shift the focus from the preoccupation, evident in much media/cultural studies, with the text in and of itself, to the audience. It is also to stress 'popular culture', rather than accept the reservation of the term culture for artistic pursuits associated with particular values and standards, sometimes referred to as elite or high culture – Williams' third definition. In addition to this emphasis on the audiences and consumption aspects of popular culture, I am concerned with the relationship between the creation of cultural products and the economic context of that creation, a process which involves creating or targeting audiences, and an active engagement between texts and their consumers. This is to recognize that neither texts nor their consumers exist in isolation.

In short then, the main concern of this study is with the interrelationship of context, texts, and consumption, as demonstrated by the manufacture, distribution, and consumption of popular music, primarily in its various recorded forms. But what is popular music?

Popular music

Popular music defies precise, straightforward definition. The terms 'rock' and 'pop' are frequently used to stand for 'popular music', when they are meta-genres within a broader musical soundscape. While some writers on popular music slide over the question of definition, and take a 'common sense' understanding of the term for granted, various attempts to provide a definition can be identified:

1   Definitions that place an emphasis on 'popular'. Historically, the term popular was used in relation to 'the ordinary people'. It was first linked in a published title to a certain kind of music that conformed to that criterion in William Chapple's *Popular Music of the Olden Times* published in installments from 1855. Not until the 1930s and 1940s did the term start to gain wider currency. Middleton observes that the question of 'what is popular music' is 'so riddled with complexities ... that one is tempted to follow the example of the legendary definition of folk song – all songs are folk songs, I never heard horses sing 'em – and suggest that all music is popular music: popular with someone' (1990: 3). However, the criteria for what counts as popular, and their application to specific musical styles and genres, are open to considerable debate. Classical music clearly has sufficient following to be considered popular, while some forms of popular music are quite exclusive (e.g. death metal).

2   Definitions based on the commercial nature of popular music, and embracing genres perceived as commercially oriented. Many commentators argue that it is commercialization that is the key to understanding popular music: 'When we speak of popular music we speak of music that is commercially oriented' (Burnett, 1996: 35). This approach is related to the emphasis on the popular, arguing that such appeal can be quantified through sales, charts, radio airplay, and so forth. In such definitions, certain genres are identified as 'popular music', while others are excluded (e.g. Clarke, 1990; Garofalo, 1997; and of course the same process of selection is at work in this volume). However, this approach can suffer from the same problems as those stressing popularity, since many genres have only limited appeal or have had limited commercial exposure. Moreover, popularity varies from country to country, and even from region to region within national markets. It needs to also be noted that this approach is largely concerned with *recorded* popular music, which is usually listened to in a fairly conscious and focused manner. Kassabian makes the useful point that what she terms 'ubiquitous musics' are frequently left out of such discussions: music in films, in stores, on the phone, in the office, on television, and so on. 'These are the kinds of music that no one chooses for herself or himself but that nevertheless wash our everyday lives with sound' (1999: 113). This acoustic wallpaper is the subject of Joseph Lanza's book *Elevator Music* (1995), while 'Muzak' is a corporate trademark.

3   Identification by general musical and non-musical characteristics. Tagg (1982), in an influential and much cited discussion, characterizes popular music according to (i) the nature of its distribution (usually mass); (ii) how it is stored and distributed, primarily as recorded sound rather than oral transmission or

musical notation; (iii) the existence of its own musical theory and aesthetics; and (iv) the relative anonymity of its composers. The last of these is debatable, and I would want to extend the notion of composers and its associated view of the nature of musical creativity. However, musicologists have usefully extended the third aspect of Tagg's definition, while sociologists have concentrated on the first two dimensions.

In sum, only the most general definition can be offered under the general umbrella category of 'popular music'. Essentially, it consists of a hybrid of musical traditions, styles, and influences, with the only common element being that the music is characterized by a strong rhythmical component, and generally, but not exclusively, relies on electronic amplification. Indeed, a purely musical definition is insufficient, since a central characteristic of popular music is a socio-economic one: its mass production for a mass, predominantly youth, market. At the same time, of course, it is an economic product that is invested with ideological significance by many of its consumers. At the heart of the majority of the various forms of popular music is a fundamental tension between the essential creativity of the act of 'making music' and the commercial nature of the bulk of its production and dissemination.

As this discussion suggests, as with a term like 'popular culture', it is misguided to attempt to attach too precise a meaning to what is a shifting cultural phenomenon. For convenience, and despite its own associated difficulties, I use the term 'popular music' throughout this study as shorthand for the diverse range of popular music genres produced in commodity form for a mass, predominantly youth, market, primarily Anglo-American in origin (or imitative of its forms), since the early 1950s.

ANALYSING POPULAR MUSIC CULTURE

The study of popular music culture is situated in the general field of cultural studies, which addresses the interaction between three dimensions of popular culture: lived cultures, the social being of those who consume popular cultures; the symbolic forms, or texts, that are consumed within the lived culture; and the economic institutions and technological processes which create the texts. My discussion of the interrelationship of these dimensions in relation to popular music draws primarily from critical media theory, contemporary political economy, and cultural studies. I regard popular cultural texts as dynamic not static, mediated by patterns of economic and social organization and the relationship of individuals and social groups to these patterns. This puts politics in a position of central importance, as culture is viewed as a site of conflict and struggle, of negotiations which constantly confirm and redefine the existing conditions of domination and subordination in society. The construction of meaning in popular music can be seen as embracing a number of factors: the music industry and

7

its associated technologies, those who create the music, the nature of musical texts, the constitution of audiences and their modes of consumption, and attempts to influence and regulate all of these.

It is, of course, not possible to deal with every aspect of popular music. Themes, topics and examples have been selected partly for their importance in exemplifying the diverse activities of the field of popular music, but primarily for their relevance to the general argument. The organizational logic of the text is to begin with issues of the economic and technological context, the music industry, music and technology. I move from these to the process of making music and issues of authorship, the nature of musical texts (songs, albums, music videos) and the cultural practices of their production. This leads on to a consideration of consumption, particularly the sites (scenes), social groups (fans, collectors, subcultures) and practices involved. I then turn to the manner in which popular music is a form of cultural politics, involving processes of regulation, restriction, and empowerment. This is to see meaning in popular music as the product of a somewhat circular process, operating at a number of cultural levels in the personal and social and institutional domains.

The discussion here draws together material from several national contexts and places this within a historical dimension, both aspects often absent from contemporary-oriented and nation-bound studies of popular media. A more historical and international perspective enables firmer conclusions to be made about the nature and impact of popular music, particularly given the continued growth of global multimedia conglomerates and the increasing evidence of the globalization of culture.

More fully, the scope of the book is as follows:

Chapter 1: the role of the music industry, in its drive to commodify performers and texts, and to maximize profits, is my starting point for the study of popular music. I look at the music industry as an example of the cultural industries, its increased concentration as part of these, and the revolutionary impact of digital music on musical production and distribution. An important aspect of how the music industry attempts to maintain its market dominance are its marketing practices, especially its use of stars and genres.

Chapter 2 considers the impact of technology on popular music, and the closely related issue of copyright. Technological changes in recording pose both constraints and opportunities in terms of the organization of production, and innovation in musical instrumentation has facilitated the emergence of 'new' sounds. New recording formats and modes of transmission and dissemination, most recently digital, alter the nature of musical production and consumption, and raise questions about authorship, the legal status of music as property and the operation of copyright.

Chapters 3 to 6 examine musical authorship and the 'success continuum', texts and genres.

Chapter 3 deals with the process of music making and sites of production; conceptions of the term 'musician'; and the status hierarchy accorded various categories of performer.

Chapter 4 provides a range of individual career profiles, both stars and auteurs, with brief examples of their work. These profiles illustrate the interaction of musical authorship with genres, audiences, and history.

Chapter 5 introduces the various textual forms popular music takes, including the graphic, the application of musicology to popular song, and the question of lyric analysis. The analysis of the main form of audiovisual text, the music video, is included here.

Chapter 6 looks at the nature and significance of genre, using rock and pop, and heavy metal as case studies. Song covers, and the album canon, illustrate the debates around authenticity, and the cultural and musical value of such forms and constructs.

Chapters 7 to 10 examine additional (to the sound recording companies) institutional mediators of music, primarily the music media, which act as gatekeepers and disseminators.

Chapter 7 is on music retail and radio, with the charts providing a central link between the two.

Chapter 8 considers the relationship between popular music and film, television, and MTV.

Chapter 9 takes up the role of the music press, a term used here for the whole corpus of writing on popular music, ranging from the popular press to cultural journalism. Within this, the focus is on music magazines and music critics as cultural gatekeepers, promotional adjuncts to the music industry, and general purveyors of lifestyles.

Chapters 10 and 11 examine the consumption of music. Two factors are seen to underpin this: music as a form of cultural capital, and as a source of pleasure and empowerment.

Chapter 10 shows the place of music in the lives of 'youth' as a general social category and as integral to fan culture. Dance and record collecting, provide examples of music consumption as a social practice.

Chapter 11 considers music as a central component of the 'style' of youth subcultures, and musical scenes and sounds, the musical geography of place.

Chapters 12 to 14 encompass aspects of music as cultural politics.

Chapter 12 is on state music policy. The validity of the 'cultural imperialism' thesis, and the concept of globalization are discussed in relation to popular music in Canada and New Zealand. The response of each to the dominance of Anglo-American music provides possible models for wider emulation, and useful insights into the question of what constitutes the 'national' in cultural forms.

Chapters 13 uses historical case studies to show how attempts to regulate popular music, its fans and performers have constituted a form of 'moral panic'.

Chapter 14: investigates popular music as a vehicle for political activism and social change, and in relation to the construction of social identities. Music as cultural politics returns us to the significance of the socio-economic context in shaping cultural meaning in the music.

Each of these topics is substantial, and clearly there is not scope to explore each one in detail; at times particular aspects can merely be introduced. Further lines of inquiry are suggested, and the Notes, and this introduction, provide a selected range of key sources for further study.

NOTES

The most comprehensive attempt to map the field of popular music studies, following a taxonomy developed by Phillip Tagg, is:

Shepherd, J., Horn, D., Laing, D., Oliver, P. and Wicke, P. (eds) (2003) *The Continuum Encyclopedia of Popular Music*, London and New York: Continuum. Particularly useful for 'mapping the field', are volumes 1 and 2.

I have found the work of Simon Frith indispensable; see especially:

(1983) *Sound Effects: Youth, Leisure and the Politics of Rock 'n' Roll*, London: Constable.

(1996) *Performing Rites. On the Value of Popular Music*, Cambridge, MA: Harvard University Press, 1996.

General overviews of the field, and discussions of key terms and concepts, include:

Middleton, R. (1990) *Studying Popular Music*, Milton Keynes: Open University Press.

Negus, K. (1996) *Popular Music in Theory*, Cambridge: Polity Press.

Horner, B. and Swiss, T. (eds) (1999) *Key Terms in Popular Music and Culture*, Oxford: Blackwell.

Shuker, R. (2005) *Popular Music: The Key Concepts* (2nd edn), London: Routledge.

Fuller treatments of particular topics and approaches can be found in:

Clayton, M., Herbert T. and Middleton, R. (eds) (2003) *The Cultural Study of Music. A Critical Introduction*, New York and London: Routledge.

Frith, S., Straw, W. and Street, J. (eds) (2001) *The Cambridge Companion to Pop and Rock*, Cambridge: Cambridge University Press.

There are a number of good collections of readings:

Frith, S. and Goodwin, A. (eds) (1990) *On Record, Rock, Pop, and the Written Word*, New York: Pantheon Books. The scope of this can be usefully set alongside and compared to later 'readers'.

Beebe, R., Fulbrook, D. and Saunders, B. (eds) (2002) *Rock Over the Edge: Transformations in Popular Music Culture*, Durham, NC: Duke University Press.

Swiss, T., Sloop, J. and Herman, A. (eds) (1998) *Mapping the Beat: Popular Music and Contemporary Theory*, Oxford: Blackwell.

Dettmar, K. and Richey, W. (eds) (1999) *Reading Rock and Roll: Authenticity Appropriation, Aesthetics*, New York: Columbia University Press.

Hesmondhalgh, D. and Negus, K. (eds) (2004) *Popular Music Studies*, London: Arnold.

Bennett, A. Shank, B. and Toynbee, J. (eds) (2006) *The Popular Music Studies Reader*, London and New York: Routledge.

On musicology:

Moore, A.F. (ed.) (2003) *Analyzing Popular Music*, Cambridge: Cambridge University Press, and the works listed in Chapter 4.

The above all make reference to the question of what constitutes 'popular music', while an intriguing virtual symposium of members of the Editorial Board of *Popular Music* on the issue is published in *Popular Music*, 24, 1, 2005.

The main journals are *Popular Music*; *Popular Music and Society*; and *Perfect Beat*.

IASPM, the International Association for the Study of Popular Music, has international and regional conferences, and publishes a newsletter; see the web site: www.iaspm. com.

Popular music history: I have drawn on the various histories of popular music throughout this study. The history of popular music has been subject to internal critiques and debates in a similar manner to other forms of historical writing. At issue are the boundaries of the field, including its tendency to privilege Western developments; the treatment of various genres within it; and the emphases that should be accorded to the context within which popular music is produced. I have found the most helpful discussions of historiography in relation to popular music, to be:

Hamm, C. (1995) *Putting Popular Music in Its Place*, Cambridge: Cambridge University Press.

Dancing in the Street, PBS/BBC 10 part series on the history of rock (and see Palmer, R. 1995).

Palmer, R. (1995) *Rock & Roll: An Unruly History*, New York: Harmony Books. This is a companion to the PBS/BBC 10-part television series, *Dancing in the Street*.

An excellent reader is:

Brackett, D. (2005) *The Pop, Rock, and Soul Reader: Histories and Debates*, Oxford: Oxford University Press.

There are many 'standard' popular music histories. A now classic account is:

Marcus, G. (1991 [1977]) *Mystery Train* (4th edn), New York: Penguin.

See also:

Bordowitz, H. (2004) *Turning Points in Rock 'n' Roll*, New York: Citadel Press.

Miller, J. (1999) *Flowers in the Dustbin: The Rise of Rock and Roll, 1947–1997*, New York: Simon & Schuster.

Friedlander, P. (1996) *Rock And Roll: A Social History*, Boulder, CO: Westview Press.

Garofalo, R.(1997) *Rockin' Out: Popular Music in the USA*, Boston, MA: Allyn & Bacon.

Chapter 1

'Every 1's a winner'
Music as a cultural industry

I begin this chapter by considering the nature of the music industry, which can best be defined as encompassing a range of economic activities, or revenue streams. I then introduce the concepts of political economy and the cultural industries, which are central to the study of the music industry. My focus then turns to the heart of the industry, the record companies, and the issue of industry concentration. The general view of the binary nature of the record companies, into 'majors' and 'independents' is problematic, but does provides insights into their ideological underpinnings, their organization, and operating practices. The Internet has radically altered the production and marketing of music, with music increasingly going on-line.

The music industry is characterized by a tendency towards oligopoly and extreme volatility, and is engaged in a constant struggle to control an uncertain market place. It does this through two main strategies: its marketing practices, using genres and stars to package and promote sound as a commodity; and through the regulation of copyright. The music industry has managed to consolidate its control of intellectual property, even in a digital age which promised greater independence for artists and audiences.

The nature of artist development and promotion is illustrated primarily through a case study of Island's marketing of Bob Marley and the Wailers in the 1970s.

WHAT IS 'THE MUSIC INDUSTRY'?

There is a tendency, especially in general discourse, to equate the 'music industry' with the sound recording companies, who develop and market artists and their 'records' in various formats, including digital. This sector has historically been at the heart of the music industry and certainly remains a very significant part of it. In a broader sense, however, the music industry embraces a range of other institutions and associated markets. The most important of these are music publishing; music retail; the music press; music hardware, including musical instruments, sound recording and reproduction technology; tours and concerts, and associated merchandising (posters, t-shirts, etc.); and royalties and rights and their collection/licensing agencies.

Below are a few indications of the nature and value of these activities (drawn from IFPI, 2006a, 2006b; and press reports):

- U2's Vertigo tour was the top box office grossing concert tour of 2005, with international revenue of $US260 million. The band's Auckland, New Zealand shows sold out in 90 minutes when they went on sale.
- The global commercial radio advertising market is worth US$30 billion a year.
- The value of portable digital music players was estimated at US$9 billion in 2005.
- Music has been the top entertainment product driving the continued growth of 3G mobile phone services, especially among the 18–35 age group.
- The two major providers of satellite radio in the US, XM and Sirius had 10.6 million subscribers in May 2006.
- The original MTV channel now reaches almost 300 million households worldwide.
- With 114 million registered users, eBay has become a primary source for music buyers generally and record collectors in particular: in the January 2006 listings, a copy of The Beatles' White Album sold for £1,550.
- In September 2006, Vivendi's Universal Music agreed to buy BMG Music Publishing for €1.63 billion; the deal is subject to review by competition authorities in the United States and Europe.

As the International Federation of the Phonographic Industries (IFPI) observes:

> The recorded music industry is the engine helping to drive a much broader music sector, which is worth more than US$100 billion globally. This is over three times the value of the recorded music market, and shows music to have an economic importance that extends far beyond the scope of record sales.
>
> (IFPI, 2006b)

The critical analysis of this situation has drawn heavily on political economy, and a view of music as constituting a cultural industry.

Music and political economy

A political economy approach to the popular mass media has as its starting point the fact that the producers of mass media are industrial institutions essentially driven by the logic of capitalism: the pursuit of maximum profit. The fact that these institutions are owned and controlled by a relatively small number of people, and that many of the largest-scale firms are based in the United States, is a situation involving considerable ideological power. Schiller (1999) has traced the pervasive and increasing inequality in access to information and cultural products due to the commercialisation and privatisation of broadcasting, libraries, higher education, and other areas of public discourse. Commenting on the United States, Bagdikian (1997) observes that 'a small number of the country's largest industrial corporations have acquired more public communications power than any private business has ever before possessed in world history', together creating 'a new communications cartel'. The music industry has been part of this process of consolidation of what Barnett and Cavanagh (1994) term 'imperial corporations'. At issue is the consequent question of control of the media and whose interests it operates in, and the relationship between diversity and innovation in the market. Within political economy, there is rich history of discussion around such questions, with the work of the Frankfurt School particularly influential.

A group of German intellectuals, active from the 1930s, the Frankfurt School theorists criticized mass culture in general, arguing that under the capitalist system of production culture had become simply another object, the 'culture industry', devoid of critical thought and any oppositional political possibilities. Adorno applied this general view more specifically to popular music, especially in his attacks on Tin Pan Alley and jazz. When he published his initial critique *On Popular Music* in 1941, the music of the big bands filled the airwaves and charts, operating within the Tin Pan Alley system of songwriting that had been dominant since the early 1900s, with the majority of songs composed in the 32-bar AABA format. At the heart of Adorno's view of popular music was the standardization associated with the capitalist system of commodity production:

> A clear judgement concerning the relation of serious to popular music can be arrived at only by strict attention to the fundamental characteristic of popular music: standardization. The whole structure of popular music is standardized even where the attempt is made to circumvent standardization.
>
> (Adorno, 1941: 17)

In this essay and his subsequent writings on popular music, Adorno continued to equate the form with Tin Pan Alley and jazz-oriented variations of it, ignoring the rise of rock and roll in the early 1950s. This undermined his critique and resulted in his views often being strongly rejected by later popular music scholars. At the same time,

Adorno's critique has remained influential, and continues to be an important point of departure for discussions of the production of popular music culture (for example: Frith, 1983: 43–8; Gendron, 1986; Miklitisch, 2006).

The influence of political economy is evident in the argument of those contemporary accounts that emphasize the power of corporate capitalism to manipulate and even construct markets and audiences. The picture of a powerful corporate capitalist music industry stresses how the music business is now an integral part of a global network of leisure and entertainment corporations, typified by a quest for media synergy and profit maximization (see Chapple and Garofalo, 1977; Eliot, 1989; Goodman, 1997). An extension of this is the classic form of the cultural imperialism thesis, popularized in the 1970s, which implied that mass manufactured popular culture, primarily from the USA, is swamping the integrity and vitality of local cultural forms.

Classical political economy tended to devalue the significance of culture, seeing it primarily as the reflection of the economic base of society, all too easily slipping into a form of economic determinism. Contemporary political economy theorists have become more sophisticated in their appreciation of the reciprocal relationships between base and superstructure, economics and social activity. As Hesmondhalgh puts it, the best accounts emphasize 'a view of the cultural industries as complex, ambivalent and contested' (2002: 3). Media institutions have been examined by asking of media texts: Who produces the text? For what audience? In whose interests? What is excluded? Such an interrogation necessitates examining particular media in terms of their production practices, financial bases, technology, legislative frameworks, and their construction of audiences. This new work has reasserted the importance of political economy, which has come into its own in the last decade in reframing popular music studies, and considering the nature of music as a cultural industry.

MUSIC AS A CULTURAL INDUSTRY

A descriptive term first coined and developed by Adorno, the cultural industries are those economic institutions 'which employ the characteristic modes of production and organization of industrial corporations to produce and dissseminate symbols in the form of cultural goods and services, generally, though not exclusively, as commodities' (Garnham, 1987: 25). In analyses situated in business economics, they are referred to as the entertainment industries. Such industries are characterized by a constant drive to expand their market share and to create new products, so that the cultural commodity resists homogenization. In the case of the record industry, while creating and promoting new product is usually expensive, actually reproducing it is not. Once the master copy of a recording is available, further copies are relatively cheap as economies of scale come into operation; similarly, a music video can be enormously expensive to make, but its capacity to be reproduced and played is then virtually limitless.

The cultural industries are engaged in competition for limited pools of disposable income, which will fluctuate according to the economic times. With its historical association with youthful purchasers, the music industry is particularly vulnerable to shifts in the relative size of the younger age cohort, their loss of spending power in a period of high youth unemployment world-wide, and their shifting modes of consumption in the era of the download. The cultural industries are also engaged in competition for advertising revenue, consumption time, and skilled labour. Radio especially is heavily dependent on advertising revenue. Not only are consumers allocating their expenditure, they are also dividing their time amongst the varying cultural consumption opportunities available to them. With the expanded range of leisure opportunities in recent years, at least to those able to afford them, the competition amongst the cultural, recreational, and entertainment industries for consumer attention has increased.

The music industry continues to demonstrate the features identified by Vogel (1994) as characteristic of the entertainment industries:

- Profits from a very few highly popular products are generally required to offset losses from many mediocrities; overproduction is a feature of recorded music, with only a small proportion of releases achieving chart listings and commercial success, and a few mega-sellers propping up the music industry in otherwise lean periods (e.g. Michael Jackson's *Thriller*, 1982, with sales of some twenty million copies through the 1980s).
- Marketing expenditures per unit are proportionally large; this applies in the music industry to releases from artists with a proven track record.
- Ancillary or secondary markets provide disproportionately large returns; in popular music through licensing and revenue from copyright (as with film soundtracks).
- Capital costs are relatively high, and oligopolistic tendencies are prevalent; in the music industry this is evident in the dominance of the majors, in part due to the greater development and promotional capital they have available.
- Ongoing technological development makes it ever easier and less expensive to manufacture, distribute, and receive entertainment products and services.
- Entertainment products and services have universal appeal, as evident in the international appeal of many popular music genres and performers; this is enhanced by the general accessibility of music as a medium, no matter what language a song may be sung in.

Calling the tune: the majors

The increased concentration of the culture industries is a feature of late capitalism, and the music industry has been part of this process of consolidation. The move into Hollywood by Japanese corporate capital in the late 1980s was a clear indication of the emerging battle for global dominance of media markets. This battle reflects companies attempts to control both hardware and software markets, and distribute their efforts across a range of media products, a synergy which enables maximization of product tie-ins and marketing campaigns and, consequently, profits. As commentator Nigel Cope observed after Sony purchased both CBS Records (for $2 billion) in 1988 and Columbia Pictures (for $3.4 billion) in 1989:

> Now Sony can control the whole chain. Its broadcast equipment division manufactures the studio cameras and the film on which movies are produced; in Columbia it owns a studio that makes them and, crucially, determines the formats on which they are distributed. That means it can have movies made on high definition televisions, and videoed with Sony VCRs. It can re-shoot Columbia's 2700-film library on 8mm film, for playing on its video Walkmans.
>
> (Cope, 1990: 56)

Such mergers reflected the economies of scale and global integration required to compete on the world media market. A small group of internationally based large corporations have spread their interests across a variety of media, including sound recording, resulting in multi-media conglomerates, such as Time-Warner. Two of the main corporate strategies used here are horizontal and vertical integration, which are neatly explained by Bishop (2005: 447) in terms of a community fish tank. Consuming, or controlling, other similar size fish in the tank is an example of horizontal integration; vertical integration occurs when a large fish owns the tank, the water, the plants, the rocks, and the food supply, which it distributes to the other fish.

German media giant Bertelsmann illustrate these processes at work. Bertelsmann owns book publishing (Random House); magazines and newspapers (Grune+Jahr); printing and media services (Arvato Printing); direct marketing groups (book and CD clubs); online interests (CDnow); and, the heart of the company, Bertelsmann Music Group (BMG). I noted earlier the sale to Universal Music in 2006 of BMG publishing, the world's third largest music publishing company, with 2005 revenue of €371 million. Yet, indicating the huge scope of Bertelsmann's interests, that figure only accounted for about two per cent of the company's total revenue.

The international record industry is dominated by a small group of large international companies, commonly referred to as the majors. In the late 1990s, there were six of these, all part of large international media conglomerates: Thorn/EMI (UK-based); Bertelsmann (German); Sony (Japan); Time/Warner (USA); MCA (with a controlling interest purchased in 1995 by Canadian-owned company Seagrams); and Philips (Holland). By 2006 further consolidation and mergers had left four: Warner Music Group, part of AOL-Time Warner; Universal Music Group, owned by Vivendi Universal SA of France; Sony-BMG, jointly owned by the Japanese Sony Corporation and Bertlesman, who merged in 2004; and EMI Ltd, a UK firm (Hull, 2004: 125).

(For an outline of the organization and activities of each of the majors, see Hull, 2004; Bishop, 2005; and for a comparison with the situation in the mid-1990s, see Burnett, 1996; Barnett and Cavanagh, 1994. For a fuller listing of record labels, including the majors, with summaries of their history and operation, see Shepherd *et al.*, 2003.) Historically, 'middle range' companies, such as Virgin, Motown, and Island, have been absorbed by the majors, while the smaller independents are often closely linked to the majors through distribution deals.

The market share exercised by the majors varies from country to country, but in some cases is over 90 per cent. There is considerable debate over the economic and cultural implications of such market dominance, especially the strength of local music industries in relation to marked trends toward the globalization of the culture industries (see the examples of Canada and New Zealand, discussed in Chapter 12). Some commentators see the natural corollary of such concentrations of ownership as an ability to essentially determine, or at the very least strongly influence, the nature of the demand for particular forms of popular culture. On the other hand, more optimistic media analysts, with a preference for human agency, emphasize the individual consumer's freedom to choose, their ability to decide how and where cultural texts are to be used, and the meanings and messages to be associated with them. The debate in this area is one of emphasis, since clearly both sets of influences or determinations are in operation.

At issue is the consequent question of control of the media and whose interests it operates in, and the relationship between diversity and innovation in the market. Free-market economists argue that innovation will occur more frequently under conditions of oligopoly (increased concentration, fewer producers), since larger firms are better able to finance innovation and pass the costs and benefits along to consumers. Conversely, other analysts argue that conditions of oligopoly mean a lack of incentive for firms to depart much from the tried and tested, resulting in a high level of product homogeneity. The crucial question in this debate is how does such concentration affect the range of opportunities available to musicians and others involved in the production of popular music, and the nature and range of products available to the consumers of popular music? In other words, what is the cultural significance of this situation, and what role does it play in the creation of meaning in popular music?

Market cycles

Initial analyses of the relationship between concentration, innovation, and diversity in popular music suggested a negative relationship between concentration and diversity in the recording industry, relating this to a cyclical pattern of market cycles in symbolic production (Peterson and Berger, 1975). This suggests that original musical ideas and styles, generated organically, are taken up by the record industry, which then popularizes them and adheres to them as the standard form. Meanwhile new creative trends emerge which have to break through the new orthodoxy. Thus develops a cycle of innovation and consolidation, a cycle reflected in historical shifts in economic concentration and market control in the music industry.

The basis for this analysis was the proportion of top selling records (as indicated by the American *Billboard* singles charts) sold by the leading companies (the majors). During periods of greatest market concentration, there were fewer top selling records. Conversely, during periods of greater market competition, with marked competition from newer/smaller record companies (the independents), there were a greater number of top selling records in the charts. Rothenbuhler and Dimmick (1982) showed that relationship continued to hold between 1974 and 1980, apparently confirming Peterson and Berger's thesis. This view was challenged by analysts who argued that a high level of concentration was actually accompanied by a high level of diversity. 'Major record companies find it advantageous to incorporate new artists, producers and styles of music to constantly reinvigorate the popular music market and to ensure that no large unsated demand among consumers materializes' (Lopes, 1992: 70; see also Ross, 2005). An important consideration here is the role of gate-keeping, the filtering processes at work before a particular piece of music reaches the charts. Building on Lopes, Christianen (1995: 91) points out the importance of the number of decision-makers within a firm, as a variable explaining the diversity and innovation generated by a major record company. In a sophisticated study of the Dutch music industry, he argues that the pattern between innovation and diversity is more complex than previous analysts had suggested.

Reviewing these, along with similar studies, Ross sees 'the question facing researchers now is where to take this approach in the future' (2005: 484). As he observes, market concentration cannot be examined purely in terms of the proportion of chart recordings issued by particular companies, and he explores how the notion needs to be expanded 'to examine further the control major record companies have on the creative process' (485). A factor here is the development of new means for delivering recorded music to consumers, especially the Internet, making it difficult to measure musical diversity in the market.

The independents

While the 'majors' dominate the recorded music market, the 'independents, or 'indies' play an important role. These are generally small record labels that are independent of the majors (at least in terms of the artist acquisition, recording, and promotion), though still reliant on a major for distribution and more extensive marketing. These labels are frequently considered to be more flexible and innovative in their roster of artists. They have been associated with the emergence of new genres: 'It is an attitude with a sound. The heart and soul of it resides in record labels such as Creation, 4AD, Sub Pop, Demon, Stiff etc.'(Larkin, 1995).

The term 'indie' denotes not just a type of economic entity, but a musical attitude. Both senses of indie are linked to a set of dominant musical values, with authenticity at their core (Azerrad, 2001; Fonarow, 2006). These values are cast as diametrically opposed to a stereotyped mainstream. Indie ideology views their music as raw and immediate, while mainstream music is regarded as processed and mediated by 'overproduction'; indie bands can reproduce their music in concert and even improve upon it, while mainstream bands use too many electronic effects to reproduce their music live. The crossover of indie bands from smaller labels into the mainstream music industry, as occurred with U2, REM, and Nirvana, led to considerable debate among their fans.

Independents have a rich and often lauded role in the history of popular music. Kennedy and McNutt (1999) provide an excellent history of what they term 'little labels', from 1920 to 1970. It has been argued that independent record companies in the 1950s did not have the corporate hierarchy of the majors, and so had greater flexibility in picking up on and promoting new trends and talent, and a greater ability to adjust record production. In combination with changes in the structure of radio and the introduction of the vinyl 45, the independents played a key role in the popularization of rock 'n' roll in the mid-1950s (Peterson, 1990). In companies such as Sun, the owner, record producer, sound technician, and promoter often were the same person (Sam Philips at Sun). 'The 1950s decade was the golden era for small independents, which embraced blues, gospel, modern jazz, country, R&B, and rock 'n' roll' (Kennedy and McNutt, 1999: xvii). From 1948 to 1954, about 1,000 new record labels were formed.

Subsequently, the independent sector continued to be an important part of the music industry, often acting as developers of talent for the majors. To maintain their market control, the music majors adopted several strategies in relation to the independents: buying out their artists' contracts (RCA and Elvis from Sun), or persuading artists to move labels; entering into marketing and other business arrangements with them, or simply buying them out. Several independents acquired a significant market share, as with Motown in the 1960s; these became mid-range companies, situated between the majors and the independents, and were subject to absorption by their larger rivals. At times, as in the 1950s, independent labels have been associated with the emergence of new styles of music: Stiff and British punk; Sub Pop and grunge; Def Jam and rap; Creation and Britpop; and Word and Christian music. While there are a huge number of independent labels, and they produce two-thirds of the titles released, their market share remains small, usually around 15–20 per cent (Hull, 2004).

The operation of the independents and the precise nature of their relationship with the majors is open to debate. For example, in a case study of Wax Trax! Records, a Chicago-based industrial dance label, Lee argued that market expansion, and the necessary links with majors for distribution, force such indies to increasingly adopt the business practices of the majors, in the process moving away from their traditional cultural goals of artistry and creativity. The result is a 'hybrid label – a privately-held company that deals with a major for important production elements or that receives some of its operating funds from a major' (Lee, 1995: 196). The interaction between the majors and independents in such situations, however, remains a dynamic process. The examples of Creation and the career of Oasis (Harris, 2004), and Rough Trade (Hesmondhalgh, 2002) in the UK during the 1990s illustrated a definite blurring of the boundaries between the independents and the major companies. Contributing to this was the advent of the Internet.

Music in cyberspace: the industry goes online

The Internet has added a major new dimension to the marketing, accessing, and consumption of popular music, while creating new problems for the enforcement of copyright. The accompanying debates are central to current popular music studies.

Created originally for military use, the Internet is a computer-linked global communications technology, with dramatically increasing numbers of people accessing it since the late 1990s. The World Wide Web (WWW), a major part of the Internet, is the graphical network that contains web sites dedicated to one topic, person, or company. These locations are known as homepages and allow seamless jumping to other locations on the Internet. The web includes sites for online retail music shops, for downloading music as digital files; for record companies and performers; online music journals; online concerts and interviews; web radio, and bulletin boards. These represent new ways of interlinking the audience/consumers of popular music, the performers, and the music industry. Discussions of the significance of such electronic commerce emphasize the business and economic aspects: the benefits to firms and consumers; the barriers and difficulties associated with doing business via the Net; the demographics of Net users; and the opportunities for companies on the Net. There are also significant cultural issues associated with popular music on the Net, which link up with on-going debates in the political economy of popular music, notably the relative importance (power) of the music industry and the consumers of popular music. The Net may create greater consumer sovereignty and choice by bypassing the traditional intermediaries operating in the music industry (primarily the record companies, but also music retail). The major record companies were initially slow to recognize its potential, but soon moved to create sites to showcase their activities and their artists.

The nature of intellectual property rights, and the regulation of these, was brought into even sharper focus with the electronic retrieval possibilities implicit in the Net. Beginning around 1999–2000, the mainstream music industry showed increasing alarm at the impact on their market share of Napster and similar sites, and practices such as the downloading of MP3s, and P2P (person-to-person) file-sharing. I shall have more to say on the industry response later.

Napster software was introduced in 1999, 'designed as a combination search engine, communication portal, and file-sharing software that facilitated the sharing process by granting users access to all other Napster users and the MP3 files they chose to share' (Garofalo, 2003: 31). Within a few months, transfers of music files using Napster reached millions per day, and, at its peak, it was estimated that as many as sixty million people were using the service. The copyright violation and consequent loss of revenue, led several artists (notably the band Metallica) and record labels to sue Napster for breach of copyright. The issues involved were complex and the litigation process was a lengthy and very public one. Napster was forced to close down, but was re-launched as a legitimate service in late 2003 (Napster 2.0). Newer technologies and providers moved things to another level:

> Whereas Napster required users first to log onto a central server to access other users' MP3 files, these newer networks allow direct user-to-user (peer-to-peer) connections involving multiple file types. These innovations expand the universe of file sharing activity and make it virtually impossible to track users or the files they choose to share.
>
> (Garofalo, 2003: 31)

The battle over P2P file-sharing continued, with the music industry targeting new, post-Napster services, and individual consumers whom they perceived as infringing copyright. An alternative industry strategy also emerged, when in 2000, record companies began establishing copyright deals with Internet music producers. In 2003 the entry of Apple into the music market place, with its iTunes service, met with considerable success, encouraging the development of further such services, most notably eMusic, which only sells music from independent labels.

There are several core issues in these developments and debates. At an immediate level has been the question of the impact of downloading on 'legitimate' recording sales. From the industry point of view, and some observers, downloading was clearly hurting the industry (e.g. Hull, 2004). Others were not so convinced, and there have been some interesting comparisons with similar earlier episodes, notably tape copying (see Jones and Lenhart, 2004). Second, market control was central to the debate around Napster and its successors: were artists and the recording companies being disempowered, and consumers (end-users) being empowered by the increasing availability of online music? (see McLeod, 2005) A related aspect is the nature of the engagement of consumers with music through on-line practices, and the formats and artists downloaded. Any new medium or technological form changes the way in which we experience music, with implications for how we relate to and consume music. In the case of the Net, an interesting question is what happens to traditional notions of the 'distance' between consumer and product, and its technological mediation?

In 2004 music continued to shift online, with legal downloading taking an increasing market share (Hull, 2004: 258–9), made even more attractive by the development of the iPod and its competitors, portable music systems capable of storing huge numbers of songs in digital format. In 2006, a major IFPI 'Report on Digital Music', a comprehensive review of the development of the digital music market internationally, presented some impressive statistical evidence. It showed the online shift had actually gained momentum, with two million songs now available online. The following summarizes the trends:

- Digital music now accounts for about six per cent of record companies' revenues, up from practically zero two years ago.
- Sales of music via the Internet and mobile phones proliferated and spread across the world in 2005, generating sales of US$1.1 billion for record companies – up from US$380 million the previous year – and promising further significant growth in the coming year.
- Music fans downloaded 420 million single tracks from the Internet last year – twenty times more than two years earlier – while the volume of music licensed by record companies doubled to over two million songs.
- The legitimate digital music business is steadily pushing back on digital piracy. In Europe's two biggest digital markets, the UK and Germany, more music fans are legally downloading music than illegally file-swapping.
- Mobile music now accounts for approximately 40 per cent of record company digital revenues. Record companies are seeing sharply increased sales of master ring tones (excerpts of original artist recordings), which account for the bulk of their US$400 million-plus mobile music revenues (IFPI, 2006a).

IFPI Chairman and CEO John Kennedy said:

> Two years ago, few could have predicted the extraordinary developments we are seeing in the digital music business today. And there will be further significant

growth in 2006 as the digital music market continues to take shape. Already in the UK and Germany – two of the biggest digital markets worldwide – legal buyers from sites like iTunes, Musicload and MSN actually exceed illegal file-swappers. We expect this trend to spread as new and pioneering legal music distribution channels open up to consumers. This is great news for the digital music market and the wider digital economy. Record companies are licensing their music prolifically and diversely. A new wave of digital commerce, from mobile to broadband, is rolling out across the world. It is generating billions of dollars in revenues, and it is being driven, to a large extent, by music – by the people who create music, who produce it and who invest in it.

(IFPI, 2006a)

He went on to observe, however, that this growth faced challenges from piracy, and called for 'more cooperation from service providers and music distributors, to help protect intellectual property and contain piracy'. As I shall show later, this view was challenged by observers not so comfortable with the shift to longer periods of copyright, and greater industry regulation and prosecution of those breaking it.

COPYRIGHT

Copyright is central to the music industry. While the global music industry is still concentrated around the production and management of commodities, the management of rights is providing an increasingly important share of its revenues.

The basic principle of copyright law is the exclusive right to copy and publish one's own work. That is, the copyright owner has the right to duplicate or authorize the duplication of their property, and to distribute it. A fuller description of the nature of copyright is beyond my scope here (see Hull, 2004, Chapter 3; and the useful summary in Frith and Marshall, 2004; 6–10). Its significance lies in its changing application and associated cultural importance. The development of new technologies of sound recording and reproduction raise issues of intellectual property rights, copyright and the control of sounds. The music industry is currently using the extension and consolidation of copyright legislation, both domestically and internationally, in an attempt to maintain market control.

The Rome Convention and the Berne Convention are the major international agreements on copyright. The IFPI, the International Federation of the Phonographic Industries, globally regulates the application and enforcement of copyright. Rights income is collected by various local and regional agencies, such as AMCOS, The Australasian Mechanical Copyright Owners Society; and APRA, the Australasian Performing Rights Association, in New Zealand and Australia. In addition to deriving income from unit sales of records, record companies, performers, songwriters and music

25

publishers derive income from the sale of rights. Ownership of rights is determined by copyright in the master tape, the original tape embodying the recorded performance from which subsequent records are manufactured. This rights income includes: (i) mechanical income: payable by record company to the owner of the copyright, for permission to reproduce a song on record; this is a fixed percentage of the recommended retail price; (ii) performance income: a license fee paid by venues, television and radio stations for the right to publicly perform or broadcast songs; and (iii) miscellaneous income: payment for the use of songs in films, adverts, etc.

As early case studies of the legal and moral arguments surrounding the sampling used in records by the JAMS, M/A/R/R/S, De La Soul, and others showed (see Beadle, 1993), the issues involved in policing copyright were extremely complex. They focused on the questions of what is actually 'copyrightable' in music? Who has the right to control the use of a song, a record, or a sound? And what is the nature of the public domain? Governmental and industry organization's attempts to ensure international uniformity in copyright laws initially met only with partial success; even within the European Community conventions and practices varied considerably. As remains the case, attitudes towards copyright diverge depending whose interests are involved. The 1990s saw an emerging hostility towards copyright among many music consumers and even some musicians, due to its regulatory use by international corporations to protect their interests. On the other hand, the companies themselves are actively seeking to harmonize arrangements and curb piracy, while the record industry associations, which are almost exclusively concerned with copyright issues, largely support the industry. The IFPI has championed digital rights management and the need for greater cooperation from Internet service providers to protect music from piracy on their network. The Federation has emphasized that: 'governments and the music industry's partners in the digital market place need to place copyright, rights management and the campaign against piracy at the top of the digital agenda' (IFPI, 2006a).

Ultimately, it is market control that is at stake. There is a basic tension between protecting the rights and income of the original artists, and the restriction of musical output. This is a contested and shifting situation, as a comparison of two edited academic collections published a decade apart shows.

The papers in Frith (1993) showed that Canada, the United States, Australia, Japan, and Ghana all demonstrated different responses to the development of copyright, depending on the nature of interest groups that make up the local performing rights societies, and national concerns about the potential exploitation of local music, the outflow of funds to overseas copyright holders, and the stifling of local performers' ability to utilize international material. Frith observed that the advent of new technologies of sound recording and reproduction had coincided with the globalization of culture, and the desire or media/entertainment conglomerates to maximize their revenues from 'rights' as well as maintaining income from the actual sale of records. What counted as 'music' was changing from a fixed, authored 'thing' which existed as property, to something more difficult to identify.

As Théberge observed in his contribution to the volume:

> The introduction of digital technologies in music production during the past decade has resulted in the development of new kinds of creative activity that have, on the one hand, exacerbated already existing problems in the conceptualization of music as a form of artistic expression and, on the other, demanded that even further distinctions be made in copyright legislation.
>
> (Théberge in Frith, 1993: 53)

The music industry's historical concern with threats to copyright has been exacerbated in the past decade, notably in the debate surrounding sampling and practices such as Internet downloading. In a further collection of papers (Frith and Marshall, 2004), the editors noted 'a recurring skepticism' about the benefits of copyright, with many of the contributors concluding that 'the current copyright regime was of limited benefit to the musical practitioners they describe' (p. 15). While the contributors at times adopted contradictory views, there was convergence on two significant points: that the role of the creators of music should be given more prominence, as a bulwark against commercial pressure; and the term of copyright has become too long.

While articles and exchanges continue to proliferate around the impact of new technologies and the Internet upon the nature and operation of copyright in an era of new technologies, the playing field is looking to be increasingly weighted in favour of the industry. As Frith and Marshall concluded: 'There currently seems to be a radical disjuncture between the law and the social practice it governs' (2004: 213). Copyright was originally conceived as a mechanism to balance private and public interests by eliminating perpetual monopolies over creative works. Today, as Bishop documents, the media conglomerates 'use their power and [intellectual] property to influence national and international laws in order to lock down culture and control creativity' (Bishop, 2005: abstract).

MARKETING AND COMMODIFICATION

Marketing has come to play a crucial role in the circulation of cultural commodities. It is a complex practice, involving several related activities: research, product planning and design, packaging, publicity and promotion, pricing policy, and sales and distribution, and is closely tied to merchandising and retailing. Central to the process is product positioning and imbuing cultural products with social significance to make them attractive to consumers. In popular music this has centred on the marketing of genre styles and stars, these have come to function in a similar manner to brand names, serving to order demand and stabilize sales patterns (Ryan, 1992: 185). Fashion is a crucial dimension. The commodity is designed to attract the attention and interest of shoppers: 'commodity aesthetics' necessitate the construction of a desirable appearance around the commodity, to stimulate the desire to purchase and possess. In the marketing process, cultural products are a contested terrain of signification.

It is noteworthy that by the 1990s the cant term for music within the industry was 'product'. Although this process was hardly new (see Frith, 1988b), it referred to popular music being an increasingly commodified product: merchandise to be packaged and sold. Recorded music can be reproduced in various formats – vinyl, audio tape, CD, DAT, and video – and variations within these: the dance mix, the cassette single, the collector's limited edition, and so on. These can then be disseminated in a variety of ways – through radio airplay, discos and dance clubs, television music video shows and MTV-style channels, and live concert performances. Accompanying these can be advertising, reviews of the record or performance, and interviews with the performer(s) in the various publications of the music press. In addition there is the assorted paraphernalia available to the fan, especially the posters and the t-shirts. Further, there is the use of popular music within film soundtracks and television advertising.

The range of these products enables a multi-media approach to the marketing of the music, and a maximization of sales potential, as exposure in each of the various forms strengthens the appeal of the others. The marketing of popular music includes the use of genre labels as signifiers, radio formatting practices, and standardized production processes (e.g. Stock, Aitken and Waterman and dance pop in the 1980s). Above all, it involves utilizing star images, linking stars and their music with the needs, demands, emotions, and desires of audiences. The case of Bob Marley and the Wailers is instructive here.

Packaging reggae

Island Records was started by Chris Blackwell, the Jamaican-born son of an English plantation owner, in 1962 to supply Jamaican music to West Indian customers in Britain. The company had its first major success when Millie Small's ska tune 'My Boy Lollipop' reached Number 2 in the English pop charts later that year. The company diversified to black music in general, setting up Sue Records in 1963 as a subsidiary to market under license American soul, blues, ska, and rhythm and blues tracks. In the later 1970s Island hooked into the commercial end of the British counterculture, releasing records by Traffic, Fairport Convention, and Free. In 1972 Blackwell signed the Wailers, with Bob Marley (see Barfe, 2004: 259–62).

Conventional histories see this move as inevitably successful, riding the burgeoning Western interest in reggae. But in fact the marketing of reggae and the Wailers is illustrative of record company attempts to maximize their investment at their most successful moment. Island shaped and marketed Marley and the Wailers as ethnic rebellion for album buyers, both black and white (Jones, 1988; White, 1989; Barrow and Dalton, 1997). The strategies used included recording *Catch a Fire* (Island, 1972) the Wailers' first album in stereo; doubling the pay rates for the session musicians involved, enabling them to record for longer; employing the latest technical facilities of the recording process to 'clean up' the music; and remixing and editing the backing tracks in London, after they had been recorded in Jamaica. Blackwell, a very hands-on label boss, also accelerated the speed of the Wailers' basic rhythm tracks by one beat, thinking that a quicker tempo might enhance the appeal of reggae to rock fans. The result was a more 'produced sound', with keyboards and guitars, moving away from reggae's traditional emphasis on drums and bass. (*Catch a Fire: Deluxe Edition*, Island/UME, includes the UK remixed and overdubbed album, along with the original, previously unreleased version recorded in Jamaica.)

Catch a Fire had an elaborate pop-art record cover, designed as a large cigarette lighter, while the Wailers' second album, *Burnin'* (Island, 1973) pictured Rastas in various 'dread' poses, and printed the song lyrics. 'These ploys seemed to confirm Island's intention to sell the Wailers as "rebels" by stressing the uncompromising and overtly political aspects of their music' (Jones, 1988: 65). At the same time, however, this stance was watered down for white consumption. The group's third album had its title changed from *Knotty Dread*, with its connotations of rasta militancy and race consciousness symbolised by dreadlocks, to *Natty Dread*, with its white connotations of fashionable style.

Island carefully promoted the Wailers concert tour of Britain in 1973 to include appearances on national radio and television. This level of exposure was new for reggae, previously constrained by the genre's limited financial support. Later marketing of the band, following only fair success for their first two albums, included pushing Bob Marley to the fore as the group's front man and 'star'. This strategy proved particularly successful during the 1975 tour of Britain, as the band – now 'Bob Marley and the Wailers' – commercially broke through to a mass white audience. Original founding members Peter Tosh and Bunny Wailer left towards the end of 1974, both feeling that too much attention was now being given to Bob. In another strategic marketing move, instead of simply replacing them with similar characteristically Jamaican male harmonies, the more gospel-inflected female backup vocals of the I-Threes were brought in to supply a sound more familiar to rock audiences at that time (Barrow and Dalton, 1997: 131). A string of record hits and successful tours followed in the late 1970s, due at least in part to the music becoming more accessible and pop-oriented. In 1981, Bob Marley and the Wailers' worldwide album sales were estimated to be in excess of $US190 million.

The success of Island with the Wailers helped usher in a period of the international commercialization of reggae. For the multinational record companies, 'reggae was a rich grazing-ground requiring low levels of investment but yielding substantial profits' (Jones, 1988: 72). Jamaican artists could be bought cheaply compared to the advances demanded by their Western rock counterparts. Yet while reggae spurred the success of dub and the ska revival of the early 1980s, and was a crucial influence on commercially successful bands like the Police, Bob Marley remained the only major star to emerge from reggae. His international success arguably owed as much to Blackwell and Island as to his personal charisma and the power of the music.

Marley's death in 1981 did little to diminish his commercial worth, as Island successfully marketed a greatest hits package, *Legend* (1984), which was Number 1 in the UK for several months. Indeed, the continued appeal of Marley was indicated by the album's remarkable longevity: by 1997 it had sold twelve million copies worldwide (Barrow and Dalton, 1997: 135), and has remained the top-selling 'catalogue' album in *Billboard* since that chart's creation in 1991. By 1984, Dave Robinson was running Island, and his market research indicated that

> You should keep the word 'reggae' out of it. A lot of what people didn't like about Bob Marley was the threatening aspect of him, the revolutionary side. So the (album cover) picture chosen was one of the softest pictures of Bob. It was a very well conceived and thought-out package. And a very well put-together record.
>
> (Chris Blackwell quoted in Stephens, 1998: 145)

This approach set the trend for the subsequent marketing of the reggae star, as his image was subtly remoulded, moving from the Rastafarian outlaw of the 1970s to the natural family man of the 1980s to the 'natural mystic' in the 1990s. This process reflected not only the incorporation of his music but also the incorporation of his image and message. A new CD compilation, *The Natural Mystic* (1995) and a four CD boxed set *Songs of Freedom* (1992), both reflected how 'The Marley of the 1970s, rude boy, revolutionary, Rastafarian, needed to be exorcised for the singer to appeal to a more mainstream white audience' (Stephens, 1998: 142). The cover *of Natural Mystic*, a profile head shot of a gently smiling Marley with his hand at his chin, was similar to that used on the *Legend* cover, and indeed came from the same photo session in 1977. The booklet accompanying the 1992 boxed set tells the story of Marley's origins as a rude boy in Trenchtown, Jamaica, the turn to Rastafari in the late 1960s, and his rise to international stardom in the 1970s, and the accompanying CDs parallel this history. The booklet and its images, and in the choice of songs for inclusion in the package, emphasize Marley's growing commitment to spiritual and social issues, playing down his increased political consciousness and desire to connect with a black audience as illness looked likely to end his career.

The marketing of popular music has become increasingly sophisticated since the efforts of Island with Bob Marley and the Wailers. The expansion of the music press, the sophistication of retail, the continued formatting of radio, the popularization of MTV and music video, and the emergence of the Internet, all contributed to the ability of the industry to coordinate marketing internationally across a range of media forms. I shall have more to say about these in subsequent chapters.

The recording industry is now entering a new post-industrial phase, characterized by the impact of digital music, and the decentralizing of the means of recording, reproduction and distribution. At the same time, there is increasing consolidation of the music industry as a whole, as part of the global cultural industry. The international conglomerates not only compete with each other, but are increasingly interconnected in complex patterns of ownership and business practices.

NOTES

Web sites
The Recording Industry Association of America: www.riaa.com.

The British Phonographic Industry: www.bpi.co.uk.

The International Federation of the Phonographic Industries: www.ifpi.org.
The IFPI promotes the interests of the international recording industry worldwide. Its members include over 1400 major and independent companies in more than 70 countries; it also has affiliated industry national groups in 48 countries.

The various 'majors', along with many 'independents', have web sites: see the list in Further Resources.

Other sources
For general analyses of the international media and the cultural industries see:
Hesmondhalgh, D. (2002) *The Cultural Industries*, London: Sage.

The music press is essential to keeping up with current changes in the industry: *Billboard*, *Variety*, and *Music Week*. Business magazine *Forbes* has included some useful material.

Published, academic, studies of the music industry are out of date by the time they appear, but provide an on-going picture of the historical changes in the industry.

I have found the most useful to be:
Burnett, R. (1996) *The Global Jukebox*, London: Routledge.
Hull, G.P. (2004) *The Recording Industry* (2nd edn), London: Routledge.

For a comprehensive listing of the sound recording companies:

Shepherd, J., Horn, D., Laing, D., Oliver, P. and Wicke, P. (eds) (2003) *The Continuum Encyclopedia of Popular Music, Volume One: Media, Industry and Society*, London and New York: Continuum.

On the operating practices of the industry, at both an international and national level, the work of Keith Negus is indispensable:
Negus, K. (1992) *Producing Pop: Culture and Conflict in the Popular Music Industry*, London: Edward Arnold.
Negus, K. (1999) *Music Genres and Corporate Cultures*, London: Routledge.

For a more current view, refer to the articles in:
Popular Music and Society, 28, 4, October 2005: 'Special Issue: The Music Monopoly'.

On the historical development of the music industry, and the rise of rock 'n' roll:
Ennis, P.H. (1992) *The Seventh Stream: The Emergence of RocknRoll in American Popular Music*, Hanover, NH and London: Wesleyan University Press (the fullest treatment of this).
Frith, S. (1992) 'The Industrialization of Popular Music', in Lull, J. (ed.) *Popular Music and Communication*, Sage. (Reproduced, though edited down, in Bennett *et al.* (eds) (2006), *The Popular Music Studies Reader*, London: Routledge (chapter 24).)
Gillet, C. (1983) *The Sound of the City: The Rise of Rock and Roll* (revised edn), London: Souvenir Press.

A solid historical account is:
Barfe, L. (2004) *Where Have All the Good Times Gone? The Rise and Fall of the Record Industry*, London: Atlantic Books.

On the impact of the Internet and online music:
Jones, S. (2000) 'Music and the Internet', *Popular Music*, 19, 2: 217–30.
Beer, D. (ed.) (2005) Special issue 'Music and the Internet', *first monday*, 10, 7.
McLeod, K. (2005) 'MP3s Are Killing Home Taping: The Rise of Internet Distribution and its Challenge to the Major Label Music Monopoly', *Popular Music and Society*, 28, 4: 521–32.
Popular Music and Society, 27, 2, June 2004: Special issue on digital music.

Chapter 2

'Pump Up the Volume'

Music and technology

The history of music is, in part, one of a shift from oral performance to notation, then to music being recorded and stored, and disseminated utilizing various mediums of sound (and, later, audio-visual) transmission. These are hardly discrete stages, but they do offer an organizing logic for the overview here. Any new medium of communication or technological form changes the way in which we experience music, and this has implications for how we relate to and consume music. Technological changes in recording equipment pose both constraints and opportunities in terms of the organization of production, while developments in musical instrumentation allowed the emergence of 'new' sounds. New recording formats and modes of transmission and dissemination alter the process of musical production and consumption, and raise questions about authorship and the legal status of music as property.

It is not possible here to cover all aspects of these topics, which have been the subject of intensive study (see Notes). Rather, I have attempted to signpost some of their cultural implications, with brief examples to illustrate the interaction of technological, musical and cultural change. As Théberge observes, 'technology' is not to be thought of simply in terms of 'machines', but rather in terms of practice, the uses to which sound recording and playback devices, recording formats, and radio, computers and the Internet are put: 'in a more general sense, the organization of production and consumption' (1999: 216–17). My discussion covers sound production, the influence of new instruments on music making; sound recording and sound formats; sound reproduction and sound dissemination.

SOUND PRODUCTION

New technologies of sound production are democratizing, opening up performance opportunities to musicians and creating new social spaces for listening to music. However, these opportunities and spaces are selectively available, and exploited by particular social groups. New instruments and modifications to instruments initiate debates around their legitimacy and place within musical culture. For instance, 'the arrival of the pianoforte into a musical culture that revered the harpsichord was for some an unwarranted intrusion by a mechanical device' (Pinch and Bijsterfeld, 2003: 537). Further examples of this process are the impact of nineteenth century brass band instruments; the microphone in the 1930s; the electric guitar in the early 1950s; the Moog synthesizer in the mid-1980s; and the MIDI (musical instrumental digital interface) since the late 1980s.

Victorian England saw an unprecedented expansion in participative music, with brass bands a major part of this. Herbert (1998) examines how and why brass bands developed, their distribution and adoption, and the nature and significance of their impact. In doing so, he illustrates the complex intersection of technology, urbanization, and musical forms at work in shaping the brass band movement. The first half of the nineteenth century was the most important period in the history of brass bands. They emerged as a new form of leisure activity, with the development of new brass instruments made possible by the invention of the piston valve: 'Suddenly brass instruments possessed a new musical facility, and potentially a new social identity' (Herbert, 1998: 110). The advent of new instruments made possible new musical techniques, and an expanded band repertoire.

The introduction of the microphone in the 1920s revolutionized the practice of popular singing, as vocalists could now address listeners with unprecedented intimacy. This led to new musical creativities and sites of authorship. Johnson traces the emergence of the microphone as a 'performance accessory' in Australia, showing how it was inscribed by gender politics. Masculine resistance to this 'artificial' aid left it primarily to women singers to exploit its possibilities in the 1930s. 'In particular, they experimented with projection, timbre and sensibility in a way that placed the intimate "grain of the voice" in the public arena, laying the foundations for the distinctive vocalisation of rock/pop' (Johnson, 2000: 81; see also Chanan, 1995: Chapter 7).

In a similar manner, the amplification of the guitar transformed popular musicianship: 'amplification allowed guitarists to play fluid and hornlike solos, while the country and jump blues genres popular in the late Forties encouraged them to elaborate a more percussive and riffing style' (Miller, 1999: 41). The Fender Esquire in 1950, the first mass-produced solid-body electric guitar, changed the range and variety of people who could play, reducing the importance of controlling each string's resonance precisely, covering fingering mistakes.

The electric guitar made it possible to play for much larger audiences, in bigger venues, creating new musical styles in the process. 'Chicago' or electric blues developed when blacks from the south moved to urban centres such as Chicago, Memphis, and New Orleans after World War II, looking for work and better lifestyles opportunities. Performers such as Muddy Waters and John Lee Hooker 'plugged in' to entertain them (Waksman, 1996: chapter 4).

The electronic synthesizer developed in the late 1960s and early 1970s, and became 'the most successful electronic instrument of the twentieth century' (Pinch and Bijsterveld, 2003: 546). Moog became the dominant manufacturer, in part because he made his machine available to as many musicians as possible and worked closely with them to constantly modify his design. His synthesizer became a keyboard device, providing an appealing feature of Moog advertising material: 'Whenever someone wanted to take a picture, for some reason or other it looks good if you're playing a keyboard. People understand then that you're making music' (Moog quoted in Pinch and Bijsterveld, 2003: 550). The acceptance of a keyboard synthesizer reflected the influence of the wider culture and the historical status of the piano and organ.

Walter Carlos, a skilled studio engineer and composer of electronic music, formed a close relationship with Moog, exchanging advice for custom-built modules. In 1968, with Rachel Elkind, he produced *Switched On Bach*, an album of Bach's 'greatest hits' performed on the Moog synthesizer. The critical and commercial success of the album helped popularize the synthesizer. Psychedelic musicians, already fascinated with unusual instruments such as the sitar and theremin, took up the synthesizer. (For example, The Byrds on *The Notorious Byrd Brothers* (Columbia, 1968) and the Beatles on later albums such as *Revolver* (Parlophone, 1966).) The production of the first portable keyboard, the cheaper and easier to use Minimoog, which became an essential part of progressive rock in the early 1970s, consolidated this popularity: 'It was the first synthesizer to have mass appeal and was sold in a new way, through retail music stores, thus laying the foundation for a retail market in synthesizers' (Pinch and Bijsterveld, 2003: 554). The Minimoog's portability, ease of use, reliability and hardwired sound, made it an important precursor to later digital instruments, notably the Yamaha DX7 (1983) with its wide array of presets.

The advent of MIDI and digital electronics completely restructured music production from 1983 onwards, marking 'a watershed in the history of popular music' (Théberge, 1997: 5; see also Hawkins, 2002). The new generation of instruments and software created fresh sound possibilities, expanded style, techniques and concepts of production, and raised the status of producers.

SOUND RECORDING

Sound recording is the process of transferring 'live' musical performance onto a physical product (the recording). The history of sound recording is one of technical advances leading to changes in the nature of the process, and the shifts in tasks and status of those working with these technologies. Such changes are not narrowly technical, as different recording technologies and their associated working practices (e.g. multi-tracking, overdubbing, tape delay) enable and sustain different aesthetics (for a detailed history, see Cunningham, 1996; for a concise overview, see Millard, 1995: Chapter 14). In the recording studio, the work of the sound mixer, or sound engineer, 'represents the point where music and modern technology meet' (Kealy, 1979: 208). Initially designated as 'technicians', sound mixers have converted a craft into an art, with consequent higher status and rewards. Zak refers to them as 'both craftsmen and shamans' (2001: 165), who are now responsible for much of what we hear on a recording, acting as a kind of translator for musicians and the other members of the recording team.

Particular recordings illustrate advances in sound recording, at times accompanied by greatly increased use of studio time. Approaching the history of popular music from this perspective creates quite a different picture of artistic high points and auteur figures, in comparison with the conventional chronologies. Compare, for example, the following recordings:

1   Les Paul and Mary Ford, 'How High is the Moon', which occupied the Number One position on the Amercian chart for nine weeks in Spring 1951, launched the concept of sound-on-sound recording, coupled with Paul's discovery of tape delay. The technique for recording Ford's voice was also innovative, as Paul recalls: 'The unwritten rules stated that a vocalist should be placed no closer than two feet from the microphone, but I wanted to capture every little breath and nuance in Mary's voice. So I had her stand right on the mic, just a couple of inches away. Then, what happened? Everybody started to record vocals that way!' (Cunningham, 1996: 25).

2   Elvis Presley, 'That's Alright Mama' (Sun, 1956), was recorded at the session in which producer Sam Philips introduced the slap-back delay sound, used on Presley's other Sun singles and the labels recordings by other rockabilly artists (see Escott, 1991).

3   The Beach Boys, 'Good Vibrations' (Capitol, 1966), Brian Wilson's 'pocket symphony', utilized a huge range of instruments, including a theremin (a pre-synthesizer electronic gadget), made possible partly by his extensive use of over-dubs.

4   Pink Floyd, *Dark Side of the Moon* (Capitol, 1973) set a new precedent in sound recording techniques; for example, in its use of noise gates, devices which

allow audio signals to be heard once they rise above a pre-determined volume threshold, and an extensive use of synthesizers.

The profound changes wrought by samplers, MIDI, and other new technological phenomena, are credited with giving new life to a moribund music industry in the 1980s. Sampling can be viewed as part of music's historic tendency to constantly 'eat itself', while also exemplifying its postmodern tendencies: 'The wilful acts of disintegration necessary in sampling are, like cubism, designed to find a way ahead by taking the whole business to pieces, reducing it to its constituent components. It's also an attempt to look to a past tradition and to try and move forward by placing that tradition in a new context' (Beadle, 1993: 24). Through the 1990s and into the 2000s, new recording technologies have continued to open up creative possibilities and underpinned the emergence of new genres, notably the variants of techno and hip hop. Most recently, technology has enabled the creation of 'mash ups': recordings combining two existing recordings, usually illegally and from radically different musical styles and performers, to create a new song.

Digital sampling allows sounds to be recorded, manipulated, and subsequently played back from a keyboard or other musical device. Introduced in the late 1970s and subsequently widely used, digital sampling illustrates the debates surrounding musical technologies. Its use is seen variously as restricting the employment of session musicians, and as enabling the production of new sounds, e.g. the use of previously recorded music in the creation of rhythm tracks for use in rap and dance remixes. The increasing emphasis on new such technologies is significantly changing the emphases within the process of producing popular music: 'As pop becomes more and more a producer's and programmer's medium, so it increasingly is a sphere of composition, as opposed to performance' (Goodwin, 1998: 130).

SOUND FORMATS

With the advent of recorded sound, music became a 'thing', with recording technology in the late nineteenth century enabling its development in commodity form, independent of its 'live' performance aspects. Subsequent shifts in the popularity of various recording formats are important in explaining the historical evolution of popular music. Each new recording format offered fresh recording and marketing opportunities, and affected the nature of consumption. Historically, these constitute a procession of formats, though some are never totally superceded, and become the preserve of collectors: the wax cylinder; the shellac 78, the vinyl 45, the EP and the LP, cassette audio tape, the compact disc, digital audio tape, the erasable compact disc, and MP3 downloads.

The shifting discourse surrounding formats reflects a search for realism, fidelity, and portability, along with the ease of access and the associated cost. Changing formats

37

usually appeal to consumers wanting better sound (though what constitutes 'better' is debatable) or greater convenience, and to those who possess a 'must have' consumerist orientation to such new technologies. New markets are created as older consumers upgrade both their hardware and their record collections. The balance sheet with regard to the declining status of the vinyl single and album, versus the ascendancy of the CD, is a mixed one. There were opportunities in this even for those still emotionally tied to vinyl, as the early 1990s saw a boom in the used record store business as CD converts sold off their record collection on their way to buying their first disc player (Plasketes, 1992). The current dematerialization of the sound recording, with MP3 downloads, represents a revolutionary cultural shift. I shall have more to say on this later.

A short history of the single

The history of the vinyl single and its successors is an example of the relationship between music making, marketing, and consumption. The introduction of the virtually unbreakable vinyl single (historically often referred to as 45s – the rpm (revolutions per minute) speed in the early 1950s was an important factor in the emergence of a proliferation of smaller independent record labels, who were significant in popularizing rock 'n' roll. The single was originally a seven-inch vinyl format, with an 'A' side, the recording considered most likely to receive radio airplay and chart 'action', and a 'B' side, usually seen as a recording of less appeal. Also important was the EP, an 'extended play' single, a vinyl seven inch, usually with four songs. In the UK the EP represented an early form of 'greatest hits' package, with attractive record covers, and outsold albums until the early 1960s.

In the early 1950s, the vinyl single overtook its shellac 78 counterpart as the dominant music industry marketing vehicle. Singles became the major selling format, the basis for radio and television programming, and the most important chart listing, with these in an apparently symbiotic relationship. Singles appealed to young people with limited disposable income, wanting to keep up with the latest chart hits. For the record companies, singles were cheaper to produce than an album, and acted as market 'testers'. While singles success was important for performers and the record companies, it was also important as a means of drawing attention to the accompanying, or subsequent album, with the release of both being closely related. With a few significant exceptions (e.g. Led Zeppelin), performers generally relied on the single to promote their album release. This approach became the 'traditional' construction of record marketing through the 1960s and 1970s. Album compilations of singles, either by one performer or from a genre or style of music, also became an important market. While some performers with high charting singles were 'one hit wonders', singles success frequently launched careers, leading to an album deal and moves from independent to major labels.

In the 1980s new single formats gained an increasingly significant market share. There was a massive increase in sales of cassette singles in America, and Swedish band Roxette's 'Listen to Your Heart' (1990) became the first single to hit Number One in the United States without being released as a vinyl 45. Twelve-inch singles, including remixes, became an important part of the dance music scene (see Straw, 2001), and, accompanying the general rise of the CD format, the CD single also began to emerge as a popular marketing form and consumer preference. Negus (1992: 65) documents the consequent decline of the vinyl single through the 1980s. In the US sales of singles between 1979 and 1990 declined by 86 per cent, from 195.5 million to 27.6 million units, and despite the growth of new formats, total sales of singles declined by 41 per cent. In Britain the single's decline was less dramatic, with total sales falling by 21 per cent, from 77.8 million in 1980 to 61.1 million in 1989. This reflected the continued industry practice in the UK of releasing one or two singles prior to the issue of an album. The relative decline of the single reflected the higher costs of the new formats, and the pressure to produce a video to accompany a single, a practice that was regarded as necessary for supporting radio airplay and chart success (see Chapter 7).

Performers were affected by the shift to the CD format. Whatever the aesthetic status of the rock/pop single, its material significance lay in its availability to artists with limited resources. The seven-inch 45 and the 12-inch dance single, with their specialist market tied to the club scene, offered such performers only a partial substitute. Linked to this, is the point that many of the independent record companies could not initially afford to produce CDs, restricting the market options available to their artists.

In the 1990s, the overall life of the single in the charts, due to radio airplay, remained important for drawing attention to the album. The single is now less important, with sales in all formats having continued to decline in the past decade. Nevertheless, it remains crucial to commodifying pop music for the teen market. The appeal of particular singles is primarily assessed by the placing achieved on the charts, as well as longevity there. (It should be noted that these are not quite the same; sustainability indicates a broader market appeal, following initial sales to a performer's niche market or cult support). Making subsequent assessments of the commercial, and thereby presumed cultural, impact of a single on the basis of total sales and the length of time spent in the charts is a common practice (see Whitburn, 1988).

In the late 1990s MP3s took the single into the digital age. A recorded sound that is technologically encoded so that it takes up much less storage space than it would otherwise, MP3 files are small enough to make it practical to transfer (download) high-quality music files over the Internet and store them on a computer hard drive: CD quality tracks are downloadable in minutes. Hardly surprisingly, MP3 soon became very popular as a way to distribute and access music. The number of people listening to digital music (primarily, but not exclusively, MP3) in the United States in June 1999 was 4 million, having grown from only a few thousand in June 1998 (Mann,

2000: xxi). By 2000, it was widely claimed that MP3 had become the most searched for word on web search engines. For consumers, MP3 enabled access to a great variety of music, most of it free, at least to begin with, and they can selectively compile their own collections of songs by combining various tracks without having to purchase entire albums. For artists, MP3 meant they could distribute their music to a global audience without the mediation of the established music industry. Yet MP3 also raised concerns about potential loss of income, and led to heated debates around copyright and access (see Chapter 1).

The physical nature of the single, and its relation to promotion and the charts, underwent a radical change during 2005–6 as the music market moved online. In the United Kingdom, by early 2006, digital singles made up some 80 per cent of the singles market as a whole, up from 23 per cent in 2004. Music mega-stores, such as Virgin in London's Oxford Street, moved their 'singles wall' to the rear of the shop, and only featured the Top Twenty singles; other record shops stopped stocking the format. This initially produced a strange situation in the weekly charts, with downloads only counting for one week before a CD single was released, and two weeks after the CD is deleted. However, many singles were available to download several weeks before their CD release, often increasing in popularity as the recording's release date approached. Recognizing this situation, the Entertainment Retailers Association began to allow all digital sales to count, so that the singles chart would remain definitive of popularity. The availability of downloads transformed the way in which consumers obtained music, giving them greater direct input into the charts, and at much less cost.

SOUND REPRODUCTION AND DISSEMINATION

The historical development of the phonograph and various subsequent sound systems (hi-fi; home stereo; the transistor radio; audio tape players; the Walkman; and the CD player) is more than simply a succession of 'technical' triumphs. Reflecting changes in the technologies of sound recording and production, each new form of sound reproduction has been accompanied by significant changes in how, when, and where we listen to music.

A talking machine

Edison invented the phonograph, a 'talking machine', in November 1877. The phonograph represented the true beginning of the reproduction of recorded sound, replacing 'the shared Victorian pleasures of bandstand and music hall with the solitary delight of a private world of sound' (Millard, 1995: 1). Edison's phonograph used cylinders and was able to record and reproduce sound. Other researchers developed the new technology further: Berliner's gramophone (1888), used a disc instead of a cylinder, while Edison considerably improved on his original in 1887.

Various commentators have identified a succession of phases in the technological history of the phonograph: an acoustic one from 1877 to the 1920s; the use of electrical/magnetic tape, from the 1920s; and the digital age, with the CD, from 1982. 'The industry built on the phonograph was driven forward by the constant disruption of innovation: new systems of recording, new kinds of machine, and newer types of recorded music' (Millard, 1995: 5–6; see also Steffen, 2005). By the 1970s, most homes in 'developed' countries had a home stereo system, the modern phonograph, consisting of an amplifier, a record player, tape recorder, and radio.

The question is the cultural significance of such developments. For example, the domestic relocation of music consumption, facilitated by the phonograph, raised questions of the nature of the listening process:

> Anyone, living no matter where, has only to turn a knob or put on a record to hear what he likes. Indeed it is just in this incredible facility, this lack of necessity for any effort, that the evil of this so-called process lies. For one can listen without hearing, just as one can look without seeing. The absence of active effort and the liking acquired for this facility make for laziness. Listeners fall into a kind of torpor.
>
> (composer Igor Stravinsky, in his autobiography, quoted in Eisenberg, 1988)

The search for 'fidelity' in sound recording continued to spark debates around the authenticity ('aura') of the cultural product (see Eisenberg, 1988; Frith, 1996: Chapter 11).

The phonograph was originally intended primarily as a business tool, but moved into entertainment initially through coin-operated phonographs (from 1889). With the development of pre-recorded cylinders in the early 1900s, the phonographic industry took off. While in 1897 only about 500,000 records had been sold in the United States, by 1899 this number had reached 2.8 million, and continued to rise. The impact of the talking machine was international. Farrell's discussion of the early days of the gramophone in India presents a fascinating story of the intersections between commerce and technological innovation and their impact on traditional Indian modes of music patronage and music making. Economics underpinned the move of GTL (Gramophone and Typewriter Ltd.) into the Indian subcontinent. As John Watson Hawf, their agent in Calcutta, put it: 'The native music is to me worse than Turkish but as long as it suits them and sells well what do we care?' (Farrell, 1998: 59). For the first time Indian musicians entered the world of Western media, as photography and recorded sound turned 'native' music into a saleable commodity.

The gramophone arrived in India only a few years after its invention in the West, and recorded sound brought many forms of classical Indian music out of the obscurity of performance settings such as the courtesan's quarter and on to the mass market. Recording these was a formidable exercise: the visits to various parts of India in the early 1900s were quite correctly termed 'expeditions', involving complex logistical problems. For the emergent Indian middle class, the gramophone was both a technological novelty and a status symbol. The images in the company catalogues, reproduced by Farrell, illustrate this , along with the use of traditional images of Hindu deities to add to the appeal of the new medium. The constraints and possibilities of the new technology affected the style and structure of the music recorded. While Farrell is cautious not to generalize from the one detailed example he presents, he suggests that one possible limitation of the brief duration of the early recordings 'was to lead artists to give greater weight to the composed or fixed parts of the performance than they would normally have done in live recitals' (Farrell, 1998: 78).

Stereo

Stereophonic sound was first developed for use in film theatres in the 1930s, with home stereo systems as scaled-down versions. In 1931 the first three-way speaker systems were introduced. The sound was divided into high, middle and low frequencies, with each band sent to three different transducers in the loudspeaker, each designed to best facilitate that part of the sound spectrum: the large 'woofer' for the bass, a mid-range driver, and the smaller 'tweeter' for the treble. Due to the Depression, and the difficulty of reaching agreement on a common stereo standard (compared with the battle over recording formats), this system was not turned into a commercial product until the late 1950s. In the 1950s, tape was the format to first introduce stereo sound into the home. Read and Welch (1976: 427) observe that the 'introduction of the stereo tape recorder for the home in 1955 heralded the most dramatic increase ever seen for a single product in home entertainment'. The increased sales of magnetic tape recorders and prerecorded tape forced the record companies to develop a competing stereo product, particularly for the classical music audiophile. By the 1960s, stereo sound was incorporated into the loudspeakers used in home stereos. December 1957 saw the first stereo records introduced to the market. These were not intended for the mass market, and sales were initially not high, but home stereos became popularized during the 1960s.

Going mobile

Mobile forms of sound reproduction have been important for decentering the listening process, and for being identified with particular lifestyles and social groups. Compact cassette audio tape and cassette tape players, developed in the mid-1960s, appealed because of their small size and associated portability. Initially a low-fidelity medium, a steady improvement of the sound, through modifications to magnetic tape and the introduction of the Dolby noise reduction system, enhanced the appeal of cassettes. The transistor radio (made possible by the invention of the transistor in 1948) and the audio cassette had become associated technologies by the 1970s, with widely popular cheap radio cassette players, and the cassette player incorporated into high-fidelity home stereos.

An efficient format for the expansion into remote markets, tape cassettes became the main sound carriers in 'developing' countries, and by the end of the 1980s cassettes were outselling other formats three to one. As a portable recording technology, the tape cassette was used in the production, duplication and dissemination of local music and the creation of new musical styles, most notably punk and rap, thus tending to decentralize control over production and consumption. Home taping is individual copying (to audio or video tape) from existing recordings, or off-air, was made possible by the development of cassette audio tape and the cassette tape player. The term 'cassette culture' has been applied to the 'do-it-yourself' ethic that underlies such practices, and the network of musicians and listeners it embraces. Such practices were seen as a threat by the music industry, with their perceived violation of copyright, a stance echoed in the later controversy over digital downloads.

The development of powerful portable stereo players (boom boxes), associated with inner-city African-American youth, created a new form of social identification and, for some, a new level of noise nuisance. The Jamaican 'sound system', large, heavily amplified mobile discos and their surrounding reggae culture, had a similar impact. These first emerged in Jamaica, from the 1950s onwards, and were transplanted to Britain with the influx of Caribbean immigrants. 'The basic description of a sound system as a large mobile hi-fi or disco does little justice to the specificities of the form. The sound that they generate has its own characteristics, particularly an emphasis on the reproduction of bass frequencies, its own aesthetics and a unique mode of consumption' (Gilroy, 1997: 342).

Another mobile form of sound system is the Walkman, which had a major impact when it was introduced during the 1980s, enabling the listener to maintain an individual private experience in public settings (see du Gay et al., 1997). 'Walkman', although a Sony Corporation trademark, became a popular generic term, for what Bull terms 'personal stereos' (Bull, 2000). As he documents, personal stereos allow their users to re-appropriate place and time, with listeners regaining control of their auditory environments by blocking out undesirable surrounding noise (and people). They also rearrange the user's experience of time, especially while waiting or during travel. Both these factors were part of the appeal of later personal stereos, but with added refinements enabled by the availability of digital music. MP3 players created practices that were not possible with earlier personal stereos, such as the Walkman and the Discman, which were tied to physical music formats. The first portable MP3 player to be released in the United States was the Rio, from Diamond Multimedia, in 1998. Since then many more have appeared on the market, but the most successful and ubiquitous is the Sony iPod from Apple Computers, launched in October 2001.

The iPod has become the sound carrier and fashion accessory of the day, a cross between the Walkman and a hard drive used to store files on a computer. The iPod does not play music from physical formats such as cassettes or CDs, but holds it internally as digital data. The iPod is not the only digital music player, but it is the most popular of the brands now on the market. In terms of use, the advantages of the iPod are presented by its marketers and supporters as threefold. First, it can store a huge quantity of music (how much depends on the capacity of the model), and all you need to carry with you is a small, self-contained device; second, 'you can listen to whatever you want, wherever you are'; and, third, it can be connected up to home stereos or car stereos: 'you can have your entire music collection instantly accessible at home, at friends' houses, when you're driving – even on holiday' (Buckley and Clarke, 2005: 4–5). In addition, using the associated iTunes, the iPod opens up access to a huge range of music: 'You can play tracks downloaded from the Internet without having the hassle of burning a CD. You can instantly compile playlists of selected songs or albums. Or have your player select your music for you, picking tracks randomly from across your whole collection or just from albums of a particular genre' (ibid.).

The extensive popular and academic discussion surrounding the iPod is reminiscent of that which accompanied the music video in the 1980s. The iPod raises questions of marketing and design, mobility and agency, consumerism, and the continued validity of the album format and associated notions of a musical canon (see Chapter 6 on this last point). The control associated with the Walkman is refined by the iPod, as the ability to create customized play lists enables listeners to create their own soundtracks. These can be used to accompany routine activities, with the selections geared to the activity, in terms of both mood generation and required duration. In his quirky take on Descartes, *iPod, Therefore I Am*, Dylan Jones (2005) celebrates the ability of his portable device to connect his past musical experiences and identity, and to thereby to construct a personal musical history. Large parts of the book are made up of song lists, and fictional constructions of meetings with pop and rock stars that influenced his formative tastes – along with those of many of his readers.

Of course, the ability to download the music collections and song selections of others can be viewed as double edged:

> There is a dark side to the iPod era. Snobbery subsists on exclusivity. And the ownership of a huge and eclectic music collection has become ordinary. Thanks to the iPod, and digital music generally, anyone can milk various friends,

acquaintances, and the Internet to quickly build a glorious song collection. We are suddenly plagued by musical parasites.

(Crowley, 2005)

The iPod has collapsed together the musical text, its production, and its consumption.

CONCLUSION

The discourse surrounding music and technology embrace divergent views about creativity and musicianship, artistic freedom, and property rights (copyright). New technologies are variously seen as democratizing or consolidating established music industry hierarchies; rationalizing or disruptive of distribution processes; confirming or challenging legal definitions of music as property; and inhibiting or enabling of new creativities and sites of authorship (Thornton, 1995: 31). These transcend national boundaries, separating music from the time, place, and social context of their production.

NOTES

It is important to acknowledge that the impact of technology upon music is not solely a twentieth-century phenomenon, associated with the advent of recorded sound. Prior to this, print was central to the transmission of music, with the circulation of hand-written songs and scores. The printing press facilitated the circulation of broadside ballads from the early sixteenth century, along with sheet music, which peaked at the end of the nineteenth century.

Good starting points on the impact of recorded sound and later technologies are the engaging and perceptive discussions in:

Eisenberg, E. (1988) *The Recording Angel: Music, Records and Culture From Aristotle to Zappa*, London: Pan Books.

Théberge, P. (1997) *Any Sound You Can Imagine: Making Music/Consuming Technology*, Hanover, NH: Wesleyan University Press.

Chanan, M. (1995) *Repeated Takes: A Short History of Recording and its Effects on Music*, London: Verso.

I have found the best historical accounts to be:

Millard, A.J. (1995) *America on Record: A History of Recorded Sound*, Cambridge: Cambridge University Press.

Day, T. (2000) *A Century of Recorded Music: Listening to Musical History*, New Haven, CT: Yale University Press.

45

Steffen, D. (2005) *From Edison to Marconi. The First Thirty Years of Recorded Music*, Jefferson, NC: McFarland.

More specifically on sound recording, see:
Cunningham, M. (1996) *Good Vibrations: A History of Record Production*, Chessington: Castle Communications.

Major recording studios are historically identified with particular producers, house bands, and sounds:
Cogan, J. and Clark, W. (2003) *Temples of Sound. Inside the Great Recording Studios*, San Francisco, CA: Chronicle Books.

On instruments:
Waksman, S. (1996) *Instrument of Desire: The Electric Guitar and the Shaping of Musical Experience*, Cambridge, MA: Harvard University Press.
Popular Music and Society, 26, 1 (October, 2003): Special Issue: Reading the Instrument.

On the impact of digital music, MP3 and the iPod:
Jones, D. (2005) *iPod, Therefore I Am*, London: Phoenix, provides an engaging personal account.

More academic discussions are:
Jones, S. and Lenmart, A. (2004) 'Music Downloading and Listening', *Popular Music*, 27, 2, 221–40.
Taylor, T. (2001) *Strange Sounds: Music Technology and Culture*, London: Routledge.

Chapter 3

'I'm Just a Singer'
Making music and the success continuum

In addressing the question of how meaning is produced in popular music, a central role must be accorded to those who actually make the music. But this is not to simply accept the 'creative artist' view of the production of cultural products, which sees 'art' as the product of the creative individual, largely unencumbered by politics and economics. Those involved in making music clearly exercise varying degrees of personal autonomy, but this is circumscribed by the available technologies and expertise, by economics, and by the expectations of their audience. It is a question of the dynamic interrelationship of the production context, the texts and their creators, and the audience for the music.

This chapter is concerned with the nature of music making and the roles and relative status of those who make music, primarily, but not exclusively musicians. While they are credited as the authors of their recordings, their ability to 'make music' is, to varying extents, dependent on the input of other industry personnel, including session musicians, songwriters, record producers, sound engineers and mixers, along with those who regulate access to the infrastructure of the industry (such as venue owners, promoters). For convenience, and reflecting their historical prominence, I am largely concerned with 'mainstream' rock and pop, and the demarcations present within their musical production as sounds. Other genres, notably disco and dance music, and 'musicians' such as the contemporary dance DJ, subvert many of the traditional assumptions of the 'rock formation' about the nature of musicianship (see Straw, 1999).

My discussion begins with the initial creation of a musical text. For performers 'starting out', this is through learning to first play one's instrument and reproduce

47

existing songs, a form of musical apprenticeship. If the intention is to move beyond this, attention then turns to songwriting and the 'working up' of an original composition, for performance and (possibly) recording. The role of the producer is central to the preparation of the musical text as a material product – the sound recording. The second part of the chapter considers the differing roles and status of those who create music. I examine the distinctions frequently used by musicians themselves, as well as critics and fans, to label various performers. There is an obvious hierarchy of values at work here, both between and within various categories, and in the discourse around the application of terms such as creativity and authenticity (see Negus and Pickering, 2004).

MAKING MUSIC

As most biographies demonstrate, the career trajectory of popular musicians involves skill and hard work, not to mention a certain amount of luck. The few detailed ethnographic accounts we have, suggest that most bands and performers are 'precariously balanced between fame and obscurity, security and insecurity, commerce and creativity' (Cohen, 1991: 4). It is a Darwinian struggle, and there are thousands of unsigned artists:

> Most bands never make it beyond the start-up and early momentum phases of the drive to success. The obstacles prove to be too great to surmount. Disharmonies within the group, lack of financial resources, personal problems, fatigue, waning enthusiasm in the face of frustration, inability to make hard decisions to sacrifice weaker members, and lack of the requisite talents and skills all contribute to failure.
>
> (Weinstein, 1991: 75)

Weinstein's later discussion (2004) suggests not much has changed. Even if a band gets signed to a major label, it has only a small chance of breaking even.

Our detailed knowledge of this process, of how performers actually create their music and attempt to create an audience for their efforts, was initially sparse. Writing in 1990, Cohen's summary of the available literature observed that there had been a lack of ethnographic or participant observer study of the process of making music:

> What is particularly lacking in the literature (on rock) is ethnographic data and micro sociological detail. Two other important features have been omitted: the grassroots of the industry – the countless, as yet unknown bands struggling for success at a local level – and the actual process of music making by rock bands.
>
> (Cohen, 1991: 6)

In addition to Cohen's *Rock Culture in Liverpool*, there are now a handful of 'classic' accounts, along with a large body of biographical profiles of varying usefulness. To these we can add several compendiums of reflections from musicians; in-depth studies of the making of particular recordings; further accounts of musicians involved in local musical scenes; and several insightful discussions of musical creativity (see Notes).

The 'musician'

To begin with, the term 'musician' is not as straightforward as it seems. Finnegan, in her study of music-making in Milton Keynes, found it difficult to distinguish 'amateur' from 'professional' musicians:

> local bands sometimes contained many players in full-time (non-musical) jobs and others whose only regular occupation was their music; yet in giving performances, practising, sharing out the fees and identification with the group, the members were treated exactly alike (except for the inconvenience of those in jobs that had to plead illness or take time off work if they traveled to distant bookings).
>
> (Finnegan, 1989: 13)

Furthermore, the local musicians tended to use 'professional' in an evaluative rather than an economic sense, to refer to a player's standard of performance, musical knowledge and qualifications, and regular appearances with musicians themselves regarded as professional. Later studies (Shute, 2005), and my own conversations with local musicians, also demonstrate this more expansive use of the term.

While the term 'musician' has been associated with singing or playing an instrument, the development of sampling technology, computer-based composition, and DJ/mixer culture have undermined such easy equations. Accordingly, the concept of musician is best regarded as 'an open category that can subsume any kind of musical competence' (Wicke, 2003: 193). Since the end of the 1950s, the demarcation between the performer, the songwriter, and producer has become blurred. Currently, while the three roles can be distinct, the term musician frequently embraces all three activities.

The realities of practice

There are still few formal study or apprenticeship programmes for aspiring popular musicians, in sharp contrast to the opportunities for classical and jazz instrumentalists. Learning the required musical skills takes time and perseverance as well as inclination and talent:

The hardest thing to dawn on us was that if you practice a lot you get better a lot faster. I didn't realize that maybe there was a big distance between an hour and five hours of practice a day. We went through a transitional stage from being proud of being a garage band to really seeing the limitations and wanting to take it one step further.

(Dan Zanes, guitarist, the Del Fuegos quoted in Pollock, 2002: 30–1)

Even the proficiency of a 'genius' like Jimi Hendrix has its pragmatic foundation:

Practicing his guitar was the central activity of Jimi's life that year [1962]. He went to bed practicing, he slept with the guitar on his chest, and the first thing he did upon rising was to start practicing again. In an effort to find even more time to practice, he occasionally bought cheap amphetamines so he could stay up all night.

(Cross, 2005: 98–9)

Bennett's detailed account, 'The Realities of Practice', showed that 'song-getting' for most rock musicians was a process of 'copying a recording by playing along with it and using the technical ability to play parts of it over and over again' (Bennett, 1990: 224). The two Liverpool punk bands which Cohen studied demonstrated a complex process of musical composition, rehearsal, and performance. Their creative process was typically incremental and participatory (Cohen, 1991). Later (auto)biographical accounts of rock performers show a similar process at work. Reflecting the limitations of conventional notation when applied to rock music, little use is made of sheet music: 'It's so simple just to get things off the record, sheet music is just for people who can't hear' (piano player; cited Bennett, 1990: 227). Composition and song copying initially takes place in private, with the next step the expansion of the song-getting experience to the group situation – transforming the song into a performable entity – and its extension to the creation of 'sets' of songs:

We work in blocks of three or four songs that fit well together, usually taken right off the records in that order. It's a matter of pacing, knowing your material, knowing how your material is going to affect people. We traditionally come out for about twenty-five or thirty minutes of solid blasting, where it's really loud and pretty up-tempo and aggressive. We'll take it down for about fifteen or twenty just to give people a little bit of a breather

(Bob Mould, guitarist, Husker Du; Sugar quoted in Pollock, 2002: 160)

These blocks of material, usually consisting of ten to fifteen songs to be played over a live set are constructed for specific audiences and contexts (gigs), and, as such, usually represent a compromise between what bands want to play, what audiences want to hear, and what is marketable.

The role of the songwriter: 'Wrote a Song', Bob Seger

With its romantic connotations of creativity and authenticity, composition is at the heart of discourses surrounding authorship in popular music. Examples of artistic and commercial success frequently accord songwriting a key place:

> Kurt Cobain's ability to write songs with such strong hooks was the crucial ingredient in Nirvana's eventual world wide appeal. The melodies he wrote were so memorable, people found themselves singing along without even knowing or understanding the lyrics.
>
> (Berkenstadt and Cross, 1998: 63)

A canonical meta-list of 'The Top Thirty Albums' shows that, with one exception, all were composed by the musicians responsible for the recording (Von Appen and Doehring, 2006; and see Chapter 7. The exception was The Beach Boys' *Pet Sounds*, where Peter Asher contributed most of the lyrics).

While composing popular music can encompass several modes, most recently the bricolage of electronic practices underpinning dance music, I am interested here in songwriting in mainstream, chart-oriented rock and pop music. In comparison with the writing on other roles in the music industry, and the nature of the creative process in popular music, the role of the songwriter has received only limited attention. Published work has concentrated on song composition and the process of songwriting, and the contributions of leading songwriters (see Flanaghan, 1987; Stock, 2004; Zollo, 1997).

There are numerous personal accounts of the process of songwriting. For example, Paul McCartney's recollections of his collaboration with John Lennon (Miles, 1997), Mike Stock's account of his work as part of the Stock Aitken Waterman production team (Stock, 2004); and Cantin's discussion of the collaboration between Alanis Morissette and Greg Ballard:

> she would sit on the floor. Ballard would perch on a chair. They'd both take acoustic guitars and fool around with melodies and lyrical ideas and see what happened. When they really got rolling, Alanis would fall into a kind of trance-like state.
>
> (Cantin, 1997: 126)

Kiedis describes writing 'Under the Bridge':

> I started freestyling some poetry in my car and putting the words to a melody and sang all the way down the freeway. When I got home, I got out my notebook and wrote the whole thing down in a song structure, even though it was meant to be a poem to deal with my own anguish.
>
> (Kiedis, 2004: 265)

Such accounts place songwriting in the realm of romantic views of creativity, but this must be tempered with an appreciation of the social conditions under which it takes place, and the sheer graft involved:

> But it wasn't easy. The secret of our success lay in hard work, long hours and those magical 'eureka' moments. Our success rate didn't happen by accident. We knew exactly what we were doing on each record and, having discussed the artist and the song, we understood the audience we were trying to reach.
>
> (Stock, 2004: 100)

Songwriters have historically exercised considerable influence over artists/styles. In the 1950s Leiber and Stoller got an unprecedented deal with Atlantic to write and produce their own songs; the resulting collaborations with performers such as the Drifters and Ben E. King produced sweet soul, a very self-conscious marriage of R&B and classical instruments, notably the violin. In the 1960s Holland, Dozier, Holland contributed to the development of the distinctive Motown sound. In the 1970s Chinn and Chapman composed over 50 British Top Ten hits in association with producers Mickie Most and Phil Wainman, 'using competent bar bands (Mud, Sweet) on to whom they could graft a style and image' (Hatch and Millward, 1987: 141), to produce highly commercial power pop, glitter rock, and dance music. In the 1980s, Stock Aitken Waterman wrote and produced successful dance pop for performers such as Kylie Minogue: 'Down at the Hit Factory, Matt and I were the band and the singers were the guest vocalists. The songs were doing the selling and the artists were an adjunct' (Stock, 2004: 100).

During the late 1950s and early 1960s a factory model of songwriting, combined with a strong aesthetic sense, was evident in the work of a group of songwriters (and music publishers) in New York's Brill Building: 'the best of Tin Pan Alley's melodic and lyrical hall marks were incorporated into R&B to raise the music to new levels of sophistication' (AMG, 1995: 883). The group included a number of successful songwriting teams: the more pop-oriented Goffin and King; Mann and Weil; and Barry and Greenwich; the R&B-oriented Pomus and Shuman, and Leiber and Stoller. Several also produced, most notably Phil Spector, Bert Berns, and Leiber and Stoller, who wrote and produced most of the Coasters hits. One factor that distinguished the group was their youth: mainly in their late teens or early twenties, with several married couples working together, the Brill Building songwriters were well able to relate to and interpret teenage dreams and concerns, especially the search for identity and romance. These provided the themes for many of the songs they wrote, especially those performed by the teen idols and girl groups of the period. Pomus and Shuman, and Leiber and Stoller also wrote some of Elvis Presley's best material.

Collectively, the Brill Building songwriters were responsible for a large number of chart successes, and had an enduring influence (see Shaw, 1992). The role of such songwriters, however, was challenged by the British invasion and the emergence of a tradition of self-contained groups or performers writing their own songs (most notably the Beatles), which weakened the traditional songwriting market. The 1980s and 1990s saw a new visibility for professional songwriters, often also producing, working with or for the proliferation of manufactured pop performers. Among the most successful recent examples of this process is 'Can't Get You Out of My Head' (2002). Written by Cathy Dennis and Rob Davis, for Kylie Minogue, the song topped the charts internationally, revived Minogue's career, and the two songwriters won the British 2002 Ivor Novello Award.

Singer songwriters

Some songwriters have been accorded auteur status, partially when they have later successfully recorded their own material (e.g. Carol King: *Tapestry*, Ode, 1971; Neil Diamond), or are performing as singer songwriters. The term 'singer songwriters' has been given to artists who both write and perform their material, and who are able to perform solo, usually on acoustic guitar or piano. An emphasis on lyrics has resulted in the work of such performers often being referred to as song poets, accorded auteur status, and made the subject of intensive lyric analysis (see Chapter 5). The folk music revival in the 1960s saw several singer writers come to prominence: Joan Baez, Donovan, Phil Ochs, and, above all, Bob Dylan. Singer songwriters were a strong 'movement' in the 1970s, including Neil Young, James Taylor, Joni Mitchell, Jackson Browne, and Joan Armatrading; most are still performing/recording. In the 1980s the appellation singer songwriter was applied to, among others, Bruce Springsteen, Prince, and Elvis Costello; in the 1990s to Tori Amos, Suzanne Vega, Tanita Tikaram, Tracy Chapman, and Toni Child; and more recently to performers such as Dido, James Morrison, and David Gray. This female predominance led some observers to equate the 'form' with women performers, due to its emphasis on lyrics and performance rather than the indulgences associated with male-dominated styles of rock music. The application of the term to solo performers is awkward, in that most of those mentioned usually perform with 'backing' bands, and at times regard themselves as an integral part of these. Nonetheless, the concept of singer songwriter continues to have strong connotations of greater authenticity and 'true' authorship.

Once a song is composed, even if only in a limited form (partial lyrics, or a riff to build on), it becomes 'worked up' for live performance and recording. Beyond creating a distinctive musical sound and original material, successful performers must also develop the different skills required of the live and studio recording settings. It is during the latter process that the role of the producer comes to the fore.

Producers: 'Lookin' for that million-dollar sound' (Bruce Springsteen, 'The Promise')

The occupation of producer emerged as a distinct job category and career path in the popular music industry during the 1950s, initially as someone who directed and supervised recording sessions, and who also frequently doubled as sound engineer (e.g. Sam Phillips at Sun Records). Successful producers, such as songwriters Leiber and Stoller at Atlantic, and George Martin at EMI, began exerting pressure on their recording companies to receive credits (on recordings) and royalties. By the mid-1960s, the studio producer had become an auteur figure, an artist employing multi-track technology and stereo sound to make recording 'a form of composition in itself, rather than simply as a means of documenting a performance' (Negus, 1992: 87). The most prominent example of this new status was Phil Spector (see his profile in Chapter 4). In the 1970s and 1980s, the important role of producers as cultural intermediaries was consolidated with the development of new technology: synthesizers, samplers, and computer-based sequencing systems: 'Of course, technology helped. By the late 1980s we were using 48-track recording facilities and filling virtually every track ourselves' (Stock, 2004: 101). Producers became central figures in genres such as dub and techno, and, above all, with disco and dance pop.

Currently, the way producers operate, their contribution to the session, and the level of reward they are accorded vary widely, depending on the stature of the musicians they are working with and the type of music being recorded. Producers approaches to recording vary from the naturalistic, 'try it and see what happens', to a more calculated, entrepreneurial attitude. Production practices represent an amalgam of established techniques and the possibilities offered by the new technologies. Moorefield makes a case for three central developments in current production:

> One: recording has gone from being primarily a technical to an artistic matter. Two: recording's metaphor has shifted from one of the 'illusion of reality' (mimetic space) to the 'reality of illusion' (a virtual world in which everything is possible). Three: the contemporary producer is an *auteur*.
>
> (Moorefield, 2005: xiii)

Public performance: 'Live and Dangerous' (Thin Lizzy)

Once a band or performer has 'learned' some music, assuming ambition and confidence, they will usually seek to perform live in public. Playing live is important to develop and trial new material, and to popularize and promote recordings, especially upon their initial release. It is also central to rock ideology, with its connotations of authorship and creativity, and the physical energy, emotional tension and release associated with live acts:

> That's what keeps you going. Those two hours on stage where everybody's in complete sync and it's like the universe is perfect. There's no flaw in the universe until the next morning. And then you can't find your breakfast and you gotta travel twelve hours in a day [to the next gig].
>
> (Joe Ely, in Pollock, 2002: 111)

I use the term 'live' performance for those situations where the audience is in close physical proximity to the performance, and the experience of the music is contiguous with its actual performance. Historically of course, prior to the advent of recorded sound, all music was live, and was experienced as such. Live music is made in a variety of settings: by buskers in the streets or subways, in clubs and concert halls, and in the 'open air', most notably at outdoor concert venues and festivals.

'Pseudo-live' performances take place at one remove, as it were, from the original or actual performance, and are usually experienced through intermediary technology: on film and television, or in one of the various recorded formats via radio and sound reproduction systems, the Internet or web broadcasts. The pseudo-live experience of music is not usually in the same time frame as the original performance, although this can be the case with radio and satellite TV linkups with 'live' events. For both fans and musicians there is a perceived hierarchy of such performances, with a marked tendency to equate an audiences' physical proximity to the actual 'performance' and intimacy with the performer(s), with a more authentic and satisfying musical experience.

Various forms of performance, and associated venues, mediate the music, creating a diegetic link between performer, text, and consumer. Their significance in determining meaning in popular music lies in the interrelationship of ritual, pleasure, and economics in the music. Performance in its various guises operates to create audiences, to fuel individual fantasy and pleasure, and to create popular music icons and cultural myths. At times, performance events have had the capacity to encapsulate and represent key periods and turning points in popular music. The Woodstock festival (1969) represented the peak of the 1960s counterculture, at least at an ideological level, while the Rolling Stones' Altamont concert in December that same year signalled its passing. The significance of such events is indicated by their use in a cultural shorthand fashion among fans, musicians, and writers – 'Woodstock' – with an assumed set of connotations.

Public performance venues are significant indicators of the nature of genre styles, the economic and critical status of performers, and the nature of their audience/fans. They range along a continuum, from impromptu performances on street corners and other public spaces, clubs and pubs, to smaller concert halls, to outdoor stadiums. Clubs and pubs remain the main venues for live music on a regular and continuing basis. Both serve as training grounds for aspiring performers operating at the local level, and provide a 'bread and butter' living for more established artists, often through being part of an organized 'circuit' of venues. Club appearances include 'showcase' evenings, similar to variety style concerts, with a number of performers featured; 'one-nighters', and extended engagements. All are important for gaining experience in live work, building an audience, and making contacts in the music industry. Clubs also remain the main site for most music fans' engagement with live music, particularly in smaller towns not on the national concert itinerary of touring performers.

The equation of live performance with musical authenticity and 'paying your dues' as a performer remains a widely held ideology among fans, musicians, and record company executives. Clubs have historically assumed mythic importance for breaking new acts, as in the 1960s with the Who at the Marquee in London, and the Doors at the Whisky in LA. They can also establish and popularize trends and musical genres, as in the 1970s with American punk at New York's Max's and CBGBs, and Cleveland's Clockwork Orange and the Viking Saloon, and English punk at London's 100 Club and the Roxy, and Manchester's Electric Circus (see Heylin, 1993; Savage, 1991), and disco in the 1980s, DJ culture and techno and its various genres in the 1990s (Thornton, 1995), and indie rock during the past decade (Fonarow, 2006).

Where there is not a strong club scene, pubs will sometimes take on the same role. In the process they can legitimate a particular sound and performance ethos. In Australia, the strongly masculine 'Oz Rock' historically dominated the local music scene, and was defined by its association with the pub circuit in the 1980s (Homan, 2003; Turner, 1992). A local network of clubs or pub venues can foster a local scene and arguably create a 'local' sound (see Chapter 13).

'On the Road Again' (Canned Heat): tours and concerts

As with club and pub gigs, concerts, usually part of a tour, expose performers and their music to potential fans and purchasers, building an image and a following. Tours were important historically, for helping 'break' English bands in the United States during the 1960s, and for the commercial breakthrough of Bob Marley and the Wailers in the UK in the 1970s (discussed in Chapter 1), and remain a crucial part of the present national and international music scenes. During the 1990s, purely promotional 'tours' became significant in building a fan base, for example Shania Twain's shopping mall stops in 1993–4; and the importation of name DJs from the UK has been a major factor in consolidating the present dance music scenes in Australia and New Zealand.

The nature of tour concerts is an oddly ambivalent one. On the one hand, for the fan it is a rare opportunity to see a performer, especially if you live in locations where the opportunity may be literally a once in a lifetime one. On the other hand, for the performer each concert blurs into a series of 'one night stands' and the challenge is to maintain freshness at each performance. Tour books, band biographies, and many classic rock songs document 'life on the road', with its attendant excesses, and exhilaration at audience enthusiasm coupled with fatigue.

> It's funny; the road's like that. You never know what to expect. Especially when you're out of the country and you have all of these communication problems. You have transportation problems, and problems with the food and hotel reservations, and then you hit these places in the middle of nowhere and it turns into a memorable night.
>
> (Joe Ely, in Pollock, 2002: 112–13)

The monotony of touring is well captured in *The Big Wheel,* a 'novel' about a band's tour of America, written by Bruce Thomas, the bass player with Elvis Costello and the Attractions:

> I slept through some of the most spectacular scenery in the world, not because I wasn't interested but because I was bloody knackered. This was the band's third time round the world in three years. Round and round and round the world we had gone until it all blurred together.
>
> (Thomas, 1991: 20)

Concerts are complex cultural phenomena, involving a mix of music and economics, ritual and pleasure, for both performers and their audience. Different genres and performance styles create different forms of concert experience. Clearly, a slickly lit and choreographed boy or girl band pop concert is a different visual and aural experience from a drum and bass DJ's presentation in a club. At the heart of concerts is the sense of community that they engender, albeit a transient one. At their head, on the other hand, lie economics and promotion.

'Rock this town' (Stray Cats)

The traditional 'rock' concert illustrates the nature of the concert experience, from the performers' point of view. To begin with, a clear backstage–frontstage divide exists in rock concerts:

> Backstage is the world of the media, governed by functional specialization, calculations of financial interest, and instrumental rationality. Frontstage is the realm of the audience, ruled by a sense of community, adherence to the codes of a valued subculture, and expressive-emotional experience. The stage itself is the site of the mediation of these two worlds by the performing artist who binds them together with the music.
>
> (Weinstein, 1991: 199–200)

The backstage area is a highly complex work site, with a range of specialized workers. The number of personnel reflects the size of the tour and the economic importance of the performers, but can include technicians in charge of the instruments and equipment (amplifiers, etc.); stage hands, who often double as roadies, people to work the sound and lighting boards, security guards, and the concert tour manager. The successful operation of the backstage area at concerts involves the integration of these workers into a stable and impersonal time schedule, where each person does their job as and when required. The scope of this task, at its most extreme, is shown in the documentary *Rock in Rio*, on the staging of the Rolling Stones free concert in Rio de Janeiro in 2006, with an estimated audience of almost two million.

The model of the rock band, at least at the level of image, is anti-hierarchical: an anarchist commune or a group of friends, and performers conform to ritual forms of behaviour:

> On stage the players come close to one another, even lean on one another, and circulate to interact with different members of the band. Off stage they live with one another when they are on tour. The poses for the ubiquitous photographs of the group require that the members be physically close to one another.
>
> (Weinstein, 1991: 99)

This public image can conceals the personal animosities present within the group, which are frequently concealed or played down in the common interest of maintaining the group's career (for example, between Townshend and Daltrey in the Who during the 1960s; between Jagger and Richards in the Stones through the 1980s; and between the Gallagher brothers in Oasis in the 1990s). At times such clashes prove too much, and are exacerbated during the stresses of touring, and members leave and are replaced, or the group breaks up.

There exists a clear hierarchy of rock and pop tours and concerts. For a relatively unknown act, seeking to publicize a new or first release and create an audience, opportunities for live work will be few and venues will be small. The pub and university campus circuit remains essential for such performers. The scale of most 'national' tours is very localized, 'hitting' only a dozen or so centres. For established visiting bands and local acts, which have 'broken' into the charts and the market place, there are larger scale 'national' tours. These still largely play selected main centres, where venues and audiences are large enough to (hopefully) make the exercise economic. At the top end of the scale, are the global tours of the top international acts, which are massive exercises in logistics and marketing – and also hugely profitable. The Rolling Stones' 2006 tour, with more than 100 shows staged over half the world, involved effectively having three stage sets being shipped and flown at the same time, and the band's entourage included 125 technical staff.

During the record industry's affluent years of the early 1970s, tours by major acts were associated with legendary excesses and expenses. Eliot cites one publicity manager:

> I was working with Zeppelin, Bad Company, the Rolling Stones. It was the heyday of rock excess, when everybody was rolling in money and there were limousines to take you to the bathroom.
>
> (Eliot, 1989: 173)

This was unsustainable when the record industry retrenched in the mid-1970s, and companies began to cut back on tour support and set such expenditure off against band's future earnings. Nevertheless, through the 1980s and into the 1990s, live concerts remained the best way to maintain audience interest in a successful act and a key factor in breaking a new one. 'Virtually every rock group eagerly toured behind the release of a new album, with record companies assuming all expenses, paying the acts nothing more than per diems' (Eliot, 1989: 169). Tours work to strictly controlled budgets, with the act usually paying for everything out of record sales before the allocation of royalties. If record sales are good, the performer(s) make money. Yet the Grateful Dead, who toured extensively in the 1970s without 'hits', became heavily indebted to their record label, Warner Brothers, and were on the road for five years before generating any income from royalties.

Tours are about promotion as much as performance. Artists take part in radio and TV shows and make personal appearances at record stores, and tours remain central to creating consumer interest and sales. As the music press indicates, a wide range of performers are on tour at any particular time, often coming together for the major festivals held during summer holiday seasons, especially in the United Kingdom, Western Europe, and North America.

'IT'S A LONG WAY TO THE TOP' (AC/DC)

I turn now to the discourse surrounding various perceived categories of musician, and the hierarchy of value frequently attached to these. Popular music is, for the majority of its participants, an essentially 'amateur' or 'quasi-professional' activity, that may become a career option. Indeed, the great majority of people who make their living playing music live near the poverty line. In the late 1990s there were said to be 10,000 functional bands in the greater Los Angeles area alone, 'all slugging it out night after night in a never-ending cacophony of competition, strategic repositioning, and reconfiguration' (Kirschner, 1998: 250).

Writing in 1988, Frith identified a traditional model of the rock music career, which he termed 'The Rock', involving a career process that was established in the 1960s. Musicians started at the base of this pyramid model, working the local scene through clubs and pubs, building up a following. They might move up through several tiers, firstly to regional live work, recording for small, indie labels, and gaining success and recognition at the regional level. Beyond this were a major recording contract,with national exposure and hits, and touring. At the highest level, there are international hits, tours, and media exposure, and 'superstar' status. Frith regarded this model as underpinned by a dynamic and ideology emphasising 'a Horatio Alger-type account of success being *earned* by hard work, determination, and skills *honed* in practice' (Frith, 1988a: 112). However, Frith was concerned that while there were still careers (e.g. U2) that followed this model, the 1980s corporatization of the music business and the key role of video in selling new pop groups had seen the rise of an alternative success story:

> The Talent Pool: The dynamic here comes from the centre. There are no longer gatekeepers regulating the flow of stardom, but multi nationals 'fishing' for material, pulling ideas, sounds, styles, performers from the talent pool and dressing them up for world wide consumption.
>
> (ibid.: 113)

MTV, which began in 1981, played a major part in this (see Chapter 8).

As Frith acknowledged, the two models are ideal types. During the 1990s, there was both a reassertion of the significance of the traditional model and a merging of the two career paths. While video exposure remained important, it no longer had the status it enjoyed in the mid-1980s. Genre is a factor here, with clear differences between the success routes for 1990s dance pop bands such as The Spice Girls and S Club 7, and alternative and grunge performers in the early 1990s and beyond. For the latter, as the Seattle scene indicated, success at the local and regional level, or nationally on a smaller scale, with a niche or cult audience, on 'independent' labels and via college radio and the club scene, was necessary to attract the attention of the major record companies. Over the past five or six years, the proliferation of 'popstar' reality TV shows have provided fresh example of Frith's talent pool at work. At the same time, as local club scenes demonstrate, the Rock model remains applicable to genres such as indie rock and dance.

Creating and working-up new musical material for performance, studio recording and touring, and once again back to creating and recording to keep the momentum going, is the musicians' work cycle. Furthermore, musical skills are not all that is involved. While the original basis of most groups is in peer friendships, this will change once things get 'more serious', with problems created by the differing levels of ability and commitment of group members, and commitment to a practice schedule), and the need for group cohesion and leadership:

> Being successful definitely put a whole lot of pressure because the band was so communally oriented. People joined the band just 'cause of the vibe of the music. What happened once the money and the fame got involved was that everybody wanted their own manager, So everyone got management, everyone got lawyers, and everything got very complicated.
>
> (Speech, Arrested Development quoted in Pollock, 2002: 96)

Then there are the well-documented physical and emotional strains of 'the rock lifestyle', amply illustrated in many popular memoirs of drugs, sex, and music (e.g. Kiedis, 2004).

One reason, and probably the dominant one, behind the willingness of so many rock musicians to enter the Darwinian struggle for commercial success, is the ultimate possibility of stardom, with its allure of a lifestyle of glamour and affluence. This is not to ignore the appeal of gaining the approval of fans and critics, but it is clear that the majority of performers aspire to that *and* 'the money'. As Kirschner (1998: 252) observes, 'Success should be seen as a central trope in popular music, informing and motivating the entire domain of rock culture' and creating what he terms the 'continuum of success'. Talent aside, success is governed by access to the differing resources and opportunities available for making music. Accordingly, my interest now moves to the 'pecking order' of popular music.

THE SUCCESS CONTINUUM

There exists a status hierarchy among performers, a hierarchy endorsed by critics and fans, as well as by musicians themselves. This hierarchy ranges from those starting out, largely reliant on 'covers', to session musicians, to performers who attempt, with varying levels of critical and commercial success, to make a living from music. This last group has its own differentiations, with tribute bands, house bands, and notions of 'journeymen' players. There are hierarchies of 'artists' and stars, often likened to some sort of sports league table: a minor or major league band; first- and second-division performers; stars and 'megastars'. The bases for such evaluations are vague, and the status of particular performers frequently varies amongst critics and over time. Taste and subjectivity necessarily feature, as much as any elaborated artistic and musical criteria.

Cover bands

At the base of this hierarchy are cover bands, which are generally accorded little critical artistic weight. A common view is that reliance on someone else's material concedes that you have nothing of your own to say. However, playing covers fulfills aesthetic, educational and and economic roles. Some covers, as I shall show in Chapter 7, take the original recording as a starting point, and modify, reinvent, or subvert it in a creative manner. Bands starting out rely on cover versions for a large part of their repertoire out of necessity, mastering them as part of a learning process. Even 'original' performers will usually play a few covers. The distinction between 'cover' and 'original' is important, since upward career mobility is directly tied to notions of originality (Kirshner, 1998: 265). Learning such songs is part of the apprenticeship process in acquiring rock musicianship: 'song copying allows the novice to become a competent member of a musical tradition' (Hatch and Millward, 1987: 3). An example is the development of 'rock' in England in the 1960s through local bands covering imported copies of American rhythm and blues hits, as with the Rolling Stones' versions of Arthur Alexander's 'You Better Move On' (1966) and Solomon Burke's 'Everybody Need Somebody To Love' (1965).

Cover songs are literally music to the ears of the managers of smaller venues like clubs and pubs, as they are tapping into a proven product that the audience can identify with. Covers featured strongly in the charts throughout the late 1980s and into the 1990s. There is a fresh generation of listeners and a new market for the recycled song, as reissues demonstrate – for instance, boosted by the film *Ghost*, the 1990 success of the re-released Righteous Brothers 'You've Lost that Lovin' Feeling', which had originally topped the charts in 1965. Even relatively straightforward carbon copies of songs can be successful, as with Wet Wet Wet's 1990s cover of The Troggs 1967 top ten hit, 'Love Is All Around'. For a new generation of record-buyers, a 'good' song is a good song, regardless of any historical memory.

Tribute bands

The extreme example of cover bands are those performers who not only directly model themselves on established bands, but actually copy them, presenting themselves as simulacra of the originals. Such tribute bands, as the industry prefers to call them, rate few plaudits artistically, but they have become big business, with several enjoying lengthy and successful careers (Homan, 2006). Australian band Bjorn Again, primarily performing the music of Swedish band Abba, had played over 1500 shows in some 40 countries worldwide by 2000, and undertook a highly successful tenth anniversary world tour in 1999. Regionally based tribute bands may become a focus for their local community, as with the Pink Floyd tribute band the Benwell Floyd, who regularly perform in the northeast England pub and club circuit. Bennett shows how the appeal of the Benwell Floyd rests on a combination of their musical expertise, and the overlapping kinship and friendship networks shared by the band and its audience, which contribute to the construction of local identities (Bennett, 2000: Chapter 7).

There are hundreds of tribute bands internationally, imitating almost everyone from defunct groups, such as CCR, the Beatles, the Ramones, to bands which are still performing, like Metallica (see Homan, 2006: Introduction). On the positive side, the imitators are bringing the music to a new, younger audience, a generation who never saw the original performers, encouraging them to seek out the earlier material. Other views are less complimentary, pointing to the difficulties in policing copyright and the fact that the original artists are frequently having to share audiences with their imitators. The main objection made to the nostalgia and cover bands, however, is that they generally do not create new music. Ironically, the same charge has not been levelled at the industry's tendency since the 1990s to produce a steady stream of 'tribute' albums, in which various artists pay homage by covering the work of artists as varied as The Clash, Gram Parsons, and Jimi Hendrix.

Session musicians and house bands

Generally anonymous, session musicians are the pieceworkers of the music industry, yet their role is more important than is usually recognized. The label is a generic one, referring:

> to a range of practices, all of which involve the participation of a musician in a recording session featuring an artist or band with which the session musician does not regularly perform.
>
> (Bowman, 2003: 104)

The emergence of session musicians as musical labour was historically tied to greater professionalism and spiraling costs of recording sessions. During the 1960s, music centres such as Nashville, New York, and London, developed highly competitive session musician scenes, with a select group of players able to make a lucrative living playing sessions. The role could be a demanding one:

> To be a session musician, one was generally expected to be able to sight-read musical notation quickly and accurately, to be able to transpose a part from one key to another instantly, to be able to play in a wide range of styles and emulate the licks, techniques and stylistic nuances of other notable instrumentalists, and, in some genres, to be able to continuously develop appropriate and catchy grooves, riffs and lines for recording after recording.
>
> (Bowman, 2003: 105)

Session musicians remain widely used in country and pop recordings.

Some session musicians attain critical recognition for their contributions. Reggae performers Sly Dunbar and Robbie Shakespeare established themselves as 'the' rhythm section, and keyboard player Billy Preston is credited, along with the group (the only time they shared authorship), for the Beatles single *Get Back*. The efforts of a few session musicians attain near legendary status, as with Jeff Beck and Jimmy Page's guitar solos on a variety of records in the 1960s, but usually only when they later become successful in their own right, creating interest in this aspect of their back catalogue.

House bands are the backing musicians used by particular record labels at a majority of their recording sessions, usually drawn from leading session musicians in an area. Their emergence was also linked to increased musical specialization and studio costs, as well as studio recording convenience. The practice began with jazz in Chicago in the 1920s, and was revived by rock music in the 1960s. Several house bands, such as Booker T and the MGs, at Stax in Memphis, received considerable credit for their creative input. Others, equally talented, tended to remain more in the background, as with The Funk Brothers at Motown in Detroit.

Beyond the bands at the base of Frith's performance pyramid of 'The Rock', are those who are working at the middling levels of the industry. These performers are sometimes described as 'journeymen': they may enjoy a fair measure of commercial success, but they are not seen as particularly innovative, even though they may have a distinctive style and themes. But this label is unnecessarily pejorative, resting as it does on contestable (in part because they are rarely fully articulated) aesthetic distinctions. It makes more sense to talk of 'mid-level' status performers, who enjoy a mix of commercial and critical recognition. These are performers whose names are recognizable to the majority of popular music fans, even when they may not necessarily buy their records or attend their performances. Mid-level rock success is illustrated by the career of performers such as Tom Petty and the Heartbreakers, and the critical response to their work (see Shuker, 1994). Beyond this are performers who are considered stars and auteurs; the subject of the next chapter.

NOTES

For general considerations of musical authorship and creativity, see:

Straw, W. (1999) 'Authorship', in Horner, B. and Swiss, T. (eds), *Key Terms in Popular Music and Culture*, Malden, MA and Oxford: Blackwell.

Negus, K. and Pickering, M. (2004) *Creativity, Communication and Cultural Value*, London: Sage.

Toynbee, J. (2000) *Making Popular Music: Musicians, Creativity and Institutions*, London: Arnold.

On the development of musicianship, within the context of local scenes, the classic studies are:

Cohen, S. (1991) *Rock Culture in Liverpool: Popular Music in the Making*, Oxford: Clarendon Press.

Finnegan, R. (1989) *The Hidden Musicians: Music Making in an English Town*, Cambridge: Cambridge University Press.

Shank, B. (1994) *Dissonant Identities: The Rock 'n' Roll Scene in Austin, Texas*, Hanover, NH: Wesleyan University Press.

For more contemporary studies, see the Notes to Chapter 11, and:

Azerrad, M. (2001) *Our Band Could Be Your Life: Scenes from the American Indie Underground 1981–1991*, Boston, MA: Little, Brown.

Fonarow, W. (2006) *Empire of Dirt: The Aesthetics and Rituals of British Indie Music*, Middletown, CT: Wesleyan University Press.

Pollock, B. (2002) *Working Musicians: Defining Moments from the Road, the Studio, and the Stage*, New York: HarperCollins.

Shute, G. (2005) *Making Music in New Zealand*, Auckland: Random House.

The changes brought about by new technologies, and the shifting nature of the 'musician', are well demonstrated in:

Brewster, B. and Broughton, F. (1999) *Last Night a DJ Saved My Life: The History of the Disc Jockey*, New York: Grove Press.

Den Tandt, C. (2004) 'From Craft to Corporate Interfacing: Rock Musicianship in the Age of Music Television and Computer-Programmed Music', *Popular Music*, 27, 2: 139–60.

Schloss, J.G. (2004) *Making Beats: The Art of Sample-Based Hip-Hop*, Middletown, CT: Wesleyan University Press.

Warner, T. (2003) *Pop Music – Technology and Creativity: Trevor Horn and the Digital Revolution*, Aldershot: Ashgate.

Zak III, A.J. (2001) *The Poetics of Rock: Cutting Tracks, Making Records*, Berkeley, CA: University of California Press.

An insightful view of the history and role of the producer is

Moorefield, V. (2005) *The Producer as Composer: Shaping the Sounds of Popular Music*, Cambridge, MA: MIT Press.

Boyd, J. (2006) *White Bicycles: Making Music in the 1960s*, London: Serpent's Tail. Boyd's autobiography presents an entertaining insider view.

Tribute bands and their performers are given overdue recognition in:

Homan, S. (2006) *Acess All Eras: Tribute Bands and Global Pop Culture*, Maidenhead: Open University Press.

Bjorn Again: www.bjornagain.com.

While Benwell Floyd appear to no longer be active, there are a huge number of Pink Floyd Tribute bands; the best-known and most successful, include LA-based Which One's Pink? Germany's The Final Cut; and Canada's Comfortably Numb (all have web sites).

Popular biographies provide some insights into the way musicians work (rehearsal, recording, and touring), even if these sections are often subsumed under a mass of the fame and celebrity, sex and drugs lifestyle. Several DVD documentaries are worth a look:

Dig! Australia: Palm Pictures, 2003.

I Am Trying To Break Your Heart (Wilco), 2002.

Metallica: Some Kind of Monster (Metallica), 2004.

Also the series: *Classic Albums*, on the making of particular 'iconic' or classic albums.

Chapter 4

'So You Want to be a Rock 'n' Roll Star'

Auteurs and stars

At the pinnacle of the success continuum discussed in Chapter 3, are stars and auteurs.

Following an introduction to these two concepts; I provide a number of case studies of such figures in popular music, with reference to examples of their work: bluesman Robert Johnson, in the 1930s; producer Phil Spector and his 'wall of sound' in the early 1960s; rock band The Who, and Pete Townshend, their lead guitarist and primary songwriter; iconoclast Frank Zappa; the Spice Girls and manufactured pop; country crossover star Shania Twain; and dance DJ and remixer Fatboy Slim, in the late 1990s. In each profile, with brief reference to their career, I want to situate these performers in terms of their influence and status, and in relation to issues of creativity and commerce, genre and authorship.

An important starting question here is how do you 'justify' a particular figure and their music as worthy of attention? The majority of the artists included here, were selected for their innovative break with, or reworking of, established traditions and conventions. They generally exemplify two central aspects of a popular music aesthetic: first, extending the traditional form; and second, working within the form itself, breaking it up and subverting its conventions. While this is not the case with the Spice Girls, I have included them as they established a dominant approach to the production and marketing of pop in the past decade, and are an example of debates around authorship and authenticity. The musical examples included show that we must go beyond simple aesthetics to explain why particular songs 'work' in terms of creating an audience. While attention is given to the musical qualities of each performer, they are also situated in terms of genre, the music industry, the personal stance of the musicians and their place in popular music history, and the audience reception of the song.

AUTHORSHIP AND STARDOM

Auteur theory attributes meaning in cultural texts to the intentions of an individual creative source. The auteur concept is historically linked to writing and literary studies, where it has been applied to 'significant' works deemed to have value, which accordingly are considered part of high culture. An ideological construct, it is underpinned by notions of creativity and aesthetic value. The concept of auteur has been especially important in relation to film, emerging as a core part of fresh critical studies in the 1950s, with the auteur usually regarded as the director (see Hayward, 2000). The concept has since been applied to other forms of popular culture and their texts, in part in an attempt to legitimate their study *vis-à-vis* 'literature' and 'art'.

Applying auteurship to popular music means distinguishing it from mass or popular culture, with their connotations of mass taste and escapist entertainment, and instead relating the field to notions of individual sensibility and enrichment. The concept underpins critical analyses of popular music which emphasize the intentions of the creator of the music (usually musicians) and attempts to provide authoritative meanings of texts, and has largely been reserved for the figures seen as outstanding creative talents. It is central to the work of some musicologists, who identify popular music auteurs as producers of 'art', extending the cultural form and, in the process, challenging their listeners. Auteurship has been attributed primarily to individual performers, particularly singer songwriters, but has also been attributed to producers, music video directors, songwriters, and DJs. Indeed, in some cases, as Phil Spector demonstrates, these figures, rather than the musicians, may provide the dominant input. It can also be argued that, as with contemporary film making, the creative process in rock is a 'team game' with various contributions melding together, even if a particular musician is providing the overall vision. Despite this multiple authorship, however, as Straw acutely observes, 'typically we evaluate a musical recording or concert as the output of a single individual or group' (1999: 200).

In the late 1960s, rock criticism began to discuss musicians in auteurist terms. John Cawelti, for example, claimed that 'one can see the differences between pop groups which simply perform without creating that personal statement which marks the auteur, and highly creative groups like the Beatles who make of their performance a complex work of art' (Cawelti, 1971: 267). American critic Jon Landau argued that the criterion of art in rock is the capacity of the musician to create a personal, almost private, universe and to express it fully' (quoted in Frith, 1983: 53). By the early 1970s:

self-consciousness became the measure of a record's artistic status; frankness, musical wit, the use of irony and paradox were musicians' artistic insignia – it was such self commentary that revealed the auteur within the machine. The skilled listener was the one who could recognize the artist despite the commercial trappings.

(Frith, 1983: 53)

The discourse surrounding 1960s rock established a paradigm aesthetic which has, until recently, dominated the application of the concept of authorship in popular music.

At a common-sense level, auteurship would appear to be applicable to popular music, since while they are working within an industrial system, many individual performers are primarily responsible for their recorded product. There are also 'artists' – the term itself is culturally loaded – who, while working within the commercial medium and institutions of popular music, are seen to utilize the medium to express their own unique visions. Such figures are frequently accorded auteur status, and, on the basis of their public celebrity and visibility, will frequently be stars as well. The concept of auteur stands at the pinnacle of a pantheon of performers and their work, an hierarchical approach used by fans, critics, and musicians to organize their view of the historical development of popular music and the contemporary status of its performers. Auteurs enjoy respect for their professional performance, especially their ability to transcend the traditional aesthetic forms in which they work.

Popular musicians often accorded the status of auteur include The Beatles, The Rolling Stones, Bob Dylan, Aretha Franklin, James Brown, Jimi Hendrix, David Bowie, Prince, Michael Jackson, Bruce Springsteen, and Radiohead, who have all achieved commercial as well as critical recognition. (Note the general absence of women from this list, and its dominance by 1960s performers.) The status of several has waned, with their later work largely being found wanting when placed against earlier recordings, as with The Rolling Stones. However, such figures retain auteur status on the basis of their historical contribution, as do auteur figures whose careers were cut short, for example Jimi Hendrix, Janis Joplin, Kurt Cobain. There are also performers whose work has had only limited commercial impact but who are regarded as having a distinctive style and ouevre which has taken popular music in new and innovative directions, such as Frank Zappa, Eno, and Captain Beefheart. The auteur status of some star performers has been a contested issue, as in the case of Madonna (see Schwichtenberg, 1993).

Since all music texts are social products, performers working within popular genres are under constant pressure to provide their audience with more of the music that attracted that same audience in the first place. This explains why shifts in musical direction often lose a performers' established audiences, while hopefully creating new adherents. This is to emphasize the contradiction between being an 'artist' and responding to the pressures of the market, and to claim particular performers as auteurs despite their location within a profit-driven commercial industry (a similar process to that applied in film studies in the 1950s to Hollywood cinema's studio system). This leads to pantheons of musical value that are problematic, since all musical texts 'arrive on the turntable as the result of the same commercial processes' (Frith, 1983: 54). Furthermore, as in any area of 'creative' endeavour, there is a constant process of reworking the 'common stock' or traditions of generic popular forms, as continuity is self-consciously combined with change.

Stars; stardom

Stars are individuals who, as a consequence of their public performances or appearances in the mass media, become widely recognized and acquire symbolic status. Stars are seen as possessing a unique, distinctive talent in the cultural forms within which they work. Initially associated with the Hollywood film star system, stardom is now widely evident in sports, television, and popular music. While there is a large body of theoretically oriented work on film stars (see Hayward, 2000 for a helpful overview), the study of stardom in popular music is largely limited to personal biographies of widely varying analytical value.

The important question is not so much 'what is a star?' but how do stars function within the music industry, within textual narratives, and, in particular, at the level of individual fantasy and desire. What needs to be explained is the nature of emotional investment in pleasurable images. 'Stars are popular because they are regarded with some form of active esteem and invested with cultural value. They resonate within particular lifestyles and cultures' (O'Sullivan et al., 1994: 207), and represent a form of escapism from everyday life and the mundane.

Stardom in popular music, as in other forms of popular culture, is as much about illusion and appeal to the fantasies of the audience, as it is about talent and creativity. Stars function as mythic constructs, playing a key role in their fans ability to construct meaning out of everyday life (see the essays in Kelly and McDonnell (eds), 1999). Such stars must also be seen as economic entities, who are used to mobilize audiences and promote the products of the music industry. They represent a unique commodity form, which is both a labour process and a product. Audience identification with particular stars is a significant marketing device; Madonna must be viewed as much as an economic entity as she is a cultural phenomenon, as over the course of her career she has generated more than $US500 million in worldwide music sales for Time-Warner. Madonna represents a bankable image, carefully constructed in an era of media globalization. Similarly, pop star Britney Spears, whose wealth was estimated at US$123 million by Forbes magazine in 2004, has sold more than 76 million records worldwide for her label Zomba. While Spears did not release any new recordings in

2005–6, the media attention devoted to her marital split in late 2006 demonstrated her continued celebrity status.

Several popular music stars have continued to generate enormous income after their death, that freezes their appeal in time while enabling their continued marketing through both the back catalogue and previously unreleased material; e.g. Elvis Presley, Jimi Hendrix, Bob Marley, and Kurt Cobain (Nirvana).

Yet the enormous fascination with stars' personal lives suggests a phenomenon that cannot be simply explained in terms of political economy. Fans both create and maintain the star through a ritual of adoration, transcending their own lives in the process. Stars appeal because they embody and refine the values invested in specific social types; eg. Kylie Minogue in the1980s as 'the girl next door' (see Rex, 1992), and Bruce Springsteen, whose image is founded on authenticity. Contemporary 'established' stars are frequently at pains to exercise considerable control over their artistic lives, perhaps because this has often been hard won; all have an ability to retain an audience across time, either through reinventing their persona and image, or through exploring new avenues in their music. Many have produced a substantial body of work, often multi-media in form; while seeking, to varying degrees, new ways of reinterpreting or reaffirming popular music styles and traditions. In these respects, such stars are frequently considered to be autuers.

The construction of a popular music star's persona and image may change across time, at times in a calculated attempt to redefine a performers audience and appeal. A number of commentators have observed how Madonna has been able to constantly reinvent her persona, and retain a high degree of creative control over her work. Her audience appeal and commercial success lies primarily in performance, through both concerts and music video, and her ability to keep herself in the public eye, and the creation and maintenance of image is central to her success.

The two most extensively considered popular music stars are Elvis Presley and the Beatles (see the huge number of entries both generated in Leyser's 1994 bibliographic guide). The Beatles are routinely considered to be auteurs: they dramatically altered the status of popular music in the 1960s, and their commercial and critical success made them iconic public figures. Elvis was certainly a star, and, as Graceland shows, continues to be one. In *Dead Elvis*, Greil Marcus (1991b) offers a fascinating account of the on-going cultural preoccupation with 'the King' since his death in 1977. However, Presley is rarely accorded auteur status, although he has a claim to this based largely on his early career at Sun Records. Springsteen and Madonna are the popular music stars and auteurs of the past twenty years who have generated the greatest amount of academic and popular analysis and discussion. In sum, the discourse surrounding these four performers shows how authorship and stardom have become linked constructs with a number of dimensions: the economic, the cultural, and the aesthetic. This is also the case, to varying degrees, with the following examples.

'Hellhound on my trail': Robert Johnson

Robert Johnson was an auteur, who posthumously became a star. He is regarded as 'the key transitional figure working within the Mississippi Delta's blues culture. He bridged the gap between the music's rural beginnings and its modern urban manifestations' (Barlow, 1989: 45).

Born in 1911, Johnson was raised by his mother, who routinely moved from place to place in the mid South. His own adulthood was similarly restless, and provided a recurring message in his work. Fellow bluesman and travelling companion, Johnny Shines said of Johnson: 'People might consider him wild because he didn't think nothing of just taking off from wherever he was, just pack up and go. He had that about traveling.' Johnson had only limited commercial success during his short life. His only recording sessions were held in San Antonio late in 1936 and in Dallas in early 1937, when he recorded a total of just 29 blues tracks. This small output was to have an influence out of all proportion to its size, not only on the blues, but also on the development of 'rock' in the 1960s, as British bands like the Rolling Stones and Cream covered songs by Johnson (see Headlam, 1997; Weisman, 2005). The singer was murdered in Greenwood, Mississippi in 1938, poisoned by a jealous lover, aged only 27.

While Johnson started out in the blues as a harmonica player, he switched to guitar. He was strongly influenced by Son House's bottleneck slide technique, which formed the core of his own playing style, and by other contemporary Delta bluesmen such as Charley Patton and Willie Brown. But Johnson assimilated a range of other influences, incorporating them into his own distinctive style: 'His guitar work was also influenced by the recordings of Kokomo Arnold, Scrapper Blackwell, Willie Newbern, and Lonnie Johnson, who also influenced many of his vocal inflections, along with Leroy Carr, Peetie Wheatstraw, and Skip James' (Barlow, 1989: 45–6). Contemporaries commented on the breadth of Johnson's musical tastes, and marvelled at his ability to 'pick a song right out of the air. He'd hear it being played on the radio and play it right back note for note. He could do it with blues, spirituals, hillbilly music, popular stuff. You name it he could play it' (Robert Jr. Lockwood, cited in Barlow, 1989: 47).

> He'd be sitting there listening to the radio – and you wouldn't even know he was paying any attention to it – and later that evening maybe, he'd walk out on the streets and play the same songs that were played over the radio, four or five songs he'd liked out of the whole session over the radio and he'd play them all evening, and he'd continue to play them.
>
> (Johnny Shines quoted in Barlow, 1989: 46)

Johnson was influential in three areas. First, through his guitar playing:

As a guitarist he almost completely turned the blues around. His tightening of the rhythmic line was the basis for the instrumental blues scene that followed him in Chicago – letting the upper strings play a free melodic part, but using the thumb for a hard rhythm in the lower strings that was also a drum part.

(Samuel Charters, blues historian quoted in Barlow, 1989: 47)

Robert Palmer notes how Johnson made his guitar:

sound uncannily like a full band, furnishing a heavy beat with his feet, chording innovative shuffle rhythms and picking out high treble-string lead with his slider, all at the same time. Fellow guitarists would watch him with unabashed, open mouth wonder. They were watching the Delta's first modern bluesman at work.

(cited in Barlow, 1989: 47)

Second, Johnson recorded a number of strikingly original songs, which captured a timeless feeling of desperation and intensity. In songs like 'Rambling on My Mind,' 'Dust My Broom" and 'Sweet Home Chicago' Johnson celebrated mobility and personal freedom; double entendres and sexual metaphors abound in 'Steady Rolling Man', 'Terraplane Blues', and 'Traveling Riverside Blues'; and in 'Crossroad Blues' and 'Hellhound on My Trail' Johnson encouraged the legend that he had flirted with the devil.

I've got to keep moving, I've got to keep moving
Blues falling down like hail, Blues falling down like hail
And the days keeps on 'minding me
There's a hellhound on my trail

('Hellhound on My Trail')

Third, Johnson's voice is particularly effective at conveying a fatalistic sense of the social and spiritual forces he saw arrayed against him. His vocal intonation is especially compelling in his poignant 'Love in Vain', with its themes of painful departure and separation:

I followed her to the station with her suitcase in my hand
And I followed her to the station with her suitcase in my hand
Well its hard to tell, its hard to tell when all your love's in vain
All my love's in vain'.

('Love in Vain' first verse)
(On *King of the Delta Blues Singers*, volume 2, CBS Records, 1970; also available on the boxed set *Robert Johnson. The Complete Recordings*, Columbia, 1990)

An analysis based on the song lyrics would not convey the emotional impact of Johnson's voice and its interplay with guitar in the recorded version of the song. In performance, the song is stripped down to its bare essentials, making it almost minimalist in contemporary terms. Obviously, if judged by the standards of traditional, classical musicology, it would be found wanting. The vocal is weak and wavering, and the singer does not project well. Yet Johnson's voice has an edge of desperation and hints at depths of experience. This is abetted by the use of repetition, and the interplay between the amplified acoustic guitar and the voice. The piece also exemplifies the role of improvisation and performance in styles such as rock and blues. Although its contemporary impact is limited by the primitive recording technology of its day, this also contributes to the song's authenticity.

Johnson has a claim to being an auteur on the basis of his recordings and their influence, but his now iconic star status owes much to other factors. The singer was widely thought to have sold his soul to the devil in return for the ability to be an outstanding blues singer and guitarist, since he disappeared for a short period and returned amazingly proficient. This, along with his early death and the lack of details about his life, created Johnson as a mythic figure in the history of popular music. The force of this myth, and public and scholarly fascination with it, has led to a spate of books and documentaries on Johnson (for an excellent review of these, and the creation of 'the Johnson myth', see Pearson and McCulloch, 2003). When one of only two known photos of him was used on a United States commemorative stamp, the fact that it had been altered to remove the cigarette from Johnson's mouth created a good deal of controversy (Schroeder, 2004). There is continued interest in his recordings, and his performing style.

Johnson retains the ability to affect listeners today. My own students regard his recording as somewhat maudlin, yet remain conscious of its force. They also find Johnson's original of 'Love in Vain' an interesting comparison with the Rolling Stones 'cover' version (on the album *Let It Bleed*) that they are more familiar with. Certainly they concede that their 'appreciation' of the song is greatly enhanced by locating it as a key text in the development of post-1950s 'rock'. This is to emphasize the point that knowledge of the performer and their influence on 'the popular music canon' adds dimensions beyond simple listening to the piece purely on its own terms.

Phil Spector: behind the Wall of Sound

In the 1960s, producer and songwriter, and occasional performer Phil Spector was an auteur and a star. Later musicians, and popular music history, recognize his achievements despite his subsequent relative commercial decline.

Spector started by writing songs, and achieved initial success with 'To Know Him Is To Love Him', sung by the Teddy Bears, a group he created. In 1960 Atlantic

Records permitted him, at the age of 19, to produce some sessions. He created hits for Ray Peterson and Curtis Lee, wrote 'Spanish Harlem' for Ben E. King, and then founded his own label, Philles. Three years of whirlwind success followed, during which he produced a series of songs which became teen anthems: 'Then He Kissed Me', 'Be My Baby', 'You've Lost That Lovin' Feeling', 'Da Doo Ron Ron', and 'He's A Rebel'. Though these featured some great female vocalists, the performers were virtually interchangeable; the star was Spector. As a producer he celebrated the girl group phenomenon of the 1960s (see Shaw, 1992; Cyrus, 2003) while transcending it, using quality songs, first-class arrangements, and leading session musicians. The noise he created, the so-called 'wall of sound', was overwhelming in its intensity.

> Through multitracking, he made his rhythm sections seem like armies, and turned the beat into a murderous mass cannonade. No question; his records were the loudest, fiercest, most magnificent explosions that rock had yet produced, or dreamed of. And Spector stood in the center, swamped by this mayhem, twiddling the knobs, controlling everything.
>
> (Cohn, 1992: 183)

At one level the wall of sound was simply putting a lot of instrumentalists in the studio and have them all play at once. For example, on 'River Deep, Mountain High', recorded with Ike and Tina Turner in 1966, the recording sessions included:

> Four guitars
> Four basses
> Three keyboards
> Two percussionists
> Two drummers
> Two obbligato vocalists
> Six horns
> And a full string section
>
> (Ribowtsky, 1989: 221)

According to Billy Preston, one of the keyboardists, Spector 'had every machine going all at once; it was a circus and he was the ringleader' (ibid.: 155). His approach to production also incorporated extensive use of echo chamber and tape echo effects.

There is a tendency to see Spector as a pure innovator, a perception encouraged by essays such as Tom Wolfe's 1963 essay 'The Tycoon of Teen' (reproduced in the boxed set, *Back To Mono*: see Notes):

> He does the whole thing. Spector writes the words and the music, scouts and signs up the talent. He takes them out to a recording studio and runs the session himself. He puts them through hours and days to get the two or three minutes he wants. Two or three minutes out of the whole struggle. He handles the control dials like an electronic maestro.
>
> (in Phil Spector, 1991)

Spector was the dominant figure, but he was influenced by earlier producers, notably Leiber and Stoller, whom he worked with, and by Sam Phillips use of echo at Sun Records in the 1950s. Also, as did most producers, Spector worked with a group of regulars, including arranger Jack Nitzsche and engineer Larry Levine. And his song writing credits were shared, or reluctantly conceded where Spector's input to them was minimal, with Brill Building teams such as Gerry Goffin and Carole King.

A millionaire at 21, Spector was hailed by the industry as a genius, but the impetus slackened in the mid-1960s. In 1966 he made his finest record, 'River Deep, Mountain High' with Ike and Tina Turner. When it failed commercially, Spector announced his retirement. A subsequent return from several years of self-imposed exile saw a few successes. He produced 'Imagine' with John Lennon and 'My Sweet Lord' with George Harrison and albums for both the former Beatles. But the dizzy earlier heights were not to be scaled again, in part because he no longer had total control, but was working as a hired hand. His presence alone was now insufficient to virtually guarantee a record's success. Writing his profile in 1992, Cohn painted a picture of a reclusive figure whose myth had swamped his present reality.

Spector's success can be attributed to a combination of two factors. First, he established the concept of business independence, seeking to control every aspect of his own enterprise: production, publicity and distribution. Second, Spector was one of the first self-conscious rock artists, 'the first to rationalize, the first to comprehend precisely what he was up to. With him, there was immediately a totally new level of sophistication, complexity, musical range' (Cohn, 1992: 184). Paradoxically, Spector managed to raid every musical source he could and still be completely original; to be strictly commercial while concerned with the records as art. He combined the two great rock 'n' roll romances – rebellion and teen dream – into one.

Spector's achievement remains impressive, and the positive response to the 1991 reprise of his work, the CD set *Back To Mono (1950–1969)*, was indicative of the continued interest in his work. On this, Spector remastered 60 of his singles (plus his attempt to create an album as a total entity, *Christmas Gift to You*), retaining their original mono sound. Spector's claim to auteur status rests on a combination of initial musical innovation and the aura of mystery and controversy created by his 'star' lifestyle; a mix of eccentricity (episodes with guns in the studio), a messy divorce in the 1970s, and his increasing social isolation. His arrest on suspicion of murder in 2003, added to this mystique, yet, ironically, prompted fresh interest in his work. As Moorefield concludes: 'By taking total artistic control of a recording, Spector in fact redefined what it meant to produce a record. He changed forever the way the producer's role would be viewed' (Moorefield, 2005: 12).

'Talkin' About My Generation': Pete Townshend and The Who

Always very self-reflexive in his attitude towards rock in the early years of The Who, their lead guitarist and main songwriter Pete Townshend was concerned to promote rock as an art form, capable of inspiring and promoting social change. However, as Marsh observes, he mixed 'incredibly pompous statements about the artistic importance of rock with disingenuously self-effacing ones about the triviality of the whole thing' (Marsh, 1983: 288).

Townshend wrote a string of hits dealing with the frustrations of youth, most notably the anthemic 'My Generation', a Number 2 chart success in the UK in 1965. In the United States, where The Who had yet to perform, and receiving limited promotion, it only reached Number 74 on the Billboard chart. The record established The Who as one of the most innovative of the new British rock groups in the wake of the Beatles; it became the endpiece of the band's concerts, and provided the title song on their first album (on Brunswick in the UK): 'Suddenly The Who went from being one, albeit the most promising, of a mass of beat groups to spokesmen, stuttering on behalf of an entire generation' (Perry, 1998: 30). While the song had a very spontaneous sound to it, 'My Generation' had actually been laboriously developed by Townshend, through a number of intermediate stages.

The Who and 'My Generation' were linked to the mod subculture, which began in London around 1963. In a deliberate marketing move by the group's managers, The Who were originally called The High Numbers, whose first single, 'I'm the Face/Zoot Suit' (1964) drew on mod slang and dress. A youth subculture, mod was basically a working-class movement with a highly stylized form of dress, the fashions of which changed frequently, and an interest in American R&B music. Living for weekend partying, the mods took pep pills, particularly 'purple hearts' (amphetamines). Several class-based strains of mod appeared, each with distinctive styles: an art school, high camp version; mainstream mods; scooter boys; and the hard mods, who developed into skinheads. The mod lifestyle parodied and subverted the respectable conventions of their class backgrounds and the relatively unskilled office jobs many of them held (see Barnes, 1979; Hebdige, 1979: Chapter 4).

'My Generation', claims Herman, 'epitomises everything that Mod meant to the mods themselves and to a whole generation of kids for whom mod was the only adequate expression of their feelings' (Herman, 1971: 62). The song presents a picture of a confused and inarticulate adolescent, with lead singer Roger Daltrey singing the vocal in a stuttering fashion that mimics the speed-induced verbal stoppages associated with mod Methedrine use.

> People try to put us down
> (Talkin 'bout my generation)
> Just because we get around
> (Talkin 'bout my generation)
> Things they do look awful cold
> (Talkin 'bout my generation)
> Hope I die before I get old
> (Talkin 'bout my generation)
>
> (The Who, 'My Generation', Brunswick/Decca, 1965;
> 'My Generation' (single: Brunswick/Decca;
> also available on numerous compilations, and the Deluxe
> Edition of the album, My Generation, Polydor, 2002)

The song itself employs what Townshend called 'The Who brag form', with its self-assertive aggressiveness concealing a basic insecurity. Its pace is fast and frantic. It is a combination of bravado and inarticulateness; the stuttering conveys a mix of rage and frustration – as if the singer can't get the words out. Today's youth still find 'My Generation' of interest. It is seen as having clear links with the later 'three chord thrash' of late 1970s punk and the recent revival of 'garage rock', which many students listen to. This, and the mod association, acts as a nostalgic prompt to further investigation of the song and The Who.

'My Generation' was a logical progression from the earlier Who singles, 'I Can't Explain' and 'Anyway, Anyhow, Anywhere'. Like them, it opened with a series of power chords and rustling drums, which Keith Moon subsequently develops into a slashing attack on his kit, and John Entwistle's rumbling bass ('perhaps the most prominently recorded electric bass in rock up to that time', Marsh, 1983: 186). This style had developed because The Who had no rhythm guitarist, accordingly Townshend's lead guitar is strongly rhythmic, emphasizing chord structures rather than melodic lines. A series of simple chord changes keep the momentum going. The song builds in intensity, with a crescendo of feedback, climaxing with sounds reminiscent of the demolishing of lead guitar and drum kit which formed part of The Who's auto-destructive stage act. But what was most revolutionary about the song was its use of feedback. Rather than being used 'as a gimmick separate from the basic flow of the music', 'My Generation' uses feedback 'for the first time as an integral part of a rock composition – without it, the song would be incomplete' (Marsh, 1983: 187).

This indicates Townshend's reputation as a lead guitarist, in addition to his standing as the writer of some of the most memorable lyrics in rock. The Who toured exhaustively through the 1960s, particularly in the US where explosive stage appearances at the Monterey Pop Festival (1967) and Woodstock (1969) consolidated their standing as one of rock's premiere live acts. Townshend's guitar work earned him recognition amongst his peers and fans, and he consistently placed well in performers' polls in the music press. What made his playing distinctive was his incorporation of it into the group's stage act, with his trademark propeller-arm playing style earning him the nickname the Birdman. Townshend's destruction of his guitar at the end of many of The Who's early concerts became a performance trademark, as did his experimentation with feedback.

The reputation of The Who, and Townshend, rests largely on these early hits:

> musical acid bombs, uniquely summing up that Sixties teenage attitude which compounded swaggering confidence with spluttering frustration [and which] are still touched by a magic that has rarely been duplicated in English rock.
>
> (Sinclair, 1992: 381–2; see also Perry, 1998)

Townshend's subsequent work mined this vein, but also dealt with more personal themes and the politics of popular music. Much of this was characterized by innovation: the album A Quick One (1966) included the mini-opera of the title; The Who Sell Out (1967) featured the use of adverts between the tracks to give the feel of pirate radio (then making an impact), and experimented with psychedelia ('Armenia City in the Sky'). Townshend's magnum opus was Tommy (1969), a milestone attempt to develop a rock opera, which was a major commercial and critical success. Tommy was performed in concert by The Who, and turned into a film. A subsequent conceptual work, Quadrophenia, was a retrospective look at the 1960s English mod movement, which The Who were initially closely associated with. Although not as successful, it too was filmed. In 1971 The Who produced their finest album, Who's Next, consolidating their status as members of rock's 'superleague', outranked in the UK only by the Beatles and The Rolling Stones. In resonating with a major fraction of the 1960s rock audience, Townshend became a generational voice, in a manner similar to Bob Dylan in the early 1960s.

The Who split up in 1983, but subsequently reformed in 1989 for a reunion tour. They have continued to sporadically perform since, even after the death of bassist John Entwistle in 2002, and toured and released a well-received new album (Endless Wire, Polydor) in late 2006. In the various albums with The Who in the late 1970s and early 1980s, Townshend's work arguably provided a form of catharsis for the traumas he and the group experienced through that period, including the death of drummer Keith Moon in 1978. Townshend's songs explored more personal themes, especially the rock lifestyle, and his Bahai religious beliefs, and the majority of his best material appeared on his solo albums, especially Rough Mix, 1977, and Empty

Glass, 1980. The now famous line, 'Hope I die before I get old', is an echo of his past, but remains staple fare for interviewers. Townshend is an example of an auteur who enjoyed both considerable artistic recognition and commercial success. This status is due to a combination of his intellectual appeal as 'rock's premier theorist and moralist' (Marsh, 1992: 165), and his songwriting distillation of, firstly, youthful frustrations, and, secondly, of aging angst.

Frank Zappa: 'We're Only In It For the Money'

Auteur status is not always dependent on chart success; indeed, the absence of 'significant market volume' is sometimes almost a necessary corollary of cult status and critical recognition. Frank Zappa, who died in 1993, is an example of such a cult figure. Zappa was a rock iconoclast whose career comprised over 50 albums (including many double and triple sets), three feature films, three feature length videos, and numerous side projects, including record labels and a merchandising operation. Zappa self-consciously played with a variety of musical traditions, mutating them into something unique, often with 'weird' and not easily accessible results. Although best known for his guitar playing, he was proficient on a range of instruments.

In the mid-1960s, with his group the Mothers of Invention, Zappa developed a musical style that was musically wildly eclectic, and thematically weighted to political debate and satire. His subsequent work included many milestones in rock. *Freak Out* in 1966 was the first rock double album, one of the first concept LPs, and an acknowledged influence on the Beatles' *Sergeant Pepper's Lonely Hearts Club Band*. Freak Out also introduced Zappa's brand of political parody and social commentary, with songs like 'Who Are the Brain Police?' The album reached *BillBoard*'s Top 200 album chart, and established Zappa and the Mothers as 'underground' figures. *Absolutely Free* (1967) is a contender for the first rock opera, and carried on Zappa's lampooning of American hypocrisy and conservatism: 'Plastic People' and 'America Drinks and Goes Home'. In the same year, the album *We're Only In It For The Money* satirised psychedelia and the hippy era, and sent up the Beatles' Sergeant Pepper.

In subsequent work, on solo albums and with the Mothers of Invention, Zappa continued to explore the same themes. He mixed satire and send-ups with 'serious' political commentary and dazzling musicianship, while milling a miscellany of musical genres and utilizing the talents of well-known musicians, including violinist and composer Jean-Luc Ponty, Little Feat's Lowell George, drummer Aynsley Dunbar, vocalists Mark Volman and Howard Kaplan (both ex-Turtles, later Flo and Eddie), and guitar virtuoso Steve Vai. The breadth of this group of performers is indicative of Zappa's range of musical interests. He formed his own labels, on which he recorded and promoted Alice Cooper (whose debut LP is on Straight), and Captain Beefheart, whose *Trout Mask Replica* Zappa also produced. Zappa's score for rock group and orchestra,

200 Motels, was launched in 1970, while the London Symphony Orchestra recorded two albums of Zappa's work in 1983.

The keystones of Zappa's work were his control over this variety of projects, his composing skills, and his mastery of production technology. In his autobiography, Zappa recounts the problems the Mothers of Invention had with their record company, MGM, and industry sharp practices such as pressing plant overruns: 'We went through a major legal struggle with MGM over royalties on those first LPs. It took about eight years to resolve'. There were also problems caused by MGM censoring the Mothers' lyrics without their knowledge or consent. By 1984, Zappa had sued two industry giants, CBS and Warners, and had learned a lot more about 'creative accounting practices' (Zappa, 1990: 83). Such experiences led Zappa to emphasize retaining control over all facets of his work. Indeed, Zappa's degree of control over the musicians in his bands, and the extent of his involvement in particular projects, became legendary.

Zappa was the most prominent rock musician to speak out against moves in the United States to censor rock. He argued for the basic right of free speech under the Constitution, seeing the PMRC (Parents' Music Resource Center) proposals for record ratings as 'ill-conceived nonsense' based on totally false notions of the effects of popular music (Zappa, 1990; and see Chapter 13). Zappa, as always, injected a sense of humour into a serious message: his subsequent 1986 Grammy award-winning *Jazz From Hell* carried a sticker warning against offensive lyrics; the album is purely instrumental!

Though seen primarily as a cult figure, receiving critical acclaim from music critics and his fellow musicians, Zappa also achieved some commercial success: his 1974 solo album *Apostrophe (')* was certified gold in the US, making Number 10 in the Billboard chart, while the single from it, 'Don't Eat the Yellow Snow', was Zappa's first in *Billboard*'s Hot 100 (even if only reaching Number 86). His classical compositions, particularly *The Perfect Stranger and Other Works*, and his electronic recordings sold well. Interest in his work remained steady, even after his death in December 1993, as indicated by the current availability of the bulk of his albums on CD and the success of the compilation *Strictly Commercial* (1995). But commercialism is not what Zappa was primarily about. At times, he almost deliberately eschewed success by opting for 'bad taste' and its attendant lack of airplay. Rather he fulfilled the criteria of the genuinely creative artist – conceding the ultimate subjectivity and social construction of 'creativity' – and was concerned with exploring and extending the dimensions of the 'rock' form. Accordingly, although his output was variable in quality, Zappa's talent and auteur status in popular music is widely recognized.

The Spice Girls

As with Madonna, the Spice Girls success story raises issues of the status of musical genres, image and representation, the commodification of popular music, and the nature and operation of celebrity in pop culture more generally.

The Spice Girls were originally put together by the management team of Bob Herbert and his son Chris. Chris drew up a flyer, which he distributed in London and the south-east of England: 'R.U. 18–23 with the ability to sing/dance. R.U. streetwise, outgoing, ambitious, and dedicated?'. Four hundred showed up for the auditions at Danceworks studios, just off London's Oxford Street. The original five Spice Girls (including Michelle Stephenson, who dropped out and was replaced by Emma Bunton) met for the first time in March 1994. Victoria Adams, Melanie Brown, Emma Bunton, Melanie Chisholm, and Geri Halliwell came from varying backgrounds, and the combination of personalities to make up the group were chosen quite deliberately. The press, and their fans, later referred to them as Posh (Victoria), Sporty (Mel C), Baby (Emma), Scary (Melanie Brown), and Ginger (Geri); labels which became pervasive public signifiers, and helped consolidate the Girls' image.

Chris Herbert used Trinity, a dance/rehearsal/recording studio in Woking, Surrey as a base for the group, who spent almost a year there, working on their singing and developing embryonic songwriting skills, and beginning the process of selling themselves to the music industry. The Herberts had no official contract with the Girls, and were a relatively small company, and the band, now increasingly confident in their abilities, looked around for a deal that offered greater support to their increasing ambitions. In April 1995 they left manager Chris Herbert and signed with Simon Fuller's 19 Management. In 1996, they signed to Virgin Records for a reported £2 million advance.

Fuller commissioned three teams of songwriters, all of whom had considerable music industry experience, credits, and success, to work with/for the group, to develop their song ideas. Their input is shown on the group's debut album. Stannard and Rowe, who had previously written material/hits for East 17 and Take That, came up with three of the Girls' four Number 1 singles: 'Wannabe', '2 Become 1', and 'Mama', and also wrote 'If U Can't Dance'. Absolute (Paul Wilson and Andy Watkins) provided 'Who Do You Think You Are', 'Something Kinda Funny', 'Naked', and 'Last Time Lover'. The remaining two songs on the first album, 'Say You'll Be There' and 'Love Thing' were written by Eliot Kennedy (one with Cary Bayliss). The Spice Girls get songwriting credit on all of the songs on the *Spice* album, but Davis (1997) claims that the Girls only get about one-twentieth of the composer's royalties apiece.

The debut single 'Wannabe' was released in July 1996. It went to Number 1 in the UK within a few weeks and stayed there for two months – a record for a debut single by a UK girl group. Subsequently it reached the Number 1 chart position in 31 countries, including the USA, selling four million copies worldwide. The Spice Girls next three singles also topped the UK charts, making them the only group to have had four UK Number 1s with their four first singles, and already the most successful British girl group ever. The appeal of the group was enhanced by their videos and energetic dance routines and performances on leading music television show *Top of the Pops*. The *Spice* LP went triple platinum in the UK within three weeks of its release, and by mid-1997 had sold over ten million copies worldwide. The Girls' personal lives, notably earlier modelling efforts and personal relationships, came under intense scrutiny by first the British, then the international press, especially the tabloids. The group's slogan, 'Girl Power', 'a hybrid of 90s feel-good optimism and cheery fun-pub feminism which alienates no one' (Davis, 1997: 35), attracted considerable debate (see Lemish, 2003).

During 1996 and into 1997, the Spice Girls solidified their success in Britain, and then tackled America. A carefully orchestrated marketing campaign was undertaken by Virgin in the USA, partly to offset initial critical reception of the records. For example, the *Rolling Stone*'s negative March 1997 review of *Spice*, which labelled the music a watered down mix of hip-hop and pop, and accorded it only one and a half stars (on a five-star scale). 'Despite their pro-woman posing', wrote reviewer Christina Kelly, 'the Girls don't get bogged down by anything deeper than mugging for promo shots and giving out tips on getting boys into bed' (quoted in Dickerson, 1998: 205). Virgin marketed the band with heavy emphasis on their videos and the Girls visual appeal, largely avoiding the more potentially awkward print media. This meant 'high profiles for MTV, short interviews for television, and staged events where cameras could only get passing glimpses of the Spice Girls in controlled situations'. MTV was crucial, 'showing the Girls' nipple-friendly video (for "Wannabe") at every opportunity' (Dickerson, 1998: 205). In July 1997, Spice topped the *Billboard* album charts, and, *Rolling Stone* ran a cover story headlined 'Spice Girls Conquer the World', a nine-page article, which told readers everything they could possibly want to know about the Spice Girls (10 July 1997 issue). All this without playing a concert, and not playing live, except on the television show *Late Night with David Letterman*.

The Spice Girls filled a market niche. As Chris Herbert observed:

> The whole teen-band scene at that time was saturated by boy bands. I felt that if you could appeal to the boys as well, you'd be laughing. If you could put together a girl band which was both sassy, for the girls, and with obvious sex appeal, to attract the boys, you'd double your audience.
>
> (Davis, 1997: 35)

The Spice Girls also provided an antidote to the 'laddish' culture of UK Britpop in the early 1990s, associated with performers such as the Gallagher brothers (Oasis). The Spice Girls were the subject of considerable hostility from many 'rock' critics/fans, who saw them as a media artefact, a view underpinned by the historical denigration of dance pop as a genre.

Their success was made possible by a combination of their music, their marketing, and their personalities. The Spice Girls' music is 'a mixture of dance, hip-hop, R&B, and smooth-as-silk pop ballads. Technically solid. Middle of the road. Nothing extreme' (Dickerson, 1998: 203). This is to overlook the appeal of the clever and catchy lyrics of songs such as 'Wannabe', with its catchphrase 'Zig-a-zig-ah' for sex, and the highlighting of ongoing friendship and a streetwise attitude toward relationships.

> Yo, I'll tell you what I want, what I really really want,
> So tell me what you want, what you really really want,
> I'll tell you what I want, what I really really want,
> So tell me what you want, what you really really want,
> I wanna, I wanna, I wanna, I wanna,
> I wanna really
> really really wanna zig-a-zig-ha.
> If you want my future forget my past,
> If you wanna get with me better make it fast,
> Now don't go wasting my precious time,
> Get your act together we could be just fine.
> If you wanna be my lover, you gotta get with my friends,
> Make it last forever friendship never ends,
> If you wanna be my lover, you have got to give,
> Taking is too easy, but that's the way it is.
> What do you think about that now you know how I feel,
> Say you can handle my love are you for real,
> I won't be hasty, I'll give you a try
> If you really bug me then I'll say goodbye.
> (The Spice Girls, 'Wannabe', Virgin, 1996)

However, this well-crafted pop is not the foundation for their mega-success, which was due mainly to the band's public image, which they partly created for themselves through force of personality and an irreverent attitude to the music industry and the media. They were seen as five 'sassy' individuals who combined girl-next-door appeal with considerable sex appeal. 'They introduced the language of independence to a willing audience of pre-teen and teenage girls – girl power' (Whiteley, 2000: 215). In a discourse reminiscent of Madonna's early career, critics pointed to a contradiction between the Spice Girls' self-expression and their subversion of standard 'feminine' images, and their incorporation into a male-dominated industry. The group themselves, and their defenders, in response claimed that this was of their own choosing and on their own terms.

The franchising (through product endorsements) of a huge range of Spice Girl products added to the Girls' ubiquitous presence through 1997 and 1998. In December 1997 *Q* magazine rated the Spice Girls the 'biggest rock band in the world', based on the amount of airplay they had received, total income from record sales, concert tickets, etc., and the number of appearances on national magazine covers (both music and 'general' titles). In 1998 the Spice Girls released their second album, *Spice World*, again topping the charts internationally, and a movie of the same name. In August 1998, 'Viva Forever' became their seventh UK Number 1 single, and they sold out a forty concert 'world' tour. During 1999 and into 2000 the group's momentum eased: Gerry departed, and was not replaced; the remaining members devoted themselves to individual projects (e.g. Mel C's *Northern Star*); and Victoria and Mel B became mothers. A third Spice Girls album was released in November 2000; its limited success contributed to the effective breakup of the band.

On her way: Shania Twain

Country emerged in the US as a major market force in popular music in the 1990s (see Sernoe, 1998) and classic stereotypes associated with the genre (especially its maudlin themes and limited appeal) no longer hold up. *Billboard* placed Garth Brooks as Top Country Album Artist and Top Pop Album Artist for the years 1990, 1991, and 1993. In 1993, all six of his albums were included among the 100 most popular albums of the year, with two – *No Fences* and *Ropin' the Wind* – having sold about ten million copies each. His crossover success opened the way on the pop charts for other country artists, often referred to as 'new country', with Billy Ray Cyrus, Dwight Yoakum, Mary Chapin Carpenter, and Reba McEntire among the best-selling artists of the early to mid-1990s. This contributed to a general market dominance by women performers, who in 1996 and 1997 had approximately 60 per cent of the releases to make the Top 20 in the *Billboard* album charts (Dickerson, 1998). At the same time, country radio became the second most listened to music format in the United States, second only to adult contemporary, and video channel CMT (Country Music Television) achieved a significant market share. The success of Shania Twain during the late 1990s was in part made possible by this aggressive resurgence of country music, and the receptive context which it created. Her crossover to the commercial mainstream and massive success, however, lifted the 'country' tag from her, and by 1998 she was an international figure.

Shania Twain was born in Canada. Her life story has, slightly cynically, been compared to a fairy tale: 'A country girl from Timmins, Ontario, is raised dirt poor, starts performing in bars as a child, loses her parents at age 22 when their car collides with a logging truck, sings to support her three teenage siblings, then finds her prince

– reclusive rock producer Robert John (Mutt) Lange – who gives her a studio kiss of stardom' (Brian Johnson, 'Shania Revealed'; cover story in *Maclean's*, Canada's leading magazine, 23 March 1998; Hager (1998) provides a detailed and balanced biography). Her success is based on a combination of her songwriting, her striking and attractive looks, her music videos, and, as Johnson suggests (above), the role of Mutt Lange in her recordings. The weighting variously accorded to these factors, illustrate the controversy that has surrounded her status as a star and a popular music 'auteur'.

Twain moved to Nashville in 1991 after signing a deal with Mercury Nashville, changing her name from Eilleen to Shania, which means 'I'm on my way' in Ojibwa (the language of her stepfather). Her self-titled debut album (1993) featured only one of her own compositions, her producers opting instead for songs from established songwriters, a common practice in Nashville. The debut was respectable, without making a major impact: it sold around a hundred thousand copies, two singles from it got to Number 55 on the Billboard Hot Country Singles Chart, and Shania made *Billboard*'s 1993 list of promising new artists. The accompanying music video for 'What Made You Say That', her own composition, broke with country tradition, celebrating her 'wholesome' sexuality, as she frolicked on a tropical beach with a male 'hunk'. It featured her bared navel, which became a 'trademark' on later videos and magazine covers. Screened on CMT Europe, the video also brought Shania to the attention of leading English producer Mutt Lange. The two started collaborating on songwriting, became close friends, and were married in December 1993.

Shania's second album, *The Woman in Me* (1995), was produced by Lange, who also partially financed it. Featuring a number of the songs turned down for the first album. *The Woman in Me* took a year and a half and more than half a million dollars to complete, a recording effort which stunned Nashville, where budgets of one-tenth of that amount were standard (Hager, 1998: 54). It sold twelve million copies by the end of 1998. Of the twelve songs, ten were co-written by Shania and Mutt, and there was a solo contribution from each. As Hager describes it, this was a creative collaboration, with each contributing from their strengths and complementing the other. In producing *The Woman in Me*, Lange drew on the 'rock' style which he had used for very successful records with Def Leppard, AC/DC, and Bryan Adams. The album was a combination of 'Irresistible songs, sassy lyrics, all backed by Lange's onion-skin production, which reveals more of each song with each play' (*Q* review, November 1999). Her third album, *Come on Over* (1998) sold 4.2 million during its first five months of release. The first single from it, 'You're Still the One', topped the *Billboard* country chart in May 1998, and went on to reach Number 1 on the pop chart. Both the album and the several singles from it topped charts internationally.

This success was achieved, her critics observed, without Twain performing 'live'. This claim conveniently overlooked the fact that she had been performing in public from the age of three, but really referred to the singer not initially undertaking a concert tour to promote her albums. Instead, Shania did a series of promotional appearances, in shopping centres, on talk shows, and at industry showcases. This led to claims that her songs were largely the product of the recording studio, and raised questions about her ability to present them in performance. Twain was also frequently accused of being a 'packaged' artist, created by her high-powered management (Jon Landau, who also represents Bruce Springsteen). The success of her extensive touring in 1998 and into 1999, and the quality of her stage performance, erased these questions. The tour also enabled the production of a best-selling concert video.

Cover stories (for example, *Rolling Stone*, 3 September 1998; *Q*, November 1999) accentuated Shania's 'natural' physical appeal, particularly her bare midriff, a feature of several of her early videos. In her songs and videos, Twain combines a flirtatious glamour and self-empowerment: 'a country singer who looks like a supermodel' who 'on camera projects a playful allure that is part come-on, part come-off-it' (Johnson, *Maclean's*, 23 March 1998: 50). This is feminism very much in the mould of the Spice Girls.

Her songs, mainly co-written with Lange, reinvigorate tired county formats. They range from ballads of domestic bliss ('You're Still the One'), and feisty reassurance ('Don't Be Stupid. You Know I Love You'), to clever assertions of women's rights ('Honey I'm Home', is a neat role reversal). Within its pop ballad format and catchy tune, 'Black Eyes, Blue Tears' alerts listeners to domestic violence:

Black eyes, I don't need 'em
Blue tears, gimme freedom
Positively never goin' back
I won't live where things are out of whack
No more rollin' with the punches
No more usin' or abusin'
I'd rather die standing
Than live on my knees
Beggin' please – no more
Black eyes, I don't need 'em
Blue tears, gimme freedom
Black eyes – all behind me
Blue tears'll never find me now
(Shania Twain, 'Black Eyes, Blue Tears',
from album *Come On Over*, Mercury/Polygram, 1998)

Come On Over established Shania Twain as a successful crossover artist. Remixed versions of singles from the album placed less emphasis on country-style instrumentation, creating greater airplay on non-country radio. Her next album, after a two-year 'time out' suffering from exhaustion, continued this marketing strategy. *Up!* (2002), a double album, featured 29 songs in a country mix on one disc, and the same songs in pop mixes on the other. The album, and several singles from it, topped the charts. A *Greatest Hits* album, in 2004, maintained Twain's commercial success. Shania Twain is a popular music auteur whose work and marketable image have made her a star, although her success illustrates the frequent contribution of others to musical authorship.

Fatboy Slim: multiple authorship

One factor common to the auteur and star figures I have considered so far is the value attached to the retaining of a consistent identity across time, the creation of a 'brand name' persona, through ongoing changes of style and genre. Straw makes a persuasive case that such a view of authorship has been challenged by the manner in which 'so much popular music now unfolds within highly specialized cultural niches – complex clusters of influence and cross-fertilization marked by tiny moves ahead or to the side' (Straw, 1999: 206). The dance music scene and the work of Norman Cook, provide an example of a different style of 'career'. (The following draws on Stuart Hutchins' Profile of Cook, in *Juice Magazine*, March 1999; Reynolds, 1998; James, 2002.)

Cook first came to public notice in the UK, when he played bass with the indie pop band the Housemartins, who had some chart success in the mid-1980s; 'Caravan of Love' was a UK Number 1 in December 1986. When they broke up in the late 1980s, Cook formed Beats International, and had another British Number 1 with 'Dub Be Good to Me'. But Beats International were castigated for 'trying to play black music', Cook's marriage ended, he declared bankruptcy, and was diagnosed as clinically depressed. A dance floor epiphany, aided by 'E' (the drug ecstasy), led him to form Freakpower, a retro-funk band, who had a top five hit in Britain when 'Turn On Tune In Drop Out' was used for a Levi's ad. Cook also started releasing records as Pizzaman and the Mighty Dub Katz. Inspired by the Chemical Brothers and London clubs such as Heavenly Social, he became a leading DJ and recording figure in the scene that became known as big beat (Reynolds, 1998: 384–6). His first album as Fatboy Slim, *Better Living Through Chemistry* (1996), and a series of singles during 1997–8 made him an international figure, especially in the dance music community. His remixes of Cornershop's 'Brimful of Asha' and Wildchild's 'Renegade Master' both reached Number 1 in the UK, and his own 'The Rockafeller Skank' and 'Gangsta Trippin' also charted. Both the last were on his commercially highly successful album *You've Come a Long Way Baby* (1998), while another single from this, 'Praise You', also went to Number 1.

The Fatboy Slim sound has been described as 'a mix of speeded up hip-hop beats, [Roland] 303 driven bass lines and big sampled hooks', and by Norman himself as 'big dumb music for drunken students' (Stuart Hutchins, *Juice Magazine*, March 1999: 46).

Cook is an auteur, by virtue of his overall vision and creativity. However, since the late 1980s, he has consistently worked with others, notably studio and sound engineer Simon Thornton. Cook has also had several contributing vocalists; for example, *Halfway Between the Gutter and the Stars* (2000) featured two collaborations with Macy Gray. Later albums saw Cook branching out stylistically, mixing his previous loop and sample-based compositions with more conventional song structures and 'real' instruments, and with more vocal collaborators, including rapper Lateef (*Palookaville*, 2004).

Norman Cook has kept up a bewildering array of aliases (indeed, Norman Cook is itself a pseudonym), in part because he believes his musical past meant that some people would not approach his music with an open mind. This failure to let each stylistic change add to his musical persona over time, as it has with Madonna for example, is 'strategically appropriate' in the field of contemporary dance music, where 'such changes are read as signs that the individual's origins in (or commitment to) any one style are not genuine, that the individual's participation in that genre's unfolding history is merely a momentary visit' (Straw, 1999: 206).

The auteurs and stars I have considered here share a number of characteristics. At a fairly self-evident level, in their musical careers they all exercise considerable control over their artistic lives, perhaps because this has often been hard won. All have an ability to retain an audience across time, either through reinventing their persona/ image, or through exploring new avenues in their music. They all have produced a substantial body of work, often multimedia in form; and they have all been, to varying degrees, seeking new ways of reinterpreting or reaffirming popular music styles. These characteristics apply to both auteurs and stars, but the latter go beyond them, to function as mythic constructs, related to their audiences collective and individual relationship to the music and performer (Marshall, 1997: 163). Popular music stars and auteurs also represent economic entities, a unique commodity form which is both a labour process and product. The continuity of their careers contributes to stability in the marketplace, thereby enhancing the cultural and potential commercial value of their musical 'texts'.

NOTES

For general considerations of musical authorship and creativity, see the reading suggested in Chapter 3. Biographical material, often situated around interviews and new releases, is a staple part of the music press. The brief career profiles included here can be supplemented by the entries on each in Wikipedia, and official artist web sites. Also:

MOJO (2004) ICONS *The Greatest Music Stars of All Time.*

On stardom generally, and in relation to film stars (useful parallels can be drawn with rock and pop stars):

Hayward, S. (2000) *Key Concepts in Cinema Studies*, London and New York: Routledge.

Robert Johnson and the blues

Robert Johnson. The Complete Recordings, Columbia, 1990 (boxed set).

The two known photos of Johnson can be seen at: www.deltahaze.com.

Pearson, B. and McCulloch, B. (2003), *Robert Johnson: Lost and Found*, Urbana, IL: University of Illinois Press; especially chapter 13: 'Who was he, really?'

Weisman, D. (2005) *Blues: The Basics*, New York & London: Routledge.

Documentaries:

The Search for Robert Johnson, Sony, 1992 (DVD).

Can't You Hear The Wind Howl? The Life and Music of Robert Johnson, Shout, 1997 (DVD).

Phil Spector

Back To Mono (1958–1969), Spector/Abko, 1991 (boxed set).

Thompson, D. (2005) *Wall of Pain: The Biography of Phil Spector*, London: Sanctuary.

Ribowtsky, M. (1989) *He's A Rebel*, New York: E.P. Dutton.

Moorefield, V. (2005) *The Producer as Composer: Shaping the Sounds of Popular Music*, Cambridge, MA: MIT Press (includes a case study of The Ronettes, 'Be My Baby').

Pete Townshend and The Who

The Who, Then & Now, Polydor, 2004 (CD).

Marsh, D. (1989) *Before I Get Old: The Story of The Who*, New York: St Martin's Press.

Q. (2004) *The Who: Special Edition*, London: EMAP Metro.

Perry, J. (1998) *Meaty, Beaty, Big & Bouncy: The Who*, New York: Schirmer Books.

Documentary: *Who's Next*, Classic Albums, Isis, 1997.

Official web site: www.petetownshend.co.uk.

Frank Zappa

Miles, B. (2004) *Frank Zappa: A Biography*, London: Atlantic.

Zappa, F. (1990) *The Real Frank Zappa Book*, London: Pan Books.

Strictly Commercial. The Best of Frank Zappa, Ryodisc, 1995 (compilation CD).

Official web site: www.zappa.com.

The Spice Girls

Lemish, D. (2003) 'Spice World: Constructing Femininity the Popular Way', *Popular Music and Society*, 26, 1: 17–29.

Whiteley, S. (2000) *Women and Popular Music: Sexuality, Identity and Subjectivity*, London: Routledge.

Of the numerous biographies, I prefer:
Golden, A.L. (1997) *The Spice Girls*, New York: Ballantine Books.
Movie: *Spice World*, Virgin, 1997.

Shania Twain and country
Come On Over, Mercury Records, 1998.
Greatest Hits, Mercury, 2004.
Hager, B. (1998) *On Her Way: The Life and Music of Shania Twain*, New York: Berkley Boulevard.

Fatboy Slim
James, M. (2002) *Fatboy Slim: Funk Soul Brother*, London: Sanctuary Publishing.
Why Try Harder (2005) A greatest hits compilation; the eighteen tracks include Cook's ten Top 40 UK singles.
Official web site: www.fatboyslim.net/.

Chapter 5

'Message Understood?'
Musical texts

The term 'text' has traditionally been used to refer to an author's original words, or a prose work – especially one recommended for student reading. More recently, as a cultural studies term, text refers to any media form that is self-contained and conveys cultural meaning, including television programmes, recordings, films, and books. Popular music texts are quite diverse, and include recordings, record sleeve covers, and music videos. The most prominent are sound recordings, in various formats, and their packaging (album covers, box sets, etc). In addition, there are several other important forms of popular music texts: music magazines, posters, T-shirts, tour brochures, and fan club merchandise. Musical performances, especially concerts, and DJ discourse, have also been analyzed as forms of musical text. These various forms are frequently interconnected and mutually reinforcing.

Following a brief consideration of the nature of textual analysis, I identify three broad types of musical text, and, with reference to examples, discuss approaches to their analysis. (Chapter 6 considers texts as 'collectivities', through discussions of genre, cover songs, and the album canon). The three forms of text are: graphic (with an emphasis on album cover art); musical (with particular reference to issues surrounding musicology and the analysis of song lyrics); and music video, as the main example of an audiovisual music text. It is obviously difficult to express through language qualities that are often visual and aural, rather then linguistic. Accordingly, in the chapter Notes, I have provided details of websites where album cover art, song lyrics and recordings, and music videos can be accessed.

TEXTUAL ANALYSIS

Textual analysis is concerned with identifying and analysing the formal qualities of texts, their underpinning structures and constituent characteristic. As such, it has become closely associated with various approaches to content and discourse analysis, including semiotic analysis. In the case of popular music, textual analysis takes several forms. The most important is the examination of the musical components of songs, including their lyrics, in their various recorded formats. Musicology is central here, although its traditional approach has been modified in relation to popular music. While texts are usually analysed independently, they can also be considered collectively, as with content analysis of chart share in terms of genres, or record labels (majors compared to independents: see the discussion of market cycles in Chapter 1). A similar approach has been applied to radio and MTV airplay, especially in relation to relative shares of local content and imported repertoire (see Chapter 14).

Intertextuality is important here: the idea that a text communicates its meaning only when it is situated in relation to other texts; it is often characterized as meaning that 'arises' between texts (Gracyk, 2001: 56). Examples of this process are the dialogue that occurs between cover versions of songs and their antecedents (see Chapter 6: covers), and fan discourse around preferred styles and performers. Intertextuality is also implicit in the repackaging of recordings as generic compilations and boxed sets. Gracyk (2001: Chapter 3) provides a number of interesting musical examples, making the point that such 'influences, connections, and allusions create nuances of meaning that cannot be grasped simply through a general intertextuality' (p. 59).

A point of debate around popular culture is its ideological role in reinforcing and reproducing dominant values through their representation in popular texts. Critics who concentrate on the text itself, often using concepts from semiotic and psychoanalytic analysis, argue that there frequently exists in the text a preferred reading, that is, a dominant message set within the cultural code of established conventions and practices of the producers/transmitters of the text. However, while many consumers may, at least implicitly or subconsciously, accept such preferred readings, it must be kept in mind that it is not necessarily true that the audience as a whole do so. In particular, subordinate groups may reinterpret such textual messages, making 'sense' of them in a different way. The Strawbs' 'Part of the Union', intended as a direct attack on trade unionism, achieved the opposite effect when sung by striking Coventry car workers. As Herman and Hoare (1979: 53) concluded: 'Because records are interpreted, because they stimulate song, their consumption is not merely passive. A song's meaning is not immutable, independent of context'. The study of pop fans similarly suggests that cultural meanings are ultimately made by consumers, even if this process is under conditions and opportunities not of their own choosing (see Chapter 11). This opens up the idea of popular resistance to, and subversion of, dominant cultures, a view that has informed analysis of the nature and reception of popular song lyrics, and music videos.

GRAPHIC TEXTS: ALBUM COVER ART

Popular music graphic texts include concert posters, street flyers, and even t-shirts, but the most prominent form is the packaging of recordings, including boxed sets and album and CD cover artwork. While present on the sleeves of singles, as with the distinctive artwork of several punk and indie labels (see Borthwick and Moy, 2004; Chapter 5), cover art is primarily associated with albums, especially in their vinyl format. The album became prominent as a format in the 1960s. Although its vinyl form was largely displaced by CDs in the 1980s, the format continued to be produced, most notable as ten inch singles for the dance market, and as limited pressings of 180 gram vinyl albums for the collector and audiophile. Album covers convey meaning through the semiotic resources they draw on and display, via language, typography, images, and layout.

Part of the appeal of albums was the development of their covers as an art form, with some creative packaging, including supplementary material, in releases during the 1960s. Prominent examples are the replica tobacco tin of The Small Faces' *Ogden's Nut Gone Flake* (Sony, 1968); and The Who's, *Live at Leeds* (MCA, 1970) which included reproductions of concert posters, performance invoices, etc. in a stapled folder cardboard cover. The album covers of the Beatles recordings were especially notable: 'groundbreaking in their visual and aesthetic properties (and) their innovative and imaginative designs' (Inglis, 2001:83). They forged a link with the expanding British graphic design industry and the art world, while making explicit the connections between art and pop in the 1960s. The prestigious Grammy's began including an award for best album cover, won by the Beatles in 1966 for *Revolver* and again in 1967 for *Sgt. Pepper's Lonely Hearts Club Band*, undoubtedly the most celebrated album cover (on its genesis, and artist Peter Blake's work with the Beatles, see Miles, 1997).

Album covers perform several important functions: they are a form of advertising, alerting consumers to the artist(s) responsible, and thereby sustaining and drawing on an auteur/star image; and they make an artistic statement in relation to the style of music by association with particular iconography, for example the use of apocalyptic imagery in heavy metal, and the fantasy imagery of progressive rock (Ochs, 1996; Weinstein, 2000). Album cover liner notes function as a literary and advertising form, while the practice of printing song lyrics on covers often signals a 'serious' genre and artist. As I showed in Chapter 1, Island's marketing of Bob Marley and the Wailers, with album covers constructing Marley as a star figure and the band as politically authentic style rebels, was important to their commercial success and the mainstreaming of reggae in the 1970s.

Cover art has become considered as an artform, with the publication of collected volumes of covers that are considered exemplars, along with collections of the work of artists such as Roger Dean, best known for his work with progressive rock band Yes. Particular record companies are associated with a 'house' style of covers, for instance the jazz label Blue Note from the mid-1950s employed a talented graphic artist, Reid Miles, to design most of its album sleeves. (Nearly 400 examples are reproduced in Marsh and Callingham, 2003). The covers represented sophisticated images of fashion, and combined with Miles' personal flair and the pioneering use of typography to signal taste and integrity as a key part of the label's appeal.

MUSICOLOGY AND POPULAR SONG

Clearly the central textual form in popular music is the song, primarily reproduced as individual sound recordings; the single. The analysis of these has been dominated in popular discourse by fans, the music press and music critics (see Chapter 10), and in academic work by musicology.

Traditional musicology privileges the text by placing the emphasis firmly on its formal properties. Musicologists investigate genres such as pop and rock as music, using conventional concepts derived from the study of more traditional/classical forms of music: harmony, melody, beat and rhythm, along with vocal style and the lyrics. A major debate in popular music studies has been around the value of a traditional musicological approach to music texts. Indeed, there is an argument as to whether popular music even merits such a 'serious' analysis. This was clearly evident in the 1980s, in the bemused reaction of the mainstream British press to the emergence of 'popular music studies' (see Frith, 1983: 4; Tagg, 1982), reflecting conservative notions of high culture set against the mass society critiques of popular music.

Academic musicologists at first largely ignored rock and pop music. A notable early exception was Mellers' sympathetic study of the Beatles, *Twilight of the Gods* (1974); his example was followed by Tagg (1982). Most musicologists, however, were reluctant to engage with a form of music accorded low cultural value in comparison with 'serious' music. At the same time, many sociologists writing on popular music were wary of musicology. This was due to its tendency to be distant from the mechanics of much actual composition of rock, its 'vague pretentiousness' and 'chronic failure to address what is really at stake in the tunes' (McClary and Walser, 1990: 277). As Frith noted, both rock musicians and rock commentators generally lack formal musical training: 'They lack the vocabulary and techniques of musical analysis, and even the descriptive words that critics and fans do use – harmony, melody, riff, beat – are only loosely understood and applied' (Frith, 1983: 13).

Frith saw rock critics as essentially preoccupied with sociology rather that sound, and identified what has been too ready a willingness to dismiss musicology as having little relevance to the study of popular styles. The arguments here were well rehearsed through the 1980s: traditional musicology neglects the social context, emphasizes the transcription of music (the score), and elevates harmonic and rhythmic structure to pride of place as an evaluative criterion. Popular music, on the other hand, emphasizes interpretation through performance, and is received primarily in terms of the body and emotions rather than as pure text. Many rock musicians observed that classical music operated according to a different set of musical criteria, which has little validity for their own efforts. Indeed, it can be argued that much popular music is largely a music of the body and emotions, and its influence can not easily be reduced to a simple consideration of its formal musical qualities.

Certainly, attempts to apply traditional musicological criteria could all too easily appear pretentious, as shown by Frith's comparison of two explanations of the Animals' 1964 hit 'I'm Crying'. Richard Middleton, a musicologist, in his explanation emphasized the formal musical qualities of the composition, including the point that:

> The cross relations in the ostinato (which is melodic and harmonic) are the equivalents of blue notes, arising from a similar conflict between melodic and tonal implications. The modal melodic movement of the ostinato, with its minor thirds, clashes with the tonal need for major triads imposed by the 12-bar blues structure.
>
> (Frith, 1983: 13)

Compare this with Alan Price's description: 'I wrote the music and Eric (Burdon) did the words and we just threw it together in rehearsal in Blackpool., We just stuck it together and recorded it and by chance it was successful' (Frith, 1983: 13). Middleton's analysis, while accurate, places considerable demands on the reader, while Price's casual explanation reflects a romantic rock ideology, with its ideal of spontaneous and inspired creativity.

In the early 1990s, there were signs that the largely negative attitude toward applying musicology to popular music was changing. Several musicologists engaged with popular music genres and texts, while popular music scholars generally began to accord musicology more weight in their analyses. This work varies in the degree to which such analysis simply takes as a given the concepts and tools of traditional (e.g. more classical-music-oriented) musicology (e.g. Mellers, 1986), or modifies these in relation to popular music (e.g. Moore, 1993; Tagg and Clarida, 2003). The past decade has produced a substantial body of what can be termed 'popular musicology'.

Much of this discussion recognizes that the traditional conception of musicology remains inadequate when applied to popular music in any straightforward manner (equating the two forms). For example, a concentration on technical textual aspects alone – the score – fails to deal with how the effects listeners celebrate are constructed, what McClary and Walser (1990: 287) term 'the dimensions of music that are most compelling and yet most threatening to rationality'. This takes into consideration the role of pleasure, the relationship of the body, feelings and emotions, and sexuality in constructing responses to genres such as dance, rock, and the blues. Recent popular musicology has engaged further with the more affective domains of the relationship between the text and its listeners, and into the generic and historical locations of texts and performers (Hawkins, 2002, provides a helpful overview and critique of this work).

It is worth remembering that people are more 'musical' than is usually credited. Radio listening – switching stations in search of something recognizable or engaging–– and selecting and downloading which music to play on one's personal stereo involves an ability to distinguish between different types of music. This is to utilize a more extended definition of 'musical', where what is crucial is the link between musical structures and people's use of them. As Hawkins observes, 'the task of interpreting pop is an interdisciplinary task that deals with the relationship between music and social mediation. It is one that includes taking into account the consideration of the sounds in their relationship to us as individuals' (2002: 3).

WHY DO SONGS HAVE WORDS?

Even when there has been a concern to address popular genres such as 'rock' as music, this has largely concentrated on its lyrical component, an approach I have cautiously followed here. In his insightful historical discussion, 'Why Do Songs Have Words?' Frith shows how through the 1950s and 1960s the sociology of popular music was dominated by the analysis of the words of songs. This was largely because such an approach was grounded in a familiar research methodology – content analysis. It did make a certain amount of sense given the dominance of popular music by the 'bland, universal well-made song' (Whitcomb, 1972) of Tin Pan Alley, but assumed, however, 'that it was possible to read back from lyrics to the social forces that produced them' (Frith, 1988b: 106).

Such an approach is evident in the extensive efforts of writers such as Cooper, who demonstrates the use of lyrics to approach social, political and personal issues:

> The attitudes and values portrayed in modern tunes demand the reflective consideration of students because they strike at the heart of the major social and political issues of our time: ecology, women's liberation, political cynicism, militarism, drug abuse, and others.
>
> (Cooper, 1981: 8; see also Cooper, 1990)

This assumes that the words of the songs indeed express general social attitudes, and, given that songwriters are social beings and presumably conscious of changing cultural norms etc. this view does have some validity. As Frith points out, however, content analysis treats lyrics too simply:

> The words of all songs are given equal value, their meaning is taken to be transparent; no account is given of their actual performance or their musical setting. This enables us to code lyrics statistically, but it involves a questionable theoretical judgement: content codes refer to what the words describe – situations and states of mind – but not to how they describe, to their significance as language. Even more problematically, these analysts tend to equate a song's popularity to public agreement with its message.
>
> (Frith, 1988b: 107)

Let us consider three instructive examples of such difficulties.

Stand by your lyric

'Stand By Your Man', co-written (with Billy Sherrill) and sung by Tammy Wynette, was a Number 1 hit upon its release in 1968, and the song remains one of the best selling records by a woman in the history of country music. Wynette adopted it as her theme song, performing it in all her concerts, and using it as the title for both her autobiography and the television movie about her life. The song even sparked a Number 1 hit response: Ronnie Milsap's Grammy-winning '(I'm A) Stand By My Woman Man' (1976). The popularity of 'Stand By Your Man' was matched by the controversy and critical response it created. This focused on the song's apparently sexist message:

> Stand by your man
> Give him two arms to cling to
> And something warm to come to
> On nights he's cold and lonely
> Stand by your man
> And tell the world you love him
> Keep giving all the love you can
> Stand by your man.

This chorus was generally interpreted as a simple clarion call for women to subserviently support their male partners, reducing the woman's role essentially to a physical one, providing 'arms' and 'something warm'. *Newsweek* headlined a 1971 article on Wynette's music: 'Songs of Non-Liberation', while other reviewers labelled her work 'pre-feminist' and equated it with traditional views of women's 'allegiance to the stronger sex'. But while the dynamics of the song emphasize the chorus, the lyrics to its only verse make its interpretation more problematic:

> Sometimes it's hard to be a woman
> Giving all your love to just one man
> You'll have bad times
> And he'll have good times
> Doin' things you don't understand
> But if you love him
> You'll forgive him
> Even though he's hard to understand
> And if you love him
> Be proud of him
> 'Cause after all he's just a man.

The verse is presenting the hardships women face in their relationships with men, with the last line a neatly condescending assertion of women's superior gender status. A literal reading of the lyrics (especially in print, as here) is misleading. The slightly maudlin and world-weary tone of Wynette's recorded vocal suggests an ironic stance. Another dimension which reinforces this emphasis, was Tammy Wynette's personal life. Then a twice-divorced mother of three, several of her previous hits had asserted the views of a wronged and righteous single woman: especially her song 'D-I-V-O-R-C-E'. Furthermore, her subsequent tortured personal life (she died in 1998), including three additional marriages, and further songs elaborating the earlier pro-woman themes, suggested Wynette was using 'Stand By Your Man' to make an ironic statement about the contradictory dimensions of women's experience of relationships. The verse and chorus of the song represent the dilemma women face of meeting their gender obligations, while anticipating their ideal achievement. The song, argues Morris (1992), must be understood as a totality.

The Sherrill-Wynette song-writing partnership was mirrored in the song, with the male mandated chorus providing the main theme, which is countered by the female-authored verse. It is also significant that Wynette dissassociated herself from the interpretations of the song as sexist:

> I never did understand all the commotion over the lyrics of that song. I don't see anything in that song that implies that a woman is supposed to sit home and raise babies while a man goes out and raises hell.
>
> (Wynette, 1980: 193)

To validate this interpretation of 'Stand By Your Man', it would be necessary to ask women (and men?) how they respond to and interpret the song, given that listeners respond in a variety of ways to the same musical text. This simple but essential point is also illustrated by the song 'Spoonful'.

A spoonful of drugs?

Willie Dixon's 'Spoonful' (based on Charlie Patton's 'A Spoonful of Blues', 1929), recorded by a number of artists, demonstrates the social meanings that may be ascribed to various renditions of a song.

> Could fill spoons full of diamonds,
> Could fill spoons full of gold,
> Just a little spoon of your precious love
> Satisfies my soul
> (chorus) That spoon that spoon that spoonful (repeats)
>   ('Spoonful', Willie Dixon)

Many listeners, myself included, initially interpreted the song as being about drug use, focusing on 'a little spoon of your precious love' as a metaphor for drugs, possibly even heroin. This reading reflected our exposure to the song as part of the 1960s counter-culture, usually heard through Cream's studio and live versions. Dixon rejects this view as simply incorrect, describing the inspiration for the song as:

> The idea of 'Spoonful' was that it doesn't take a large amount of anything to be good. If you have a little money when you need it, you're right there in the right spot, that'll buy you a lot. If a doctor give you less than a spoonful of some kind of medicine that can kill you, he can give you less than a spoonful of another one that will make you well.
>
> (Dixon, 1989: 148)

Again meaning is ultimately dependent on the associations listeners attach to any particular work, and the period in which particular renditions of it are situated.

Patriotism and irony in the USA

Songs create identification through their emotional appeal, but this does not necessarily mean that they can be reduced to a simple slogan or message, although some listeners may do just that. This is evident in Bruce Springsteen's song 'Born in the USA'. Springsteen was a dominant figure in 1980s rock music. His song 'Born in the USA' represents one of his most powerful political statements, reflecting the self-consciously political stance evident in his work, and his view that 'I don't think people are being taught to think hard enough about things in general, whether its about their own lives, politics, the situation in Nicaragua, or whatever' (1987 interview quoted in Pratt, 1990: 177). 'Born in the USA' is a bitter narrative of life in the American underclass. The first person singer-narrator, Springsteen, joins the army to avoid 'a little hometown jam', fights in Vietnam, where his brother is killed, and returns to unemployment, seemingly with no hope or future.

> Born down in a dead man's town,
> The first kick I took was when I hit the ground
> You end up like a dog that's been beat too much
> Til you spend half your life just covering up
> (Bruce Springsteen, 'Born in the USA')

The music has a militaristic flavour, especially in the upbeat chorus sections, with the anthemic refrain:

> BORN IN THE USA
> I was BORN IN THE USA
> I was BORN IN THE USA
> BORN IN THE USA

It is an open question to what extent Springsteen's listeners appreciate the song as a resigned and ironic comment on the United States. Springsteen himself was highly conscious of this:

> I opened the paper one day and saw where they had quizzed kids on what different songs meant to them and they asked them what 'Born in the USA' meant. 'Well, it's about my country', they answered. Well, that is what it's about – that's certainly one of the things it's about – but if that's as far in as you go, you're going to miss it, you know?
>
> (Pratt, 1990: 177)

Casually listening to the song, many of my own students regard it simply as a homage to America, picking up on the celebratory anthem-like chorus, rather than the verse narrative.

A provocative comparison with the original recorded version of the song is provided by Springsteen's live acoustic version, which appears on *Tracks*, 1999. Here, due to Springsteen's vocal and guitar being fairly constant throughout, the verses 'compete' on an equal footing with the chorus, and listeners are more conscious of the song's ironic celebration of the United States.

'Stand By Your Man', 'Spoonful', and 'Born in the USA' all demonstrate that listeners use songs for their own purposes, and the popularity of particular performers is only in part derived from the substantive content of their work.

'THE POETRY OF ROCK', SONG AND SOCIAL REALISM

Part of the argument for 1960s rock's superiority over pop and earlier forms of popular music rested on the claim that its major songwriters were poets. Richard Goldstein's *The Poetry of Rock* (1969) and similar anthologies helped to popularize this view, which emphasized a particular form of rock lyrics – those akin to romantic poetry with lots of covert and obscure allusions, as in the work of Bob Dylan. This approach validated 'rock' in terms of established 'art' forms, elevating the role of the songwriter to that of an auteur figure with the ability to work in a recognizable high cultural mode (an approach linked to the early years of *Rolling Stone* magazine, established in 1967). An extension of this position is the relegation of mainstream commercial pop lyrics to banality and worthlessness. Yet clearly such lyrics do in some sense matter to their listeners: *Smash Hits,* focusing on the words of the latest chart entries, has been one of Britain's biggest selling music magazines. Frith (1988b: 121) suggests that a critical question here is 'how do words and voices work differently for different types of pop and audience?' This necessitates addressing how song lyrics work as ordinary language.

One of the issues here is the realism of song. A notion of lyrical realism asserts 'a direct relationship between a lyric and the social or emotional condition it describes and represents' (Frith, 1988b: 112). This is evident in the study of folk song and the analysis of blues lyrics. Garon (1975) compares blues to poetry, arguing that the blues convey pleasure 'through its use of images, convulsive images, images of the fantastic and of the marvelous, images of desire'. Charles Keil interpreted American post-war urban blues lyrics as expressing their black singers' personal adjustment to their move to urban ghettos:

> a more detailed analysis of blues lyrics might make it possible to describe with greater insight the changes in male roles within the Negro community as defined by Negroes at various levels of socio-economic status and mobility within the lower class.
>
> (Keil, 1966: 74)

The lyric content of city, urban and soul blues also reflects varying sorts of adjustment to urban conditions generally, as does Jamaican reggae (see Jones, 1988; Hebdige, 1990), and much contemporary rap music (Forman, 2002).

Even if blues lyrics and reggae do reflect social realities, is their role to confirm oppression or do they encourage struggle? And why do we still enjoy them, even while identifying with the singer's emotions of anger, disillusionment, or sadness? One answer to the latter question is that most listeners simply don't listen too carefully to the lyrics. Reflecting back on his influential book *The Sociology of Rock* (1978), Frith observed that he had gone so far as to ignore lyric analysis altogether, and 'simply assumed that the meaning of music could be deduced from its users' characteristics' (Frith, 1988a: 119). As I have demonstrated, the same popular culture texts are 'heard' in varying ways and for different purposes by different audiences. My own students' responses to particular songs support the view that popular music audiences listen primarily to the beat and the melody – the sound of the record – and make their own sense of songs; accordingly, meaning can not be simply read off from the lyrics. Indeed, it is not uncommon for lyrics to be misconstrued, sometimes with comic results: in the 1960s Bob Dylan heard the Beatles 'I get by with a little help from my friends' as 'I get high etc', assuming they were already 'turned on' to marijuana.

LISTENING TO POPULAR SONG

There is much to be said for utilizing musicology, provided that such analysis is kept easily accessible to those who have never encountered music theory, and that its ambit is extended. To begin with, it is necessary for students to get a grasp of the meaning of basic musical terms: rhythm, beat, and so forth (see Appendix 2; also Beard and Gloag, 2005). Once this is established, students can move on to the examination of individual pieces. This involves identifying those formal properties which 'stand out' for the listener, i.e. whether or not the piece has a strong rhythm, the nature of its vocals, the use of particular instruments, and so on. Second, the emotional and physical response of the listeners to each piece must be identified and discussed. This is to emphasize the individual's reaction to popular music essentially at the affective, personalized level. Third, and most important, these first two aspects must be brought together by considering how particular stylistic and musical techniques serve to encourage certain responses from their listeners, and the role of genre in determining musical meaning.

The Sex Pistols' 'Anarchy in the UK', and punk rock, illustrate how songs are situated in terms of a combination of their formal musical properties, genre, social context, along with listeners' responses to them.

Sex Pistols, 'Anarchy in the UK' (EMI, UK, 1976)

Punk rock was a musical style with a closely associated youth subculture. The historical roots and antecedents of punk have been much debated, as has its subsequent influence (see Lentini, 2003; Sabin, 1999). Punk emerged in response to a specific social and political context in the United Kingdom in 1976 and 1977: 'the fault line between the two dominant conjunctures of postwar Britain: the postwar social democratic consensus and Thatcherism' (Borthwick and Moy, 2004: 83). Punk rock affirmed a politics of dissatisfaction with this political shift, and its accompanying social and economic upheaval, which included sharp rises in youth unemployment, racism, and industrial unrest.

Evaluation then and since gives 'Anarchy in the UK' (EMI, 1976) and the Sex Pistols debut album *Never Mind the Bollocks* (Virgin, 1977), which for many listeners was their first exposure to the song, a key place in the advent of punk rock in 1977–8 in the UK and accords it a lasting influence. For Marsh, it illustrates the musical fracture presented by punk in the late 1970s: 'somebody had figured out how to make artistically and commercially viable pop music based on a rhythmic process outside R&B, a feat unequalled since the advent of Elvis Presley; consequently, things were fundamentally different thereafter. It was a true historic disjuncture' (Marsh, 1989: 72). For Savage (1991), it was 'an index of their increasing ambition ... a call to arms, delivered in language that was as explosive as the group's name'. For Marcus (1992: 594), it was part of the Sex Pistols' rupturing of rock 'n' roll, as they 'broke the story of rock & roll in half, turning it back on itself, and recasting key questions as to its cultural weight' (see also the contemporary reviews collected in Heylin, 1998: 137ff).

Savage traces the genesis and impact of 'Anarchy', giving it a definite political intent, and accusing John Lydon (Johnny Rotten) of 'deliberately using inflammatory imagery' particularly the terms 'antichrist' and 'anarchist', both conveying images of apocalypse, the second coming, and social chaos: 'there seems little doubt that Lydon was fed material by Vivienne Westwood (McLaren's designer partner) and Jamie Reid (the Pistol's graphic artist), which he then converted to his own lyric' (Savage, 1991: 204).

The raw sound of the song is hardly accidental, as it went through a number of versions and recording sessions. 'Anarchy in the UK' was one of seven songs recorded by the group in July 1976, and it was these tapes that their manager Malcom McLaren took to the recording companies. With a stagnant music industry largely reacting to trends rather than initiating them, the Pistols material at first created little interest.

> When production values were complex and smooth, the Goodman [producer, Dave Goodman] tapes capture the group's live sound 'of broken glass and rusty razor blades'. In 1976, they must have sounded to the uninitiated like a rougher, more inept version of the new wave of Pub Rock bands, none of whom had reached the attention of the industry.
>
> (Savage, 1991: 206; see also Heylin, 1998)

Two days after they signed for EMI, the Sex Pistols again recorded 'Anarchy in the UK', which was to be their first single. The first attempts 'to get the spirit of live performance' (bass player Glen Matlock) proved unsatisfactory, and it was eventually re-recorded with a different producer, Chris Thomas replacing Dave Goodman. On 26 November 1976 the single was finally released: 'A much cleaner, more mainstream version, it was by that stage so loaded with expectation that it was difficult to listen objectively' (Savage, 1991: 255). Following the infamous Grundy interview on Thames Television on 2 December, and the subsequent controversy and distribution problems, the single climbed to Number 43 on the *NME* British chart and eventually reached Number 27 in late December; it never charted in the United States.

The ingredients of 'Anarchy in the UK' typify punk rock (the following discussion is based largely on Laing, 1988). First, punk bands relied on live shows to establish an identity and build a reputation, consequently 'techniques of recording and of arrangement were adopted which were intended to signify the "live" commitment of the disc' (Laing, 1988: 74). In short, punk records generally sound 'live', as if the studio had not come between the intentions of the musicians and their listening audience. Second, the use of the voice is in an identifiably punk mode, blurring the lyric with the singer's aggressive vocal, which lies between ordinary speech and singing. This makes the sound of the recording (voice plus instruments) more important than the actual identifiable lyric. Thus, for Laing 'any hope for the pure message, vocals as reflector of meaning, is doomed', which makes it 'possible (if difficult) to find pleasure in this celebrated punk rock song without the necessity of agreeing with the message' (Laing, 1988: 75–6, 78). This is rather at odds with Savage's view of 'Anarchy' as a political text, but is the dominant impression of the song retained by most casual listeners. Indeed, how 'seriously' are we to take punk lyrics like 'Anarchy'? The ideology of sincerity was central to punk, and in interviews, 'the stated beliefs of musicians, and their congruence with the perceived messages of their lyrics, became routine topics' (ibid.: 90). But, as various analyses demonstrate, in many cases punk lyrics are like collages, a series of often fractured images, with no necessarily correct reading (Sabin, 1999).

Third, there is punk's mode of address. Compared with much popular music, the confidential stance is rare in punk rock, and 'Anarchy' is strongly in a sardonic, declamatory mode. As with other punk songs, there is also an emphasis on addressing individuals other than 'lovers', and a 'plural specific' address. Fourth, the tempo of punk is usually described as 'basic' and 'primitive'. As a musically minimalist genre, punk rock eschewed the growing use of electronic instruments associated with 'progressive' rock, and featured a strict guitar and drums instrumental line-up: 'this was a sound best suited to expressing anger and frustration, focusing chaos, dramatizing the last days as daily life and ramming all emotions into the narrow gap between a blank stare and a sardonic grin' (Marcus, 1992: 595). What also set punk apart from other rock styles, was its rhythmic patterns, the main reason for the 'undanceability' of much punk rock. This 'provided a feeling of unbroken rhythmic flow, enhanced by the breakneck eight to the bar rhythm of much punk rock' (Laing, 1988: 85), adding to the urgency which the voice and aggressive vocals evoked. The lack of emphasis on instrumental virtuosity reflected punk's frequent association of skill with glibness. The frequently alleged musical incompetence of punk bands, however, was largely a myth, often fuelled by the bands themselves. (On this point, see McNeil and McCain, 1996; and Marcus Gray's study of the Clash, *Last Gang in Town*, 1995, which takes issue with much of the received wisdom regarding punk's supposed values).

As even this abbreviated discussion indicates, 'Anarchy' indicates the congruence between punk as music and the social location and values of the associated punk subculture (see Hebdige, 1979: 114ff). Music here exists very much within a broader set of social relations.

MUSIC VIDEO

The most pervasive and significant form of musical audiovisual text is the music video. The primary focus in the study of music video (MV) has been on their nature as audio-visual texts. Various attempts to read music videos have necessarily adopted the insights and concepts of film and television studies, although these have had to be modified in the light of the different functions they often play in MVs, particularly in relation to the music. There is also some recognition, at times rather belated, of the point that MV's are not self-contained texts, but reflective of their nature as industrial and commercial products, and their close association with MTV (see Chapter 9).

I sketch some basic considerations that usefully inform specific 'textual' readings of MV, and, with particular reference to the influential work of Anne Kaplan, examine the difficulties endemic in constructing a classificatory typology of music videos. Three case studies of music videos follow: Madonna's 'Justify My Love' and Duran Duran's 'Hungry Like the Wolf', two classic videos from the 1980s that helped establish the conventions of the form; and Nelly's 'Tip Drill' (2005), which raises questions of the representation of ethnicity and gender. My consideration of these can only be a preliminary and abbreviated one; (for extended discussions of music videos as texts and examples of close readings, see the references in the Notes at the end of the chapter).

'Reading' music video

Individual music video clips follow the conventions of the traditional 45 single: they are approximately two to three minutes long, and function, in the industry's own terms, as 'promotional devices', encouraging record sales and chart action. These clips are the staple component in music television, especially the MTV channel, and the long form music video compilation, increasingly available on DVD.

Two general points frequently made about MVs as individual texts are their preoccupation with visual style, and, associated with this, their status as key exemplars of 'postmodern' texts. Music videos were pioneers in video expression, but their visual emphasis raises problems for their musical dimensions. As some three-quarters of sensory information comes in through the eye, the video viewer concentrates on the images, arguably at the expense of the soundtrack. This combination has been accused of fuelling performers' preoccupation with visual style, which can dominate over content. Since the 1980s MV has been a crucial marketing tool, with the music often merely part of an overall style package offered to consumers.

Cultural historian and theorist Fredric Jameson (1984) saw music videos as 'meta entertainments' that embody the postmodern condition. It is certainly clear that MVs do indeed merge commercial and artistic image production and abolish traditional boundaries between an image and its real life referent. In this respect, their most obvious characteristic is their similarity to advertisements, making them a part of a blatantly consumerist culture. Kaplan (1987) went so far as to suggest that the MV spectator has become decentred and fragmented, unable any longer to distinguish 'fiction' from 'reality', part of postmodern culture. This conflation of MV and postmodernism is, however, difficult to sustain. While many MV's display considerable evidence of pastiche, intertextuality and eclecticism, this does not in itself make them postmodern (for an insightful discussion of this point, see Goodwin, 1993). Further, by the 2000s, the nature of MV's was arguably becoming more traditional and clichéed, as just a few hours watching MTV made clear.

Considering music videos as texts means applying some stock topics and questions. These are derived partly from film studies, and include cinematic aspects, such as camera techniques, lighting, use of colour, and editing. Different styles of video utilize different conventions; heavy metal videos, for example, make considerable use of wide-angle lens and zoom shots in keeping with their emphasis on a 'live concert' format. A major focus of MV analysis that draws on film studies is the nature of the gaze in MV – who is looking at who, how, and what do these conventions convey in terms of power relations, gender stereotypes, and the social construction of self?

In more general thematic terms, there is a need to also consider:

1   The mood of the video – the way in which the music, the words and the visuals combine to produce a general feeling of nostalgia, romanticism, nihilism, or whatever.
2   The narrative structure – the extent to which the video tells a clear time-sequenced story, or is a non-linear pastiche of images, flashbacks, etc.
3   The degree of realism or fantasy of the settings or environments in the video, and the relationship between genres and particular physical settings, as with rap and the street.

4   The standard themes evident – for example, the treatment of authority, love and sex, 'growing up' and the loss of childhood innocence, political and social consciousness.

5   The importance of performance – why does this format better suit particular genres such as heavy metal?

6   Different modes of sexuality – the female as mother/whore figure; androgyny and the blurring of dress codes; and homoeroticism.

7   The nature of MVs as a star text, centred on the role played by the central performer(s) in the video and the interelationship of this to their star persona in rock more generally.

8   The music – what we hear and how it relates to what we see.

The last is often a critical absence from visual-oriented readings of M.V. Goodwin goes so far as to argue that 'a musicology of the music video image is the basis for understanding how to undertake a credible textual study. Issues relating to the sound–vision relation, the formal organization of music videos, questions of pleasure and so on, need to be related to the musical portion of the text' (Goodwin, 1993: Introduction). In a substantial, music-based study of recent music videos, Vernallis (2004) sees them as utilizing visual images to represent and enhance the music, while continuing to play a commercial role as industry promotion.

These are not simply signposts to viewing individual MVs, they are also factors that can be utilized to categorize them. Although much criticized, the most thorough attempt to categorize MVs remains that developed by Kaplan, in her study *Rocking Around the Clock: Music Television, Postmodernism, and Consumer Culture* (1987). While Kaplan is primarily concerned with analyzing MTV, she also constructs an interesting typology of individual MVs. Her five categories here are derived from combining a reading of rock history with theoretical tools taken from psychoanalytic and film theory, a combination that at times sits awkwardly. Her five typical video forms are: the Romantic, the Socially Conscious, the Nihilist, the Classical, and the Postmodern. Critics have found this categorization 'confusing and ultimately not very helpful' (Goodwin, 1987: 42), as have my students and myself when attempting to apply the typology to particular videos.

Kaplan's schema is weak partly because it mixes the bases for each category: the first three are situated in pop history – the romantic clips drawing from 1960s soft rock; the socially conscious from 1970s rock, and the nihilist from 1980s new wave and heavy metal music. But then the remaining two categories are based in film theory (with the classical category related to realist film texts), and the postmodern in some sort of catch-all residual category in which postmodern motifs, evident in practically all MVs, are simply more plentiful. The result is that clips placed in one category might just as easily be located in another. It is also questionable to collapse the history of pop/rock music into a series of decades, each dominated by and identified with a certain style of music. Further, the schema ignores the significance of genre and auteurship in the music industry, both of which sit awkwardly with it. What would be a viable alternative schema? Perhaps the eclectic nature of music video makes impossible anything other than a basic distinction between performance and fictional narrative MVs? Having raised some issues surrounding the analysis of music videos, I now want to relate these to three examples.

Duran Duran, 'Hungry Like the Wolf' (music video, director: Russell Mulcahy, 1981)

The early career of Duran Duran provides an example of the need to consider music videos as promotional devices as much as mini visual texts. Formed in 1978, UK pop quartet Duran Duran achieved considerable early commercial success, with several hits in the British Top 20 in 1981, but initially failed to dent the US market. Despite intensive touring in North America and the photogenic male group's considerable exposure in the teen music press, their self-titled debut album on Capitol/EMI failed to yield a hit single and had only risen to Number 150 on the album charts. Exposure on MTV changed this dramatically.

The group had already attracted attention with their first video: 'Girls On Film' (1980) directed by leading video auteurs Godley and Creme. The group barely appear in the MV, which features a series of soft-porn style scenes, including attractive, scantily clad (nude in the uncensored version) women pillow-fighting on a phallic pole covered in whipped cream! Kevin Godley acknowledges the sexism of the video, but explains: 'Look, we just did our job. We were very explicitly told by Duran Duran's management to make a very sensational, erotic piece that would be for clubs, where it would get shown uncensored, just to make people take notice and talk about it' (quoted in Shore, 1985: 86). That bands were increasingly making two versions of their videos, one for mainstream television shows and MTV, and one for more adult cable outlets and clubs, demonstrates the market-driven nature of the video text, and any reading of MV must take this intention into account.

The 'Hungry Like the Wolf' video also raises the issue of authorship in MVs. While it is customary to refer to MVs as being the product of the particular performer featured, and some artists take a major role in determining the nature of their MVs, 'the directors most often are responsible for the concepts, the vision, the imagery, and the editing rhythm that coalesce into a look that keeps people watching' (Shore, 1985: 97). This is still the case, particularly with 'new' performers unfamiliar with the medium. There are a number of MV directors who can be considered pioneers and auteurs in the field, including Godley and Creme, Russell Mulcahy, David Mallet,

Brian Grant, and Julian Temple. Several, most notably Mulcahy and Temple, went on to direct major feature films.

In August 1981, as MTV began broadcasting in North America, EMI invested $200,000 to send Duran Duran to Sri Lanka to shoot three video clips with director Russell Mulcahy. One of them, 'Hungry Like the Wolf', became an MTV favourite. Less than two months after the two-week shoot, the clip was in heavy rotation on MTV, was getting heavy radio airplay, and this exposure helped propel the single into the Top 10 and Duran Duran's second album, *Rio*, into the upper reaches of the album charts. MTV confirmed Duran Duran as a teenage sensation (Hill, 1986). In 1983, in conjunction with Sony that was promoting its new video 45s (which included the Duran's 'Girls On Film' – the uncensored nightclub version – and 'Hungry'), along with Duran Duran's compilation, 'sell through', video cassette, the group undertook a highly successful video tour of major clubs across North America; 'Each date on the video tour sold out, and in every city the video tour hit, Duran Duran's records sold out within days' (Shore, 1985: 93–4).

In 'Hungry like the Wolf' Singer Simon LeBon's head rises in slow motion out of a river as rain pours down. He then chases a beautiful Indian woman, clad only in an animal skin(?) through a Sri Lankan tropical jungle and open air market. During the chase, he has his brow mopped by a young Indian (boy?) and overturns a barroom table. When he catches the beast/woman they have an encounter suggestive of both sex and violence:

> Mulcahy's ravenously tracking and panning camera, insinuating erotic ambiguity, and editing wizardry (frames slide in from the left or right, double and split-screen edits on and around the beat, etc) which have been the real stars of the show all along, come into full play … we've been dazzled, seduced and abandoned.
>
> (Shore, 1985: 178)

The nature of the narrative is almost irrelevant here, serving merely to showcase LeBon, and add an aura of exotic appeal and sexuality to the song. Indeed, a satisfactory analysis of 'Hungry' as a text must acknowledge this 'focus on the star' aspect of it. Duran Duran were the pin-up band of the mid-1980s, particularly amongst young girls. Watching the video even now, women students focus on the physical appeal of the singer, who is variously described as 'delicious', a 'hunk', and 'sexy'. Young male viewers acknowledge that LeBon is 'conventionally handsome' and some even tentatively point to his rather androgynous appeal. The star appeal of LeBon is fed on and enhanced by the technical virtuosity of the director, already then recognized as a leading auteur of the music video form. Mulcahy is arguably the star as much as LeBon – though not, of course, to the young fans of Duran Duran in the mid-1980s.

Even purely at the level of text, 'Hungry like the Wolf' is difficult to categorize in Kaplan's terms. It has elements of the 'classical', with the male as subject and the woman as object: 'I'm on the hunt I'm after you' sings LeBon – though there is a case for reversing this distinction? Further, the video's narrative structure is a mini-drama, based loosely around LeBon's chase while his friends are being enticed by lithe beauties back in the town, a narrative that never fully realizes closure. But in Kaplan's terms, the video also has strongly 'postmodernist' features. The rapid editing creates a series of disjointed images, which disrupt linear time and leave the viewer uncertain about the sequence of the events and even if there is indeed a 'plot' to follow.

Kaplan pays little attention to the music in her analysis of music video, an absence that is significant in the case of 'Hungry' (even if it is admittedly not one of the MVs she examines). The sharp rhythm and strong beat of the song, along with the single male voice, match the rapid editing and sheer physical aggression of the video. It is the music that links and 'makes sense of' the images, which would not have the same impact on their own.

Madonna, 'Justify My Love' (music video, director: Jean-Baptiste Mondino, 1990)

Madonna is a central example of the significance of the star image in the construction and appeal of MVs: 'Singled out for identification, but also for homo- as well as heteroerotic and narcissistic pleasures, the star takes on the role of originator of the work, the absent centre of its production, the core of the economy of desire established in the tape or the body of work mapped out by the artist as auteur' (Cubitt, 1991: 57). In the case of star performers, their specific videos do not stand alone, but are intimately related to their established public persona.

Madonna's MVs have been the subject of considerable public controversy and academic analysis. In December 1990, American MTV rejected the 'Justify My Love' MV, even though it was shown in its entirety on ABC's *Nightline*, where it generated the programme's largest audience of the year. In the UK, 'Justify My Love' was screened only on a late-night MV show on Channel 4, and the video was accorded similar treatment internationally.

The MV features Madonna in bra and garter belt in an erotic encounter with a lover, played by her then real-life boyfriend Tony Ward, along with several other androgynous figures, in a Paris hotel (for a full description, see Henderson, 1993). The video portrays a series of fantasies: bisexuality, voyeurism, group sex, cross-dressing and mild sadomasochism, and icons abound: chains, black leather, and crucifixes. As Henderson observes, the video was almost revolutionary:

In its sexual stances, 'Justify My Love' defies some of music videos' worst cliches, opening up an aesthetic and political corner for other ways of envisaging sex in popular culture. Unlike most MTV clips (ZZ Top's come to mind), it eroticizes all its characters – female, male, and those in between, black and white – fondly entangling them in a collective fantasy even as it foregrounds its star. Madonna's voice, *her* voice, orchestrate that fantasy, whose polymorphism slips and slides around conventional video images of sensation and arousal.

(Henderson, 1993: 111–12)

Madonna herself defended the video as being 'about honesty and the celebration of sex. There's nothing wrong with that' (press report, December 1990).

Primarily at issue in the public and academic debates during the 1980s and since, over MVs such as 'Justify My Love' was whether Madonna was simply appealing, through the sexual 'explicitness' of her videos, to male (and female) voyeurism, or was in fact a proto-feminist. Madonna herself adopted the latter position: 'I may be dressing like the typical bimbo, or whatever, but I'm in charge of my fantasies. I put myself in these situations with men' (press report, December 1990). Several academic commentators identified with this claim: Frith argues that 'selling women as stars means showing them in charge of their femininity (and its construction as a way of looking)', not just as available objects for the male gaze (Frith, 1988a: 217); and Kaplan regarded Madonna as 'the female star who perhaps more than any other embodies the new postmodern feminist heroine in her odd combination of seductiveness and a gutsy sort of independence' (Kaplan, 1987: 117).

Similar arguments surround Madonna's use of religiously charged icons. To some it was simply read as blasphemy, and another facet of the performer's deliberately courting controversy to gain increased public exposure; this was part of a wider body of public criticism that regarded the singer as exemplifying the worst aspects of 'low culture'. Conversely, while offering a semiotic analysis sympathetic to Madonna, Fiske writes:

Combining the crucifix with the signs of pornography is a carnivalesque profanity, but the new combination does not 'mean' anything specific, all it signifies is her power over discourse, her ability to use the already written signifiers of patriarchal Christianity, and to tear them away from their signifieds is a moment of empowerment.

(Fiske, 1989: 252–3)

Although analyses which present readings of Madonna and 'Justify My Love' (and her other videos) as potentially empowering for women viewers are plausible, they tend to assume that this removes her from the patriarchal gaze. Rather, observation of, and discussions with, male viewers suggest that her early videos do still function as voyeuristic texts, albeit in a complex fashion. While they enjoyed looking at Madonna as an object of sexual desire, adolescent males were perturbed by the confidence she expressed in her own sexuality, and as such at times labelled her a 'tart' or 'slut'. Analysing Madonna's equally controversial video 'Open Your Heart', Bordo (1993) concluded that the dominant position in the video is in fact still that of the objectifying gaze. This gaze, however, is hardly a unitary 'male' one. Madonna's videos are variously read off by particular ethnic groups, by different sections of the gay community, and by both differentially socially located fans and critics of the singer (see the essays in Schwichtenberg, 1993; also Brown and Schulze, 1990; Vernallis, 2004).

Nelly, 'Tip Drill' (music video, director: Benny Boom, 2005)

As the two examples above demonstrate, music videos can consolidate or even establish gender role stereotypes. Several authors have observed that the male address in music videos activates 'textual signs of patriarchal discourse, reproducing coded images of the female body, and positioning girls and women as the objects of male voyeurism' (Lewis, 1990: 43; see also Goodwin, 1993: Chapter 4; Kaplan, 1987: Chapter 5). Male hip-hop artists' songs and their accompanying music videos are frequently constructed around three types of women: the sexually promiscuous, the financial predator, and the girlfriend, with all three characteristics often present within the narrative of the video. As Vernallis observes, for African-American women, the imagery of contemporary hip-hop music videos 'stridently argues that their bodies are for ogling and sex' (Vernallis, 2004: 72). An example of this is the lyrics and imagery in the video for Nelly's song 'Tip Drill'.

As a performer, Nelly's work had already attracted criticism for songs and videos such as 'Hot in Here' (The singer exhorts a woman at a dance club to 'take off all your clothes', since it is getting so hot, with a not too subtle subtext suggesting sex is to follow?). 'Tip Drill', drawing its title from slang for group sex, or a 'gang bang', added to the controversy. The video is set at a house party, with shots alternating between the inside and outside. Dance is a central part of the loose narrative, with the performers typical of hip-hop videos:

> One brown-skinned sister, wearing painted-on jeans and four-inch stilettos, is as tall as a runway model but with an ample booty and sleepy almond eyes. Another woman is baby-doll petite with olive skin, long bleached-blonde curls and supersized cleavage bursting out of the tiny piece of fabric that is her top. When they finally shoot a take, it goes like this: the music starts bumping, the

camera rolls, and the girls all break into dance, rubbing their hips, shaking their hair, leaning their heads back and looking coyly at the camera. This is the work of the video girl.

(Amber, 2005: 164)

For Vernallis, 'When we consider the imagery of African-American women, we need to be sensitive to the ways their bodies are used in each video, where they fall within the music, and what other kinds of imagery surrounds them' (Vernallis, 2004: 72). The women at the party exemplify the tendency for such videos to reduce them to body parts, with numerous close-ups of buttocks and breasts. Money is thrown at them to encourage sexually explicit actions, and, at the end of the video, Nelly swipes a credit card between the butt cheeks of one woman. There is 'a play between the visual and the musical codes' at work here (Vernallis, 2004: 199). When Nelly raps 'if you see a tip drill, point her out', the crowd of men respond: 'there she at', pointing to the women's buttocks. The video exhibits elements of the pimp lifestyle that permeate mainstream hip-hop culture. The figure of the pimp is 'a signifier of charisma, power and wealth. Pimp is domination in the bedroom, respect on the streets, a romantic illusion of male greatness' (Amber, 2005: 164). Nelly's screen persona embodies this, and he has even marketed a drink, 'pimp juice', named after one of his songs.

To what extent is Nelly the 'author' of the video? Although the director clearly played a role, as in most videos, those in hip-hop function as star texts. As George puts it: 'Hip-hop's typical narrator is a young, angry, horny male who is often disdainful of or, at least uninterested in, commitments of any kind' (George, 1999: 184). The misogynist lyrics and negative representation of African-American women (and 'white' women too), as generally unintelligent and oversexed, in hip-hop videos, reinforce social attitudes, especially among young viewers: 'whereas hip-hop has spiritually and financially empowered African-American males, it has boxed young women into stereotypes and weakened their sense of worth' (George, 1999: 186–7).

While 'Tip Drill' could be seen as a sophisticated comment on contemporary capitalism and the increasing commodification of sex, the dominant impression is one of simple sexual exploitation. My students, both male and female, see the video in these terms, and regard it as resembling the soft-porn film genre.

The videos examined here are arguably typical of the MV form, and illustrative of the difficulties of textual classification. To explain the nature of their appeal it is necessary to go beyond their purely textual aspects, and consider their function as polysemic narratives and images of viewer fantasy and desire. As are other popular culture texts, MVs present a semiotic terrain open to cultural struggles over meaning. This illustrates the general point that meanings and pleasures are not purely embedded 'in' MV texts, but are produced in the act of viewing.

Having looked at musical texts as individual entities, in the next chapter I want to extend the discussion by considering them as 'collectivities', through an examination of genre, cover songs, and the album canon.

NOTES

Textual analysis in general:
Barker, C. (2002) *Making Sense of Cultural Studies. Central Problems and Critical Debates*, London: Sage Publications.

For links to web sites featuring song lyrics:
http://www/music-sites.net/mediasearch/lyrics.html.

On album covers:
Marsh, G. and Callingham, G. (2003) *Blue Note Album Cover Art: The Ultimate Collection*, San Francisco, CA: Chronicle Books.
Inglis, I. (2001) '"Nothing You Can See That Isn't Shown": The Album Covers of the Beatles', *Popular Music*, 20, 1: 83–98.
Ochs, M.(1996) *1000 Rock Covers*, Cologne: Taschen.

For links to web sites featuring album covers:
http://tralfaz-archives.com/coverart/coverartlinks.html.

Popular musicology:
There are several edited volumes containing extensive discussion and examples:
Covach, J. and Boone, G.M. (1997) *Understanding Rock. Essays in Musical Analysis*, New York: Oxford University Press.
Middleton, R. (2000) *Reading Pop: Approaches to Textual Analysis in Popular Music*, Oxford and New York: Oxford University Press.
Moore, A. F. (2003) *Analyzing Popular Music*, Cambridge: Cambridge University Press.

Studies reflecting their author's sustained engagement with the field are:
Tagg, P. and Clarida, B. (2003) *Ten Little Title Tunes: Towards a Musicology of the Mass Media*, New York and Montreal: The Mass Media Musicologists' Press.
Moore, A. F. (2001) *Rock: The Primary Text – Developing a Musicology of Rock*, 2nd edn, Buckingham: Open University Press.
Hawkins, S. (2002) *Settling the Pop Score: Pop Texts and Identity Politics*, Aldershot: Ashgate.

Music video:
To view music videos:
http://music.yahoo.com/musicvideos/.

The major studies of music video, which can be usefully read chronologically, are:

Kaplan, E.A. (1987) *Rocking Around the Clock: Music Television, Postmodernism, and Consumer Culture*, New York: Methuen.

Goodwin, A. (1993) *Dancing in the Distraction Factory: Music, Television and Popular Culture*, Minneapolis, MN: University of Minnesota Press.

Vernallis, C. (2004) *Experiencing Music Video: Aesthetics and Cultural Context*, Columbia, OH: Columbia University Press.

A still useful compilation, is

Frith, S., Goodwin, A. and Grossberg, L. (1993) *Sound and Vision: The Music Video Reader*, London: Routledge.

Now hard to find, but still a useful early history of the form, and its main creators, is:

Shore, M. (1985) *The Rolling Stone Book of Rock Video*, London: Sidgwick and Jackson.

Chapter 6

'It's Still Rock and Roll to Me'

Genre, covers and the canon

Genre, its nature and significance, are a central aspect of popular music studies. I distinguish here between metagenres, genres, and subgenres. Rock and pop, often situated in opposition to each other, provide examples of metagenres. Heavy metal shows a common pattern of genre differentiation, with a range of subgenres developing during the history of the form. Rap demonstrates a similar pattern, along with the shift to the commercial mainstream of once marginal musical styles. Song covers, and the album canon, illustrate debates around the authenticity and cultural value of different popular music texts.

GENRE AND MUSIC

'Genre' can be basically defined as a category or type. A key component of textual analysis, genre is widely used to analyse popular culture texts, most notably in their filmic and popular literary forms, as with thrillers, science fiction, and horror. The various encyclopedias, the standard histories, and critical analyses of popular music use genre as a central organizing element. Some accounts tend to use style and genre as overlapping terms, or prefer style to genre (e.g. Moore, 1993). The arrangement in retail outlets also suggests that there are clearly identifiable genres of popular music, which are understood as such by consumers. Indeed, fans will frequently identify themselves with particular genres, often demonstrating considerable knowledge of the complexities of their preferences (subgenres). Similarly, musicians will frequently situate their work by reference to genres and musical styles.

The usual approach to defining musical genres is 'to follow the distinctions made by the music industry which, in turn, reflect both musical history and marketing categories' Frith (1987: 133). Another approach, suggested by Frith, is to 'classify them according to their ideological effects, the way they sell themselves as art, community or emotion' (1987: 133). He gives the example of a form of rock termed 'authentic', exemplified by Bruce Springsteen:

> The whole point of this genre is to develop musical conventions which are, in themselves, measures of 'truth'. As listeners we are drawn into a certain form of reality: this is what it is like to live in America, this is what it is like to love or hurt. The resulting work is the pop equivalent of film theorists' 'classic realist' text.
>
> (Frith, 1987: 147)

Against and in interplay with authentic genres can be placed a tradition of artifice, as in glam rock.

Critical analysis of popular music genres has concentrated on the tension between their emphasis on 'standardized codes that allow no margin for distraction' (Fabbri, 1999), and their fluidity as these codes are elaborated on and challenged and displaced by new codes. Currently, while musical genres continue to function as marketing categories and reference points for musicians, critics and fans, particular examples clearly demonstrate that genre divisions must be regarded as highly fluid. Further, no style is totally independent of those that have preceded it, and musicians borrow elements from existing styles and incorporate them into new forms. Performers have always absorbed influences across genre (and ethnic) lines. In the 1920s, country pioneer Jimmie Rogers drew extensively from the blues and popular music traditions just as, in the 1990s, Oasis reworked the imagery and sounds of British 1960s rock. Further, many performers can fit under more than one classification, or shift between and across genres during their careers (e.g. Neil Young; see Echard, 2005). There is also considerable genre bending: subverting or playing with the conventions of existing musical genres, or adopting an ironic distance from those same conventions. This process is strongly present in hybrid genres, where different styles inform and engage with each other, as in jazz rock or rap metal. Moreover, 'while the surface styles and fashions of popular music change rapidly, the underlying structures move far more slowly' (Hardy and Laing, 1990: i).

It is useful to distinguish between metagenres, which are rather loose amalgams of various styles, overarching labels, notably rock, pop, and 'world music', and genres, which arguably exist in a purer, more easily understood and specified form (e.g. disco). It is also important to acknowledge the significance of subgenres, which are particularly evident in well-established and developed styles or genres, and qualify any simplistic depiction of a genre; the blues, heavy metal and techno provide good examples of strongly differentiated genres. 'Mainstream' musical genres are operating within a commercial system of record companies, contracts, marketing, publicity, management, support staff and so on; within this context performers tour and perform, make recordings, and create an image often following the conventions of the genre with which they are identified.

In the light of the above, a number of distinguishing dimensions of popular music genres can be identified. First, genres need to be placed in the context of their historical roots and antecedents and performers, along with the social and political context that they emerge out of. Second, there are the stylistic traits present in the music: their musical characteristics, 'a code of sonic requirements … a certain sound, which is produced according to conventions of composition, instrumentation and performance' (Weinstein, 1991: 6). These may vary in terms of their coherence and sustainability, as examples such as Christian rock, and glam rock clearly demonstrate, and particularly in metagenres. Along with other aspects of genre, particular musical characteristics can be situated within the general historical evolution of popular music. Important here, as we saw in Chapter 2, is the role of technology, which establishes both constraints and possibilities in relation to the nature of performance, and the recording, distribution, and reception of the music. Third, there are other, essentially non-musical, stylistic attributes, most notably image and its associated visual style. This includes standard iconography and record cover format; the locale and structure of performances, especially in concert, and the dress, make-up, and hair styles adopted by both the performers and their listeners and fans. Musical and visual stylistic aspects combine in terms of how they operate to produce particular ideological effects, a set of associations which situate the genre within the broader musical constituency. Fourth, there is the primary audience for particular styles. The relationship between fans and their genre preferences is a form of transaction, mediated by the forms of delivery, creating specific cultural forms with sets of expectations. Finally, there is the question of the style's durability and subsequent influence. Genres are historically located; some endure, others spring briefly to prominence then fade away (e.g. Britpop in the 1990s; surf rock in the 1960s).

Genres are accorded specific places in a musical hierarchy by both critics and fans, and by many performers. This hierarchy is loosely based around the notions of authenticity, sincerity and commercialism. The critical denigration of certain genres, including disco, dance pop, and the elevation of others, such as alternative country, reflects this, and mirrors the broader, still widely accepted, high/low culture split. The shifting status and constituency of genres, and the ultimately subjective nature of these concepts, must be acknowledged.

In terms of the identification and delineation of various genres, it is instructive to see which have, or have not, been accorded separate treatmen in major overviews and histories of popular music. For example, Gammond (1991) excludes, among others, art rock, Christian rock, folk rock, and glam rock; Clarke (1990) concentrates on performers, and 'major' genres: blues, country, folk, heavy metal, jazz, reggae, rock, and soul, with considerably briefer entries on several other genres (e.g. doo wop; bubblegum). DeCurtis and Henke (1992) have no separate contributions for country, the blues, and jazz, though these are necessarily referred to where they have influenced and fused with rock and roll. Hardy and Laing (1990) include a fairly inclusive glossary of styles and genres, with the brief entries supplemented by the discussions of associated artists. This approach works quite well, and is illustrative of how genres defy static/academic definition independent of those making the music.

Histories of popular music also privilege some styles, notably classic rock, and neglect others, such as 1960s garage rock (Friedlander, 1996).

Studies that focus on genres also make such selections, often with limited explanation of the basis for choice (Shuker, 2005). Borthwick and Moy (2004) provide a comprehensive discussion of genre as a concept, along with chapter-length case studies of soul music, funk, psychedelia, progressive rock, punk rock, reggae, synthpop, heavy metal, indie, rap, and jungle. This is a reasonable selection, but grunge, placed here under punk rock, has a stronger claim as a distinctive genre with a wider fan base and influence than several of those included as chapters.

ROCK, POP AND AUTHENTICITY

The terms 'pop' and 'rock' are often used as shorthand for 'popular music', at the same time as there is a tendency to contrast and polarize the two styles. They are best regarded as broadly constituted metagenres, and as commercially produced music for consumption by a mass market. Similarities of production aside, there are important ideological assumptions behind the distinctions between pop and rock.

Pop: 'Silly Love Songs' (Paul McCartney)

As Ennis (1992) documents, pop music was evident in three of the defining 'streams' which eventually overlap and fuse in the evolution of American popular music:

1   Pop as the commercial music of the nation, associated with Tin Pan Alley, musical theatre, the motion picture, and the rise of radio.
2   'Black Pop', the popular music of black Americans, commercially domesticated around 1900, and from 1920 to 1948 known as 'race music'.
3   'Country Pop', which was the popular music of the American white south and Southwest.

Alongside these were three smaller streams: jazz, folk, and gospel.

Collectively, these six streams were the basis for the emergence in the 1950s of what Ennis, in common with many other commentators, terms 'rock 'n' roll'. Rock 'n' roll grafted together the emotive and rhythmic elements of the blues, the folk elements of country and Western music, and jazz forms such as boogie woogie. Pop is seen to have emerged as a somewhat watered-down, blander version of this, associated with a more rhythmic style and smoother vocal harmony, characteristic of the period of teen idols in the late 1950s and early 1960s.

Musically, pop is defined by its general accessibility, its commercial orientation, an emphasis on memorable hooks, or choruses, and a lyrical preoccupation with romantic love as a theme. The musical aesthetics of pop are essentially conservative: 'It is about providing popular tunes and cliches in which to express commonplace feelings – love, loss, and jealousy' (Frith, 2001: 96). Along with songwriters, producers are often regarded as the main creative force behind pop artists. Accordingly, as a genre in the market place, pop's defining feature is that 'It is music produced commercially for profit, as a matter of enterprise not art' (Frith, 2001: 94). Over the past half-century it has frequently been collapsed into and equated with 'popular', and includes a range of styles under labels such as 'chart pop' and 'teen pop'. Much of pop is regarded as disposable, for the moment, dance music; the best of it survives as 'golden oldies' and 'classic hits'.

While pop has a long musical history, predating the 1950s, it became used in a generic sense as the umbrella name for a special kind of musical product aimed at a teenage market, especially in the United Kingdom. Reflecting the dominance of teen pop in the late 1950s, pop became used in an oppositional, even antagonistic sense, to rock music. This was linked to notions of art and commerce in popular music; for example:

> Pop implies a very different set of values to rock. Pop makes no bones about being mainstream. It accepts and embraces the requirement to be instantly pleasing and to make a pretty picture of itself. Rock on the other hand, has liked to think it was somehow more profound, non-conformist, self-directed and intelligent.
>
> (Hill, 1986: 8; see also Dettmar, 2006: Introduction)

Subsequently the term pop was used to characterize chart and teenage audience oriented music, particularly the genres of dance pop, bubblegum, power pop, and the New Romantics, and performers such as the girl groups of the 1960s, their 1990s equivalents, and the ubiquitous boy bands of the modern era. Pop is also currently prominent in reality television shows such as 'Pop Idol'. The most significant of these styles has been chart-oriented, dance pop. As with pop generally, dance pop is often maligned, in part because of its perceived commercial orientation and its main audience of adolescent girls – teenyboppers (although for a positive analysis of such consumption, see Baker, 2002). Commercially highly successful exponents include Kylie Minogue, Paula Abdul, and Bananarama in the 1980s; the Spice Girls and Britney Spears in the 1990s.

The debate around the Spice Girls, who had enormous international success in the late 1990s, exemplified the discourse around dance pop, especially regarding its commodification and authenticity. The Spice Girls 'introduced the language of independence to a willing audience of preteen and teenage girls – girl power' (Whiteley, 2000: 215); stressing female bonding, a sense of sisterhood, friendship, and self-control in their personas, press interviews, and the lyrics to their songs. However, critics pointed to the contradictions between the Spice Girls professed self-expression and their subversion to standard sexualized 'feminine' images, and their incorporation into a male-dominated music industry, thereby sustaining dominant gender ideologies (see the career profile in Chapter 4).

The success of these pop performers was frequently attributed to the Svengali-like influence of producers and professional songwriters (e.g. Stock Aitken Waterman and Kylie Minogue), and exposure through MTV and energetic video performances (e.g. Britney Spears), as much as or more than musical talent. Today, pop is increasingly identified with the wider culture of celebrity. Current pop performers capitalize on their prior public visibility in film and television, fashion and society, using this to, hopefully, launch a recording career (Paris Hilton, Hillary Duff).

'Rock On' (Gary Glitter)

Rock 'n' roll emerged in the United States in the early 1950s, when black rhythm and blues songs began to get airplay on radio stations aiming at a wider, predominantly white audience, and white artists began rerecording black R&B songs. R&B, American country music, and 1940s and 1950s boogie-woogie music were all elements of early rock 'n' roll. Alan Freed, a Cleveland disc jockey, is usually given credit for coining the phrase rock 'n' roll in the early 1950s. However, the style had been evolving well prior to this, and the term 'rock 'n' roll', with its sexual connotations, was first popularized in the music of the 1920s. In 1922, blues singer Trixie Smith recorded 'My Daddy Rocks Me (With One Steady Roll)' for Black Swan Records, and various lyrical elaborations followed from other artists through the 1930s and 1940s. Rock became the broad label for the huge range of styles that have evolved out of rock 'n' roll since the mid-1960s; these include hard rock, blues rock, progressive rock, punk rock, psychedelic or acid rock, heavy metal, country rock, glitter rock, new wave, indie rock, and alternative rock (see Regev, 2004; Shuker, 2005).

Rock is often considered to carry more 'weight' than pop, with connotations of greater integrity, sincerity, and authenticity: 'in rock, there is the ethos of self-expression which draws an intimate tie between the personal and the performance. Rock and pop stars play to different rules' (Street, 1986: 5). Similarly, for Strong:

> Rock music is written by the artist(s) for him or herself, not with the initial intention of making money, but to make music – and, possibly, to stretch its limits and boundaries a little further. This is music that may last forever, becoming 'classic' in the process. On the other hand, POP music is written with the sole intention (normally) of making a quick buck, either for the artists(s) or (more than likely) their record label.
>
> (Strong, 1998: Preface)

This attempts to keep commerce and artistic integrity apart on a central yardstick to identify particular artists with either pop or rock 'n' roll. It reflected a tendency in the 1980s (and still evident) to view popular music in terms of a series of dichotomies: mass v. community/local; commerce v. creativity; manufactured v. authentic; major record companies v. independents. This is a legacy of the mythology of 'rock' which was a product of the 1960s, when leading American critics – Landau, Marsh, and Christgau – elaborated a view of rock as correlated with authenticity, creativity and the Romantic cultural tradition (Pattison, 1987), and a particular political moment: the 1960s protest movement and the counterculture. Closely associated with this leftist political ideology of rock was *Rolling Stone* magazine, founded in 1967.

The distinction between pop and rock is difficult to maintain, given the commercial production and marketing of both metagenres. Even the frequent refusal of rock musicians and fans to admit to commodity status, and its attempt to position itself as somehow above the manufacturing process, all too easily have become marketing ploys – 'the Revolution is on CBS' slogan of the late 1960s being perhaps the best example. Nevertheless, using authenticity to distinguish between rock and pop continues to serve an important ideological function, helping differentiate particular forms of musical cultural capital. Such distinctions also occur *within* the two metagenres, as with indie rock setting itself apart from mainstream rock music (see Fonarow, 2006).

HEAVY METAL

Heavy metal (HM) began in the late 1960s, its origins variously being traced to several key recordings: Blue Cheer's 1968 reworking of Eddie Cochran's 1950s hit 'Summertime Blues', which turned Cochran's great acoustic guitar riff into distorted metallic sounding electric guitar chords, accompanied by a thumping percussion; Steppenwolf's 'Born To Be Wild' (1968) with its reference to 'heavy metal thunder' (from the William Burroughs' novel *Naked Lunch*) in the song's second verse; and the release of British metallers Black Sabbath's eponymous debut album (1970), which reached Number 8 in the UK album chart and spent three months on the US album chart.

HM was a logical progression from the power trios of 1960s groups such as the Jimi Hendrix Experience and Cream, who played blues-based rock with heavily amplified guitar and bass reinforcing each other. The commercial success of the British bands Black Sabbath, Deep Purple and, above all, Led Zeppelin, Grand Funk and Mountain in the US – despite the general critical 'thumbs down' for their efforts – consolidated heavy metal as a market force in the early 1970s, and established a heavy metal youth subculture. Even this short list of performers demonstrates the difficulties of bounding the genre. Led Zeppelin performed more traditional blues-based material and combined acoustic outings with electric guitars, yet are accorded the HM tag chiefly because they were played at a very loud volume.

Although Deep Purple and their American counterparts may be considered HM bands, they can just as easily be classified as 'hard' or 'heavy' rock. In the 1980s, there was a clear distinction possible between the more overtly commercially oriented MTV-friendly HM bands, such as Bon Jovi and Poison with their glam rock images, and mainstream HM bands, whose styles merge into hard rock, such as Guns 'n' Roses, and Aerosmith. Consequently, the musical parameters of heavy metal (HM) as a diverse genre cannot be comfortably reduced to formulaic terms. It is usually louder, 'harder' and faster-paced than conventional rock music, and remains predominantly guitar oriented. The main instruments are electric guitars (lead and bass) drums and electronic keyboards, but there are numerous variants within this basic framework.

Once established, heavy metal demonstrated the common pattern of genre fragmentation and hybridization. The most successful of the early hybrid genres to develop was thrash or speed metal. Largely a US phenomenon to begin with, thrash developed out of hardcore and punk, and became a journalistic convenience for guitar-based non-mainstream metal, usually played faster and louder. This metal subgenre initially developed in the San Francisco Bay area in the mid-1980s, with groups like Metallica drawing their inspiration from British HM bands such as Def Leppard and Iron Maiden. Other bands emerged, most notably Suicidal Tendencies and Slayer in Los Angeles, and Anthrax in New York. This new subgenre was apocalyptic in its visions of negation, and constructed through the live concert as much as its recorded forms. The crossover success of Metallica brought the style to mainstream attention (see Kotarba, 1994; McIver, 2000). Speed metal remained popular, especially in Europe, where the names of leading bands indicate their social and musical stance: for example, Sodom, Kreator, and Destruction (see *Record Collector*, January 2002: 'Speed Kills – Again').

During the 1990s, these established subgenres of HM were joined by new variants (e.g. death metal) and further hybrid forms (e.g. funk metal). The most recent variants of metal include 'rap metal', 'extreme metal', itself with a range of styles, including grindcore and pagan metal (see McIver, 2000); and hybrids such as progmetal. Metal maintained its high market profile into the 2000s, despite frequent critical derision and a negative public image. Its latest variant, nu metal, breathed new life into the genre, achieving considerable commercial success (e.g. Limp Bizkit; Linkin Park). There are now a number of identifiable heavy metal subgenres, or closely related styles. Although these are historically specific, each has continued to be represented in the complex range of contemporary heavy metal, now often referred to simply as 'metal' (see Christe, 2003).

HM is frequently criticized as incorporating the worst excesses of popular music, notably its perceived narcissism and sexism, and it is also often musically dismissed. Even Lester Bangs, one of the few rock critics to favourably view the emergence of HM, wrote of the genre:

> As its detractors have always claimed, heavy-metal rock is nothing more than a bunch of noise; it is not music, it's distortion – and that is precisely why its adherents find it appealing. Of all contemporary rock, it is the genre most closely identified with violence and aggression, rapine and carnage. Heavy metal orchestrates technological nihilism.
>
> (Bangs 1992: 459)

HM was one of the main targets of moves to censor popular music in the 1980s (see Chapter 13). Reprising earlier controversies around heavy metal, but in more attenuated form, extreme metal raises questions of free speech, censorship, and 'the limits of musical expression' (Kahn-Harris, 2003: 81).

Until the publication of Weinstein's comprehensive sociological study (1991), and Walser's more musically grounded treatment (1993), there were few attempts to seriously discuss the genre. Yet HM displays a musical cogency and enjoys a mass appeal, existing within a set of social relations. Some forms of the genre have enjoyed enormous commercial success, and have a large fan base; other 'harder' sub-genres have a cult following. Many HM fans are working-class, white, young and male, identifying with the phallic imagery of guitars and the general muscularity and oppositional orientation of the form (there is some debate here: see Walser 1993). The symbols associated with HM, which include Nazi insignia and Egyptian and biblical symbols, provide a signature of identification with the genre, being widely adopted by metal's youth cult following (see Christe, 2003).

The much-debated question is why a genre generally panned by the critics (and many other music fans) as formulaic noise, associated with a negative social stance and consequent public controversy, is so popular? What is the basis of HM's appeal? Breen argued that the rise of HM in the 1980s was linked to 'firstly, a search for substance and authenticity in rock music and, secondly, to advanced methods of marketing music for mass consumption' (Breen 1991: 194; see also Weinstein 1991: Chapter 4). The theatrical aspects of glam metal, plus its musical accessibility, remain part of its commercial appeal and success. The genre's performers present an achievable image of flounced hair and torn jeans, a rock lifestyle whose surface aspects at least are affordable to its followers. The fans are also attracted by HM's sheer volume, the 'power' of the music, the genre's problem-oriented lyrics, and many performers general lack of a commercial image. This is a form of authenticity, with metal fans seeking greater 'substance' than what they see in mainstream, chart-oriented music. Authenticity is also central to the appeal of extreme metal to its fans (Kahn-Harris, 2006).

CROSSOVER: FROM THE MARGIN TO THE MAINSTREAM

Genres can develop and become part of the musical 'mainstream', usually through 'crossing over' into the pop and rock mainstream and charts. During the 1990s, this occurred with grunge, beginning with the huge success of Nirvana's album *Nevermind* (Geffen, 1991), and with country, and performers such as Shania Twain (see Chapter 4). Crossover has commonly occurred with black music in the United States, with debate over whether this has compromised the authenticity of the music, or can be seen more positively as part of the integration and upward social mobility of the black community (Garofalo, 1994; George, 1989). An example of crossover at its most successful is rap, which shifted from New York in the late 1970s, with a local following, to large-scale commercial success internationally in the late 1990s.

The antecedents of rap lie in the various story-telling forms of popular music: talking blues, spoken passages and call-and-response in gospel. Its more direct formative influences were in the late 1960s, with reggae's DJ toasters, and stripped-down styles of funk music, notably James Brown's use of stream-of-consciousness raps over elemental funk back-up. Initially a part of a dance style which began in the late 1970s among black and Hispanic teenagers in New York's outer boroughs, rap became the musical centre of the broader cultural phenomenon of hip hop: the broad term that encompassed the social, fashion, music and dance subculture of American's urban, black and Latino youth of the 1980s and 1990s. It embraces rap, break-dancing, graffiti art, athletic attire – baseball caps, basketball boots, etc. (see Potter, 1995).

Rappers made their own mixes, borrowing from a range of musical sources – sampling – and talking over the music – rapping – in a form of improvised street poetry. This absorption and recontextualizing of elements of popular culture marked out rap/hip-hop as a form of pop art, or postmodern culture. The style was commercially significant, as black youth were 'doing their own thing', bypassing the retail outlets: 'By taping bits of funk off air and recycling it, the break-dancers were setting up a direct line to their culture heroes. They were cutting out the middlemen' (Hebdige, 1990: 140). Many of the early rappers recorded on independent labels, initially on twelve inch singles, most prominently Sugar Hill Records in New York. The label's 1982 release, Grandmaster Flash and the Furious Five, 'The Message', was one of the first rap records to have mainstream chart success, and led to greater interest in the musical style (see Shuker, 2001: 163–4). Run DMC, *Raising Hell* (London, 1986) was the first rap album to crossover to the pop charts, and brought rap into wider public consciousness.

As with other maturing musical styles, a number of identifiable sub genres emerged within rap (see Krims, 2000; Shuker, 2005). These included the blander commercial rap of performers such as M.C. Hammer, Kris Kross, and Vanilla Ice; gangsta rap, with its accompanying controversy and censorship (see Chapter 13); and the serious political 'hardcore rap' of Public Enemy. The genre was soon taken up by white youth, white artists (Eminem), and the major record labels, in a familiar process of the appropriation of black musical styles.

By the late 1990s, rap and hip-hop became bracketed together as part of mainstream American culture. A *Time* magazine cover story, featuring Lauryn Hill, proclaimed the arrival of the 'Hip-Hop Nation', referring to 'the music revolution that has changed America' (*Time*, 8 February 1999: 40–57). The Fugees, *The Score* (Sony/Columbia, 1996), was a huge international success, with sales of seven million by early 1997. In adding elements of R&B, soul, and ragga rock to the genre, it foreshadowed the contemporary orientation of rap. By 1998, rap was the top-selling music format in the US market. Its influence pervaded fashion, language, and street style. The *Time* story noted that the two terms, rap and hip-hop, were now 'nearly, but not completely, interchangeable' (ibid.).

This conflation was cemented through the next few years. The record sales, product endorsements, associated fashion merchandising, and public celebrity of artists such as Beyoncé (and her former group Destiny's Child), Nelly, and Eminem made rap and hip-hop in effect the mainstream. The broad genre also became globalized. In a major edited study, *Global Noise*, Mitchell argued that 'Hip-hop and rap cannot be viewed simply as the expression of African-American culture; it has become a vehicle for global youth affiliations and a tool for reworking local identity all over the world' (2001: Introduction).

I now want to look at a body of work that constitutes a loose form of genre: the cover version.

'NOT FADE AWAY': COVER VERSIONS

Cover versions are performances and recordings by musicians not responsible for the original recording. Historically, these were often 'standards', and were the staples of singers repertoire for most of the 1940s and 1950s. Reflecting industry competition and as part of marketing strategy, record companies would release their artists cover versions of hits from their competitors. In the 1950s, white singers covered the original rock 'n' roll recordings by black artists, often sanitizing them in the process (e.g. Pat Boone's cover of Little Richard's 'Tutti Frutti'), in an effort by record companies to capitalize on the ethnic divide in American radio. Criticism of this frequently exploitative practice led to covers being equated with a lack of originality, and regarded as not as creative, or authentic, as the original recording. This view was reinforced by the aesthetics and ideology of 1960s rock culture, valuing individual creativity and the use of one's own compositions (Keightley, 2003).

There is an economic dimension to covers, since they are a proven product that an audience can often identify with. Accordingly, many covers, especially when played by cover and tribute bands, seek to replicate the original as closely as possible. Covers have also featured strongly in the charts, especially since the late 1980s. There is a fresh generation of listeners and a new market for a recycled song, as reissues, compilation albums and film soundtracks demonstrate

Such marketing practices and career choices can undermine the status of covers, but the negative image of the cover is undeserved. Interpretation of the original recording aside, covers have provided a training ground for musicians, and have often served as a form of homage to the original artists. Playing and recording covers is a way for artists to authenticate themselves with their audience, through identification with respected original artists. Elvis Presley's Sun performances of 'That's Alright Mama' (Sun, 1955), originally recorded by R&B singer Arthur 'Big Boy' Crudup, and his version of the bluegrass classic 'Blue Moon of Kentucky', rehearsed the singer's influences and contributed to the formation of rockabilly and rock 'n' roll in the 1950s.

At times, song covers have been creative in their own right. To illustrate how artists 'seek to define themselves in relation to traditions and genres other than their own' (Butler, 2003: 1), Butler examines two covers by the Pet Shop Boys: 'Where the Streets Have No Name', originally by rock band U2 (1987), and 'Go West', originally by the disco/dance group the Village People (1979). The musical sound, performance style, and lyrical themes of each pair of songs, and the discourse surrounding their production and reception, show how these covers provide an intertextual commentary on the original works. He argues that the Pet Shop Boys subvert the U2 song, 'poking fun at certain common ways of exposing authenticity in 1980s rock', and their cover of 'Go West', as a 'stomping disco record', repositions disco as a form of roots music for the gay community of the 1990s.

In the UK in the late 1950s and early 1960s, a number of musicians became intensely interested in Black American performers, including those whose work provided the antecedents of rock 'n' roll. Groups such as The Rolling Stones, the Yardbirds, and the Animals began playing covers or reworked versions of American R&B and blues, gradually transforming the music into what became known as 'rock'. A significant audience emerged for this music, stimulated by tours of England by several leading American bluesmen, including Howlin' Wolf and Muddy Waters (see Hatch and Millward, 1987: 94–107). Guitarist Eric Clapton, formerly with the Yardbirds and John Mayall's Bluesbreakers, was prominent among those reaching back beyond 1950s rock 'n' roll to country and electric blues for inspiration and musical texts. In 1966, with two other key figures in the British rhythm and blues movement, Ginger Baker (drums) and Jack Bruce (bass), both from the Graham Bond Organisation, Clapton formed Cream. The trio came together in a conscious attempt to push the boundaries of rock through developing the potential of blues-based music, and performed and recorded versions of blues classics. (Headlam (1997) instructively traces these back to their original sources in Chicago and Delta blues.)

For other performers, covers are a significant part of their repertoire, with the ability to 'mine' and revise the musical past, regarded as a virtue. Joan Jett, who played lead guitar in the teenage female hard rock band the Runaways, initiated a solo career with 'I Love Rock 'n' roll' (Boardwalk, 1982). A remake of an obscure B-side by British band The Arrows, Joan Jett and the Blackhearts' version was one of the biggest hits of the 1980s, spending seven weeks at Number 1 on the US *Billboard* chart. The song provided the title track for a successful album, which also included 'Crimson and Clover', originally a Number 1 hit for Tommy James and the Shondells in 1967. Released as a single, Jett's cover of this reached Number 7. She had further chart success with a cover of Gary Glitter's 'Do You Wanna Touch Me (Oh Yeah)', and subsequently released an album of covers, *The Hit List* (Epic, 1990), featuring songs she had frequently played in concert. As a quirky footnote to this, the Arrows' version of 'I Love Rock 'n' roll' was itself an oblique form of cover, being written in response to the rather cynical and world-weary tone of the Rolling Stone's single, 'Its Only Rock 'n' Roll'.

At the beginning of her music career, punk poet Patti Smith attempted a 'radical feminization of rock' (Whitelely, 2000: 7) by appropriating and adapting songs associated with masculinity and the romantic rebel tradition in rock. In her first single, a cover of 'Hey Joe', Smith replaced the original wife-murderer in the song with female terrorist and media celebrity Patti Hurst. On her critically acclaimed debut album *Horses* (Arista, 1975), Smith covered Van Morrison's 'Gloria' (originally recorded by Them in 1966). Them had recorded 'Gloria' in a proto-punk, garage rock style, with a basic beat, Van Morrison's growled vocals, and a ragged chanted chorus: 'G-L-O-R-I-A: Gloria'. The song's lyrics emphasize the appeal of Gloria – 'she'll make you feel alright' – and cater to the male fantasy of seduction by a female temptress.

Them's 'Gloria' can be considered an example of male-coded rock and roll, sometimes referred to as 'cock rock'. This became an alternative term for hard rock, highlighting the genre's often explicit and aggressive expression of male sexuality, its mysogynist lyrics, and its phallic imagery. Cock rock performers were regarded as aggressive, dominating and boastful, a stance, it was argued, evident in their live shows (Frith and McRobbie, 1990; Reynolds and Press, 1995). Against this tradition, Smith reworks the song from a female point of view, exposing Morrison's macho stance with an exaggerated leering 'male' vocal performance, and using gender ambiguities to parody the 'maleness' of Morrison's song. At various points in the song, Smith slips into gendered 'characters', undermining the dominant male rock vocal of the original, along with its numerous cover versions by male rock bands (Daley, 1997: 237).

On stage and in personal style, Smith emulated the toughness of male rebellion, but regarded her band's music as 'feminine music' (Press and Reynolds, 1995: 356). In her striking photograph on the cover of *Horses* (Arista, 1975), Smith is dressed in jeans and a white shirt, with a tie draped around her neck, conveying an air of self-assurance and sexual ambiguity. Along with her music, this stance enabled Smith to challenge patriarchal control and attempt to bridge rock's gender gap, as have later performers such as Björk, P.J. Harvey, and Tori Amos (Whiteley, 2005).

THE ROCK CANON

Art forms are typically discussed in terms of a canon, where works are 'typically presented as peaks of the aesthetic power of the art form in question, as ultimate manifestations of aesthetic perfection, complexity of form and depth of expression which humans are capable of reaching through this art form' (Regev, 2006: 1). The canon embraces value, exemplification, authority, and a sense of temporal continuity (timelessness). Critics of the concept point to the general social relativism and value judgments embedded in it, and the often associated privileging of Western, white, male, and middle-class cultural work.

Notions of canon are frequently present in popular music discourse, implicitly in everyday conversations among fans, and more directly in critical discourse. As Regev puts it: 'Canonisation in popular music has gone hand in hand with its very recognition as a legitimate art form' (ibid). Music critics and the music press are major contributors to the construction of a musical canon, with the use of ratings systems for reviews, annual 'best of' listings, and various 'guidebooks' to key recordings (Dimery, 2005; Irvin, 2000). The canon also underpins accounts of the history of popular music.

General coverage of historical figures, musical trends, and recordings are standard content in music magazines (see Chapter 9), especially those aimed at an older readership, for example *MOJO* and *UNCUT*. In addition, many of these titles have begun publishing special issues and series. Given that many of these are rapidly sold out, this is a lucrative market, tapping into and reinforcing popular memory. Examples here include the *NME Originals*, the *UNCUT Legends*, and the *Rolling Stone* special issues, such as *The 50th Anniversary of Rock: IMMORTALS. The 100 Greatest Artists of All Time* (Issue 642, August 2005). These frequently draw on rich source material: 'Distilled from the archives of the NME, the collectable NME Originals document the history of music'.

In addition to their economic motivation, these publications are playing an important ideological role. They contribute to the identification and legitimating of a canon of performers, in the same way as lists of 'greatest albums', which of course, they are closely aligned with. The selection process at work here is an interesting one, indicative of particular views of creativity and authorship. The title IMMORTALS: The 100 Greatest Artists of All Time, displays no lack of ambition and confidence, but the choices of artists from the 1950s excludes Bill Haley, presumably as his image does not conform to a notion of 'rock' authenticity.

The gendered nature of the musical canon and its dominance by Anglo-American performers and recording has been strongly critiqued. Citron (1993) examines the question: 'Why is music composed by women so marginal to the standard "classical" repertoire?' Her study looks at the practices and attitudes that have led to the exclusion of women composers from the received 'canon' of performed musical works, important elements of canon formation: creativity, professionalism, music as gendered discourse, and reception. This historical absence of women has also been noted in popular music studies. For example, the marginalization of women in popular music histories (see O'Brien, 2002); the privileging of male performers and male-dominated or -oriented musical styles/genres in discussions of authorship (Whiteley, 2000); and the consequent domination of popular music canons by male performers.

The nature of the canon and the difficulties surrounding it, are evident in the recurring presentation of a 'mainstream' canon of rock and pop recordings in 'Best Of/Greatest Albums of All Time' lists. Von Appen and Doehring (2006) provide a metaanalysis of such lists, drawing on thirty-eight rankings made between 1985 and 1989 and 2000–4 (see Appendix 3). This 'top thirty', is dominated by artists rock albums of the 1960s and 1970s, notably the Beatles, and there is an absence of women and black artists. The list represents the staple musical repertoire for 'classic rock' radio, which both reflects and reinforces the visibility and value accorded to such performers and albums.

Why does this pattern emerge? They suggest that two criteria are important: aesthetic and sociological. The aesthetic places a premium on artistic authenticity, and there is at times a limited relationship between such rankings and sales and chart success. The exclusion of compilation and greatest hits albums from most of the lists included reflected the view that the album must represent a showcase of the work of an artist at a particular point in time. Von Appen and Doehring's discussion of the sociological factors at work here shows the role of the music press and industry discourse in shaping taste, and the cultural capital and social identities of those who voted on the lists. The following chapters engage with some aspects of these.

NOTES

Starting points for studying music and genre are:

Frith, S. (1996) *Performing Rites:On the Value of Popular Music*, Cambridge, MA: Harvard University Press.

Fabbri, F. (1999) 'Browsing Music Spaces: Categories and the Musical Mind' (paper delivered at IASPM (UK) conference. Available online at: www.tagg.org/others/ffabbri9907.html.

Borthwick, S. and Moy, R. (2004) *Popular Music Genres: An Introduction*, Edinburgh: Edinburgh University Press. This is an excellent reference. The authors develop a general schema for studying musical genre, apply this to a number of major genres, and provide a useful list of further resources in relation to each.

Other books covering a range of genres and associated performers are:

Shuker, R. (2005) *Popular Music: The Key Concepts* (2nd edn), London and New York: Routledge.

Charlton, K. (1994) *Rock Music Styles: A History* (2nd edn), Madison, WI: Brown & Benchmark.

Prendergast, M. J. (2003) *The Ambient Century: From Mahler to Moby – The Evolution of Sound in the Electronic Age*, London: Bloomsbury.

Heavy Metal

A comprehensive popular overview is:

Christe, I. (2004) *Sound of the Beast: The Complete Headbanging History of Heavy Metal*, New York: HarperEntertainment.

The major academic studies are:

Arnett, J. (1996) *Metalheads. Heavy Metal Music and Adolescent Alienation*, Boulder, CO: Westview Press.

Walser, R. (1993) *Running With the Devil: Power, Gender and Madness in Heavy Metal Music*, Middletown, CT: Wesleyan University Press.

Weinstein, D. (2000) *Heavy Metal. The Music and Its Culture*, Boulder, CO: Da Capo Press.

Kahn-Harris, K. (2006) *Extreme Metal: Music and Culture on the Edge*, Oxford: Berg.

Kahn-Harris also provides an extensive bibliography on metal and related genres at his web site: www.kahn-harris.org

Documentaries:

Decline of Western Civilization. Part 2: The Heavy Metal Years, 1988.
American Hardcore.

Rap and hip-hop

Forman, M. (2002) *The Hood Comes First*, Middletown, CT: Wesleyan University Press.

Krims, A. (2000) *Rap Music and the Poetics of Identity*, Cambridge: Cambridge University Press (especially Chapter 2: A genre system for rap music).

Chang, J. (2005) *Can't Stop, Won't Stop: A History of the Hip Hop Generation*, New York: St Martin's Press.

Song covers

Plasketes, G. (2005) *Popular Music and Society*, 28, 2. 'Special issue: Like a Version – Cover Songs in Popular Music'.

Keightley, K. (2003) 'Covers', in Shepherd, J., Horn, D., Laing, D., Oliver, P. and Wicke, P. (eds) *The Continuum Encyclopedia of Popular Music*, Volume 1. London and New York: Continuum.

Weinstein, D. (1998) 'The History of Rock's Past Through Rock Covers', in Swiss, T., Herman, A. and Sloop, J.M. (eds) *Mapping the Beat: Popular Music and Contemporary Theory*, Malden, MA and Oxford: Blackwell Publishers.

The Wire, 'The singer not the song', Issue 261, November 2005: 44–51. Profiles of 69 covers that rattle the state of the song, plus Alan Licht investigates the motives for covering other artists' work.

The canon

Popular Music, 25,1, 2006. Special Issue on Canonisation.

Of the many anthologies bringing together a canon of recordings I like:

Irvin, J. (ed.) (2003) *The MOJO Collection: The Ultimate Music Companion*, Edinburgh: Canongate.

Marsh, D. (1989) *The Heart of Rock and Soul: The 1001 Greatest Singles Ever Made*, New York: Plume/Penguin.

See also the regular music press 'best of' lists.

Chapter 7

'Shop Around'
Retail, radio and the charts

The music industry includes a series of gatekeepers, people and institutions that 'stand between' consumers and the musical texts, once it has been produced as a commodity. The sound recording companies have a number of such 'cultural intermediaries' (Bourdieu, 1984) making the initial decision about who to record and promote, and filtering material at each step of the process involving the recording and marketing of a song. In this chapter, and Chapters 8 and 9, I outline the role of other gatekeepers, primarily various music media. There is an historical progression of these. Based in the established sector of sheet music sales, retail shops were where sound recordings could first be listened to and purchased. Later, film and radio provided cultural spaces where music could be experienced, informing and shaping consumption. The music press, established in the 1920s, played a similar role, especially in the emergence of 'rock culture' in the 1960s. The introduction of television in the 1950s, followed by MTV in the 1980s, provided new sites of mediation. Most recently (as indicated in Chapters 1 and 2), the Internet has dramatically altered the relationship between the sound recording industry and the manufacture, distribution and consumption of music.

I use the phrase 'stand between' as shorthand for what are complex processes of marketing and consumption. The concepts of 'gatekeepers' and 'cultural intermediaries' have been used to analyse the way in which media workers select, reject, and reformulate material for broadcast or publication. Based on a filter-flow model of information flow, gatekeepers 'open the gate' for some texts and information, and close it for others. The concept of gatekeeper became critiqued for being too mechanistic, as oversimplified, and of limited utility (O'Sullivan *et al.*, 1994: 126–7; Negus, 1992); following the work of Bourdieu (1984), other analysts prefer the concept of 'cultural intermediaries' due to its greater flexibility. I have drawn on both concepts here.

RETAIL

Music retail includes the sale of sheet music, musical instruments, music-related merchandise, concert tickets, music DVDs, music magazines and books. Primarily, however, the term 'music retail' refers to the sale of sound recordings to the public. Information on this topic is sparse, and there is a history of music retail yet to be written, but a quick sketch is possible.

Sound recordings were first available through shops selling sheet music and musical instruments. In the early 1900s, chains of department stores began supplying hit songs, along with sheet music. Later, smaller, independent and sole proprietor shops (the 'mom and pop' stores in the United States) emerged. By the 1950s, and the advent of rock and roll, record retailers included independent shops, often specializing in particular genres; chain stores; and mail order record clubs. The subsequent relative importance and market share of each of these has reflected the broader consolidation of the music industry, along with shifts in recording formats and distribution technologies. Retailers have had to adapt to changes as mundane as the need for different shelf space to accommodate new formats. The advent of electronic bar coding in the 1990s enabled retail, distribution, and production 'to be arranged as an interconnected logistic package', allowing 'music retailers to delineate, construct and monitor the "consumer" of recorded music more intricately than ever before' (du Gay and Negus, 1994: 396). A similar process now occurs with the tracking of browsers and purchasers preferences in on-line shopping.

Retail chains have, at times, also assumed a direct gatekeeping role, by censoring or not stocking particular artists, genres, and recordings (for example Wal-Mart in the US). Record company sales and distribution practices can be directly tied to music retail. Several leading mail order record clubs in the 1950s were adjuncts of labels, receiving discounts on stock, a situation successfully challenged legally by their competitors (Barfe, 2004). Linked independent record stores have been part of labels, such as Rough Trade and Beggars Banquet in the UK, although the importance of such arrangements declined in the 1990s.

As with the culture industries generally, increased concentration of ownership has been a feature of the music retail industry. An increasing proportion of recordings are sold through general retailers (e.g. Woolworths, Wal-Mart), and megastores such as Tower and HMV. This concentration influences the range of music available to consumers, and the continued economic viability of smaller retail outlets. The general retailers frequently use music as a loss-leader: reducing their music CD and DVD prices to attract shoppers whom they hope will also purchase other store products with higher profit margins. This situates music as only one component of the general selling of lifestyle consumer goods. This marketing strategy is central to the Warehouse national chain, New Zealand's largest music retailer. The Warehouse has used their bulk purchasing power, along with heavy advertising of discounts through blanket media coverage (the press, flyers to home mailboxes, TV, radio advertising), to secure market dominance. What this means for consumers, however, is a relatively restricted range of music on offer, with a heavy emphasis on the discounted chart-oriented recordings, which are available only on CD. Smaller local music chains have been forced to retrench by consolidating shops and 'downsizing' staff, or have kept operating through niche marketing and their increased use of the Internet.

Brennan (2006) documents how the increased concentration of music retail in Britain constrains the availability of releases from indie and specialist genre labels. In addition to central buying, the five major chain stores have introduced the use of 'retail packs', with only a limited number of sales spaces available:

> At HMV there's 24 non-pop retail packs up for grabs every month. And that's for folk, world music, classical *and* jazz. If you don't get one of them, you're not going to sell even 1000 records.
>
> (Tom Bancroft, owner of jazz label Caber Music;
> interviewed and quoted by Brennan, 2006: 224)

As Brennan observes, this 'can mean almost guaranteed commercial failure for independent artists not offered a pack' (ibid). Further, the central buyer's decision to offer a pack will be based on an artist and labels 'track record': a combination of favourable press coverage; radio airplay; band tours and promotional activities; and previous retail history. Obviously, there is a process of validating existing advantages likely to occur here: to those who have, shall be given.

Second-hand record shops form a minor but culturally significant part of record retail. They have been hit by the same trends as their mainstream counterparts, along with the gentrification and higher rents of their traditional central city locations. They have managed to survive, and in some cases even flourish, by using the Internet, by catering to specialist interests, and continuing to stock vinyl. Through their ambience and knowledgeable staff, they retain a loyal collector following.

THE CHARTS

The charts provide a crucial link between music retail and radio. The popular music chart is a numerical ranking of current releases based on sales and airplay, usually over a week; the top ranked album/single is No.1 and the rest are ranked correspondingly. The first UK chart appeared in 1928 (the *Melody Maker* 'Honours List'); in the US,

Billboard, the leading trade paper, began a 'Network Song Census' in 1934. Such charts quickly became the basis for radio 'Hit Parade' programmes, most notably the 'Top 40' shows.

The popular music charts represent a level of industry and consumer obsession with sales figures almost unique to the record industry. The charts are part of the various trade magazines (e.g. *Billboard*, *Variety*, *Music Week*), providing a key reference point for those working in sales and promotion. The record charts also play a major role in constructing taste: 'to the fan of popular music, the charts are not merely quantifications of commodities but rather a major reference point around which their music displays itself in distinction and in relation to other forms' (Parker, 1991: 205).

The precise nature of how contemporary charts are compiled, and their basis, varies between competing trade magazines, and national approaches differ. In the United States, singles charts are based on airplay, while the album charts are based on sales. Current releases are generally defined for the singles charts as up to 26 weeks after the release date. In the UK, the charts are produced by market research organizations sponsored by various branches of the media. In both countries, data collection is now substantially computerized and based on comprehensive sample data (Hull, 2004: 201–2). Airplay information is compiled from selected radio stations, sales information from wholesalers and retailers, assisted by bar coding.

This represents a form of circular logic, in that the charts are based on a combination of radio play and sales, but airplay influences sales, and retail promotion and sales impacts on radio exposure. Historically there has been frequent controversy over attempts to influence the charts (see payola, below), and debate still occurs over perceived attempts to manipulate them. The charts continue to provide the music industry with valuable feedback and promotion, and help set the agenda for consumer choice.

Changes in the presentation of the charts can have important repercussions for the relative profile of particular genres/performers. The charts are broken down into genre categories; these can change over time, acting as a barometer of taste, as with the change in *Billboard* from 'race' records to R&B in 1949. The decline of the single has influenced the way the charts are constructed. In the UK, in 1989 the music industry reduced the number of sales required to qualify for a platinum award (from one million to 600,000) to assist the promotional system, and ensure charts continued to fuel excitement and sales. In 2006, greater chart recognition of on line sales of singles reflected their increasing market share (see Chapter 2).

RADIO

Radio developed in the 1920s and 1930s as a domestic medium, aimed primarily at women in the home, but also playing an important role as general family entertainment, particularly in the evening. Radio in North America was significant for disseminating music in concert form, and helped bring regionally based forms such as western swing and jazz to a wider audience (Ennis, 1992). Historically the enemy of the record industry during the disputes of the 1930s and 1940s around payment for record airplay, radio subsequently became its most vital promoter. Until the advent of MTV in the late 1980s, radio was indisputably the most important broadcast medium for determining the form and content of popular music.

The state has played a significant, yet often overlooked, role in radio. First, in shaping the commercial environment for radio, primarily through licensing systems, but also by establishing broadcasting codes of practice – a form of censorship. This state practice has at times been challenged, most notably by pirate radio (see below). Second, the state has at times attempted to encourage 'minority' cultures, and local music, with the two frequently connected, through quota and other regulatory legislation. Examples of this are attempts to include more French-language music on Canadian radio (Grenier, 1993), a case illustrating the difficulties of conflating 'the national' in multicultural/ bilingual settings; and the New Zealand government's recent introduction of local content quotas for radio (see Chapter 12).

The organization of radio broadcasting and its music formatting practices have been crucial in shaping the nature of what constitutes the main 'public face' of much popular music, particularly rock and pop and their associated sub genres. Radio has also played a central role at particular historical moments in popularizing or marginalizing music genres. Two examples of this follow: the popularizing of rock 'n' roll in the 1950s; and the impact of British pirate radio in the 1960s.

Radio meets rock 'n' roll: payola and the cult of the DJ

The reshaping of radio in the 1950s was a key influence in the advent of rock 'n' roll. Radio airplay became central to commercial success, especially through the popular new chart shows. Hit radio was 'one of America's great cultural inventions', revitalising a medium threatened by television (Barnes, 1988: 9). The DJ (disc jockey) emerged as a star figure, led by figures such as Bob 'Wolfman Jack' Smith and Alan Freed.

The place of radio in the music industry was brought to the fore by the debate around payola, a term used for the offering of financial, sexual, or other inducements in return for promotion. In 1955 the US House of Representatives Legislative Oversight Committee, which had been investigating the rigging of quiz shows, began looking at pay-to-play practices in rock music radio. Payola, as the practice was then known, had long been commonplace, but was not illegal. 'Song plugging', as the practice was originally termed, had been central to music industry marketing since the heyday of Tin Pan Alley in the 1920s. By the 1950s, DJs and radio station programmers frequently supplemented their incomes with 'consultant fees' and musical credits on records, enabling them to receive a share of songwriting royalties.

During the committee hearings, Dick Clark admitted to having a personal interest in around a quarter of the records he promoted on his influential show *American Bandstand*. He divested himself of his music business holdings and was eventually cleared by the committee. A clean-cut figure, Clark survived the scandal because he represented the acceptable face of rock 'n' roll. Pioneer DJ Alan Freed was not so fortunate; persecuted and eventually charged with commercial bribery in 1960, his health and career were ruined.

Payola did not target all music radio, but was rather 'the operative strategy for neutralizing rock 'n' roll' (Garofalo, 1997: 170), and part of a conservative battle to return to 'good music'. The campaign against payola was underpinned by economic self-interest. The American Society of Composers, Authors and Publishers (ASCAP) supported it by attacking rivals BMI (Broadcast Music, Inc.), whose writers were responsible for most rock 'n' roll. The majors supported it as part of a belated attempt to halt the expansion of the independents. Hill goes so far as to conclude that one way to see the payola hearings was as an attempt – ultimately successful – 'to force a greater degree of organization and hierarchical responsibility onto the record industry so that the flow of music product could be more easily regulated' (Hill, 1991: 667). The involvement of conservative government officials, and a number of established music figures (including Frank Sinatra), was largely based on an intense dislike of rock 'n' roll, a prejudice with only loosely concealed racist overtones, given the prominence of black performers associated with the genre.

Payola did not disappear, merely becoming less visible and concealed under 'promotion' budgets. In the United States in 2005, echoing the earlier controversy, New York Attorney-General Eliot Spitzer initiated a sweeping payola investigation, implicating all four major record labels in play for pay practices. Sony-BMG and Warner Music Group settled for US$10 million and US$5 million respectively, while the cases against Universal and EMI are ongoing. In March 2006, Spitzer filed a lawsuit charging Entecom Communications, owner of WKSE and 104 stations nationwide, with trading airtime for cash and goods, providing numerous examples of the practice. Prompted by Spitzer's inquiries, the Federal Communications Commission opened its own investigation (*Rolling Stone*, 6 April 2006: 14. 'Payola Probe Branches Out').

Pirate radio and the BBC

Pirate radio broadcasts are those made by unlicensed broadcasters as an alternative to licensed, commercial radio programming. However, the pirate stations usually rely on the same popular music that is programmed on commercial radio, rarely programming music other than the main pop and rock styles. A major exception was in the 1960s, when the British pirates challenged the BBC's lack of attention to pop/rock music. British pirate radio in its heyday, 1964–8, was an historical moment encapsulating the intersection of rock as cultural politics and personal memory with market economics and government intervention. Twenty-one different pirates operated during this period, representing a wide range of radio stations in terms of scale, motives, and operating practices.

Chapman (1992) argues that the myth of the pirates is that they were about providing pop music to their disenfranchised and previously ignored youthful listeners, representing a somewhat anarchic challenge to radio convention and commerce, but the reality was rather more commercial. However, given that the BBC's popular music policy was woefully inadequate in the early 1960s, the pirates did cater for a largely disenfranchised audience; they also pioneered some innovative programmes and boosted the careers of leading DJs of the time Kenny Everett and John Peel. As their programming indicated, they were never predominantly about popular music, and were heavily oriented toward advertising. All the pirates were commercial operations: 'though work-place and legal judicial circumstances were not typical, in all other respects these were entrepreneurial small businesses aspiring to become entrepreneurial big businesses' (Chapman, 1992: 167). This was particularly evident in the case of Radio London, set up with an estimated investment of £1.5 million, whose 'overriding institutional goals were to maximize profit and bring legal commercial radio to Great Britain' (Chapman, 1992: 80). In this respect, the station succeeded, with the BBC's Radio One, established in 1967 as the pirates were being closed down, borrowing heavily from the practices of pirate radio, and even hiring pirate DJs.

From FM to web radio

FM radio was developed in the early 1930s, using a frequency modulation (hence FM) system of broadcasting. It did not have the range of AM, and was primarily used by non-commercial and college radio until the late 1960s, when demand for its clearer sound quality and stereo capabilities saw the FM stations become dominant in the commercial market. They contributed to what became a dominant style of music radio in the 1970s and 1980s (radio friendly; high production values; relatively 'easy listening': 'classic rock', exemplified by The Eagles and Fleetwood Mac). The appeal of FM witnessed a consolidation of the historically established role of radio in chart success. Independent programme directors became the newest power brokers within the industry, replacing the independent record distributors of the early 1960s (Eliot, 1989). Most radio stations now followed formats shaped by consultants, with a decline in the role of programme directors at individual stations, a situation that persisted into the 1990s, and continues today.

Though video became a major marketing tool in the 1980s, radio continued to play a central part in determining and reflecting chart success (This is illustrated in the shifting attitude of radio to heavy metal; see Weinstein, 1991: 149–61). Web radio and new broadcasting technologies have fostered an explosion of radio stations, even although many have a very localized signal. In the commercial sector, digital technologies have produced new production aesthetics, and reshaped the radio industry (Dunaway, 2000; Hull, 2004). Terrestrial radio's audience has dropped 13 per cent in the past decade. In response to this dwindling market share, and its serious impact on advertising revenue, eight of the top radio companies in the North American market formed the HD Digital Radio Alliance in 2005, and began launching digital radio stations in key markets. These new stations offered listeners near-CD-quality sound and up to three additional channels per frequency, along with alternate versions to their primary format (*Rolling Stone*, 23 February 2006: 18. 'Radio's Next Generation').

Stations and formats

Radio stations are distinguishable by the type of music they play, the style of their DJs, and their mix of news, contests, commercials and other programme features. We can see radio broadcasts as a flow, with these elements merging. The main types of radio station include college, student, pirate, and youth radio (e.g. the US college stations; New Zealand's campus radio, and Australia's Triple J network); state national broadcasters, such as the BBC; community radio; and, the dominant group in terms of market share, the commercial radio stations. There is a longstanding contradiction between the interests of record companies, who are targeting radio listeners who buy records, especially those in their teens and early twenties, and private radio's concern to reach the older, more affluent audience desired by advertisers. To some extent, this contradiction has been resolved by niche marketing of contemporary music radio.

Station and programme directors act as gatekeepers, being responsible for ensuring a prescribed and identifiable sound or format, based on what the management of the station believes will generate the largest audience – and ratings – and consequent advertising revenue; (the classic study here is Rothenbuhler, 2006 [1985]). The station's music director and the programme director – at smaller stations the same person fills both roles – will regularly sift through new releases, selecting three or four to add to the playlist. The criteria underpinning this process will normally be a combination of the reputation of the artist; a record's previous performance, if already released overseas; whether the song fits the station's format; and, at times, the gut intuition of those making the decision. Publicity material from the label/artist/distributor plays an important role here, jogging memories of earlier records or sparking interest in a previously unknown artist. Chart performance in either the US or UK is especially significant where the record is being subsequently released in a 'foreign' market. In choosing whether or not to play particular genres of popular music, radio functions as a gatekeeper, significantly influencing the nature of the music itself. (See Hendy

(2003) on UK Radio 1's playlist, and Neill and Shanahan (2005) on New Zealand's commercial networks.)

Historically, radio formats were fairly straightforward, and included 'Top 40', 'soul', and 'easy listening'. Subsequently formats became more complex, and by the 1980s included 'adult-oriented rock', classic hits (or 'golden oldies'), contemporary hit radio, and urban contemporary (Barnes, 1988). Urban contemporary once meant black radio, but now includes artists working within black music genres. In the USA, black listeners constitute the main audience for urban contemporary formats, but the music also appeals to white listeners, particularly in the 12–34 age group. Today, radio in most national contexts includes a range of formats: the dominant ones, reflecting historical developments in addition to current demographics, are rock, contemporary chart pop, adult contemporary, and classic hits.

As channel switching is common in radio, the aim of programmers is to keep the audience from switching stations. Common strategies include playing fewer commercials and running contests which require listeners to be alert for a song or phrase to be broadcast later, but the most effective approach is to ensure that the station does not play a record the listener does not like. While this is obviously strictly impossible, there are ways to maximize the retention of the listening audience. Since established artists have a bigger following than new artists, it makes commercial sense to emphasize their records and avoid playing releases from new artists on high rotation (ie. many times per day) until they have become hits, an obvious catch-22 situation.

The most extreme example of this approach is the format classic rock, or classic hits, which only plays well-known hits from the past and is dominated by performers such as Led Zeppelin, Pink Floyd, The Who, The Rolling Stones, Jimi Hendrix, and Queen. This popular format capitalizes on the nostalgia of the demographic bulge who grew up during the 1960s, and who now represent a formidable purchasing group in the market. Classic rock is also gaining support among younger listeners: 'nine per cent of kids age twelve to seventeen listened to classic rock radio in any given week in 2005, marking a small but significant increase during the past three years' (Radio ratings company Arbiton, reported in *Rolling Stone*, 23 February 2006: 11).

The concern to retain a loyal audience assumes fairly focused radio listening. Paradoxically, while the radio is frequently 'on', it is rarely 'listened' to, instead largely functioning as aural wallpaper, a background to other activities. Yet high-rotation radio airplay remains vital in exposing artists and building a following for their work, while radio exposure is also necessary to underpin activities like touring, helping to promote concerts and the accompanying sales of records. The very ubiquity of radio is a factor here. It can be listened to in a variety of situations, and with widely varying levels of engagement, from the Walkman to background accompaniment to activities such as study, domestic chores, and reading.

NOTES

Retail

Barfe, L. (2004) *Where Have All the Good Times Gone? The Rise and Fall of the Record Industry*, London: Atlantic Books.

Brennan, M. (2006) 'This Rough Guide to Critics: Musicians Discuss the Role of the Music Press', *Popular Music*, 25, 2: 221–34.

Du Gay, P. and Negus, K. (1994) 'The Changing Sites of Sound: Music Retailing and the Composition of Consumers', *Media, Culture and Society*, 16, 3: 395–413.

The British Phonographic Industry website includes data on retail: www.bpi.co.uk.

The charts

Strachan, R. and Leonard, M. (2003) 'The Charts', in Shepherd, J., Horn, D., Laing, D., Oliver, P. and Wicke, P. (eds) *The Continuum Encyclopedia of Popular Music, Volume 1*, and New York: Continuum.

Radio

Hendy, D. (2003) *Radio in the Global Age*, London: Polity Press.

Ennis, P.H. (1992) *The Seventh Stream*, Hanover, NH and London: Wesleyan University Press; Chapter 5: 'The DJ Takes Over, 1946–1956'.

Rothenbuhler, E. (2006 [1985]) 'Commercial radio as Communication', in Bennett, A. Shank, B. and Toynbee, J. (eds) *The Popular Music Studies Reader*, London and New York: Routledge.

Neill, K. and Shanahan, M. (2005) *The Great New Zealand Radio Experiment*, Southbank, Victoria: Thomson/Dunmore Press.

Chapter 8

'U Got the Look'
Film, television and MTV

This chapter deals with the relationship of popular music production, dissemination, and consumption in relation to film and television. With film, my focus is on commercial feature film and popular music, primarily the popular/rock musicals that followed in the footsteps of the classic Hollywood musicals. With television, I am interested in the impact of the new medium on the impact of rock and roll, and the subsequent role of mainstream television music shows, including those that are a form of reality television. Both film and television have screened popular music documentaries, validating and mythologizing particular performers, styles, and historical moments. A final section on MTV illustrates, once again, the global reach of the music industry, and the synergy between music, marketing, and audiences.

FILM

Film has an important historical relationship to popular music. Early silent films often had a live musical accompaniment (usually piano); and with the 'talkies' musicals became a major film genre in the 1930s, and continued to be important into the 1960s. Composers and musicians, primarily stars, provided a source of material for these films, as did Broadway musicals. The various genres of popular music, its fans and performers have acted as a rich vein of colourful, tragic and salutary stories for filmmakers. A new form of musical, the 'rock musical', played an important part in rock 'n' roll in the mid-1950s. Allied with such musicals were youth movies, with a range of sub-genres. Over the past 35 years or so, considerable synergy has been created between the music and film industries; film soundtracks and video games represent another avenue of revenue for recordings, including the back catalogue, and help promote contemporary releases.

The classic Hollywood musical was a hybrid film genre, descended from European operetta and American vaudeville and the music hall. While *The Jazz Singer* (Alan Crosland, 1927) was the first feature film with sound, the first 'all-talking, all-singing, all dancing' musical was *The Broadway Melody* (Harry Beaumont, 1929), which was important also for establishing the tradition of the backstage musical. The musical soon became regarded as a quintessentially American or Hollywood genre, associated primarily with the Warner and MGM studios, and RKO's pairing of Fred Astaire and Ginger Rogers. Mainly perceived as vehicles for song and dance, the routines and performance of these became increasingly complex, culminating in the highly stylized films of Busby Berkeley. *The Wizard of Oz* (Victor Fleming, 1939) introduced a new musical formula, combining youth and music. Other new forms of the musical were introduced during the 1940s, including composer biographies, and biographical musicals of 'show biz' stars. The vitality and audience appeal of the musical continued into the 1950s, with contemporary urban musicals such as *An American in Paris* (Vincent Minnelli, 1951), which portrayed the vitality of the Paris music scene, with a cast including musical stars Frank Sinatra and Bing Crosby.

Although the 1960s did see several blockbuster musicals, notably *The Sound of Music* (Robert Wise, 1965), the heyday of the classic musical had passed, with fewer Broadway hits now making it to the screen. The 1960s saw a move towards greater realism in the musical, exemplified by *West Side Story* (Robert Wise, Jerome Robbins, 1961), an updated version of Romeo and Juliet. The classic musical established a link between music and the screen, featuring stars from both media and creating a market synergy between them, a relationship which rock and roll was able to build upon.

Popular and rock musicals

The classical musical's place was taken by a plethora of new forms associated with the popular musical genres spawned by the advent of rock and roll. These films are frequently treated as a generic group: Szatz calls them 'popular musicals', although this term could apply equally to their historical predecessors, and they are also accorded the more appropriate label 'rock film'. There is now a substantial body of such films, including a number of identifiable subgenres, with a considerable literature on them.

During the 1950s, the decline of the Hollywood studio system and a dwindling cinema audience, led to the need to more systematically target particular audience demographics. Hollywood linked up with the record industry to target youth, with a spate of teenage musicals. Many of these starred Elvis Presley, with his song and dance routines in films such as *Jail House Rock* (Richard Thorpe,1957). Most early popular musicals had basic plots involving the career of a young rock performer: *Rock Around the Clock* (Fred Sears, 1955), *Don't Knock the Rock* (Fred Sears, 1956), and *The Girl Can't Help It* (Frank Tashlin, 1957). These were frequently combined with the other stock forms, films serving purely as contrived vehicles for their real-life stars. Most of Elvis Presley's movies, from *Love Me Tender* (Robert Webb, 1956) onward, were of this order, while British examples include Cliff Richard in *The Young Ones* (Sydney Furie, 1961), and Tommy Steele in *The Tommy Steele Story* (Gerard Bryant, 1957).

The single 'Rock Around the Clock', by Bill Haley and the Comets, provides an example of the market power of cinema. Originally released in May 1954, it barely dented the *Billboard* chart, peaking at Number 23, where it stayed for only one week. Greater success came when the song was prominently used on the soundtrack for *Blackboard Jungle* (Richard Brooks, 1954). One of the most successful and controversial films of the period, the film used the new genre of rock 'n' roll to symbolize adolescent rebellion against the authority of the school. Re-released in May 1955, 'Rock Around the Clock' went to Number 1 in the UK and the USA. By the end of 1955 it had become the most popular recording in the US since 'The Tennessee Waltz', selling six million copies (Miller, 1999: 91).

Any interest such films retain is largely due to their participant's music rather than their acting talents, though they did function as star vehicles for figures like Presley. In helping establish an identity for rock 'n' roll, the teenage musicals placed youth in opposition to adult authority, and for conservatives confirmed the 'folk devil' image of fans of the new genre, associating them with juvenile delinquency, a major concern internationally through the 1950s. Thematically, however, the popular musicals actually stressed reconciliation between generations and classes, with this acting as a point of narrative closure at the film's ending. Such musicals also helped create an audience and a market for the new musical form, particularly in countries distant from the initial developments. These related roles continued to be in evidence in the subsequent development of the popular rock musical.

British beat and the British invasion of the early 1960s were served up in a number of films. Gerry and the Pacemakers brought a taste of the moment to a broader audience with *Ferry Across the Mersey* (J. Summers, 1964). This stuck to what had already become a standard formula – struggling young band makes good after initial setbacks – which was only shaken when the Beatles enlisted director Richard Lester to produce the innovative and pseudo-biographical *A Hard Day's Night* (1964). Along with Lester's *Help* (1965), this consolidated the group's market dominance, and extended the rock film genre into new and more interesting anarchic forms. In the mid–late 1960s, with the emergence of the counter-culture, popular music was a necessary backdrop and a cachet of cultural authenticity for films such as *Easy Rider* (Dennis Hopper, 1969) and *The Graduate* (Mike Nichols, 1967). Both fused effective rock soundtracks with thematic youth preoccupations of the day: the search for a personal and cultural identity in contemporary America.

149

During the 1970s and 1980s there was a profusion of popular musicals: the realist Jamaican film *The Harder They Come* (Perry Henzel, 1972); the flower power and religious fantasy of *Godspell* (David Greene, 1973) and *Hair* (Milos Forman, 1979); the disco-dance musicals of *Saturday Night Fever* (John Badham, 1977), and *Grease* (Radnal Kleister, 1978), and the dance fantasies of *Flashdance* (Adrian Lyne, 1983), and *Dirty Dancing* (Emile Ardolino, 1987) The 'rock lifestyle' was the focus of *That'll Be The Day* (1973) and Ken Russell's version of *Tommy* (1975). Nostalgia was at the core of *Amercian Graffiti* (George Lucas, 1973), *The Blues Brothers* (John Landis, 1978), *Quadrophenia* (Franc Rodham, 1979), and *The Buddy Holly Story* (Steve Rash, 1978). The success of these popular musicals helped prepared the ground for the success of MTV, launched in 1981, by reshaping the political economy of popular music, shifting the emphasis from sound to sound *and* images.

Since the 1980s, popular musical films have continued to mine a range of themes: youth subcultures (*River's Edge*, Tim Hunter, 1987); adolescent and young adult sexuality and gender relations (*Singles*, Cameron Crowe, 1992); class and generational conflict; nostalgia; stardom and the rock lifestyle (*Backbeat*, Iain Softley, 1995; *The Doors*, Oliver Stone, 1990; *Sid and Nancy*, Alex Cox, 1986; *Rock Star*, Stephen Herek, 2001; *Purple Rain*, Albert Magnoli, 1984); dance fantasies such as *Strictly Ballroom* (Baz Luhrman, 1992) and *Take the Lead* (Liz Friedlander, 2006); and fandom and the joy of making music, as in *High Fidelity* (Stephen Frears, 2000) and *School of Rock* (Richard Linklater, 2004). *The Rocky Horror Picture Show* (Jim Sharman, 1975) created a new subgenre: the cult musical, with the audience becoming an integral part of the cinematic experience, an indulgence in fantasy and catharsis. The film went on to became the king of the 'midnight movies' – cult films shown at midnight for week after week, usually on Friday and Saturday nights (Samuels, 1983).

The storylines of such musicals involve popular music to varying extents, ranging from its centrality to the narrative theme, to its use as soundtrack. These films articulate with the hopes and dreams, and fantasy lives, which popular music brings to people. When an actual artist is drawn on, or featured, such films help the process of mythologizing them, as with Elvis Presley, the Beatles, and Jim Morrison. Dominant themes include youth and adolescence as a rite of passage, frequently characterized by storm and stress, and using subcultural versus 'mainstream' affiliations to explore this; reconciliation, between generations, competing subcultures, and genders, frequently expressed through the emergence of couples; and the search for independence and an established sense of identity. Given such themes are ones identified in the literature as central adolescent 'tasks' and preoccupations, they clearly appeal to youthful cinema audiences, and to film makers looking for box office success.

Soundtracks and marketing

As mentioned above, *Rock Around the Clock* (1956) and many of the films featuring Elvis Presley demonstrated the market appeal of popular musical soundtracks, as had many Hollywood musicals before them. Mainstream narrative cinema has increasingly used popular music soundtracks to great effect, with accompanying commercial success for both film and record; e.g. the soundtrack to *The Commitments* (Alan Parker, 1991), featuring some impressive covers of soul classics and the powerful voice of Andrew Strong (who plays the part of the lead singer Deco), charted internationally, reaching Number 1 in a several countries.

Such soundtracks feature popular music composed specifically for the film, or previously recorded work which is thematically or temporally related to the film, as with *American Graffiti* (1973), *The Big Chill* (1983), *Boyz N The Hood* (1991), and *High School Musical* (2006). This enables multimedia marketing, with accompanying commercial success for both film and record. Several musicians better known for their band recordings have followed Ry Cooder's example and moved into composing music for such films; e.g. Trent Reznor (Nine Inch Nails) for *Natural Born Killers* (1994), and Kirk Hammett (Metallica) and Orbital for *Spawn* (1999). Television series have also provided a vehicle for music soundtracks. *Northern Exposure* (1990–5) set the pattern for later shows, using a local radio station and the local bar's jukebox to get artists from Nat King Cole to Lynyrd Skynyrd into the programme. Films aimed at children (and the parents who take them to the movies) have had some of the biggest selling soundtrack albums in recent years: *The Lion King*, and *Tarzan*. Prince's soundtrack for the film *Batman* (1989) was part of a carefully orchestrated marketing campaign, which successfully created interest in the film and helped break Prince to a wider audience, primarily through exposure (of the promotional video clip) on MTV.

TELEVISION

Television has been an important mode of distribution, promotion and formation for the music industry. The discussion here is of free-to-air, broadcast television, and the popular music programmes which form part of its schedules: light entertainment series based around musical performers, music documentaries, and the presentation of musical acts as part of television variety and chat/interview shows. (MTV and similar cable channels are dealt with later.) Popular music plot themes, music segments and signature tunes are also an important part of many television genres, including those aimed at children (e.g. *Sesame Street*) and adolescents (*The Simpsons*, *The X Files*), but also 'adult' dramas such as *The Sopranos* and *Grey's Anatomy*, with the accompanying release of soundtrack albums from these series.

A contradictory relationship initially existed between television and popular music. Television is traditionally a medium of family entertainment, collapsing class, gender, ethnic, and generational differences in order to construct a homogeneous audience held together by the ideology of the nuclear family. In contrast, many forms of popular music, especially rock 'n' roll and its various mutations, have historically presented themselves as being about 'difference', emphasizing individual tastes and preferences. The introduction of public broadcast television in the United States and the United Kingdom in the 1950s coincided with the emergence of rock 'n' roll. Television helped popularize the new music, and established several of its performers, most notably Elvis Presley, as youth icons. Indeed, for some fans, along with film television was their only access to 'live' performance. Television was quick to seize the commercial opportunities offered by the emergent youth culture market of the 1950s. 'Television became devoted, at least in part, to the feature of televisual musical products for an audience that spent much of its leisure time and money in the consumption of pop music goods' (Burnett, 1990: 23). This led to a proliferation of television popular music shows.

The better-known of these on US television included *American Bandstand*, one of the longest running shows in television history (1952–), *Your Hit Parade* (1950–9), and *The Big Record* (1957–8). Britain had *Juke Box Jury* and *Top of the Pops*, both starting in the late 1950s, and *The Old Grey Whistle Test* (launched by the BBC in 1971, and aimed at more album-oriented older youth). In 1963 *Ready Steady Go!* (RSG) began showcasing new talent, who usually performed live, compared with the *Top of The Pops* staid studio lip-synchs with backing from a house orchestra. In addition to the music, such shows have acted as influential presenters of new dances, image, and clothing styles. Several of these shows are now marketed as sell-through videos or DVDs, documenting historically significant performers and styles (e.g. *The Best of the Old Grey Whistle Test*, BBC DVD, 2001), and showcasing contemporary acts (*Later, with Jools Holland*).

Television's presentation of rock music prior to the advent of music video was generally uninspiring. Performers either straightforwardly performed, even if at times in an impressively frenetic manner (as with The Who's debut effort on *RSG*) or mimed to their recordings in a pseudo-live setting. There were a few notable experiments through the 1960s and 1970s to incorporate additional visual elements (see Shore, 1985, for a full history of the development of music video in relation to television). The 1980s success of MTV boosted televised music videos, reshaping the form and the broadcast programmes that relied on music videos for their content. In the United States and Canada, nearly every major city had its own televised music video show, with several nationally syndicated. MV-based programmes also became a stock part of television channel viewing schedules in the United Kingdom and Western Europe, and New Zealand and Australia. These shows were significant because of their importance to advertisers, drawing a young audience whose consuming habits are not yet strongly fixed. The increased popularity of MTV and the digital delivery of music undermined music on mainstream television. Only in New Zealand and Australia, which recently acquired cable television and do not yet have widely available satellite reception, did these programmes retain the high audience ratings they achieved during the 1960s through into the 1990s. Many shows have now ended, including the iconic *Top of The Pops* in the United Kingdom in 2006. Today, Popular music on television is increasingly competing against other genres for scheduling space and advertising revenue, while the demographic significance of the youth audience has declined since the 1990s.

A number of studies have illustrated the factors at work in the emergence and nature of popular music programmes on commercial television, particularly their place within scheduling practices and the process of selection of the performers and music videos for inclusion on them. Of particular interest are the links between screen space, advertising, and record sales. While it is difficult to prove a direct causal link, as with radio airplay and chart 'action' there is evidence that the television exposure has an influence on record purchases. The nature of such shows, and their tendency to play music videos which are shortened versions of the associated song, have exercised considerable influence over the way in which videos are produced and their nature as audio-visual and star texts. Also significant, especially in small nations such as Australia, New Zealand, and the Netherlands, is the often marginalized status of locally produced music videos which are competing for screen space compared with their imported counterparts, a form of cultural imperialism (Shuker, 2001: 183–5; Stockbridge, 1992).

Reality television: from 'S Club 7' to 'Rock Star Supernova'

'Reality television' describes a variety of programming ranging from crime and emergency-style shows, to talk shows, docu-soaps, and some forms of access-style programming. Emerging in the 1980s in the United States, it established itself as a central part of mainstream, popular television by the mid-1990s. In the 2000s reality television became a leading programme format, with many shows internationally franchised (e.g. *Survivor*; *Big Brother*). A hybrid genre, reality television draws on and reworks generic codes and conventions from a variety of sources, using new technology (e.g. camcorders) to convey as sense of immediacy and authenticity to viewers. Reality television has been criticized for being reliant on shock value and pandering to viewer voyeurism and the lowest common denominator; and celebrated as a form of 'democratainment', with its emphasis on viewer participation (Casey *et al.*, 2002). Popular music has provided a significant vehicle for reality television. Popular series like *The Monkees* in the 1960s (Stahl, 2002) and *S Club 7 in Miami* in the late 1990s, reinforced the public profiles and commercial success of their performers.

Initial TV and 19 Management (who managed the Spice Girls) conducted a nationwide search in the UK to develop a group to star in a teen-oriented television show for BBC1. Reflecting their name, the assembled group S Club 7 consisted of seven members whose public image was very much that of a supportive friendship group. The television show, *S Club 7 in Miami*, debuted in the UK during 1999, and went on to be screened internationally. Its success led to the show being re-screened (on BBC 2 in 2000), and to its marketing as two 'sell-through' video compilations of several episodes. A follow up series, with S Club 7 now in Los Angeles (*LA7*), first screened in the UK on BBC 1 in early 2000, and was also sold overseas. S Club 7 appeared frequently in the teen music magazines, with several cover stories (e.g. *Smash Hits*, 5 April 2000), and on shows such as *Top of the Pops*.

Further media coverage was generated through the group's own magazine, *S Club*, and a sophisticated official website that introduced visitors to 'the S Club experience' in an interactive and engaging manner. The site enabled fans to find out personal details about each member of the group, the recordings and television shows, and their other activities. Fans could register to receive advance information about all of these, and leave messages for the groups' members. The website consolidated S Club 7's fan base, and was an early example of what has become a valuable adjunct to more traditional forms of music marketing. This fan base appeared to largely consist of young girls, and some boys, aged between eight and twelve, a significant 'demographic' with considerable spending power.

Helped by such exposure, the group's debut single 'Bring it All Back' topped the UK chart, and enjoyed modest success when it was released in the United States. A second single, 'S Club Party', also charted, as did the groups self-titled first album. In March 2000, a second album and the first single from it ('Reach') charted in the UK, and overseas. The group enjoyed further chart success through 2001 and 2003, and made a third television series, *Hollywood 7*. In mid-2002 Paul Cattermole left the band, which continued as S Club. In 2003, after their movie *Seeing Double* and a greatest hits album (*Best*) were released, the group broke up.

S Club 7 foreshadowed the later *Pop Idol*, *Popstars* and *Rock Star* series. These musical talent quests, based on audience votes but with a key role played by judging panels (especially in the initial selection of participants), have become an international phenomenon. They have created new pop and rock stars in a number of countries, although the career of some has been short-lived (e.g. True Bliss in New Zealand). Hear'Say, put together through *Popstars*, topped the UK album and singles charts in 2001. *Pop Idol* launched the careers of Will Young and Gareth Gates in the UK, and Ruben Studdard in the US. INXS successfully toured in late 2006 with their new lead singer J.D. Fortune, the winner of the television show *Rock Star INXS*. The popularity of such shows, their audience, and the discourse of commodification and authenticity surrounding them are topics now being investigated.

DOCUMENTARIES AND ROCKUMENTARIES

'Constructed as a genre within the field of non-fictional representation, documentary has, since its inception, been composed of multiple, frequently linked representational strands' (Beattie, 2004: 2). Popular music documentaries include concert, tour and festival films; profiles of performers, and scenes; and ambitious historical overviews. Such documentaries can be produced for either film or television (as both 'one-offs' and series). The various forms of popular music documentary have served a number of economic and ideological functions. As a form of programming, they create income for their producers and those who screen them, via rights and royalties. They validate and confirm particular musical styles and historical moments in the history of popular music as somehow worthy of more 'serious' attention. While celebrating 'youth' and the mythic status of stars, they also confirm their status as 'the other' for critics of these sounds and their performers.

Concert, tour, festival, and scene documentaries demonstrate a close link between the documentation of musical performance and observational modes of documentary film-making. Referred to in the United States as 'direct cinema', and evident from the early 1960s, these documentaries have a well-established tradition (see Beattie, 2004), exemplified in the work of director D.A. Pennebaker (*Don't Look Back*, 1966; *Monterey Pop*, 1968; and *Down From the Mountain*, 2002). Direct cinema has recently mutated into 'docusoap' and other variants of reality television, as in MTV's *The Real World* series (which frequently featured participants who were seeking musical careers), and *Meet the Osbournes*, a fly on the wall depiction of the family life of aging heavy metal rocker Ozzy Osbourne.

Films of music festivals have consolidated the mythic status of events such as *Monterey Pop* (1968) and, especially, *Woodstock* (1969), with the 1970 film a major box office success . A number of other concert and concert tour films have had a similar but more limited commercial and ideological impact; for example: *The Last Waltz* (Martin Scorsese,1978), a record of The Band's final concert; *Hail, Hail Rock and Roll* (Taylor Hackford, 1987), featuring Chuck Berry and other seminal rock 'n' roll performers; *Stop Making Sense* (Jonathan Demme, 1984), featuring Talking Heads; Prince's *Sign O' The Times* (Prince,1987); and Neil Young and Crazy Horse in *Year of the Horse* (Jim Jarmusch, 1998). Such films capture particular moments in 'rock history', while at the same time validating particular musical styles and performers.

Other documentaries consolidate particular historical moments: the Beatles first tour of America '*What's Happening! The Beatles in the USA*' (Albert and David Maysles, 2004); the Rolling Stones Altamont concert of 1969 (*Gimme Shelter*, 1970; released on DVD by Criterion in 2000); and Julian Temple's examination of the Sex Pistol's phenomenon, including the television interview that sparked off controversy (*The Filth and the Fury*, 2000). Documentaries have also been important in exposing particular scenes, sounds, and performers to a wider audience, as in *The Decline of*

155

Western Civilization, Part One (1981) on the Los Angeles punk/hardcore scene circa 1981, featuring Black Flag, the Circle Jerks, X, and the Germs; its 'sequel', *The Decline of Western Civilization, Part Two: The Metal Years* (1988), featuring Aerosmith, Alice Cooper, Ozzy Osbourne, Kiss, Metallica, and Motorhead; and *Hype* (1996) on the Seattle grunge scene. The success of *Buena Vista Social Club* (1999) introduced Cuban jazz to an international audience, and led to massive sales of the accompanying soundtrack album (which had initially gone largely ignored following its first release in 1996). *Genghis Blues* (2000) consolidated the appeal of world music, and *Down From the Mountain* (D.A. Pennebaker, 2002) did the same for contemporary bluegrass. Documentaries have reminded us of the important role of session musicians and 'house bands', for example the Funk Brothers in *Standing in the Shadows of Motown* (Paul Justman, 2002). Other popular music documentaries have celebrated major performers; for instance, The Who in *The Kids Are Alright* (Jeff Stein, 1979; released as a Special DVD Edition, 2004) As with any genre, the ultimate accolade is parody, best represented by *This is Spinal Tap* (Rob Reiner, 1984).

Documentary series on the history of popular music, made for television, include the joint BBC and US co-production *Dancing in the Street* (1995); *Walk on By* (2003), a history of songwriting; Ken Burns *Jazz* (2000); the Australian series *Long Way to the Top* (ABC, 2001); and the Martin Scorsese series, *Legacy of the Blues*, screened as part of the 'Year of the Blues' celebrations in the USA in 2003 (see Weissman, 2005, for an informed discussion of the seven programmes). In addition to the income from their initial screenings and international licensing, such series have produced accompanying books (Palmer, 1995), soundtracks, and video and DVD boxed sets. Through the selection of material depends heavily on the nature and quality of what is available, they visually construct particular historical narratives, reframing the past. In the case of *Dancing in the Street*, for example, the emphasis is on 'authentic artists' rather than commercial performers: in the episode 'Hang on to yourself', Kiss get barely a minute, while 'punk icon' Iggy Pop features throughout. In sum, as with the music press, music documentary history is situated primarily around key performers and styles, a form of canonization.

MTV

In North America, the 24-hour, non-stop commercial cable channel, 'MTV: Music Television', founded in 1981, has made its logo synonymous with the music video form. Originally owned by the Warner Amex Satellite Company, the channel was subsequently sold to Viacom International in 1985. Viacom, which still owns MTV and MTV 2, also has interests in broadcast and cable television, radio, the Internet, book publishing, and film production and distribution. In 2005, it was the third largest communications conglomerate in the world, with annual revenues of US$26.6 million (Bishop, 2005: 452).

After a slow start, with many detractors who did not think a dedicated music video channel would have an audience, MTV became enormously popular and highly profitable. The channel is credited with boosting a flagging music industry in the 1980s. Not only did it eventually capture a considerable share of the advertising directed at the youth and young adult/yuppie market, as Goodwin observes, MTV solved the perennial problem of cable television – how to generate enough revenue for new programming – by having the record companies largely pay for the 'programmes' by financing the video clips (Goodwin, 1993).

In the late 1980s it was reaching nearly 20 million American homes, and was regularly watched by 85 per cent of 18 to 34 year olds (Kaplan, 1987). In November 1991, *MTV 10*, an hour-long celebration of MTV's tenth anniversary, was screened in prime time on the North American ABC TV network. The show asserted the cultural centrality of MTV over the networks, opening with a performance of 'Freedom 90' by George Michael: 'We won the race/Got out of the place/Went back home/Got a brand new face/For the boys on MTV'. Performers on the show included Michael Jackson, Madonna, and REM, and *MTV 10* was subsequently screened worldwide, while the 1992 MTV Music Awards were seen in 139 countries.

By the early 1990s, MTV had 28 million subscribers, and was adding 1–3 million new subscribers every year. MTV's success spawned a host of imitators in the United States, and a number of national franchises and imitations around the globe. These raised the issue of the place of local music in a context dominated by international repertoire, especially from the North American music market (Hanke, 1998). After an initial struggle to untangle cable and satellite regulations in dozens of countries, MTV Europe, launched in 1988, broke even for the first time in February 1993, and became the continent's fastest growing satellite channel. By 1993, its 24-hours-a-day MV programming was available in more than 44 million homes, and it was adding subscribers at the rate of almost a million a month. Thirty per cent of its airtime was reserved for European performers, and while the programme format was similar to that of its parent station, 'a genuine effort was made to play a substantial number of "European" music videos' (Burnett, 1990: 24). MTV-Asia began broadcasting in late 1991, with a signal covering more than 30 countries from Japan to the Middle East. The channel's English-language broadcasts reached more than 3 million households with a programme dominated by MVs by Western stars, but with an approximately 20 per cent quota of Asian performers. MTV channels continued to proliferate international; there are now 38, with New Zealand the latest to be added in August 2006 (see the MTV web site: www.mtv.com).

The influence of MTV on the North American music industry during the 1980s – and, therefore, by association, globally – was enormous. By 1991, claimed Riordan,

80 per cent of the songs on *Billboard*'s Hot 100 were represented by a video (Riordan, 1991: 310). MTV became the most effective way to 'break' a new artist, and to take an emerging artist into star status. Performers who received considerable exposure on MTV before they were picked up by radio include Madonna, Duran Duran, the Thompson Twins and Paula Abdul. Rimmer argues that the new 'invasion' of the American charts by British groups, in the mid to late 1980s was directly attributable to MTV (Rimmer, 1985: 71).

Given their crucial role in determining commercial success, a key question is how particular MVs are chosen for the MTV play list. Evidence on this point is sparse, and it is clearly an area for further inquiry. Surprisingly, Kaplan's (1987) study of the channel ignores the selection issue, as do most commentators preoccupied with the videos as texts. Rubey (1991) noted that MTV's top 20 lists are compiled from national album sales, video airplay, and the channel's own research and requests, building circularity and subjectivity into the process. In the most thorough study of the operation of MTV, Banks (1996: Chapter 9) looked at the gatekeeper role of the American MTV channel, the operation of its Acquisitions Committee and the standards, both stated and unstated, which they apply. He concluded that major companies willingly edit videos on a regular basis to conform to MTV's standards, even coercing artists into making changes to song lyrics, while smaller, independent companies cannot usually get their videos on MTV. It would be worthwhile to know if such practices remain the case a decade on, but an update of Banks' work is lacking.

Despite the heady growth of the 1980s, the American MTV channel began the 1990s by retrenching. MTV executives claimed that the format had lost its freshness and was becoming clichéd, that the clips submitted to them 'are often simplistic to a fault. They're too literal, depriving viewers of their own interpretations' (press report, 15 January 1990). The channel initiated a programme overhaul designed to lessen its reliance on videos; new shows included *Vidcoms,* combining comedy and MV, and *Unplugged,* a 30-minute Sunday programme featuring live acoustic performances by bands such as Crowded House. *Unplugged* has proven highly successful, particularly through associated chart-topping album releases (Eric Clapton, Mariah Carey). These programme changes were a direct response to research on viewing patterns, which indicated, not surprisingly, that people tuned in to MTV for only as long as they enjoy the clips. With MVs making up some 90 per cent of the channel's broadcast day, negative reaction to a few clips can spell problems for audience retention and the sale of advertising time. This is a situation MTV shares with 'mainstream' television and radio, which have always been in the business of delivering audiences to advertisers in a highly competitive market.

Today, while MVs are still the staple of MTV channel's programming, the channel also screens concerts, interviews, and music-oriented news and gossip items, acting as a visual radio channel. Although owned by a global media giant (Viacom), 'localization' is almost a mantra for the nationally situated MTV channels, who use local VJs, play locally produced music videos, and air local programming.

NOTES

Film and television

Corner, J. (2002) 'Sounds Real: Popular Music and Documentary', *Popular Music*, 21, 3: 357–66.

Mundy, J. (1999) *Popular Music on Screen: From the Hollywood Musical to Music Video*, Manchester: Manchester University Press.

Romney, J. and Wootton, A. (1995) *Celluloid Jukebox: Popular music and the Movies since the 50s*, London: BFI.

Hayward, S. (2000) *Off The Planet: Music, Sound and Science Fiction Cinema*, London: John Libbey Perfect Beat Publications.

Popular Music, 21, 3, 2002. 'Special issue: Music and Television'.

MTV

On the operating practice of the channel, international impact, and its relation to local music, see:

Banks, J. (1996) *Monopoly Television: MTV's Quest to Control the Music*, Boulder, CO: Westview Press.

Hanke, R. (1998) '"Yo Quiero Mi MTV!": Making Music Television for Latin America', in Swiss, T., Sloop, J. and Herman, A. (eds) *Mapping the Beat: Popular Music and Contemporary Theory*, Malden, MA and Oxford: Blackwell.

And the website: www.mtv.com.

Chapter 9

'On the Cover of
The Rolling Stone'
The music press

T he music press plays a major part in the process of selling music as an economic
   commodity, while at the same time investing it with cultural significance. In one
of the first extended critical discussions of the music press, Frith correctly argued for
its central role in 'Making Meaning': 'the importance of the professional rock fans
– the rock writers', and the music papers, whose readers 'act as the opinion leaders,
the rock interpreters, the ideological gatekeepers for everyone else' (Frith, 1983: 165).
In spite of this significance, until recently, the music press has received little critical
attention.

My discussion begins with a general consideration of just what constitutes 'the
music press', which is viewed as a diverse range of publications, with music journalism
a literary genre in which any distinction between 'rock journalism' and academic
writing on popular music is frequently blurred. Music magazines include industry
reference tools, musicians' magazines, record collector magazines, fanzines, 'teen
glossies', 'the inkies', style bibles and the new tabloids. Although these publications
have many features in common, each serves a particular place in a segmented market,
in which journalism becomes collapsed into, and often indistinguishable from, music
industry publicity. Despite this symbiosis, popular music critics continue to function
as significant gatekeepers and as arbiters of taste, a role examined in the concluding
section of the discussion here.

The music press includes a wide range of print publications, with many now online.
General magazines and newspapers will also cover popular music, with regular review
columns. More specifically, however, the music press refers to specialized publications:
lifestyle magazines with major music coverage, music trade papers, and weekly and

monthly consumer magazines devoted to popular music, or particular genres within it. In addition to these are privately published fanzines, usually peripheral to the market economy of commercial publishing but nonetheless significant. There is also a variety of book-length writing on popular music, which has been drawn on extensively throughout this study, and to which I now turn.

'EVERYDAY I WRITE THE BOOK' (ELVIS COSTELLO)

An extensive, annotated bibliography published in 1985, covering the writing on popular music since 1955, revealed a considerable body of literature, which had increased dramatically during the early 1980s (Taylor, 1985). Subsequent published bibliographic guides showed rapid growth continued during the following decade (Shepherd *et al.*, 1997). More recently, the review columns of both the leading popular music academic journals and music magazines reveal a steady stream of books. Many are from specialist publishers of popular music titles, notably Da Capo, Omnibus, and Backbeat. In June 2006, the British *Observer Weekend* magazine included an article on the '50 best music books', and a further 50 could have been comfortably added.

Although categories frequently overlap, various categories of publication can be distinguished. They include popular (auto)biographies, histories, and genre studies; various forms of consumer guides, including encyclopedias and dictionaries, and chart listings and compilations; and discographies, usually organized by artist, genre, or historical period. The last represent an important aspect of popular music history, which they constitute as well as record, and are important texts for fans and aficionados. There are also more esoteric publications, such as rock quiz books, genealogical tables plotting the origin and shifting membership of groups, and 'almanacs' dealing with the trivia and microscopic detail of stars' private lives. Taylor's summary of all this is apposite: 'The variety of these publications is matched by the variation in the quality of their writing, accuracy and scholarship, which means one must approach them with a degree of discrimination and care' (Taylor, 1985: 1). Some twenty years on, this judgement still stands.

Initially, popular music journalism included a proliferation of 'quickie' publications, cashing in on the latest pop sensation. This was very much the case with the pop annuals accompanying the emergence of chart pop in the 1950s, which were largely rewritten public relations handouts. Emphasizing the pictorial aspect and providing personal information about performers rather than any extended critical commentary, these were often little more than pseudo-publicity. They reinforced the star aspect of pop consumption, feeding fans' desire for consumable images and information about their preferred performers, as did pop and rock magazines aimed at the teenage market (*Record Mirror*, UK, which began publication in 1953; and *Disc*, UK, 1958).

In the 1960s this changed with the impact of two factors: first the rise of a 'rock culture' with serious artistic intentions; second, the emergence of the 'New Journalism', associated with the writing of figures such as Hunter S. Thompson and Tom Wolfe. The New Journalism set out to move journalism beyond simple factual reporting, by using conventions derived from fiction. 'Stylistic traits pioneered by the new journalists such as scene by scene construction, third person point of view, recording of everyday detail and the inclusion of the figure of the journalist within the text were appropriated by US and UK music critics from the end of the 1960s' (Leonard and Strachan, 2003: 254). There was also a commitment to treating popular culture as worthy of serious analysis, an approach that has continued to be influential. The newly established *Rolling Stone* (US) magazine and a revamped *NME* in the UK, exemplified this, and elevated several rock critics to star status (Greil Marcus, Lester Bangs, Dave Marsh).

The 1980s saw a continuation of this trend, with a proliferation of articles and book-length studies of a more serious vein and intent. As McRobbie observed:

> Two kinds of writing now feed into the study of youth and popular culture. These are the more conventional academic mode, and what might be called a new form of cultural journalism. Each is marked by its own history, its debates and disputes.
>
> (McRobbie, 1988: xi)

Her edited collection, *Zoot Suits and Second-Hand Dresses*, showed serious popular music journalism had changed dramatically during the 1980s, 'with interest shifting from the music itself to a more general concern with the cultural phenomena which accompany it'. This new focus was strongly evident in the new 'style bibles' of the 1980s, especially *The Face*. Some of this journalism also colonized the 'mainstream' press and the more 'serious' weekly and monthly magazines.

Alongside this, developed a similar, though more historically situated, identifiable body of journalistic work on popular music, not only aimed at a broader readership, but also thoughtful and critically analytical of its subjects. Indicative of the commercial and ideological significance of this work is its appearance in book form, as sustained, in-depth studies of genres and performers; collected reviews and essays; several encyclopedias of popular music, aimed at a broad readership; and anthologies. Also significant, are a number of more thematic historical studies. For example, in *Mystery Train*, Greil Marcus uses a handful of rock artists, including Elvis Presley, Sly Stone, The Band, and Randy Newman, to illuminate the 'question of the relationship between rock 'n' roll and American culture as a whole'. His concern is with 'a recognition of unities in the American imagination' (Marcus, 1991a: Introduction). In a similar fashion, Miller's *Flowers in the Dustbin* (1999) documents the development of rock 'n' roll through a succession of key artists, recordings, technologies, and moments, relating all these to broader cultural currents in American life.

MUSIC MAGAZINES

We can usefully distinguish between industry-oriented, performer-oriented, and consumer-oriented music magazines. The music trade papers keep industry personnel informed about mergers, takeovers, and staff changes in the record and media industries, and changes in copyright and regulatory legislation and policies; advise retailers about marketing campaigns, complementing and reinforcing their sales promotions; and provide regular chart lists based on extensive sales and radio play data (the main publications are *Billboard*, *Music Business International*, and *Music Week*). Musicians' magazines (e.g. *Guitar Player*) inform their readers about new music technologies and techniques, thereby making an important contribution towards musicianship and musical appropriation (Théberge, 1991).

The various consumer- or fan-oriented music magazines play a major part in the process of selling music as an economic commodity, while at the same time investing it with cultural significance. Popular music and culture magazines don't simply deal with music, through both their features and advertising they are also purveyors of style. At the same time, these magazines continue to fulfil their more traditional function of contributing to the construction of audiences as consumers.

The majority of popular music magazines focus on performers and their music, and the relationship of consumers and fans to these. These magazines fall into a number of fairly clearly identifiable categories, based on their differing musical aesthetics or emphases, their sociocultural functions, and their target audiences. 'Teen glossies' emphasize vicarious identification with performers whose music and image is aimed at the youth market (e.g. *Smash Hits*); *Melody Maker* and *New Musical Express* (the 'inkies') have historically emphasized a tradition of critical rock journalism, with their reviewers acting as the gatekeepers for that tradition; and the 'style bibles' (*The Face*) emphasize popular music as part of visual pop culture, especially fashion. Several relatively new magazines offer a combination of the inkies' focus on an extensive and critical coverage of the music scene and related popular culture, packaged in a glossier product with obvious debts to the style bibles (*MOJO, Q, UNCUT*). Currently, there is a clear split between inclusive magazines, attempting to cover a broad range of musical styles, and those magazines that are genre specific.

Such magazines can be studied and compared in relation to a series of generally common features:

1   Their covers: the cost, the title, and the featured artists are all indicative of the magazine's scope and target audience. Further 'clues' are in the visual design

(layout, graphics, typeface), the level of language, and the use of promotional give-a-ways (e.g. *Smash Hits* key rings compared with the compilation CDs used with *Q*).

2 The general layout and design: e.g. the use or absence of colour, boxed material, sidebars, visuals, and even the actual size and length of the magazine.

3 Scope: the genres of music included; other media covered (the increasing reference to Internet sites, X Games, video game culture); the relative importance accorded particular artists; language used; gender representation (including in the advertising).

4 Reviews: length/depth, tone and language used e.g. *Rolling Stone's* stars system; *Hot Metal's* skull rating system. (For a helpful analysis of the evaluative criteria and rating systems underpinning reviews in Australia's *Rolling Stone* and *Juice*, see Evans, 1998.)

5 Adverts: which products feature? The links to a target readership; e.g. teen magazines, feminine hygiene ads; the proportion of the content which is adverts; and the values and associated lifestyles projected by the advertising. Often the distinction between adverts and 'real' content is blurred, with much content rewritten press copy.

6 The readership involvement: letters to the editor; competitions; reader questions answered (*Q's* 'where are they now?'); the use of their readers to survey taste and the popularity of artists and genres.

In sum, the answers to such questions provide a profile of particular music magazines, and an indication of their relationship to the wider music industry – a combination of gatekeeper and symbiotic marketing tool. While there is obvious overlap – and market competition – amongst these various types of music magazine, they each have distinctive qualities. The following examples illustrate this.

The inkie tradition: NME

Typical of the more serious 'inkie' rock press is the *New Musical Express* (NME), which began publication in 1952, marketed to the new generation of teenage record buyers in the UK. As with its main competitor, *Melody Maker*, the NME was closely tied into the record industry. In 1952, NME published 'the first regular and reasonably accurate list of British record sales'; the *Melody Maker* soon followed with a similar 'hit parade' based on retailers' returns, and both charts became closely tied to the industry's stocking and promotional policies (Frith, 1983: 166). Through the 1950s, the NME focused on the stars of popular music, with little critical perspective on the music covered. This clearly met a market demand, and by 1964 the magazine was selling nearly 300,000 copies per week.

The orientation of the UK music press, including *NME*, changed with the emerging and critically self-conscious progressive rock market of the mid-1960s, and the development in the USA of new, specialist music magazines such as *Creem* and *Rolling Stone*, characterized by their serious treatment of rock as a cultural form. In 1972 the *NME* was reorganized, with a new team of writers recruited from Britain's underground press. After a slump in the face of a late-1960s market assault by the now 'progressive' *Melody Maker*, by 1974 *NME* was back to 200,000 sales (Frith, 1983). Biting 'new journalist' prose for many readers became part of *NME*'s appeal – whether you agreed or not with the evaluations on offer was almost incidental.

Increasingly, the *NME* became associated with the British 'alternative' or indie music scene (see the recollections of its staff in Gorman, 2001). To a degree, *NME*'s very hipness and cynicism in the 1980s proved its undoing, as two new groups of readers emerged in the music marketplace: ageing fans, no longer into clubbing and concerts, with an eye to nostalgia, Dire Straits, their CD collections, and FM 'solid rock'/'golden oldies' radio; and younger yuppies and style-oriented professionals. Both groups of consumers were largely uninterested in the indie scene, and turned instead to the lifestyle bibles and the new glossies like *Q*, and (later) *MOJO*. This competition saw a decline in *NME*'s circulation, but it maintained its role as the essential chronicler of indie music.

NME remains indispensable for those wanting to keep up with this scene, and invaluable for those performers and labels working within it. The magazine sticks closely to its traditional format: a tabloid-style layout, although now using better quality paper and with much greater use of colour. It continues to feature a mix of features: reviews of records and concerts, as well as film, book, and video reviews; competitions and classifieds; an extensive U.K. gig guide and tour news; and chart listings, including retrospectives of these.

Rolling Stone: from counter culture icon to industry staple

The American inspiration for the outburst of the rock press in the late 1960s, and its reorientation, *Rolling Stone* was launched in San Francisco on 9 November 1967. Jann Wenner, its founder, wanted the publication to focus on rock music, but it was also to cover the youth culture generally. The first issue of the new fortnightly established that it was aiming at a niche between the 'inaccurate and irrelevant' trade papers and the fan magazines, which were viewed as 'an anachronism, fashioned in the mould of myth and nonsense'. *Rolling Stone* was for the artists, the industry, and every person who 'believes in the magic that can set you free'; it was 'not just about music, but also about the things and attitudes that the music embraces' (quoted in Frith, 1983: 169).

This rather earnest ideological mission resulted in considerable tension in the early years of *Rolling Stone* (see Draper, 1990), as it attempted to fuse in-depth and sympathetic reporting of youth culture and the demands of rock promotion. In its struggling early years, *Rolling Stone* was supported by the record companies, and the concern with radical and alternative politics was soon suborned by the dependence on the concerns of the music industry. In August 1973, *Rolling Stone* changed its format, becoming 'a general interest magazine, covering modern American culture, politics and art, with a special interest in music' (Frith, 1983: 171). However, it retained its now pre-eminent place as an opinion leader in the music business, mainly because its ageing, affluent, largely white male readership continued to represent a primary consumer group for the record industry.

The development of 'regional editions' of *Rolling Stone*, beginning with Britain in 1969 and followed by an Australian monthly edition, along with subsequent Japanese and German language editions reflects the increasing internationalization of popular music, and the global predominance of Anglo-American artists. In format, *Rolling Stone* retains its distinctive character through its famous cover picture feature (immortalized in the Doctor Hook single of 1972, which gained the band a cover story), but contents and presentation-wise it is similar to its newer competitors such as *Q* and the hip-hop bibles *The Source* and *VIBE*. This is hardly surprising, given that these magazines are oriented to older consumers with sufficient disposable income to allow them to purchase the music, clothes, spirits, and travel opportunities which *Rolling Stone* advertises.

The zines

At this point, I want to make a few comments on a type of magazine often not regarded as part of the music press, but whose importance is considerable: the fanzines. Fanzines are overlooked in discussions of the music press, due to their largely non-commercial nature, but play an important role in it. They are typically part of alternative publishing, which is characterized by the centrality of amateurs, readers as writers; non-mainstream channels of distribution; a non-profit orientation; and a network based on expertise from a wide base of enthusiasts. Produced by one person, or a group of friends, working from their homes, popular music fanzines are usually concentrated totally on a particular artist or group, and are characterized by a fervour bordering on the religious. This stance can be a reactionary one, preserving the memory of particular artists/styles, but is more usually progressive. Many of the original punk fanzines were characterized by a broadly leftist cultural politics, challenging their readers to take issue with the views presented by bastions of the status quo and reasserting the revolutionary potential of rock. Fanzines like *Crawdaddy* in the 1960s and *Sniffin' Glue* in the 1970s had tremendous energy, reflecting the vitality of live performances and emergent scenes.

The impact of punk rock was aided by a network of fanzines and their enthusiastic supporters. Savage argues that in the early days of punk in the UK, nobody was defining 'punk' from within:

> the established writers were inevitably compromised by age and the minimal demands of objectivity required by their papers. The established media could propagandize and comment, but they could not dramatize the new movement in a way that fired people's imagination.
>
> (Savage, 1991: 200)

With photocopying cheap and accessible for the first time, the fanzines were a new medium tailor-made for the values of punk, with its do-it-yourself ethic and associations of street credibility, and there was an explosion of the new form. These fanzines provided a training ground for a number of music journalists (e.g. Paul Morley; Jon Savage; Lester Bangs), and in some cases useful media expertise for those who, taking to heart their own rhetoric of 'here's three chords, now form a band', subsequently did just that (for example Bob Geldof, The Boomtown Rats; Chrissie Hynde, The Pretenders). Fanzines producers/writers did not have to worry about deadlines, censorship, or subediting, and 'even the idea of authorship was at issue, as fanzines were produced anonymously or pseudonymously by people trying to avoid discovery by the dole or employers' (Savage, 1991: 279).

Fanzine readers tend to actively engage with the publication: they debate via the 'letters to the editor', contribute reviews of recordings and concerts, provide discographies, and even interviews with performers. A number of studies have demonstrated the value of fanzines to producing and maintaining particular musical styles and scenes, as with Seattle in the early 1990s. In the case of progressive rock, fanzines maintain interest long after the genre had been discarded by the mainstream (Atton, 2001).

Despite their essentially non-commercial and often ephemeral nature, fanzines remain a significant part of the popular music scene. They represent a cultural space for the creation of a community of interest. The Internet has provided a new medium for the international dissemination of fanzines; through their 'printing' of contemporary concert reviews and tour information, such 'e-zines' have an immediacy that provides a form of virtual socialization for fans.

GATEKEEPERS AND INDUSTRY PUBLICITY

Writing in 1983, Frith saw the music papers and their writers as operating in a symbiotic relationship with the record industry, with the blurring of the boundary between rock journalism and rock publicity reflected in the continuous job mobility between them: 'record company press departments recruit from the music papers, music papers employ ex-publicists; it is not even unusual for writers to do both jobs simultaneously' (Frith, 1983: 173). The situation Frith describes has become even more firmly consolidated. Popular music magazines have developed in tandem with consumer culture, with the variations evident amongst them reflecting the diversity of readers' tastes and interests. They have also become part of a general magazine culture; while they are to be found in a separate section in the magazine racks, they are competing for advertising with a proliferating range of magazines. Accordingly, the market profile (especially the socio-economic status) of their readership must guarantee advertisers access to their target consumers. The advertising each carries firmly indicates their particular market orientation. They are providing not just an adjunct to popular music – though that dimension remains central – but a guide to lifestyle, especially leisure consumption.

The ideological role of the music press in constructing a sense of community and in maintaining a critical distance from the music companies had already become muted by the late 1980s: 'The music press has abandoned its pretensions of leading its readership or setting agendas, and contracted around the concept of "service": hard news, information, gossip, consumer guidance' (Reynolds, 1990: 27). During the 1990s the music press largely abandoned any residual post-punk sense of antagonism towards the industry, realizing that they share a common interest in maintaining consumption. This is achieved by sustaining a constant turnover of new trends, scenes, and performers, while also mining music's past using the links between older consumer's nostalgia, younger listeners' interest in antecedents, and the back catalogue.

It remains influential as gatekeeper of taste, arbiter of cultural history, and publicist for the record industry. This influence can sometimes be spectacular, as with *Billboard* editor Timothy White's decision upon first hearing *Jagged Little Pill*, to make Alanis Morissette the focus of his 'Music to My Ears' column before the album' s release; and then influencing the editors of *Spin* and *Rolling Stone* to follow suit. White's column (in the 18 May 1995 issue), was distributed with some review copies of *Jagged Little Pill*, helping set the tone for the generally positive press and magazine reviews the record received. The album was exceptional, but this coverage provided a helpful initial boost (Cantin, 1997: 142, 151).

Such episodes aside, there is general agreement that music critics don't exercise as much influence on consumers as, say, literary or drama critics. The more crucial intermediaries are those who control airtime (DJs and radio programmers) and access to recording technology and reproduction and marketing facilities (record companies and record producers). Nonetheless, I would argue that the critics do influence record buyers, particularly those who are looking to make the best use of limited purchasing power. Many buyers purchase the latest manufactured pop band or Norah Jones release as a matter of course, acting as confirmed followers of that artist, style, or scene. But others are actively exploring the byways of fresh talent, new musical hybrids, or the back catalogue.

Such searches are aided by the way in which 'rock critics' don't so much operate on the basis of some general aesthetic criteria, but rather through situating new product via constant appeal to referents, attempting to contextualize the particular text under consideration:

> Canadian Angela Desveaux combines a nice mix of gentle Gillian Welch countrified flavours with a few Lucinda Williams-like rockier moments. However, unlike, say, Jenny Lewis, she ultimately falls short of her two main inspirations on her debut, Wandering Eyes. While Williams – and Loretta Lynn, Neko Case, and Emmylou Harris – is comfortable to wallow in the depths of despair as yet another man has used her and cast her aside, Desveraux takes a far more restrained approach, like on Familiar Times. And when she does decide to take a rockier route ... it owes more to the Dixie Chicks.
>
> (Lindsay Davis, review of *Wandering Eyes*,
> *Dominion Post*, 9 November 2006)

In the process, popular music critics construct their own version of the traditional high–low culture split, usually around notions of artistic integrity, authenticity, and the nature of commercialism. The best of such critics – and their associated magazines – have published collections of their reviews; most prominently the various editions of *The Rolling Stone Record Guides*. Along with recent series such as the *All Music Guides* and *the Rough Guides* (to rock, reggae, hip-hop, etc.), these reference tools have become bibles in their fields, establishing orthodoxies as to the relative value of various styles or genres and pantheons of artists. Record collectors and enthusiasts, and specialist and secondhand record shops, inevitably have well-thumbed copies of these and similar volumes close at hand.

Yet, this body of criticism is a field in which highly idiosyncratic and disparate standards are the norm. Particular performers and their efforts will be heaped with praise by one reviewer and denigrated by another. Evaluations reflect personal preferences and matters of taste. Rarely are evaluative criteria laid bare for critical scrutiny, and even where this occurs it creates as well as resolves difficulties (see McLeod, 2001).

Popular music critics, and their histories, encyclopedias and consumer guides are playing a key role in defining the reference points, the highs and lows in the development of 'rock' and other styles of popular music. They imbue particular performers, genres, and recordings with meaning and value, and even their internecine arguments strengthen an artist's or record's claim to being part of a selective tradition. The consumers of the music themselves frequently reflect (even if only to reject) such distinctions.

This is also a strongly gendered field of writing (Evans, 1994). An example of this is the manner in which gender is marked in the press coverage of Ani DiFranco, a self-produced indie artist, who records on her own label, Righteous Babe Records. Drawing on a corpus of 100 articles on DiFranco, appearing between 1993 and 2003, in a wide range of print sources and on-line reports, Feigenbaum shows 'how language employed in rock criticism frequently functions to devalue and marginalize women artists musicianship, influence on fans, and contribution to the rock canon' (Feigenbaum, 2005: 37). She concludes that it is necessary to move away from 'gendered binaries', to 'challenge and reconstruct the conventional language that dominates rock criticism' (2005: 54).

Music magazines play their part in the economics of popular music, encouraging readers to buy records (and posters, T-shirts, etc.), and generally immerse themselves in consumer 'pop' culture. Similarly, music critics act as a service industry to the record industry, lubricating the desire to acquire both new product and selections from the back catalogue. Music press reviews form an important adjunct to the record company's marketing of their products, providing the record companies (and artists) with critical feedback on their releases. In the process, they also become promotional devices, providing supportive quotes for advertising and forming part of press kits sent to radio stations and other press outlets.

Both the press and critics, however, also play an important ideological function. They distance popular music consumers from the fact that they are essentially purchasing an economic commodity, by stressing the product's cultural significance. Furthermore, this function is maintained by the important point that the music press is not, at least directly, vertically integrated into the music industry (i.e. owned by the record companies). A sense of distance is thereby maintained, while at the same time the need of the industry to constantly sell new images, styles and product is met.

NOTES

For general analyses of the music press and music journalism, including their history, see:

Jones, S. (2002) *Pop Music and the Press*, Philadelphia, PA: Temple University Press.

Leonard, M. and Strachan, R. (2003) 'Music Press' (pp. 38–42), 'Music Journalism' (pp. 253–7), in Shepherd, J., Horn, D., Laing, D., Oliver, P. and Wicke, P. (eds) *The Continuum Encyclopedia of Popular Music, Volume One: Media, Industry and Society*, London and New York: Continuum.

More specific analysis of magazines and their journalists can be found in:

Gorman, P. (2001) *In Their Own Write: Adventures in the Music Press*, London: Sanctuary Publishing.

Strausbaugh, J. (2001) *Rock Til You Drop: The Decline from Rebellion to Nostalgia*, New York: Verso, 2001 (Chapter on *Rolling Stone* magazine).

Thornton, S. (1994) 'Moral Panic, the Media and British Rave Culture', in Ross, A. and Rose, T. (eds) *Microphone Fiends: Youth Music & Youth Culture*, New York: Routledge.

McLeod, K. (2001) '*1/2: A Critique of Rock Criticism in North America', *Popular Music*, 20, 1: 29–46.

For good examples of the collected writings of music/rock critics:

Bangs, L. (1990) *Psychotic Reactions and Carburetor Dung*, ed. G. Marcus, London: Minerva.

Da Capo Best Music Writing: an annual book series, published since 2001.

Hoskyns, B. (2003) *The Sound and the Fury; A Rock's Back Pages Reader – 40 Years of Classic Rock Journalism*, London: Bloomsbury.

Rock's back pages (an archive of reviews, interviews, and features on artists; articles are full text): www.rocksbackpages.com/.

On the gendered nature of the music press, and women working in it:

Feigenbaum, A. (2005) '"Some guy designed this room I'm standing in": marking gender in press coverage of Ani DiFranco', *Popular Music*, 24, 1: 37–56.

Chapter 10

'My Generation'
Audiences, fans and collectors

The chapter begins with an introduction to the general nature of audiences and of cultural consumption. I then consider the various modes of popular music consumption, the social categories associated with these (notably age, gender, and ethnicity), and the variety of social practices through which such consumption occurs. I argue that two factors underpin the consumption of popular music: the role of popular music as a form of cultural capital, with records as media products around which cultural capital can be displayed and shaped, and as a source of audience pleasure. To emphasize these is to privilege the personal and social uses people make of music in their lives, an emphasis that falls within the now dominant paradigm of audience studies. This stresses the *active* nature of media audiences, while also recognizing that such consumption is, at the same time, shaped by social conditions.

Beyond patterns of demographic and social preferences in relation to popular music, there exists a complex pattern of modes of consumption. These include buying recorded music, viewing MTV and music videos, listening to the radio, home taping, and downloading music from the net. To these could be added the various 'secondary' levels of involvement, or the social use of music texts: reading the music press, and decorating your bedroom walls with its posters; dancing and clubbing; and concert-going. Several of these have been dealt with elsewhere in this study; here I want to examine how we actually access music texts in their various modes, and the associated social practices, through two examples: dance and record collecting.

FROM THE MASS AUDIENCE TO ACTIVE CONSUMERS

The study of media audiences is broadly concerned with the who, what, where, how, and why of the consumption of individuals and social groups. Historically, a range of competing media studies approaches to the investigation of audiences can be identified. At the heart of theoretical debates has been the relative emphasis placed on the audience as an active determinant of cultural production and social meanings. Music is a form of communication, and popular music, as its very name suggests, usually has an audience.

Social theorists critical of the emergence of mass society/culture in the later nineteenth and early twentieth centuries first used the term 'mass audience', alarmed at the attraction of new media for millions of people. Their fears were based on a conception of the audience as a passive, mindless mass, directly influenced by the images, messages, and values of the new media such as film and radio (and, later, TV). This view emphasized the audience as a manipulated market. In relation to popular music, it is a perspective evident in the writings of high-culture critics, and of the Frankfurt School.

The high-culture tradition, as it emerged during the nineteenth century, was essentially a conservative defence of a narrowly defined high or elite 'culture', in the classic sense of Arnold's 'the best that has been thought and said' (Arnold, 1869). Such views asserted an artistic conception of culture: the only real and authentic culture is art, against which everything else is set. It views the valued civilized culture of an elite minority as constantly under attack from a majority or mass culture, which is unauthentic and a denial of 'the good life'. Its analytic emphasis is on evaluation and discrimination; a search for the true values of civilization, commonly to be found in Renaissance art, the great nineteenth-century novels, and so on.

The high cultural critique of popular culture has frequently vehemently attacked popular music. While such a view can be traced back to Plato, it emerged more forcefully with the massive social changes of the nineteenth century. By way of illustration, writing in 1839, Sir John Herschel claimed: 'Music and dancing (the more's the pity) have become so closely associated with ideas of riot and debauchery among the less cultivated classes, that a taste for them, for their own sakes, can hardly be said to exist, and before they can be recommended as innocent or safe amusements, a very great change of ideas must take place' (quoted in Frith, 1983: 39). Various commentators since have regarded much popular music as mindless fodder, cynically manufactured for mindless youthful consumers. Bloom (1987), for instance, claimed that rock presents life as 'a nonstop commercial prepackaged masturbational fantasy', which he charges as responsible for the atrophy of the minds and bodies of youth.

Underpinning such views are assumptions about the potentially disruptive nature of 'the popular', and the need for social control and the regulation of popular pleasures. The high-culture view of popular culture has been criticized for failing to recognize the active nature of popular culture consumption; failing to treat the cultural forms seriously on their own terms; biased by aesthetic prejudices, which are rarely explicated; and resting on outmoded class-based notions of a high–low culture split. The traditionally claimed distinctions between high and low culture have become blurred. High art has being increasingly commodified and commercialized, while some forms of popular culture have become more 'respectable', receiving state funding and broader critical acceptance. Nonetheless, the high-culture perspective remains evident in the application of aesthetics to popular music, and the tendency of traditional musicology to ignore or dismiss popular music. It also underpins some state attitudes towards the funding and regulation of cultural forms. At an everyday level, it is implicit in the manner in which musicians, fans and critics make distinctions of value both between and within particular genres (see Frith, 1996; Gracyk, 1996).

In a similar manner, but from a Marxist perspective, in the 1930s and 1940s the Frankfurt theorists criticized mass culture in general, arguing that under the capitalist system of production culture had become simply another object, the 'culture industry', devoid of critical thought and any oppositional political possibilities. Adorno applied this general view to popular music, especially in his attacks on Tin Pan Alley and jazz (see the discussion in Chapter 1).

Later analyses placed progressively greater emphasis on the uses consumers (the term represents a significant change of focus) made of media: uses and gratifications, which emerged in the 1960s, largely within American media sociology; reception analysis, and cultural analysis all stressed the active role of the audience, especially fans and members of youth subcultures. More recently there has been an emphasis on the domestic sphere of much media consumption, and the interrelationship of the use of various media forms. The emerging information age is seeing a reorganization of everyday life: 'people are integrating both old and new technologies into their lives in more complex ways', and within an increasingly cluttered media environment, this means 'being an audience is even more complicated' (Ross and Nightingale, 2003: 1). Related to this is an emerging literature on music and everyday life, in a variety of settings, including the workplace and in public space. ✳ 2

The opposition between passive and active views of audiences must not be overstated. What needs highlighting is the tension between musical audiences as collective social groups and, at the same time, as individual consumers. The concept of consumer sovereignty is useful here, emphasizing the operation of human agency. Advocates of consumer sovereignty consider that people's exercise of their 'free' choice in the market place is a major determinant of the nature and availability of particular cultural and (economic) commodities. While the elements of romance and imagination that have informed individual personal histories and the history of popular musical genres are frequently marginalized in the commodification process, they remain essential to the narratives people construct to help create a sense of identity. As an influential approach within cultural studies during the 1980s, consumer sovereignty was tied to the notion of the active audience, to produce a debated view of semiotic democracy at work (see Fiske, 1989).

An emphasis on consumer sovereignty as the primary factor underpinning how social meaning is created in music, is in contra-distinction to the view that the process of consumption is constrained by the processes of production: production determines consumption. Yet production and consumption are not to be regarded as fixed immutable processes, but must be regarded as engaged in a dialectic. While economic power does have a residual base in institutional structures and practices; in this case, the record companies and their drive for market stability, predictability and profit, this power is never absolute.

THE DEMOGRAPHY AND SOCIOLOGY OF MUSIC CONSUMPTION

Studies of the audience(s) and consumer(s) of popular music reflect such broad shifts in the field of audience studies. Such studies have drawn on the sociology of youth, the sociology of leisure and cultural consumption to explore the role of music in the lives of 'youth' as a general social category, and as a central component of the 'style' of youth subcultures and the social identity of fans. Music consumption is closely related to age, gender, and ethnicity.

The study of audiences in popular music focuses largely on 'youth'. Historically, the main consumers of contemporary (post-1950) popular music, especially rock music, have been young people, between 12 and 25. One factor youth have in common internationally is an interest in popular music. Cultural surveys since the 1970s, in North America, the United Kingdom, and New Zealand all indicate youth's high levels of popular music consumption, along with a clear pattern of age and gender-based genre preferences, often also inflected with ethnicity. Younger adolescents, particularly girls, prefer commercial pop; older adolescents express greater interest in more progressive forms and artists. High-school students tend to be more interested in alternative/indie genre tastes, and less interested in the more commercial expressions of popular music. As youthful consumers get older, their tastes in music often become more open to exploring new genres and less commercial forms. This trend is particularly evident amongst tertiary students, reflecting the dominant forms of musical cultural capital within their peer groups.

The straightforward association of genres such as 'rock' and 'pop' with youth, however, needs qualifying. Certainly, the music was initially aimed at the youth market in the 1950s, and young people have continued to be major consumers of it, and for the products of the leisure industries in general. At the same time, the market extended to those who grew up with the music in the 1950s and 1960s, and who have continued to follow it, aging along with their favoured surviving performers of the 1960s. As Dave Marsh puts it:

> Rock and soul-based music has become more sustaining, not less, as I've aged. It may be true that young people were the first people to realize that rock and soul had a serious message to convey, but that message has little or nothing to do with youth per se.
>
> (Marsh, 1989: xxiii)

Accordingly, attempts to locate the audience for popular music primarily amongst 'youth', once historically correct, no longer applied with the same force by the 1990s. The head of Polygram Records, Rick Dobbis, observed in 1993:

> The lament in the industry a few years ago was that older buyers are listening to news radio and not buying records anymore. But research shows that they're actually spending a lot of money on a wide variety of music. They make multiple purchases and buy boxed sets.
>
> (New Zealand Press Association report, July 1993)

He referred to surveys undertaken by the Recording Industry Association of America, which showed that in the previous five years, the music-buying power of 30-somethings has risen 6.4 per cent, while purchases by those under 24 have fallen by 12.1 per cent; music consumers over 30 now make up 42 per cent of the American market.

These trends have continued, and demographics are partly responsible for the continued success of performers as diverse as the Rolling Stones, Bonnie Raitt, the Buzzcocks, and Bob Dylan, all still touring and recording. Older consumers, in part at least, also account for the present predominance of 'golden oldies' radio formats, though their tastes do not remain fixed purely at the nostalgic level. Throughout the 1990s, 'nostalgia rock' was prominent in popular music, with the release of 'new' Beatles material (*Live at the BBC*, etc); the launch of the magazine *MOJO*, placing 'classic rock' history firmly at its core and with 35 per cent of its readers aged 35-plus; and successful tours by the Rolling Stones, Pink Floyd, and the Eagles, among other aging performers. The changing nature of the 'rock' audience has implications for musical styles: turned off by rap metal, techno, and hip-hop, older listeners return to the familiar styles and artists of their own adolescence, or contemporary music that is 'easy on the ear', such as the work of Celine Dion, Shania Twain, and Norah Jones.

Given that relative generational size is an important explanatory variable of generational experience, the demographic significance of 'youth' in the overall age structure influences their importance socially, economically, and politically. In most Western societies, following the peaking of the post-war 'baby boom', the absolute numbers of young people entering the labour market for the first time declined during the 1980s, and continued to fall until the end of the century. In the United States, for example, in July 1983, the number of Americans over the age of 65 surpassed the number of teenagers (Dychtwald, 1989: 8). Consequently, as Frith argued, a key explanation for what he perceived as the rock genres lack of vitality by the late 1980s, was the decline of the youth market: 'In material terms, the traditional rock consumer – the "rebellious" teenager – is no longer the central market figure' (Frith, 1988b: 127). This decline in youth as a market force – both as consumers and as producers – has significantly altered youth's social visibility. The consequent clash with established expectations became increasingly evident, as did youth's relative political powerlessness.

That said, the demographic decline of youth must not be exaggerated. As marketing analysts continue to observe, young people remain a major consumer group with considerable discretionary income for the leisure industries to tap. *Time* magazine noted in a 1997 cover story on 'Generation X', that there were 45 million X-ers born in the United States between 1965 and 1977, and this group represented annual purchasing power of some $125 billion a year (*Time*, 9 June 1997).

Today, many adolescents continue to spend up to four to five hours a day downloading, playing, and listening to music and watching music videos; often while 'multi-tasking': doing schoolwork at the same time. This involvement extends beyond sheer time spent:

> Music alters and intensifies their moods, furnishes much of their slang, dominates their conversations, and provides the ambience at their social gatherings. Music styles define the crowds and cliques they run in. Music stars provide models for how they act and dress.
>
> (Christenson and Roberts, 1998: 8)

The great majority of this music is popular music, with its range of genre styles. Only a minority of students regard classical music as one of their interests, a situation which stands in sharp contrast to the continued classical music orientation of most school music syllabus prescriptions. Younger listeners remain a substantial market, as the marketing of various pop stars continues to show.

The various attempts to profile music consumption also show a clear pattern of age- and gender-based genre preferences. An obvious example is what has been termed 'teen pop', which is preferred by younger adolescents, particularly girls. That girls enjoy chart pop music more than boys reflects the segmented nature of the market. Performers such as Kylie Minogue in the 1980s, New Kids on the Block in the early 1990s (see Marshall, 1997), and Hillary Duff in 2006, are oriented toward younger listeners, particularly girls, and are being marketed as such. Music magazines such as *Smash Hits*, are aimed at the young adolescent market. The majority of their readers are girls, who buy them partly for their pin-up posters, reflecting their frequent obsession with particular stars and what has been termed 'teenybopper' bedroom culture (Baker, 2002).

In studies of music consumption in ethnically mixed or diverse populations, black adolescents are more likely (than their white or Asian counterparts) to favour black music genres, most notably soul, R&B, blues, reggae, and rap. Such genres are carriers of ideology, creating symbols for listeners to identify with. Rap has emerged as a major genre preference among black youth internationally (Mitchell, 2001). For instance, such differences are clear in New Zealand, a multicultural society, with almost fifteen per cent of the population being either descendants of the indigenous Maori people or Pacific (Polynesian) Islander, and the majority population descendants of the British and European immigrants ('Pakeha'). Strong Maori and Polynesian support for reggae, soul and rap music is hardly surprising, since these categories (along with the blues) have become virtually synonymous with 'black music' and black culture. Reggae does not simply describe an experience, but it politicizes it through creating symbols for listeners to identify with. Many Maori and Polynesian youth are knowledgeable about rasta, and familiar with some of the metaphors in the music (Babylon, Jah, etc.). They regard reggae as relevant to the structural location of Maori and Polynesian as a major part of New Zealand's socially dispossessed working class. Similar views are expressed by black youth in England and North America.

Rap has also established a strong following in Auckland, which has New Zealand's main concentration of Polynesians. There are several prominent local performers, specialized record labels, clubs, festivals, and radio stations catering for the genre and its audience. Rap's appeal is in part through its links to dance and street culture, but adherents are also frequently conscious of the genre's history, and the politicized work of performers such as Public Enemy and Ice-T (Zemke-White, 2000).

MODES OF CONSUMPTION

Studies of the process and nature of music consumption have used qualitative methodologies to examine individual record buyers, concert-goers, radio listeners, and music video viewers. These reveal a complex set of influences upon the construction of individual popular music consumption. Even younger adolescent consumers, who are often seen as relatively undiscriminating and easily swayed by the influence of market forces, see their preferences as far from straightforward, with the views of their friends' paramount. Whatever their cultural background or social position, young people's musical activities rest on a substantial and sophisticated body of knowledge about popular music. Most have a clear understanding of its different genres, and an ability to hear and place sounds in terms of their histories, influences and sources. Fans, and young musicians, have no hesitation about making and justifying judgements of meaning and value. Modes of consumption are complex, overlapping and reinforcing one another. They include record buying, music television and video viewing, listening to the radio, home taping (historically) and downloading from the Internet. There are also various secondary levels of involvement, through the music press, dance, clubbing, and concert going.

Making copies of recordings has historically been a significant aspect of people's engagement with popular music. During the 1970s and 1980s this was primarily through audio tape. Aside from the convenience of ensuring access to preferred texts, selected (particularly with albums) to avoid any 'dross' or material not liked sufficiently to warrant inclusion, there is an economic aspect to such home taping:

> Home taping of music was, in one sense, a strategy directly tailored to recession conditions. The tape cassette has proved to be a practical, flexible and cheap way of consuming and distributing music.
>
> (Willis *et al.*, 1990: 62)

Home taping was primarily from the radio, but

> Young people frequently rely on friends, with larger record collections to make tapes for them. There is something of an informal hierarchy of taste operating here.
>
> (ibid.: 63)

Home taping was significant as an aspect of consumption largely beyond the ability of the music industry to influence tastes. The modern forms of home taping are 'burning' CDs on one's home computer, and downloading digital recordings from the Internet (see Chapter 2).

Despite the impact of the Internet on consumption practices, the purchase of recorded music in its various formats from physical sites (shops) remains important. This search includes second-hand record shops, which are currently thriving because of the limited purchasing power of students and unemployed youth and the high prices of new CDs and albums. It can also be seen in the retail bargain bins and at record sales. Radio remains a major source for most people's engagement with popular music, with surveys indicating that young people in particular frequently 'listen to the radio' (and watch less television). Although this is generally listening at an unfocused level, with the radio acting as a companion and as background to other activities, at times listening to the radio – including web radio while 'multi-tasking' – is deliberately undertaken in order to hear and copy new music. This is frequently done in relation to particular specialist shows or DJs. Preferences for particular radio formats and their associated stations are related to factors such as age and ethnicity.

MUSIC AS CULTURAL CAPITAL

Music consumption is not simply a matter of 'personal' preference. It is, in part, socially constructed, serving as a form of symbolic or cultural capital. Following Bourdieu (1984), we can see 'taste' as both conceived and maintained in social groups efforts to differentiate and distance themselves from others, and underpinning varying social status positions. Music has traditionally been a crucial dimension of this process. Writing in 1950, Riesman astutely distinguished between two teenage audiences for popular music. First, a majority group with 'an undiscriminating taste in popular music (who) seldom express articulate preferences', and for whom the functions of music were predominantly social. This group consumed 'mainstream', commercial music, following the stars and the hit parade. Second, Riesman identified a minority group of 'the more active listeners', who had a more rebellious attitude towards popular music, indicated by:

> an insistence on rigorous standards of judgment and taste in a relativist culture; a preference for the uncommercialized, unadvertized small bands rather than name bands; the development of a private language ... (and) a profound resentment of the commercialization of radio and musicians.
>
> (Riesman, 1950: 412)

Among Swedish youth in the 1980s, Trondman found rock to be split between two major genres: a mature 'artistic' rock, and a commercial 'idol rock' (Trondman, 1990). In such a distinction, one form of rock – the mature – is identified with what Bourdieu refers to as legitimate culture, while the other expresses distance from legitimate culture. Trondman, utilizing data from a large-scale Swedish survey, teased out the more precise functioning of this core distinction. The adherents of artistic rock were found primarily among university students and graduates, people who have good prospects of becoming part of the legitimate culture. For them, there is an emphasis on music that satisfies demands of 'intellectuality', 'aesthetic appeal', and 'association with tradition'. Linking these qualities to 'legimate culture', Trondman (1990: 81) argues that the acquisition of such musical culture capital can assist its holders in becoming assimilated into the dominant social elite. This process, and the distinctions upon which it is based, is very similar to the operation of fandom within contemporary popular music genres, notably the various forms of 'alternative' music, especially indie (Fonarow, 2006).

Acquiring any form of popular music cultural capital involves developing a knowledge of selected musical traditions, their history, and their associated performers. With this background, an individual can knowledgably discuss such details as styles, trends, record companies, and the biographies of artists, and even nuances such as associated record producers and session musicians. Such cultural capital does not necessarily have to be part of the dominant, generally accepted tradition, but can instead function to distance its adherents from that tradition, asserting their own oppositional stance. This is the pattern with many youth subcultures, which appropriate and innovate musical styles and forms as a basis for their identity (see Chapter 11: subcultures and scenes).

FANS, FANDOM, AFICIONADOS

Popular music fans avidly follow the music, and lives, of particular performers/musical genres, with various degrees of enthusiasm and commitment. Fandom is the collective term for the phenomenon of fans and their behaviour: concert going, record collecting, putting together scrapbooks, filling bedroom walls with posters, and discussing stars with other fans. Music industry practices help create and maintain fandom; record labels and the artists themselves have frequently supported official fan clubs and appreciation societies. Many fan clubs (especially those associated with the Beatles and Elvis Presley) conduct international conventions, even well after the performers celebrated are dead, or groups have disbanded

Writing in 1991, Lewis correctly observed that while fans are the most visible and identifiable of audiences, they 'have been overlooked or not taken seriously as research subjects by critics and scholars' and 'maligned and sensationalized by the popular press, mistrusted by the public' (Lewis, 1992:1). Although there has been considerable study of fandom since Lewis wrote, and academic discussions emphasize a less stereotyped image, the popular view of fans has arguably not changed much. This reflects the traditional view of fandom, which situates it in terms of pathology and deviance, with the label 'fans' used to describe teenagers who avidly and uncritically following the latest pop sensation. These fans are often denigrated in popular music literature and, by those favouring rock styles of popular music. Their behaviour is often described as a form of pathology, and the terms applied to it have clear connotations of condemnation and undesirability: 'Beatlemania', 'teenyboppers'. An early example of this, was the media treatment of the 'bobby soxers', Frank Sinatra's adolescent female fans, in the 1940s. An extreme form of fandom are 'groupies' – also a largely negative term – who move beyond vicarious identification and use their sexuality to get close to the stars, even if the encounter is usually a fleeting one.

Fandom is best regarded as an active process: a complex phenomenon, related to the formation of social identities, especially sexuality. Fandom offers its participants membership of a community not defined in traditional terms of status. Fiske (1989)

sees it as the register of a subordinate system of cultural taste, typically associated with cultural forms that the dominant value system denigrates, including popular music. Grossberg defines fandom as a distinct 'sensibility', in which the pleasure of consumption is superseded by an investment in difference: 'Fandom is located within a sensibility in which the fan's relation to cultural texts operates in the domain of affect or mood' (Grossberg, 1992: 54, 56). Pleasure and difference are central to fandom. Hills distinguishes 'cult fandom' as a form of cultural identity, partially distinct from that of the 'fan' in general, related to the duration of the fandom concerned, especially in the absence of new or 'official' material in the originating medium or persona (Hills, 2002: Preface, x). Pop fans commitment may last only as long as an often brief career, as with the Spice Girls, whereas the fans of performers such as Bruce Springsteen (Cavicchi, 1998) maintain their fandom over time, as did the Deadheads (see below).

A distinction can also be made between fans and aficionados, with the latter more focused on the music, and with different affective investments present. Aficionados are those who see themselves as 'serious' devotees of particular musical styles or performers. They are fans in terms of the word's origins in 'fanatic', but their emotional and physical investments are different from mainstream 'fans', as are the social consumption situations in which they operate. Aficionados' intense interest is usually at more of an intellectual level and focused on the music per se rather than the persona of the performer(s). Aficionados prefer to describe themselves as 'into' particular performers and genres, and often display impressive knowledge of these. They seek out rare releases, such as bootlegs; read and contribute to fanzines in addition to buying commercial music magazines; are regular concert-goers; and have an interest in record labels and producers as well as performers. They may also be involved in music-oriented subcultures. Aficionados frequently become record collectors on a large scale, supporting an infrastructure of specialist and second-hand record shops. At times, their record collecting can become a fixation bordering on addiction; I will have more to say about this later.

Fans, in the more widely accepted, perjorative sense of the term, will collect the records put out by their favoured stars, but these are only one aspect of an interest that focuses rather on the image and persona of the star. For example, studies of the post-punk British 'New Pop' performers of the 1980s (Culture Club, Duran Duran, Wham!, Spandau Ballet, Nik Kershaw, and Howard Jones), showed how they drew upon a fanatical female following. As such, fans' consumption becomes a significant part of the star system. These fans represent a merchandising dream, buying up practically anything associated with the group, with their support in extreme cases bordering on the pathological. At the same time, such 'Pop fans aren't stupid. They know what they want. And ultimately, all the media manipulation in the world isn't going to sell them something they haven't got any use for' (Rimmer, 1985: 108). This is to argue that whatever the press of 'context' – the intentions of the industry, the pop press, and musicians themselves – meaning in the music is ultimately created by the consumers.

Fans are often fiercely partisan. Such strong identification with the star becomes a source of pleasure and empowerment. For many fans, their idols function almost as religious touchstones, helping them to get through their lives and providing emotional and even physical comfort. Elvis fandom has been understood as a secular form of religion, with Elvis acting as a religious icon (Doss, 1999). Duffett argues that this is too simplistic, that such an emphasis means 'we miss the complexity, the diversity of investments, and the rich array of informal institutions that support fans' interests' (Duffett, 2003: 520).

'By participating in fandom, fans construct coherent identities for themselves. In the process, they enter a domain of cultural activity of their own making which is, potentially, a source of empowerment in struggles against oppressive ideologies and the unsatisfactory circumstance of everyday life' (Lewis, 1992: 3). Most fans see themselves as part of a wider community, even if their own fan practices are 'private', individual activities undertaken alone. Examples of such empowerment are as diverse as heavy metallers, and fans of the Bay City Rollers, the Grateful Dead (Deadheads), and Bruce Springsteen. There is an assertion of female solidarity evident in the activities of girl fans, for example, those of the Spice Girls in the 1990s. Similar cultural self-assertion is present in many adherents of youth subcultures' knowledge of the associated music.

The Deadheads, fans of the American band the Grateful Dead, provide an example of long-term fandom. The band were leading figures in San Francisco's psychedelic scene in the early 1960s, and continued to tour and record extensively until the death of band leader Jerry Garcia in 1996. Deadheads attended large numbers of the band's concerts, often making extensive tape compilations of the various performances, or purchasing bootlegs of these performances, with the band unofficially condoning such practices. The Grateful Dead's concerts functioned as secular rituals for the band's hardcore followers, who were also frequently identified with the broadly counterculture values and style of the band. This led some municipalities to ban Dead concerts, because of the 'undesirable elements' attending them (Sardiello, 1994).

Beyond possible empowerment, popular music fandom as a form of cultural activity has a number of pleasurable dimensions common to both fans and afficionados: dance and its associated rituals of display and restraint; the anticipatory pleasure of attending a concert or playing a new purchase; the pleasure of acquiring a new recording; the sheer physical pleasure of handling records/tapes/CDs; and the intellectual and emotional pleasures associated with 'knowing' about particular artists and genres valued by one's peers and associates. Fans actively interact with texts 'to actively assert their mastery over the mass-produced texts, which provide the raw materials for their own cultural productions and the basis for their social interactions', becoming 'active participants in the construction and circulation of textual meanings' (Jenkins, 1997: 508).

The rise of interactive media (e-mail, list servers, and the Internet) have added a new dimension to fandom, aiding in the formation and maintenance of fan bases for performers and musical style. At the same time, digital music raises questions of the different consumption experiences and practices involved when the physical object, the 'record', lacks materiality.

I turn now to two examples of the consumption of popular music: dance, and record collecting.

DANCE

Dance is an example of the active nature of our engagement with popular music, and its wider social importance. As a social practice dance has a long history, closely associated with music, ritual, courtship, and everyday pleasure. Historically, organized social dancing dates back at least to the sixteenth century and the private balls of the aristocracy, with ballroom dancing popularized in the early nineteenth century (the waltz). 'The demands of the dancer tended to shape the course of ragtime and jazz rather than the obverse', and 'this status has continued into the rock age' (Gammond, 1991: 144). Dance is associated with the pleasures of physical expression rather than the intellectual, the body rather than the mind. At times, the closeness and implied sexual display of dance has aroused anxiety and led to attempts to regulate dance, or at least control who is dancing with whom.

Forms of dance subject to considerable social criticism include the charleston, jitterbugging, rock 'n' roll in the 1950s, the twist in the 1960s, and disco dancing in the 1970s. Adorno saw jitterbugging, a popular and flamboyant form of dance in the 1940s, as a 'stylized' dance style whose performers had 'convulsive aspects reminiscent of St. Vitus's dance or the reflexes of mutilated animals' (1991: 46). As Negus (1996) observes, such responses reflected a distaste for overt expressions of sexuality, a racist fear of 'civilized' behaviour being undermined by 'primitive rhythms', and a concern that young people are being manipulated and effected by forms of mass crowd psychology.

Dance is central to the general experience and leisure lives of young people, and many adults, through their attendance at, and participation in, school dances, parties, discos, dance classes, and raves. The participants in the dance break free of their bodies in a combination of 'socialised pleasures and individualised desires', with dancing operating as 'a metaphor for an external reality which is unconstrained by the limits and expectations of gender identity and which successfully and relatively painlessly transports its subjects from a passive to a more active psychic position' (McRobbie, 1991: 194, 192, 201). Dance also acts as a marker of significant points in the daily routine, punctuating it with what Chambers (1985) labels the freedom of Saturday night. These various facets of dance are well represented in feature films such as *Flashdance* (1983), *Strictly Ballroom* (1995), and *Take the Lead* (2006).

Dance is associated with some popular musical genres to a greater extent than others, notably disco, rap, and rock 'n' roll. Chambers (1985) documented the clubs and dance halls of English postwar urban youth culture, referring to 'the rich tension of dance' in its various forms, including the shake, the jerk, the Northern soul style of athletic, acrobatic dance, and the break dancing and body-popping of black youth. There are forms of dance that are genre and subculture specific, such as line dancing in country, slam-dancing and the pogo in punk, break dancing in some forms of rap, and headbanging and 'moshing' at concerts by heavy metal and grunge and alternative performers.

The last represented new forms of dance, less formally constrained than traditional dance forms. While the audience does not 'dance' at heavy metal concerts, as the subculture stresses male bonding rather then male–female pairing, it is 'nonetheless engaged in continuous kinesthetic activity' (Weinstein, 1991: 216), moving the body in time with the beat. This includes 'headbanging', which involves keeping the beat by making up-and-down motions of the head, and 'moshing', a form of circle dance: 'a hard skipping, more or less in time to the music, in a circular, counterclockwise pattern. Elbows are often extended and used as bumpers, along with the shoulders' (Weinstein, 1991: 228). There is a moshing circle, the 'pit', located close to center stage, and visible to both performers and the audience.

Similar dance styles are linked to indentifiable subcultures in the alternative scene. Slam dancing mirrors an 'apolitical punk ideology of rebellion' in the breakdown of symbolic order which seems to occur in the pit, with its 'assertions of individual presence and autonomy'. At the same time, it creates and reinforces unity through concern with the welfare of others, with practices such as the picking up of fallen dancer (Tsitsos, 1999: 407). Moshing, in contrast, lacks the elements, such as circular motion, which promote unity in the pit, and is identified with a 'straight edge ideology of rebellion' (ibid.: 410). Through their participation in (and rejection of) these dances, 'members of the scene pledge allegiance to the rules which govern their rebellion' (ibid.: 413). There is a process of gender discrimination at work in the maintenance of such male-dominated dance practices.

A detailed history of American dance music, from 1970 to 1979, traces the development of 'a new mode of DJing and dancing that went on to become the most distinctive cultural ritual of the decade' (Lawrence, 2003: Preface). Drawing in part on interviews with the key figures involved, Lawrence provides a narrative web of clandestine house parties and discotheques, traced back to legendary pre-disco New York dance clubs The Loft and the Sanctuary. Similar dance scenes are present around subsequent locales and musical genres.

There are three pillars of contemporary dance music: the venues, the DJs, and the music.

The close link between these and popular music is indicated in the title of a major documentary series on popular music, *Dancing in the Street* (1995), which shows an historical progression of dance styles and their associated musical genres.

RECORD COLLECTING

Buying recorded music in its various formats is central to the consumption of popular music. Most people purchase or otherwise acquire 'records', in a limited and generally unsystematic fashion; record collectors represent a more extreme version of this practice. 'Record collecting' can be considered shorthand for a variety of distinct but related practices. Foremost is the collection of sound recordings, in various formats, by individuals; the dimension focused on here. Such recordings include various official releases, in a variety of formats; bootleg recordings (largely of concerts); radio broadcasts, and sound with visuals – the music video or DVD. Individual collecting also frequently includes the collection of related literature (music books and magazines) and music memorabilia (e.g. concert tickets and programmes, tour posters). The interest from both private collectors and the Hard Rock Café chain have stimulated interest – and prices – in the collecting of such memorabilia, with several major auction houses starting to conduct regular sales during the 1980s. There is also the record collecting undertaken by museums, including the various 'rock museums' (such as The Experience Museum in Seattle). Such collecting frequently includes sheet music and other printed music literature, in addition to recordings, musical instruments, and popular music ephemera.

Record collecting has a now extensive, although largely unexplored history. During the mid to late nineteenth century, a mix of capitalism and consumerism, increased leisure time and disposable income, and nostalgia, made collecting a significant aspect of social identity for the new middle classes of Europe, Britain and its colonies, and the United States (Pearce, 1995). Record collecting was a logical extension of such activities. Sound recording, and its reproduction as a cultural and economic artifact around the turn of the century, produced the 'record' in what became a succession of formats. In the early years of the twentieth century, cylinders and their successors, 78s, along with the equipment necessary to play them, became an important part of mass, popular culture. The gramophone became a major fashion accessory of the day, and sound recordings became collectibles. Today, record collecting is a major form of collecting. It includes an associated literature (the music press generally, but especially the specialist collector magazines, fanzines, discographies, and general guidebooks); the recording industry targeting of collectors (reissue labels; promotional releases, remixes, boxed sets); and dedicated sites of acquisition (record fairs, second-hand and specialist shops, e-Bay, and high-profile auctions).

The popular image of contemporary record collectors is of obsessive males, whose 'train spotting' passion for collecting is often a substitute for 'real' social relationships. This image can draw on some support from academic discussions of collectors and collecting. Straw shows how, for male collectors, the social role of collecting can be a significant part of masculinity, providing a point of difference and 'confirmation of a shared universe of critical judgement' (Straw, 1997: 5). In common with other forms of collecting, record collecting can represent a public display of power and knowledge, serving as a form of cultural capital within the peer group. Collecting also provides a private refuge from the wider world and the immediate domestic environment. In Nick Hornby's novel *High Fidelity*, Rob Fleming in times of stress re-catalogues his album collection:

> Is it so wrong, wanting to be at home with your record collection? It's not like collecting records is like collecting stamps, or beer mats, or antique thimbles. There's a whole world in here, a nicer, dirtier, more violent, more colourful, sleazier, more dangerous, more loving world than the world I live in.
>
> (Hornby, 1995: 73)

Muesterberger (1994) has theorized that collecting is a way of overcoming childhood anxiety by creating a sense of order and completion. This can border on the obsessional: Eisenberg describes the case of 'Clarence', a New York record collector crippled with arthritis and on welfare, living in an unlit, unheated 14-room house 'so crammed with trash that the door wouldn't open – and with three-quarters of a million (vinyl) records'. 'Clarence' had inherited the house from his parents, along with a considerable inheritance, now gone, which enabled him to pursue his dream of owning a complete collection of jazz, pop, and rock recordings, along with ethno-musicological field recordings and various recorded ephemera (Eisenberg, 1988: 1ff)

It has been claimed that 'Collectors themselves – dedicated, serious, infatuated, beset – cannot explain or understand this all-consuming drive … is it an obsession? An addiction? Is it a passion or urge, or perhaps a need to hold, or possess, to accumulate?' (Muensterberger, 1994: 3). This is an overstatement. While it is true that many collectors find it difficult to pinpoint the precise set of motivations that drive their collecting, they are frequently well aware of the various explanations offered for it. This was particularly evident in my study of record collectors, a well-educated group, whose responses to two central questions covering self-definition, and perceptions of collectors and the collecting process showed considerable awareness of the 'High Fidelity' stereotype, along with a concern to distance personal practice from this. These collectors demonstrated a complex mix of characteristics: a love of music; obsessive-compulsive behaviour, accumulation and completism, selectivity and discrimination; and self-education and scholarship. For many of these collectors, record collecting was a core component of their social identity and a central part of their lives (Shuker, 2004).

The landscape of record collecting has changed dramatically in the past thirty years. The range of collectibles has increased, with promotional material and memorabilia more prominent. Record collecting has become more organized, more intense (and, at times, more expensive). The Internet has added a major new dimension to collecting, adding increased opportunity but also fuelling price rises. Reflecting such developments, the record collecting press has mushroomed. The shift to online music has raised questions about the nature of collecting, especially its privileging of the album (McCourt, 2005).

CONCLUSION

A major theoretical issue with the consumption of popular music – be it by fans, members of subcultures, or 'mainstream' youth – is the problem of authenticity: the relationship between popular culture and market forces, especially the extent to which styles and tastes are synthetically produced for a deliberately stimulated mass market. As I have previously argued, we need to see culture as a reciprocal concept, an active practice which shapes and conditions economic and political processes, as well as being conditioned and shaped by them. The various types of consumers of popular music genres considered here illustrate this reciprocity, occupying a critical social space in the process whereby the music acquires cultural meaning and significance. The following chapter examines further the role of music in the construction of social identity, in relation to youth culture, subcultures and music scenes.

NOTES

On audiences and cultural/media consumption generally:
Ross, K. and Nightingale, V. (2003) *Media and Audiences*, Buckingham: Open University Press.

On fans and fandom:
Lewis, L. (1992) *The Adoring Audience: Fan Culture and the Popular Media*, London: Routledge.
Hills, M. (2002) *Fan Cultures*, London and New York: Routledge.
Marcus, G. (1991b) *Dead Elvis: A Chronicle of a Cultural Obsession*, New York: Penguin.

Informative and amusing personal accounts of fandom include:
Aizlewood, J. (1994) *Love is the Drug*, London: Penguin.

Hunter, S. (2004) *Hell Bent For Leather: Confessions of a Heavy Metal Addict*, London and New York: Fourth Estate.

Klosterman, C. (2002) *Fargo Rock City: A Heavy Metal Odyssey in Rural North Dakota*, London: Simon & Schuster.

Smith, G. (1995) *Lost in Music*, London: Picador.

On dance, dance music, and club culture:

Thornton, S. (1995) *Club Cultures: Music, Media and Subcultural Capital*, London: Polity Press.

Straw, W. (2001) 'Dance Music', in Frith, S. and Street, J. (eds) *The Cambridge Companion to Pop And Rock*, Cambridge: Cambridge University Press.

Wall, T. (2006) 'Out on the Floor: The Politics of Dancing on the Northern Soul Scene', *Popular Music*, 25, 3: 431–46.

Record collecting:

Dean, E. (2001) 'Desperate Man Blues', in Guralnick, P. and Wolk, D. (eds) *Da Capo Best Music Writing 2000*, printed and published in the USA. (An entertaining profile of Joe Bussard, self-styled 'King of the Record Collectors'. There is also a DVD documentary based on this: *Desperate Man Blues*, Cube Media, 2004.)

Hornby, N. (1995) *High Fidelity*, London: Random House.

Milano, B. (2003) *Vinyl Junkies: Adventures in Record Collecting*, New York: St Martin's Press.

Shuker, R. (2004) 'Beyond the "High Fidelity" Stereotype: Defining the (Contemporary) Record Collector', *Popular Music*, 23, 3: 311–30.

Straw, W. (1997) 'Sizing Up Record Collections: Gender and Connoisseurship in Rock Music Culture', in Whiteley, S. (ed.) *Sexing the Groove: Popular Music and Gender*, London: Routledge.

Chapter 11

'Sound of our Town'
Subcultures, sounds and scenes

The preceding chapter has sketched some aspects of the consumption of popular music, and its fans. A related area of study has been the nature and significance of youth subcultures, the initial focus of this chapter. Emerging out of the earlier study of 'youth culture', subcultural analysis was prominent in popular music studies through the 1980s and 1990s. Its theoretical utility was then challenged, and, some would argue, displaced by greater attention to musical sounds and scenes, the focus of the second part of the chapter.

FROM YOUTH CULTURE TO YOUTH SUBCULTURES

The concept of youth culture developed in the 1950s. It assumed that all teenagers shared similar leisure interests and pursuits and were involved in some form of revolt against their elders. The emergence of a distinctive youth culture was linked to the growing autonomy of youth (particularly working-class youth) because of their increased incomes. Greater spending power gave youth the means to express their own distinct values and separate ideals, and large markets were developed for teenage interests, most notably music and clothes. Advertising analyst Mark Abrams, in a pamphlet aptly titled *The Teenage Consumer* (1959), estimated that in Britain there was available 'a grand total of 900 million pounds a year to be spent by teenagers at their own discretion'. In real terms, this was twice the pre-war figure. In the US, the consumer potential of the new teenagers outstripped that of any other segment of the population, as between 1946 and 1958 teenage buying potential grew to an estimated $10 billion. A further explanation for the prominence of this youth or teenage culture was the dramatic growth of secondary and university education in Western countries, as young people spending longer periods in educational institutions encouraged youth separateness and solidarity (Coleman, 1961).

While academic sociology now began to display considerable interest in 'youth' as a social group, it was slower to more specifically explore the relationship between music and its adolescent audience. Initially, youth were seen as a relatively passive consumer group, with 'youth culture' shaped by the burgeoning leisure industries. Hall and Whannell reflected British anxiety about the effects of the emergent teenage culture, especially in its imported American forms:

> Teenage culture is a contradictory mixture of the authentic and the manufactured: it is an area of self-expression for the young and a lush grazing ground for the commercial providers.
>
> (Hall and Whannell, 1964; see also Hoggart, 1957)

Similarly, in the United States the work of Riesman (1950) acknowledged the varied bases for American youth's musical tastes, but still saw the majority of adolescents as fodder for commercial interests.

The 1960s saw the growth of a youth counter culture, with youth protests in the universities and on the streets against the Establishment and the war in Vietnam. It seemed to some that a major division in society was the so-called 'generation gap', usually believed to be between the age of 25 and 30. Youth were now viewed as a definite social block, belonging to a generational culture that transcended class, status, and occupation. Popular music, particularly emergent genres such as psychedelic or acid rock, was regarded as an age-specific means of cultural expression, uniting young people and confirming their radical potential (Reich, 1967).

By the 1970s, this view of a homogeneous youth culture, offering a radical challenge to the established social order, was obviously untenable. The radicalism of the 1960s' protest movement had become defused through its commercialization, including the marketing of 'alternative rock' by the Major record companies, and the counter-culture's continued identification with middle-class rather than working-class youth. The emphasis on an age-based youth culture obscured the key fact that a major shaper of adolescents' values and attitudes was the social class background of those involved. Rather than being part of a coherent youth culture, it became clear that youth consisted of a 'mainstream' majority, and minority subcultures whose distinctiveness was shaped largely by the social class and ethnic background of their members. Sociological interest now concentrated on the various youth subcultures, whose members were seen to rely on leisure and style as a means of winning their own cultural space, and thus represented cultural oppositional politics at the symbolic level.

Subcultures

General consumption patterns and modes demonstrate a structural homology between the audience and various social indicators. Such homology is evident at its most extreme in youth subcultures. As the contributors to a major edited reader demonstrate, while there is no consensus about the definition of a subculture, they can be broadly considered to be social groups organized around shared interests and practices (Gelder and Thornton, 1997: part 2). Subcultures often distinguish themselves against others; fractions of the larger social group, they usually set themselves in opposition to their parent culture, at least at a cultural level.

Music is one of a complex of elements making up subcultural style. Its role in terms of pleasure and cultural capital is similar to that played out among more mainstream youth, but in an accentuated form. The relationship between popular music and youth subcultures was comprehensively explored in a number of influential studies during the 1970s and early 1980s. Collectively, these argued what became a frequently asserted thesis: that youth subcultures appropriate and innovate musical forms and styles as a basis for their identity, and, in so doing, assert a counter-cultural politics. This perspective was primarily associated with writers linked to the influential Birmingham (UK) Centre for Contemporary Cultural Studies (BCCCS) whose views became more widely accepted (see Bennett, 2000, for a succinct but comprehensive overview; and Stahl, 2003, for an informed critique drawing on the sociology of space).

For the writers associated with the BCCCS, subcultures were regarded as:

> meaning systems, modes of expression or life styles developed by groups in subordinate structural positions in response to dominant meaning systems, and which reflect their attempt to solve structural contradictions rising from the wider societal context.
>
> (Brake, 1985: 8)

Hebdige (1979), in what is now regarded as a classic text, starts from the premise that style in subculture is 'pregnant with significance', illustrating this through a comprehensive analysis of various spectacular subcultural styles: beats and hipsters in the 1950s, teddy boys in the 1950s and 1970s, mods in the early 1960s, skinheads in the late 1960s, rastas in the 1970s, glam rockers in the early to mid-1970s, and, most visible of all, punks in the mid-1970s. In his analysis, subcultures rely on leisure and style as a means of making their values visible in a society saturated by the codes and symbols of the dominant culture. The significance of subcultures for their participants is that they offer a solution, albeit at a 'magical' level, to structural dislocations through the establishment of an 'achieved identity' – the selection of certain elements of style outside of those associated with the ascribed identity offered by work, home, or school.

The expressive elements of this style offer 'a meaningful way of life during leisure', removed from the instrumental world of work:

> Subcultures are therefore expressive forms but what they express is, in the last instance, a fundamental tension between those in power and those condemned to subordinate positions and secondclass lives. This tension is figuratively expressed in the form of subcultural style.

(Hebdige, 1979: 132)

The majority of youth were seen to pass through life without any significant involvement in such subcultures. Associated aspects of subcultural fashion and musical tastes may be adopted, but for 'respectable' youth these are essentially divorced from subcultural lifestyles and values. Members of youth subcultures, on the other hand, utilize symbolic elements to construct an identity outside the restraints of class and education, an identity which places them squarely outside of conservative mainstream society. Membership of a subculture was seen to necessarily involve membership of a class culture and could be either an extension of, or in opposition to, the parent class culture (as with the skinheads). Writers such as Hebdige were at pains not to overemphasize this class dimension, and to accord due analytical weight to gender and ethnic factors.

Youth subcultures in the 1970s and early 1980s were an international phenomenon, but with marked differences. Subcultural styles in both Britain and the United States essentially developed out of their immediate social context, reworking commercial popular culture into a subcultural style which reflected and made sense of their structural social location. This process was not so clear cut in more culturally dependent societies. In Canada, for example, the situation was confused by the nation's historical links with Britain and France and the marked contemporary influence of its close proximity to the United States, a situation contributing to Canada's problem of finding a sense of national identity. Canadian youth cultures were consequently largely derivative and any potential oppositional force in them was highly muted (Brake, 1985).

For the subcultural analysts of the 1970s, homology was central to the consideration of the place of music in youth subcultures: a 'fit' between the 'focal concerns, activities, group structure and the collective self-image' of the subculture, and the cultural artifacts and practices adopted by the members of the subculture. The latter were seen as 'objects in which they could see their central values held and reflected', including music (Hall and Jefferson, 1976: 56). The most developed applications of the concept of homology to the preferred music of specific subcultures are Willis's study of bike boys and hippies, *Profane Culture* (1978), and Hebdige's various case studies in his hugely influential study *Subculture: The Meaning of Style* (1979). Willis argued that there existed a 'fit' between certain styles and fashions, cultural values, and group identity; for example, between the intense activism, physical prowess, love of machines and taboo on introspection, of motorbike boys, and their preference for 1950s rock 'n' roll. For Hebdige, the punks best illustrated the principle:

> The subculture was nothing if not consistent. There was a homological relation between the trashy cut-up clothes and spiky hair, the pogo and the amphetamines, the spitting, the vomiting, the format of the fanzines, the insurrectionary poses and the 'soulless', frantically driven music.
>
> (Hebdige, 1979: 114–15)

The BCCCS writers' socio-cultural analyses represented an original and imaginative contribution to the sociology of youth cultures, but were critiqued for their overemphasis on the symbolic 'resistance' of subcultures, which was imbued with an unwarranted political significance; the romanticizing of working-class subcultures; the neglect of ordinary or conformist youth; and a masculine emphasis, with little attention paid to the subcultural experiences of girls. And while music was regarded as a central aspect of subcultural style, its homological relation to other dimensions of style was not always easy to pin down. For example, the skinheads' preferred music changed over time, making problematic any argument for its homological role in skinhead culture. As Hebdige observed, the 'early' skinheads preference for elements of black style, including reggae and ska music, is contradictory considering their racial stance. At times, stylistic attributes were too quickly attributed to a specifically subcultural affiliation, rather than recognizing their generalizability.

A convergence between music and cultural group values continued to be evident in some contemporary youth subcultures through the 1990s, most notable in goth, heavy metal (Arnett, 1996), hip-hop, and various strains of punk. However, subsequent theoretical discussions and case studies suggested that the degree of homology between subcultures and music had been overstated. Reviewing the literature, Middleton concluded that subcultural analysis had drawn the connection between music and subculture much too tightly, 'flawed above all by the uncompromising drive to homology' (Middleton, 1990: 161). Indeed the very value of the concept 'subcultures', and particularly its conflation with oppositional cultural politics, became seriously questioned. Even Dick Hebdige, one of the central figures of 1970s subcultural theory, concluded that 'theoretical models are as tied to their own times as the human bodies that produce them. The idea of subculture-as-negation grew up alongside punk, remained inextricably linked to it and died when it died' (Hebdige, 1988: 8).

Redhead's detailed reading of events post-punk in the United Kingdom suggested that the very notion of 'subculture', and the emphasis on it as part of a tradition of 'rock authenticity' and opposition at the level of cultural politics, were in need of revision:

Such notions are not capable of capturing the changes in youth culture and rock culture from at least the late 1970s onwards. They are, moreover, unsatisfactory as accounts of pop history and youth culture in general.

(Redhead, 1990: 41–2)

For many youthful consumers during the 1980s and 1990s, the old ideological divides applied to popular music had little relevance, with their tastes determined by a more complex pattern of considerations than any 'politically correct' dichotomizing of genres. This is most evident in the constituencies for alternative/indie and dance-music (see Fonarow, 2006; Thornton, 1995).

Interest turned more to the majority of youth, those who do not join or identify with subcultures, the nature of fandom, and the study of local musical scenes. While the commercial orientation of the musical tastes of 'mainstream' youth are still, as with Riesman fifty years earlier, taken as given, this consumption is seen in more active and creative terms. Further, it is by no means a homogeneous situation, as, like the various subcultures, the 'mainstream' is revealed as a varied audience with different tastes and allegiances informed by factors such as class, ethnicity, and gender. Similarly, the phenomenon of pop/rock fandom, previously largely ignored, has been redefined and subjected to serious scrutiny.

Northern soul

The cultural studies preoccupation with youth subcultures, obscured the significance of subcultural affiliations held by older music fans. A case in point is the academically neglected (although see Wall, 2006) example of Northern soul, a regional cult in the UK Midlands, based around ballroom/club culture and all-night dancing to 1960s Motown and independent label (e.g. Cameo, Parkway, Verve) soul records chosen for their 'danceability' (e.g. The Exciters). Northern soul became prominent in the early 1970s, with the Wigan Casino, a World War I dance hall, being declared by American *Billboard* to be the world's best discotheque. The subculture has maintained itself, with fanzines, continued all-nighters, and record compilations. While rarity and exclusivity of records, and commodity exchange are integral to the Northern Soul scene, dance is at its heart.

Hollows and Milestone's case study of Northern Soul challenged orthodox subcultural theory, and its preoccupation with music as symbol and the homology between musical style and subcultural values. They demonstrated how Northern Soul produces a sense of identity and belonging based on the consumption of 'music as music', organized around a club scene. Here the records have value both as commodities and as bearers of musical meaning; the exchange, buying and selling of records is an important part of the Northern Soul scene. Indeed, the use of 'white labels' represents a unique form of fetishization of black musical culture by white consumers (Hollows and Milestone, 1998).

Northern soul illustrates how 'contemporary youth cultures are characterized by far more complex stratifications than that suggested by the simple dichotomy of "monolithic mainstream" – "resistant subculture"' (Muggleton and Weinzierl, 2003: 7). Recent research in popular music has retained elements of the subculturalist approach, but moved towards a more sophisticated understanding of the activities of music audiences, drawing heavily on the concepts of sounds and scenes.

SCENES AND SOUNDS: THE MUSIC OF PLACE

The intersection of music and its physical location has been a developing field of enquiry, with a number of distinct and original contribution to the critical examination of space and scale as significant aspects in the production and consumption of sound recordings. Cultural geographers have been doing research on music since the late 1960s, seeking to establish 'the nexus between the social, cultural, economic and political in musical analysis' (Kong, 1995: 273). Traditionally, the geographical analysis of music emphasized the dynamics and consequences of the geographical distribution of recorded music around the world, and how particular musical sounds have become associated with particular places. This work was largely characterized by the use of a narrow range of methods and theories, and focused on only a few musical styles, notably blues, folk, and country. Studies of rock and pop music, and their various genres, were notably absent from the majority of this work. In the 1990s, these musical forms, and their locales, became seen as worthy of serious study and accorded greater attention by cultural geographers and popular music scholars (see Carnoy, 2003; Leyshon et al., 1998; Stokes, 1994).

Four main agendas for geographical research into popular musical have been identified : (i) a concern with the spatial distribution of musical forms, activities, and performers; (ii) exploration of musical home locales and their extension, using concepts such as contagion, relocation and hierarchical diffusion; and the examination of the agents of and barriers to diffusion; (iii) the delimitation of areas that share certain musical traits, or, relatedly, on the identification of the character and personality of places as gleaned from lyrics, melody, instrumentation, and the general 'feel' or sensory impact of the music; (iv) pertinent themes in music, such as the image of the city. A necessary addition to these emphases is the global processes of cultural homogenization and commodification, and the intersection of these with the local (see Chapter 12 on cultural imperialism, globalization, and the relationship between local music and the international music industry).

While the cohesion of their 'common' musical signatures is frequently exaggerated, such localized developments offer marketing possibilities by providing a 'brand name' with which consumers can identify. Interest in particular sounds has concentrated on the significance of locality, and how music may serve as a marker of identity. Many histories of popular music refer to particular geographic locales, usually cities or regions, as being identified at a specific historical juncture with a sound. Examples include the Liverpool 'Merseybeat' sound associated with the Beatles, Gerry and the Pacemakers, and the Searchers in the early 1960s, San Franciso and the psychedelic rock of the Jefferson Airplane, Moby Grape, and the Grateful Dead in the later 1960s, and the various punk scenes of the 1970s. The following brief sketches illustrate the interaction of history, physical location, musical style, and the music industry.

Sounds: Dunedin and Manchester

A New Zealand example of this process is the emergence of the 'Dunedin sound' associated with the now internationally recognized Flying Nun label. In the late 1970s, a number of bands in Dunedin, a university city of then only just over 100,000 people, established a local cult following through their appearances at various pubs and university venues. National exposure and critical and commercial success followed, and several bands (the Chills, the Bats, the JPS) went on to establish international reputations, largely on the 'indie' college circuit in the UK and North America. The 'Dunedin Sound' and 'the Flying Nun Sound' became shorthand for these bands, despite the clear differentiation amongst the Flying Nun label's recorded output. The sound itself, at least in its original evocation, was largely equated with a jangly guitar-driven sound, a distinctive New Zealand accent on the vocals, and 'low-tech' recording and production, all serving to produce a specifically identifiable local product (see McLeay, 1994; Mitchell, 1996).

Manchester also provides an instructive example of the role of geography in forging a distinctive orientation to localized alternative music. The notion of a Manchester sound and scene was a loose label, popularized by the British music press in the early 1990s. Since the late 1970s, Manchester has been associated with several styles of indie and alternative music: in the late 1970s and early 1980s, the post-punk sound of Joy Division, which mutated into New Order; 'bedsit blues' in the mid-1980s with the Smiths and James; and the tempo and mood was revived around 1988, in the wake of 'Acid House', with the arrival of the club-and-ecstasy sounds of 'Madchester', led by the Happy Mondays, the Stone Roses and Oldham's Inspiral Carpets. All three periods and styles fed off the association with Manchester: the songs often had included clear geographical references and reflected localized feelings and experiences; record covers and other promotional imagery incorporated place-related references; and a network of alternative record labels (especially Factory Records), venues, and an active local press created a supportive network for the bands and their followers (Halfacree and Kitchin, 1996).

Scenes

As the previous discussion indicates, there has been considerable exploration of the role and effectiveness of music as a means of defining identity. Situated within this, the concept of scene has become a central trope in popular music studies, a key part of the 'spatial turn' evident in urban and cultural studies generally (see Stahl, 2003). To an extent, scene, as an analytical concept of greater explanatory power, is now regarded as having displaced subcultures.

Scene can be understood as 'a specific kind of urban cultural context and practice of spatial coding' (Stahl, 2004: 76). A basic reference point for later discussion was an essay by Straw (1992), which argued for greater attention to scene in popular music studies, defined as the formal and informal arrangement of industries, institutions, audiences and infrastructures. Also influential were Cohen's study of 'rock culture' in Liverpool (Cohen, 1991), and Shank's study of the rock 'n' roll scene in Austin, Texas (Shank, 1994). Researchers subsequently engaged with, refined, and applied the concept of scene to a wide range of settings and locales. Much of this work, along with theoretical discussion of the concept of scene(s) can be found in several edited collections (Whiteley *et al.*, 2004; Bennett and Kahn-Harris, 2004), while the journal *Popular Music* devoted an issue to the theme (2001, 19: 1).

To provide just one example from among many, locality, scene and youth culture are fruitfully brought together by Bennett in a series of ethnographic case studies. Among these, his study of urban dance music (including house, techno, and jungle) in Newcastle-upon-Tyne, England, shows how, through their participation in club events and house parties,

> the members of this scene celebrate a shared underground sensibility that is designed to challenge the perceived oppression and anarchism of Newcastle's official night-time economy and the coercive practices of the local police force.
> (Bennett, 2000: 68)

A particular focus, in part arising from the earlier fascination with subcultures, has been on alternative music scenes. (The term 'underground' is also used for non-commercialized alternative scenes, since the performers in them are hidden from and inaccessible to people who are not 'hooked into' the scene.) Alternative music scenes fall into two basic catagories, they are either college (US tertiary institutions) or university towns, or large cities that are somehow 'alternative', usually to even larger urban centers nearby (e.g. Minneapolis and Chicago). Most important American college towns had local music scenes self-consciously perceived as such in the 1980s, with these linked as part of an American indie underground (see Azerrad, 2001). The most prominent were Athens, Georgia (source of the B-52s, Love Tractor, Pylon and R.E.M.); Minneapolis (source of the Replacements, Husker Du, Soul Asylum and Prince), and Seattle. Sometimes a small college town and nearby large city have contributed to a shared scene; as with Boston and Amherst, MA (sources of Dinosaur Jr., the Pixies, Throwing Muses and The Lemonheads), with bands moving back and forth between the two centres. Alternative scenes worldwide appear to conform to this basic pattern (see Fonarow, 2006, on British indie).

While alternative music is often linked to particular local scenes, the question is why then and there? Such scenes have generally developed out of a combination of airplay on the local college radio stations, access to local live venues, advertisements and reviews in local fanzines and free papers and, especially, the existence of local independent record companies. Bertsch (1993) argues that there are fundamental links between alternative music scenes and high-tech areas, with both sharing a decentralized, do-it-yourself approach to production, and with indie isolationism not far removed from the entrepreneurial spirit of capitalism, with 'everyone out for himself'. Music making, equipment design and programming are undertakings one person or a small group can succeed at without much start-up capital:

Seattle in the early 1990s provides an example.

Seattle

In 1992 the Seattle music scene came to international prominence, closely linked with the mainstream breakthrough of alternative music promoted by American college radio. Nirvana's second album and major-label debut *Nevermind* (Geffen, 1991) topped the *Billboard* charts; Pearl Jam and Soundgarden were major draw cards at the second Lollapalooza touring music festival in 1992, and both bands enjoyed huge record sales. The 'Seattle Sound' broadly referred to a group of bands initially recording with Seattle's Sub Pop independent record label, which were known for their grunge sound.

The Seattle scene and the grunge music with which it was associated became the most written about phenomenon in contemporary popular music since the birth of punk. Major labels scoured Seattle for unsigned bands or internationally sought out grunge-oriented performers (for instance Australia's Silverchair). The film *Singles* (Cameron Crowe, 1992), set amidst the Seattle scene, was widely publicized and commercially successful. The popularization of grunge-related fashion saw spreads in *Elle* and *Vogue* touting $1000 flannel shirts from the world's most famous designers. The 'Seattle Sound' became a marketing ploy for the music industry, as well as an ideological touchstone for Generation X.

> 'Seattle' defines the source of the phenomenon and organizes its often disparate expression. In writing about the Seattle scene, critics are not just chronicling a random success story. They are grappling with the notion of a geographically specific scene itself.
>
> (Bertsch, 1993)

A combination of factors explained why 'Seattle' occurred at that time and place: the ability of Sub Pop to feed into the majors; many good bands of similar style; the strong local alternative scene, linked to the Universities of Washington and Evergreen State (the latter a progressive, no-grades school with an alternative-oriented radio station); and the city's considerable distance from LA (Kirschner, 1994). Critics emphasized the purity and authenticity of the Seattle scene as a point of origin, defining bands like Nirvana in opposition to the mainstream. The foundations for the success of bands such as Nirvana and Soundgarden were laid throughout the 1980s by earlier alternative music scenes. What had changed was that by the early 1990s it had become easier and quicker for new alternative or indie bands to attract the attention of major labels or commercial radio, and to move to major labels and achieve some mainstream success (Azerrad, 2001).

The specific configuration and dynamics of other indie/alternative scenes have been examined in numerous ethnographically oriented studies. Takasugi (2003), for instance, studied the development of underground musicians in a Honolulu (Hawaii) scene in the mid-1990s. His interest was in the values and norms shared by members of the scene, and the relationship of these to the socialization and identity formation of the musicians involved: the resulting networks serve to sculpt and reinforce the identity of the band members within the scene' (74). This was to conceptualize the scene as 'a kind of social movement' (ibid.), one in which the distinction between fans and musicians was not always clear, with both integral to the scene. O'Connor, in a study of contemporary punk scenes in four cities (Washington, DC; Austin, Texas; Toronto, and Mexico City), shows that clear differences exist between such scenes, explicable in terms of the social geography of each city. For the punks involved, these scenes were identified with 'the active creation of infrastructure to support punk bands and other forms of creative activity' (O'Connor, 2002: 226).

The relationship of the local to the global is a key part of the dynamic of local music scenes, alternative or otherwise. For many participants in alternative local scenes, the perceived dualities associated with indie and major record labels are central to their commitment to the local. Here 'the celebration of the local becomes a form of fetishism, disguising the translocal capital, global management, and the transnational relations of production that enables it' (Fenster, 1995). However, the 'local' is increasingly allied with other localities, for both economic and affective reasons. Fenster notes 'the degree to which "independent" non-mainstream musics, while clearly based upon local spaces, performances and experiences, are increasingly tied together by social networks, publications, trade groups and regional and national institutions in … locally dispersed formations' (ibid.: 83). A decade on, this is even more evident. This internationalization of the local is a process encouraged and fostered economically by the major record companies, who place particular local sounds within larger structures, reaching a larger market in the process. Similarly, local sounds/scenes and their followers are ideologically linked through internationally distributed fanzines, music press publications and the Internet.

CONCLUSION

The concept of scene provides a more useful way in to looking at local patterns of music making and consumption, since it has greater flexibility than subculture. I have traced a shift from the concepts of youth culture, to subcultures, to sounds, and scenes. While this is something of a progression, I would argue that aspects of each of these remain present in particular locales. Accordingly, it seems most appropriate to view particular physical locations as scenes that include subcultures, and specific sounds, with these placed within an international music and leisure market.

NOTES

Subcultures

The classic studies are:

Hall, S. and Jefferson, T. (eds) (1976) *Resistance Through Rituals: Youth Subcultures in Post-War Britain*, London: Hutchinson/BCCCS.

Hebdige, D. (1979) *Subculture: The Meaning of Style*, London: Methuen.

For reappraisals of these, see:

Muggleton, D. (2000) *Inside Subculture: The Postmodern Meaning of Style*, Oxford and New York: Berg.

Thornton, S. (1995) *Club Cultures: Music, Media and Subcultural Capital*, London: Polity Press.

On the current state of the field:

Bennett, A. and Kahn-Harris, K. (eds) (2004) *After Subcultures*, London: Ashgate

Muggleton, D. and Weinzierl, R. (eds) (2003) *The Post-subcultures Reader*, Oxford and New York: Berg.

An excellent reader is:

Gelder, K. and Thornton, S. (1997) *The Subcultures Reader*, London and New York: Routledge.

Place (scenes and sounds):

Cohen, S. (1994) 'Identity, Place and the "Liverpool Sound"', in Stokes, M. (ed.) *Ethnicity, Identity and Music*, Oxford: Berg.

Cohen, S. (1999) 'Scenes', in Horner, B. and Swiss, T. (eds) *Key Terms in Popular Music and Culture*, Malden, MA and Oxford: Blackwell.

Hamm, C. (1995) *Putting Popular Music in Its Place*, Cambridge: Cambridge University Press.

Leyshon, A., Matless, D. and Revill, G. (1998) *The Place of Music*, New York: The Guilford Press.

Stahl, G. (2004) '"It's like Canada reduced": setting the scene in Montreal', in Bennett, A. and Kahn-Harris, K. (eds) *After Subcultures*, London: Ashgate.

Whiteley, S., Bennett, A. and Hawkins, S. (2004) *Music, Space and Place: Popular Music and Cultural Identify*, Aldershot: Ashgate.

Chapter 12

'We Are the World'
State music policy, globalization, and national identity

Policy in relation to popular music is formulated and implemented at the levels of the international community, the nation-state, regions, and local government. It includes regulation and stimulation of aspects of the production and consumption of music. At an international level there are agreements on market access and copyright provisions. At the State level policies include the regulation/deregulation of broadcasting; the use of tax breaks and content quotas; support for local copyright regulation; and censorship. The local level involves venue related regulations and the policing of public space.

State attitudes and policies towards popular culture are a significant factor in determining the formulation of such policies, and the construction of meaning in popular music. At the level of attitudes, state cultural policies are indicative of the various views held about the very concept of culture itself, debates over government economic intervention in the marketplace versus the operation of the 'free market', the operation of cultural imperialism, and the role of the state in fostering national cultural identity. As the Task Force Report on *The Future of the Canadian Music Industry* (1996: 1) put it:

> Most industrialized states believe that cultural products must not be treated as commodities. The cultural exemption contained in international trade agreements reflects a recognition that it is in their diversity that the richness of human cultures is to be found and that the distinctive characteristics of each culture should be preserved.

205

This chapter begins with a general discussion of the state and music, and cultural imperialism, globalization, and music. I then consider two examples of national policy in relation to local popular music: Canada and New Zealand. The question of the relationship between such policies, and the nature of 'the local', is exemplified in the case of New Zealand's recent garage rock bands, and the Polynesian based dub-reggae performers.

THE STATE AND MUSIC

The state has often been ignored in analyses of popular music, though there is a tradition of work on cultural policy at both the central and local state level. Studies of local policy include Kenney's history of the evolution of Chicago jazz, which details how a mix of council regulations, licensing law, moral watchdog organizations and police practices influenced the particular genre form taken by jazz in that city (Kenney, 1993). In a similar project, Chevigny (1991) shows how successive New York City Councils applied a network of zoning, fire, building and licensing regulations to discipline the venues and styles of jazz within the city. Homan (2003) demonstrated the complex relationship between city zoning, licensing, and noise regulations in Sydney and the venues for rock and dance, and the styles of music associated with them. These factors are significant in shaping local music scenes, and deserve greater attention, but I concentrate here on music policy at the national level.

State cultural policies have been largely based on the idealist tradition of culture as a realm separate from, and often in opposition to, that of material production and economic activity. This means that government intervention in its various forms – subsidy, licensing arrangements, protectionism through quotas, and so on – is justified by the argument which has been clearly elaborated by Garnham:

> that culture possesses inherent values, of life enhancement or whatever, which are fundamentally opposed to and in danger of damage by commercial forces; that the need for these values is universal, uncontaminated by questions of class, gender and ethnic origin; and that the market cannot satisfy this need.
>
> (1987: 24)

A key part of this view is the concept of the individual creative artist, with the associated cultural policy problem defined as 'one of finding audiences for their work rather than vice versa' (ibid.). This ideology has been used by elites in government, administration, intellectual institutions, and broadcasting to justify and represent sectional interests as general interests, thereby functioning as a form of cultural hegemony. Seeing classical music, ballet, and the theatre as high culture or 'the arts' legitimizes both their largely middle-class consumption and their receipt of state subsidy.

Popular culture is then constructed in opposition to this, as commercial, inauthentic, and so unworthy of significant government support. Such a dichotomized high–low culture view is unsustainable, yet it nonetheless remains a widely held and still powerful ideology. A comic example was provided by civil servant Sir Humphrey Appleby, giving advice to his ministerial 'boss' in the television comedy series *Yes Minister*:

> Subsidy is for Art. It is for Culture. It is not to be given to what the people want, it is for what the people don't want but ought to have. If they really want something they will pay for it themselves. The Government's duty is to subsidize education, enlightenment and spiritual uplift, not the vulgar pastimes of ordinary people.
>
> (Episode: 'The Middle Class Rip Off', BBC Television)

In the case of popular music, government attitudes have generally, but not exclusively, tended to reflect a traditional conservative view of 'culture', a high-culture tradition, which is used to justify non-intervention in the 'commercial' sphere. Yet this non-intervention exists in tension with frequent governmental concern to regulate a medium which, at times, has been associated with threats to the social order: moral panics over the activities of youth subcultures, the sexuality and sexism of rock, and obscenity (see Chapter 13). There have been a number of cases where the state has played a significant role in relation to popular music through economically and culturally motivated regulation and intervention. This has usually been to defend national cultural production against the inflow of foreign media products, using trade tariffs, industry incentives, and suchlike.

The past two decades have seen increased governmental (state) interest internationally in the economic possibilities inherent in the social and economic value of the arts and creative industries, and popular music has been a significant part of this discourse. State and local governments have increasingly recognized the economic and social potential of popular music. Their intervention:

> is becoming increasingly explicit, increasingly programmatic and institutional ... the role of government has become a crucial factor in the structural organization of rock music at the local, the national and ultimately at the global level.
>
> (Bennett *et al.*, 1993: 9)

Popular music scholars have paid greater attention to music policy (for example: Breen, 1999, on Australia), and increasingly become involved in its development (as with a commissioned report on the music industry in Scotland: Cloonan *et al.*, 2004). This 'turn to policy' in part reflects a concern at the dominance of international music repertoire, along with desire to gain a larger share in this market.

CULTURAL IMPERIALISM, GLOBALISATION AND MUSIC

The common preference of listeners and record buyers for foreign-originated sounds, rather than the product of their local artists and labels, is associated with the cultural imperialism thesis. Cultural imperialism developed as a concept analogous to the historical, political and economic subjugation of the Third World by the colonizing powers in the nineteenth century, with consequent deleterious effects for the societies of the colonized. This gave rise to global relations of dominance, subordination and dependency between the affluence and power of the advanced capitalist nations, most notably the United States and Western Europe, and the relatively powerless underdeveloped countries. This economic and political imperialism was seen to have a cultural aspect:

> the ways in which the transmission of certain products, fashions and styles from the dominant nations to the dependent markets leads to the creation of particular patterns of demand and consumption which are underpinned by and endorse the cultural values, ideals and practices of their dominant origin. In this manner the local cultures of developing nations become dominated and in varying degrees invaded, displaced and challenged by foreign, often western, cultures.
>
> (O'Sullivan *et al.*, 1994: 62; see also Hesmondhalgh, 2002)

In terms of mass media and popular culture, evidence for the cultural imperialism thesis, as it became known, was provided by the predominantly one way international media flow, from a few international dominant sources of media production, notably the USA, to media systems in other national cultural contexts. Not only did this involve the market penetration and dominance of Anglo-American popular culture, more importantly, it established certain forms as the accepted ones, scarcely recognising that there were alternatives:

> One major influence of American imported media lies in the styles and patterns which most other countries in the world have adopted and copied. This influence includes the very definition of what a newspaper, or a feature film, or a television set is.
>
> (Tunstall, 1977: Introduction)

The cultural imperialism thesis gained general currency in debates through the 1970s and 1980s about the significance of imported popular culture. Such debates were evident not only in the Third World, but in 'developed' countries such as France, Canada, Australia, and New Zealand, all subject to high market penetration by American popular culture. Adherents of the thesis tended to dichotomise local culture and its imported counterpart, regarding local culture as somehow more authentic, traditional, and supportive of a conception (however vaguely expressed it may be) of a distinctive national cultural identity. Set against this identity, and threatening its continual existence and vitality, was the influx of large quantities of commercial media, mainly from the United States. Upholders of the cultural imperialism view generally saw the solution to this situation as some combination of restrictions upon media imports and the deliberate fostering of the local cultural industries, including music.

While the cultural imperialism thesis has generally been applied to film, television and publishing, it has rarely been examined in relation to popular music. At first sight, its application here appears warranted, given that the major record companies are the dominant institutions of the music industry, and local pressings of imported repertoire take the major share of national music markets. But to what extent can this situation be seen in terms of cultural invasion and the subjugation of local cultural identity? Such figures present only the bare bones of the structure of the music industry, and tell us little about the complex relationship of the majors to local record companies in marginalized national contexts such as Canada and New Zealand.

Although the existence of cultural imperialism became widely accepted at both a 'common sense' level and in leftist academia, its validity at both a descriptive level and as an explanatory analytical concept came under increasing critical scrutiny in the 1980s. The validity of the local/authentic versus imported/commercial dichotomy is difficult to sustain with reference to specific examples, while media effects are assumed in a too one-dimensional fashion, underestimating the mediated nature of audience reception and use of media products. More importantly, the cultural imperialism thesis is predicated on accepting the 'national' as a given, with distinctive national musical identities its logical corollary. However the globalization of Western capitalism, particularly evident in its media conglomerates, and the increasing international nature of Western popular music bring these notions into question.

There are three significant points to be made here: first, Anglo-American popular culture has become established as the international preferred culture of the young since the 1950s, with American rock 'n' roll an instance of the use of foreign music by a generation as a means to distance themselves from a parental 'national culture' (Laing, 1986: 338). Second, local products cannot be straightforwardly equated with local national cultural identity, and imported product is not to be necessarily equated with the alien. Indeed local product is often qualitatively indistinct from its overseas counterpart, though this in itself is frequently a target for criticism. Third, while specific national case studies demonstrate the immense influence of the transnational music industry on musical production and distribution globally, they just as clearly indicate that the process is rather one in which local musicians are immersed in overlapping and frequently reciprocal contexts of production, with a cross-fertilization of local and international sounds. The global and the local cannot be considered binary categories, but exist in a complex interrelationship.

More recently, reflecting the internationalization of capital – a trend particularly evident in its media conglomerates – the term 'globalization' has replaced cultural imperialism, As an explanatory concept, however, globalization is often used too loosely, and is open to similar criticisms to cultural imperialism. Although awkward linguistically, 'glocalization' emerged as a more useful concept, emphasizing the complex and dynamic interrelationship of local music scenes and industries and the international market place.

As discussed in Chapter 1, the major problem faced by record companies is the uncertainty of the music market. It is widely agreed that, at best, only one in eight (to ten) of the artists who sign and record will achieve sufficient sales to recoup the original investment and start to earn money for the artists and generate a profit for the company. This situation has led to major record companies to look for acts that are already partially developed and which indicate commercial potential, especially in the international market (Hesmondhalgh, 2002; Hull, 2004; Negus, 1999). This is an approach with considerable implications for local artists operating primarily at a regional or national level. Attempts at the national level to foster local popular music production are primarily interventions at the level of the distribution and reception of the music. They attempt to secure greater access to the market, particularly for local products in the face of overseas music, notably from the United Kingdom and the United States. Such attempts, along with the issues surrounding cultural imperialism and globalization and the status of the local, can be more fully addressed through two national examples: Canada and New Zealand.

GLOBAL MUSIC, NATIONAL CULTURE: CANADA

I want to look at governmental intervention in relation to Canada's popular music industry, taking the story up to 2000, when the place of the local music industry was more secure. Policy since has been largely a case of maintaining existing provisions, and dealing with issues of copyright in the digital age.

The history of the Canadian music industry has been shaped largely by its relationship to the international market place, especially its proximity to the dominant United States market for popular music. During the 1980s and into the 1990s, the Canadian music industry was dominated by the local branches of the majors.

> The eight largest record companies in Canada are foreign-owned; 89 per cent of the revenues from the Canadian domestic market goes to multinationals. Their interest in Canadian music is restricted to those recordings which are marketed across the continent. This preference also shapes current government programs

for subsidizing domestic recording. All other recording remains economically, spatially, and discursively marginal.

(Berland, 1988: 349; see also Robinson *et al.*, 1991: Chapter 5)

Economies of scale applied to production meant that indigenous product was far more costly to produce and frequently had inferior production values compared with imports (largely) from the United States. With record distribution also dominated by the majors, and commercial radio frequently tied to US programme formats and broadcast sound quality, the Canadian industry and musicians had only a small market share: in 1988 the independents received approximately 11 per cent of national revenues from record sales. One consequence of this situation was that only a small percentage of music bought in Canada originated there, even when it was made by Canadian artists (e.g. Bryan Adams).

This economic situation sat uneasily with the historical Canadian concern to encourage nationhood and a cultural identity via communications technology, while at the same time resisting the intrusion of American media and messages. These concerns have pushed the state to the forefront in media and cultural policy (see Dorland, 1996). The two core aspects of this policy are the 'CanCon' regulations, administered by the Canadian Radio and Telecommunications Commission (CRTC), and the Sound Recording Development Program (SRDP).

The CRTC and CanCon

The CRTC was established by Parliament in 1968. The Broadcasting Act requires the CRTC to ensure that each 'broadcasting undertaking … shall make maximum use, and in no case less than predominant use, of Canadian creative and other resources in the creation and presentation of programming' (unless the specialized nature of the service makes it impracticable). The CRTC has responsibility for establishing classes of broadcasting licences, the allocation of broadcast licences, making broadcasting regulations, and the holding of public hearings in respect of such matters.

In pursuit of this goal, a Canadian Content quota on AM radio was introduced in 1971, and extended to FM radio in 1976. These quotas took into account particular station airplay formats, and expected a reasonably even distribution of Canadian selections throughout the day and through the broadcast week. What constitutes 'Canadian' was established by the MAPLE test, in which at least two of the audio components of a recording must be:

a) 'M' – music is composed by a Canadian
b) 'A' – artist (principal performer) is a Canadian
c) 'P' – performance/production is in Canada
d) 'L' – lyrics are written by a Canadian

CanCon, as the local content requirements came to be known, proved controversial, but had an undeniably positive impact on the Canadian recording industry:

> That simple regulation was a watershed. It was the expression of a protectionist policy designed to allow Canadian musicians to be heard in their own country. The overall effect of the regulations has been the creation of an active, vigorous, self-supporting, and surprisingly creative industry – one that hardly existed prior to the regulations.
>
> (Flohel, 1990: 497)

It was generally agreed that, while the current group of Canadian international stars would have 'made it ' anyway, their early careers received a significant impetus from the airplay guaranteed by CanCon. Further, and perhaps more importantly, the quota allowed a 'middle' group of perfomers to make an impact – and a living – within the Canadian industry:

> there's a whole lot of middle ground Canadian artists who are fabulous acts and CanCon has helped to ensure that they get the airplay that allows them to become the stars that they have become in Canada and, in many cases, nowhere else in the world.
>
> (Doug Pringle, director of programming at Rawlco Communications, responsible for a number of newer radio stations, quoted in Melhuish, 1999: 73)

The Sound Recording Development Program (SRDP)

The SRDP was created in 1986 to provide support to Canadian-owned companies for the production of Canadian audio and video music and radio programs and to support marketing, international touring, and business development. This recognized that it was necessary to assist the industry to enable it to provide the local content required under the CRTC regulations. A 1991 evaluation of the SRDP found that it had had a very positive effect on the sound recording industry, but that its resources (funding was initially CAN$5 million) were inadequate to significantly strengthen the independent sector of the industry and, in particular, that it provided too little support to marketing and distribution. This was confirmed by a later report, which regarded the scheme has now substantially underfunded: 'A major concern for both English and French language industries is the inadequacy of the resources available to support the marketing of recordings by Canadian artists' (Task Force, 1996).

The Task Force (1996) recommended that the resources of the Sound Recording Development Program should be increased immediately to CAN$10 million annually and sustained at that level for a period of five years, but it was not until late 1999 that government policy began to address this, and a comprehensive review of the Program began. Speaking in 1999, Brian Chater, President of CIRPA (the Canadian Independent Record Producers Association) emphasized there remained a pressing need to get 'serious structural funding' in the local industry:

> The music business has become very much like the film business; you have to have a lot of bucks to play the game, and a lot of the time it won't work anyway. Now if you don't invest three or four hundred grand on each project, nobody thinks you're serious. Do five of those and you've spent a couple of million dollars. The reality with project funding is that you're always scrambling from A to B trying to pay the bills with the project money. What we want to see indies have access to is structural funding, so that you can operate a company rather than do projects.
>
> (Melhuish, 1999: 79)

The Canadian music industry as a whole was considerably stronger by the mid-1990s. Recordings now generated substantial economic activity: retail sales in Canada totalled CAN$1.3 billion in 1997, while the royalties paid to Canadian songwriters, composers and publishers (as public performance rights) totalled CAN$49 million in 1997, up from CAN$34 million in 1993 (DFSP, 1999). While this overall picture was impressive, the historical dichotomy remained: Canadian firms earned about 90 per cent of their revenue from selling Canadian-content recordings, while 88 per cent of the revenues of foreign-controlled firms came from selling recordings made from imported masters. Foreign firms had five times the revenue, eighteen times the profit, ten times the long-term assets, and sixteen times the contributed surplus and retained earnings of Canadian-controlled firms (Task Force, 1996).

It should also be acknowledged, however, that the majors were not simply parasitic here. Brian Robertson, President of CRIA, stressed the important investment in Canadian talent by the multinationals (majors), now around CAN$40 million a year in Canadian Content production. 'This has escalated tremendously in the last decade, and represents a huge investment per year in Canadian music and artists and their recordings' (author interview, July 1999).

Yet in the mid-1990s, while the general picture of a marginalized local sound-recording industry remained valid, there were evident contradictions (Straw, 1996). On the one hand, there was the increased international visibility and success of Canadian artists/music within the global sound-recording industry, although these artists frequently record in the United States for US-based companies; e.g. Bryan Adams; Alanis Morissette, Shania Twain. On the other hand, there was also an increased share of the local market for music of Canadian content, with commercially significant sales

213

for several locally-based performers, including Bare Naked Ladies, Our Lady Peace, (Blue) Rodeo, and Sarah McLachlan. In 1998, Our Lady Peace's CD *Clumsy* sold over 800,000 copies in Canada, along with well over half a million copies in the USA; Bare Naked Ladies had a Top Ten *Billboard* single ('One Week'), and their album *Stunt* reached sales of three million (Chauncey, 1999: 57).

At the same time the popular music market had changed dramatically, with the splintering of 'mainstream rock', once the dominant genre, into a wide range of genre styles and performers, along with the willingness of the major record companies to market/exploit these. These trends created uncertainty about the future role and status of Canada's small, locally based firms, which have traditionally nurtured and been economically dependent on new musical styles. In other words, reflecting glocalization, the relative market positions and relationship of 'majors' and 'independents' in the Canadian market had changed. The growth of foreign markets has made artist development in Canada more globally oriented. The Canadian branches of the majors, and Canadian-owned independent labels such as Nettwerk Productions, Attic Music Group, True North, and Marquis Classics were increasingly looking to develop artists with international appeal. As Randy Lennox, president of Universal Music Group (Canada) observed: 'We're watching specific market trends worldwide when signing an artist today' (LeBlanc, 1999).

In the midst of these shifts, positive government policy toward the local music industry appeared to be more necessary than ever, a view shared by the comprehensive and influential Task Force Report, on *The Future of the Canadian Music Industry* (Task Force, 1996). The Task Force was asked to develop proposals that would ensure that the industry could maintain its central role in promoting Canada's cultural identity by providing an increasing choice of Canadian music. Objectives set for the industry were to maintain its ability to compete in Canada and abroad; to be adequately compensated for use of its copyrighted material; and to benefit from new technologies. The Task Force concluded: 'While cultural objectives should provide the basis for music industry policy, measures that strengthen the creation, performance, production, distribution and marketing of Canadian music will also generate important economic benefits' (Task Force, 1996). In early 1999, after a series of public hearings and a review of radio policy by the CRTC, the Canadian content requirement was increased to 35 per cent. This change did not indicate a 'failure' of the previous requirement, but was a recognition that the local industry was now in a strong enough position to provide sufficient acceptable recordings to meet such an increase.

The Canadian case raises crucial questions about the role of music as a form of discourse actively engaged in the uniting or fragmenting of a community. Government policy presupposes that listeners consciously identify – and identify with – specifically locally produced music. However, it is misleading to automatically assume that local musicians embody and support a Canadian cultural nationalism in their work: Canada is characterized by considerable cultural diversity, with strongly developed regional music scenes and idioms. The frequent negative reaction local product provokes is an important reminder of how what counts as popular music has been identified with a particular imported form, the result of the dominance of American radio formats, music videos, and production values.

NEW ZEALAND ON AIR

These questions of the relationship between popular music, local cultural identity, and the global nature of the music industry are also present in New Zealand, a country with a small market for recorded music, a small share for local music within the major-dominated turnover of the local phonogram market, and with a relatively unimportant role for local sounds within the international music market. New Zealand's local recording companies and their products are largely marginalized by the dominant position of the international record companies (the majors), and the sheer quantity of 'imported' material – mainly New Zealand pressings of international repertoire. Given the economic and cultural significance of recorded music, this situation has been the focus of considerable public debate and Government cultural policy. The 1989–1990 debate over a compulsory quota for NZ music on the radio traversed the arguments over the importance of supporting the local music industry, the constitution of the 'local', and the relationship between airplay and commercial success (see Shuker and Pickering, 1994). When a quota was not introduced, New Zealand On Air (NZOA) was established, to administer the funds collected by the broadcasting fee. Its brief included provision for subsidizing local music – a kind of quota default option. I shall return to these schemes.

The New Zealand popular music scene has experienced periodic highs and lows through the last two decades. After a low period in the late 1980s (in terms of overall chart success), local artists made strong chart showings both at home and internationally during 1991–2, greatly assisted by the introduction of NZ On Air's music schemes. Flying Nun, the country's main independent label, saw continued sales growth, particularly in the United States. During the next few years, despite the continuation of NZ On Air's funding of videos and CD compilations of local artists, retail sales fluctuated and chart success failed to match the peak level achieved in 1992. This was followed in the mid-1990s by the international success of OMC ('How Bizarre'), Crowded House, and Neil Finn, and strong local showings by artists such as Bic Runga, Shihad, Che Fu, and The Feelers.

Despite such occasional successes, in 2001, the vital signs of the local recording industry remained mixed. The local scene was still insufficient to support full-time professional performers, there was still only limited radio and television exposure for local artists, and initiatives to support the industry remain limited. Several explanations

215

were offered for this: a general lack of effort on the part of the majors to sign and develop New Zealand artists; the general lack of an industry infrastructure, especially in terms of management and the limited opportunities for radio and television airplay, especially the absence of a local content quota (as existed in Canada). New Zealand artists who stayed 'at home' remained marginal to the international music industry, since the country lacked the population base to support a music industry on the scale of neighbouring Australia. The result is a tension between the support for the purely local, and the need to go offshore to follow up national success. Shihad, arguably New Zealand's premier rock band, in late 1998 relocated to Los Angeles:

> We're not turning our back on New Zealand. A lot of people are coming to the realisation that as a climate for making music New Zealand is tremendously wealthy in terms of what we have available to us and what people can produce here, but the actual platform for getting music out into the market place is absolutely shit. We're crippled in comparison to places like Australia where they have local content quotas.
>
> (Tom Larkin, drummer, Shihad; Rip It Up, October 1998: 14; in 2006 they are based in Melbourne)

There are a number of established NZ Independent labels, along with local branches of the majors who dominate the global music industry. According to industry sources, the subsidiaries of the multi-national record companies have traditionally supplied approximately 90 per cent of the domestic market. While any strict division between the majors and the 'indies' is difficult to maintain, with distribution deals tying the two sectors of the industry together, there are interesting questions about the dynamics of their relationship. This is particularly the case with the operation of the majors with respect to local product.

Logically, given the economies of scale involved, the majors concentrate more on promoting their overseas artists, with their local performers treated as a lower priority. The majors also, in a sense, feed off local labels, treating them in the same fashion as North American professional sports franchises use their 'farm teams' to foster talent and provide local backup as necessary. But, as in Canada, this is as much a symbiotic relationship as it is a parasitic one. The independents need the distribution and marketing support the majors can provide, particularly in overseas markets, while NZ performers who outstrip the strictly local need the majors to move up a league. This was evident with the two main New Zealand independent record labels operating in the late 1980s: Flying Nun, and Pagan (Mitchell, 1996), and continues to be the case.

Given the marginal status of New Zealand recording industry in the international arena, and the difficulties facing local artists, the initiatives taken by New Zealand On

Air (NZOA) to foster New Zealand music, in operation since July 1991, are of crucial importance. NZOA's brief is not restricted to 'popular music', but in practice this is the case, with classical music having its own sources of funding and support. NZOA is charged with ensuring that 'New Zealanders have a diverse range of broadcasting services that would not otherwise be available on a commercial basis'. A key strategy in pursuit of this goal is 'To encourage broadcasters to maintain a sustained commitment to programmes reflecting New Zealand identity and culture'. Working towards achieving this includes 'funding programming on television and radio about New Zealand and New Zealand interests, including the broadcasting of New Zealand music' (NZOA: Statement of purpose and goals).

By 2000, NZOA's popular music programme had four main schemes related to radio and television. These are ongoing, and continue to provide the basis for its support of local music:

1   RADIO HITS: which provides incentives to record companies to produce records suitable for the commercial radio playlist; and lessens the financial risk inherent in recording and releasing singles, by enabling partial recovery of recording costs.
2   THE HIT DISC, which assists record companies to get airplay for new releases, and makes sure that 'every Programme Director in every NZ radio station has access to a broadcast-quality copy of new singles which have commercial radio airplay potential'. The first of these, and still the most important, is the *Kiwi Hit Disc*, made up of 'new New Zealand music on release or about to be released by record companies'. The *Indie Hit Disc* and the *Iwi Hit Disc* are similar schemes with more of a niche market (Iwi targets Maori radio; Indie the university stations).
3   MUSIC VIDEO: 'funding NZ music videos as part of a campaign to get more NZ music on air', through subsidizing production costs of selected videos.
4   NEW ZEALAND MUSIC ON RADIO, which involves funding specialist radio programmes promoting NZ music, for commercial radio and student radio, aimed at the youth audience.

In each of the first three schemes the criteria for support is similar, or identical. First, 'It must be New Zealand music. The priority is original New Zealand music but we accept covers as well' (Guidelines for Music Video; Radio Hits; Kiwi Hit Disc). Second, there must be a confirmed record release: 'the video must backup the release of a single or EP in NZ either by an independent or a major label' (Music Video); and 'A record company – either a major or one of the independents – must be involved in releasing the record' (Radio Hits). Priority goes to projects distributed nationally usually via one of the major record companies. Third, a key consideration is broadcast potential: 'our priority is videos which are likely to generate repeat screenings on national network television' (Music Video); 'To qualify for funding, the record must attract significant airplay on commercial radio' (Radio Hits); and 'the record must be a realistic contender for significant airplay on commercial radio' (Kiwi Hit Disc). Seven radio stations are used as barometers, and the schemes use programmers from TV shows and radio as consultants to identify broadcast potential.

A mix of cultural and commercial criteria are being applied here, with an emphasis on the latter. It is important to recognize that the schemes in themselves do not guarantee exposure through local television and radio. What they do is facilitate the production of local product, including an acceptable technical quality of these videos and recordings, and make it more available to local programmers. Recognizing this, in early 1998 NZOA began employing a 'song plugger', whose role was to push (promote) the forthcoming Hit Disc to key radio station programmers. This represented a dramatic departure for NZOA, but was a necessary move given that, despite six years of effort, there appeared to have been only limited improvement in the levels of New Zealand music getting airplay on commercial radio.

Fresh initiatives

The NZOA music schemes were in effect the alternative to a local content quota. Certainly, they contributed to a gradual improvement in the proportion of local content on radio, with NZOA close to its breakthrough goal of 'double digits' (New Zealand 10 per cent of local airplay) in 2000. Yet, even with the more forceful presentation of the products of the schemes, it remained uncertain if this goal could be achieved, thus making a quota unnecessary,

It was becoming recognized in official circles, as well as in the music industry, that the continued development of the infrastructure of the New Zealand music industry was central to generating opportunities for local musicians, and for providing a launching platform for access to the international market.

In mid-2000, Helen Clarke, Prime Minister and Minister of Culture and the Arts, announced a Governmental NZ$146 million arts-recovery package, with three goals: the arts were to be nurtured for their intrinsic worth; they should help build a uniquely New Zealand national identity; and arts and culture should 'contribute to the building of strong creative industries which provide rewarding employment, opportunities for creative entrepreneurs, and good economic returns'. As part of this package, in July 2000 the funding for the NZOA music schemes was virtually doubled, from NZ$2 million to NZ$3.78 million a year, to enable the implementation of strategies to get increased airplay for local recordings. In 2001, a New Zealand Music Industry Commission was created, with funding of NZ$2 million (over five years), charged simply with 'growing the industry'.

The proportion of New Zealand music played on radio had remained small through the 1990s, varying between approximately 5 per cent on some commercial stations and 15–20 per cent on student radio. This situation improved quite dramatically in 2001, when a voluntary NZ Music Code was negotiated between the Radio Broadcasters Association and the Minister of Broadcasting, and began operating in 2002 (while not mandatory, the new targets were 'strongly encouraged' with the implicit threat of licences not being renewed). At the same time, during 2002–3 NZOA began increasingly using 'song pluggers' to promote its releases to radio playlist programmers. Boosted by the emergence of a few high profile local acts, and several performers' international success, these initiatives contributed to a marked increase in the proportion of New Zealand artists gaining local airplay, which reached some 15 per cent in 2002. In late 2002, *Billboard*, the main industry trade magazine, featured New Zealand in its high profile 'Spotlight' section, noting that the strength of the local music scene had set the stage for an international breakthrough (J. Ferguson, 'New Zealand Acts Aim for Global Impact', *Billboard*, 30 November 2002: 37–45).

In July 2004, a Government sponsored report *Creating Heat – Tumata kia white* set out a blueprint to encourage New Zealand's music industry to increase its overseas exchange earnings (from NZ$5 million in 2003–4) to NZ$50 million per year by 2014. This was to be facilitated by a new export model, 'NZ Out There', that would connect musicians of all genres more directly into overseas networks, a process coordinated by a reorganized New Zealand Music Industry Commission, with increased funding (Music Industry Development Group, 2004).

These initiatives paid off. In 2003, Hayley Westenra, Bic Runga, and Scribe had the three top-selling albums for that year in the charts, the first time three 'Kiwi' acts had taken all three top spots. Westenra also had considerable commercial success in the UK, while Runga consolidated her cult status there, and rapper Scribe topped the Australian charts. Launched in 2004, C4 the nationwide, free-to-air music channel, strongly committed itself to New Zealand programming, achieving solid viewer ratings. During 2005, Fat Freddy's Drop's album *Based On A True Story* spent a record ten weeks at Number 1 in the New Zealand album charts, selling 90,000 copies (by March 2006), and winning Worldwide Album of 2005 at the BBC's Radio 1 Giles Peterson awards. New Zealand music accounted for a record 20.8 per cent of music played on commercial radio, meeting the Code of Practice target of 20 per cent ahead of schedule (the aim was to achieve this level in 2006). Broadcasting Minister Steve Maharey hailed this as 'a fantastic result for the music industry, and it demonstrates that New Zealanders want to tune into more of their own music'. Local bands Breaks Co-op and The Feelers had the top three airplay songs for the year.

Musical style and 'Kiwi' identity

But while the New Zealand music scene is demonstrably stronger than ever, some commentators are uncomfortable that the emphasis on commercial success was 'squeezing out anything distinctively local about the music' (this section draws on Shuker, 2003/4; detailed references to the local press commentary can be found there). Such concerns are linked to the importance of popular music as an indicator of cultural identity, operating at the levels of the self, community, and the nation. Songwriters frequently draw on themes of homeland and the nation to both situate and authenticate their music, while particular geographic locales, usually cities or regions, but sometimes the nation, are identified with particular locales. Such themes and connections to local culture can arguably be lost when the preoccupation is with producing 'international repertoire'. How does the current prominence of New Zealand music sit alongside such questions of music and identity? I want to consider this with reference to two prominent aspects of the local renaissance: Kiwi 'garage' rock bands, and Urban Polynesian music.

Indie and garage rock

'Indie rock' is a broad international meta-genre, with a strong continuity in preferred sounds and rhythms, influences, and performance stances. A guitar-dominated genre, associated with groups rather than solo performers, indie represents an ideology (situated around a DIY ethic, and independence from the major recording companies), as much as musical style. The genre has a long and honourable tradition in New Zealand, associated primarily with the independent local labels of the 1980s, especially Flying Nun. The reverb-driven, drone, and 'jangly guitar' style central to many of the leading Flying Nun bands (e.g. The Bats; The Chills) was often regarded as a coherent label style (see Mitchell, 1996). This 'Flying Nun sound' also came to represent a metonym for New Zealand music in general, one with a continued legacy and contribution to the local musical canon (see *Rip It Up*, December 2000: 'The Top 100 New Zealand Albums'; Flying Nun Releases Feature Prominently'). However, its coherence and significance has been debated, and it is noteworthy that it was primarily a style dominated by white males.

The most recent manifestation of international indie guitar rock is 'garage rock'. The style combines basic rock 'n' roll of the late 1960s, especially the United States garage bands, and a fresh version of 1970s hard rock, along with punk and heavy metal overtones. Highly successful international exponents include The White Stripes (US), The Vines (Australia), and The Hives (Sweden). The success of contemporary garage rock is partly due to traditional rock audiences' disenchantment with hip-hop and dance music, and manufactured pop. For its fans, garage rock represents a confirmation of

220

the traditional rock ideology of authenticity: 'real' performers playing their instruments live, to 'real' audiences.

The leading New Zealand garage rock bands are the Datsuns and the D4. At the New Zealand Music Awards (the Tuis) in May 2003, the Datsuns won four awards: 'album of the year', for their self-titled debut; 'best group'; 'outstanding international achievement'; and 'breakthrough artist of the year'. Their album had reached Number 1 in New Zealand, 17 in the United States and 25 in Europe. Signed to Richard Branson's V2 Records, the Datsuns had been on the front of leading British indie magazine NME, and played their debut single 'In Love' on leading television chart show Top of the Pops. Critics lauded their music as a blend of Led Zeppelin and Deep Purple, Kiss, T Rex and AC/DC, 'influences' acknowledged by the band members themselves. The D4 also had an impact in the UK, offering, in the words of one critic: 'Splenetic, frenetic punk rock', with their debut album 6 Twenty 'a call to beers classic' exemplified by the single 'Rock 'n' roll Motherfucker' (Record Collector, Issue 287, July 2003: 78–80).

Like their international counterparts, both the Datsuns and the D4 were treading a well-worn musical path, a 1970s hard rock template. Their success had come after intensive gigging on the local scene and then in the UK and the United States (and Japan, in the case of the D4). This is very much part of the indie rock tradition, and is frequently referred to by band members: 'That's our thing. We like playing live and being on the road' (Datsun's rhythm guitarist Phil Buckle). The influential indie magazine NME voted the Datsuns the best live act of 2003. The success of the Datsuns and the D4 was achieved largely without initially having significant New Zealand sales, radio airplay, or support from New Zealand On Air (even though the last had been made available to them, they preferred to remain strictly independent). These were bands who had found success by leaving the country, and both continued to successfully tour and record through 2004–6.

The media frequently label them 'Kiwi rock 'n' roll' (for example, during the New Zealand tours by both bands in October 2003). The tag is justified in terms of national origin, however neither band has anything distinctively local about their music. This matters to those concerned that New Zealand music is not to simply adopt of international styles. Such a view is perhaps naïve, given that all popular music embraces a mix of the local and the global. It is more a question of the extent of the local referents, and the importance of these as national cultural signifiers. A more 'local mix' is offered by contemporary urban Polynesian music in New Zealand.

Urban Polynesian Sounds

Polynesian dominated local rap-, reggae- and hip-hop-inflected music represents a crucial example of the hybridity of much contemporary music, including elements of a distinct New Zealand identity. A few examples from what is now an extensive body of work must suffice here.

Katchafire's debut album *Revival* (2003) and subsequent recordings reflect the continued local influence of reggae icon Bob Marley (Marley and the Wailers played in New Zealand in 1979, and their recordings still dominate back catalogue sales). Lead singer and guitarist Logan Bell states, 'Bob Marley's music has always had special relevance for Maori because he sang a lot about cultural pride, about mana and about the struggle and hardships that oppressed people face – we could immediately identify with that'. Accordingly, Katchafire go for a similar sound, but 'with lyrics about our own life experiences'. Hip-hop group Nesian Mystik revel in their mixture of ethnic backgrounds, including Maori, and members from the Cook Islands, Tonga, and Samoa. Their album *Polyunsaturated*, which won the Best Urban Album Award at the 2003 Tuis, reflects New Zealand's increasing demographic 'brownness': singer Te Awanui Reeder observes that 'our music is about real things like friends and family rather than just copying that same old American sound. The messages we talk about are universal, but some of the sounds, and rhythms and harmonies you only find down here'. In similar fashion, Wellington's Trinity Roots' album *True* (2002) assimilated 'offshore influences like dub, reggae, jazz and R&B into something that sounded as indigenous as the haka' – the traditional Maori 'war dance', performed by the All Blacks rugby team (Nick Bollinger, 2004: review), a process carried further by *Home, Land & Sea* (2004), seen as 'sushi fresh', 'alive with aroha' [love], and 'proudly Pacific' (Grant Smithies, 2004: review). The songs weave together themes of land ownership, Maori spirituality and myth, and national identity: 'We'll probably be writing songs bout those two subjects for the rest of our lives: our love for New Zealand, and our love for whanua [kin, family]' (Warren Maxwell, quoted in Smithies, 2004: 26). As the comments of local reviewers demonstrate, a clear relationship existed between these performers and the national cultural context within which they were working.

The success of these performers, along with local artists such as Che Fu, King Kapisi, and Scribe, supported the view that 'urban Polynesian music' represented New Zealand's best opportunity to make a musical impact internationally. Auckland, New Zealand's main urban centre, has the biggest Polynesian population of any city in the world, while Maori and Polynesians will make up a steadily increasing share of New Zealand's population over the next decade. With youthful music consumers forming a major part of this growth, the local market increasingly provides a fertile testing ground for local Polynesian music, which can use this as a springboard to the international market. Local inflections of imported musical styles will engender international interest while maintaining a New Zealand flavour to the music.

CONCLUSION

The transformation of the global circulation of cultural forms is creating new lines of influence and solidarity which are not bounded by geographically defined cultures, and popular music is not exempt from such processes. Accordingly, we need to be conscious of the danger of too easily dichotomising the local and the global, recognize the dynamism and intertextuality of at least the best of contemporary popular music, and avoid adopting a narrowly defined cultural nationalist position. Nevertheless, there remain important economic arguments for the support of the local. The continued development of the infrastructure of the Canadian and New Zealand music industries is central to generating opportunities for local musicians, and for providing a launching platform for access to the international market.

Debates over cultural policy and popular music embrace a volatile mix of the ideological and the economic. At the ideological level, there is the maintenance of an outmoded high–low culture dichotomy, which partly serves to legitimate the general neglect of the popular, including popular music. At the same time, however, the state is also concerned to respond to the significant level of community support for local culture, and the perceived necessity of defending the local against the continued and increasing dominance of international popular media. This concern is mediated by the difficulty of establishing the uniqueness of national 'sounds', be they New Zealand or Canadian.

NOTES

The internationalization of the music industry, and its repercussions at the local level, are examined in:

Wallis, R. and Malm, K. (1984) *Big Sounds from Small Countries*, London: Constable.
Wallis, R. and Malm, K. (1992) *Media Policy and Music Activity*, London: Routledge.
Gebesmair, A. and Smudits, A. (eds) (2001) *Global Repertoires: Popular Music Within and Beyond the Transnational Music Industry*, Burlington, VT: Ashgate.
Homan, S. (2003) *The Mayor's A Square: Live Music and Law and Order in Sydney*, Newtown, NSW: LCP, is a fascinating study of the regulation of music venues in Sydney, Australia.
Cloonan, M., Williamson, J. and Frith, S. (2004) 'What is music worth?', *Popular Music*, 23, 2: 205–12. Reflecting on their commissioned report for Scottish Enterprise: *Mapping the Music Industry in Scotland*, the authors raise issues common to such projects.

Canada: National policy and the music industry:
Canadian Recording Industry Association (CRIA): www.cria.ca.
Canadian Culture Online (funding programmes): www.canadianheritage.gc.ca/progs.

Music Industries Association of Canada (MIAC): www.miac.net.

Canada's Independent Record Production Association (CIRPA): www.cirpa.ca.

New Zealand: National policy and the music industry:

New Zealand On Air (NZOA) : www.nzonair.co.nz.

New Zealand Music Industry Commission: www.nzmusic.org.nz.

Recording Industry Association of New Zealand (RIANZ): www.rianz.org.nz.

Chapter 13

'Pushin' Too Hard'
Moral panics

Particular genres of popular music have sparked controversy and opposition, both upon their emergence and sporadically since: rock 'n' roll in the mid-1950s, psychedelic rock in the late 1960s, disco and punk in the 1970s, heavy metal and gangsta rap in the 1980s, and rave culture in the 1990s, to name only the better-known examples (see Martin and Seagrave, 1988; Cloonan, 1996; Winfield and Davidson, 1999; Cohen, 1997). Criticism has centred variously on the influence of such genres on youthful values, attitudes and behaviour through the music's (perceived) sexuality and sexism, nihilism and violence, obscenity, black magic and anti-Christian nature. The political edge of popular music has been partly the result of this hostile reaction often accorded to the music and its associated causes and followers, helping to politicize the musicians and their fans.

While such episodes are a standard part of the history of popular music – music hall, jazz, and other new forms of popular music were also all stigmatized in their day – rarely are their nature and cultural significance more fully teased out. I argue here that they have constituted a form of moral panic – the social concern generated by them was greatly exaggerated, and the perceived threat to social harmony was by no means as ominous as many regarded it. Attempts to control and regulate popular music genres such as rock and rap are significant as part of the ongoing contestation of cultural hegemony, particularly with the emergence of the New Right.

MORAL PANIC AND REGULATION

The episodes dealt with here have been chosen for their value in illuminating different facets of the reaction to popular music, at particular historical moments. First, the New Zealand reaction to rock 'n' roll in the 1950s exemplifies the characteristic concerns displayed internationally towards the new form of popular music: antipathy towards it as music, the anti-social behaviour linked to concerts and rock movies, and, most importantly, the associations with juvenile delinquency. Second, the issues of obscenity and free speech are examined in the light of the establishment of the PMRC and the celebrated court action against American band the Dead Kennedys in 1986–7, and controversies surrounding the lyrics of songs by 2 Live Crew (1990) and Ice-T (1992). Third, attempts to link the Columbine massacre of 1999 to the influence of Marilyn Manson illustrate the ongoing tendency to blame 'rock' for deeper social problems. These case studies illustrate the utility of the concept of moral panic to examine how music, as a central form of popular culture, becomes invested with ideological significance.

To place such opposition to popular music in context, it is important to acknowledge that popular culture in general has historically been the target of censure, condemnation and regulation. In the 1950s, for example, psychologist Frederic Wertham's influential bestseller, *Seduction of the Innocent*, argued for a direct causal connection between comic books and juvenile delinquency. Concern over new media and the activities of their youthful consumers seems to periodically reach a peak, frequently associated with 'boundary crises', periods of ambiguity and strain in society, which lead to attempts to more clearly establish moral boundaries. In many instances, such boundary crises are forms of 'moral panic', a concept that was widely utilized in British sociology of deviance and new criminology studies of the 1970s. This writing drew on labelling theory, associated with the American sociologist Howard Becker, who argued that societies and social groups 'create deviance by making those rules whose infraction comprises deviance and by applying them to particular people, and labeling them as outsiders' (Becker, 1997: 9); that is, deviance is considered to be a social construct. The mass media are the major source for the labeling process, as they transmit and legitimate such labels, for example Cohen's 'folk devils', and contribute to the legitimation of social control. Labelling theory is evident in popular music studies of various subcultures and their perceived 'anti-social' behaviours.

The concept of moral panic was popularized by sociologist Stanley Cohen's now classic study of mods and rockers in the United Kingdom, *Folk Devils and Moral Panics*. Cohen states that a period of moral panic occurs when:

> A condition, episode, person or group of persons emerges to become defined as a threat to societal values and interests; its nature is presented in a stylised and stereotypical fashion by the mass media; the moral barricades are manned by

editors, bishops, politicians and other right-thinking people; socially accredited experts pronounce their diagnoses and solutions; ways of coping are evolved or (more often) resorted to; the condition then disappears, submerges or deteriorates and becomes more visible.

(Cohen, 1980: 9)

The second stage of Cohen's view of moral panic is particularly significant, involving as it does the repudiation of the 'common-sense' view that the media simply report what happens. Cohen's own case study of the 1960s clashes between mods and rockers in the UK (the 'folk devils' of his title), showed up just such a process of the selection and presentation of news. The media coverage of the clashes simplified their causes, labelled and stigmatized the youth involved, whipped up public feeling, and encouraged a retributive, deterrent approach by those in authority. (For a helpful discussion of the subsequent application of the concept of moral panic, see Critcher, 2003.)

Examining the historical relationship between youth, 'antisocial' attitudes and behaviours, and popular music, means considering culture as a political issue. At a deeper level, moral panics around new media are episodes in cultural politics and the continual reconstitution and contestation of cultural hegemony. Underpinning debates over popular fiction, comics, film, television, video and popular music genres and performers are a series of assumptions about popular or 'mass' culture, which is frequently seen as diametrically opposed to a 'high' culture tradition. This dichotomy is a doubtful basis for evaluating particular forms of culture. The whole notion of a 'high–low' culture distinction must be regarded as a social construct, resting on class-based value judgements. It is more appropriate to view particular cultural forms in terms of both their formal qualities and their social function for consumers, while keeping in mind the salient point that any evaluation must be primarily in terms relevant to the group that produces and appreciates it. This is particularly the case with popular music (Shepherd et al., 1977). With these general points in mind, I now turn to examples of music and moral panics.

Rock 'n' roll: the devil's music

The music industry and the social context of the early 1950s were ready for rock 'n' roll. With fuller employment, general economic prosperity, and their emergence as an important consumer group, teenagers began to demand their own music and clothes, and to develop a generational-based identity. Before 1956, popular music was dominated by American sounds, epitomised by the recurrent image of the 'crooner'. The music was largely safe, solid stuff, what Cohn terms 'the palais age – the golden era of the big bands, when everything was soft, warm, sentimental, when everything was make believe' (Cohn, 1970: 11). There was little here for

227

young people to identify with, though riot-provoking performers like Johnny Ray represented prototypes for rock.

Although rock music began with rock 'n' roll in the mid-1950s, as Tosches (1984) documents, it had been evolving well prior to this, and was hardly the sole creation of Elvis Presley and Alan Freed. The phrase 'rock 'n' roll' itself was popularized with its sexual connotations in the music of the 1920s, and was basically 'a mixture of two traditions: Negro rhythm and blues and white romantic crooning, coloured beat and white sentiment' (Cohn, 1970: 11). Negro rhythm and blues was good-time music, danceable and unpretentious. While highly popular on rhythm and blues charts and radio stations, it received little airplay on white radio stations, and was frequently banned because of the sexual innuendo of 1950s R&B songs such as Hank Ballard's 'Work With Me Annie', Billy Ward's 'Sixty Minute Man', and the Penguin's 'Baby Let Me Bang Your Box'. It is this link between sex and rock 'n' roll – the devil's music – which underpinned the moral reaction to its popularization in the 1950s.

In April 1954, Bill Haley made 'Rock Around the Clock'. The record was a hit in America, then worldwide; eventually selling 15 million copies. While it did not start rock 'n' roll, it did represent a critical symbol in the popularization of the new musical form. 'Rock Around the Clock' was featured in the MGM movie *Blackboard Jungle*, the story of a young teacher at a tough New York school. The success of the film with teenage audiences, and the popularity of Haley's song (see Miller, 1999: 87–94), led to Haley being signed to make a film of his own. *Rock Around the Clock* (1956) told how Bill Haley and his band popularized rock 'n' roll, but the thin story was really a showcase for the rock acts on the soundtrack. The film proved enormously popular internationally, but attracted controversy over its effect on audiences. In Britain, for example, local councils banned showings of the film following riots in some cinemas. According to contemporary press reports, in the Gaiety Cinema, Manchester,

> gangs of teenage youths and their girlfriends danced in the aisles, vaulted up on to the stage, and turned fire hoses on the manager when he tried to restore order. After the programme, they surged into city streets in a wild stampede, bringing traffic to a standstill in the centre of town and pounding a rock 'n' roll rhythm on buses and cars with their fists.
>
> (UK newspaper, 10 September 1956)

Haley was an unlikely hero for youth to emulate, since his image (old, balding, and chubby) hardly matched the music, but others were waiting in the wings. In this brief overview, complex developments must be reduced to their key moments. The success of Haley was one, the emergence of Chuck Berry and Little Richard another. Elvis Presley's was the biggest yet:

His big contribution was that he brought it home just how economically powerful teenagers could really be. Before Elvis, rock had been a feature of vague rebellion. Once he'd happened, it immediately became solid, self-contained, and then it spawned its own style in clothes and language and sex, a total independence in almost everything – all the things that are now taken for granted.

(Cohn, 1970: 23)

Cohn is overly enthusiastic about teenagers' independence, but by the end of 1957 Elvis had grown into an annual US$20 million industry, and the process of homogenization of both 'the King' and the music had begun.

The new music provoked considerable criticism, with many older musicians contemptuous of rock 'n' roll, and conservative commentators regarding it as a moral threat.

Viewed as a social phenomenon, the current craze for rock 'n' roll material is one of the most terrifying things ever to have happened to popular music. Musically speaking, of course, the whole thing is laughable. It is a monstrous threat, both to the moral acceptance and the artistic emancipation of jazz. Let us oppose it to the end.

(British jazzman Steve Race, quoted in Rogers, 1982: 18)

Rock 'n' roll 'down under'

Although necessarily brief, this capsule view of the early history of rock 'n' roll is apposite, since the New Zealand experience I now turn to followed developments overseas, illustrating the rapid establishment of rock as an international phenomenon. This can be seen through New Zealand's response to the film *Rock Around the Clock*, and the emergence of the antipodean folk devil, the bodgie (for a fuller discussion of these, see Shuker and Openshaw 1991; the quotes here are from contemporary press reports). The local reaction in each case contained elements of a moral panic, with youth once again being constructed as posing a social problem.

As with their overseas counterparts, by the mid-1950s New Zealand youth were more visible and more affluent. Contemporary press advertising reflected increased awareness of youth as a distinctive market, particularly for clothes and records. Dances and concerts catering for youth increased, and the nationally broadcast *Lever Hit Parade* began in November 1955.

In late 1956 *Rock Around the Clock* arrived in New Zealand, and was approved for general exhibition by the film censor, who noted that 'a somewhat compulsive rhythm pervaded the film but otherwise there was nothing unusual about it'. Anticipation of similar scenes in New Zealand to the riots accompanying screenings of the film overseas

229

were rarely met. Despite press headlines such as 'Larrikins Take Over After Film', and 'Rock 'n' Roll Addicts in Minor Disturbance', the crowds attending screenings were in fact generally restrained. Indeed, there was almost an air of disappointment. The police, prepared for trouble, were present at and following some screenings, but were rarely needed. In Auckland, the country's main centre,

> in spite of a few policemen standing by, and the expectancy that had booked the cinema out, the first night's showing passed off with nothing more rowdy than some adolescent hand-clapping, some whistling and stamping, a little squealing in the rain after the show, and one charge of obstruction.
>
> (*Here and Now*, November 1956: editorial)

This was in spite of the cinema's provocative publicity for the film, which included a foyer display of press cuttings of the riots produced by the film overseas!

For most observers, rock 'n' roll was at worst a safety valve, and a passing craze: 'It does invite one to dance with hypnotic abandon and self-display, but to listen to it is more monotonous than boogie-woogie'! As occurred overseas, there was a tendency to see rock 'n' roll as:

> not a very attractive art form for those whose tastes have made any progress towards maturity. Prime requisites appear to be that the words – or sounds – should be meaningless and repetitive, while any semblance of melody is hastily and noisily murdered.
>
> (*Here and Now*, November 1956: editorial)

Generally, however, the press ignored the new phenomenon, while popular music on the radio remained largely confined to the numerous Maori show bands of the day, supplemented by a bit of jazz.

New Zealand's first real rock 'n' roll hero emerged in 1957: Johnny Devlin, an 18-year-old bank clerk. Devlin was a self-conscious Presley imitator, a natural singer and showman. His first record, 'Lawdy Miss Clawdy' became the most successful local single of the 1950s. Successful tours, including a hugely successful five-month national tour during 1958, saw sell-out houses, Devlin mobbed by screaming girls, and several incidents of damage to theatres and injuries to the police protecting the singer. While the tour subsequently assumed almost mythic proportions in the history of rock 'n' roll in New Zealand, there was clearly an element of media promotional hype present. Devlin, for example, wore lightly stitched clothing to facilitate the incidents where the fans 'ripped the clothes from his back'.

If both *Rock Around the Clock* and Johnny Devlin's concerts failed to measure up as local moral panics, the bodgies represented New Zealand's very own folk devils of the

1950s. Bodgies and widgies, their female companions, were the local equivalent of the English teddy boys, adopting similar styles:

> The males wore unusual and exaggerated haircuts. All went to extremes in the style of suits worn. The trousers were all much tighter in the legs than usual. Some favoured extreme shortness of leg exposing garishly coloured socks. Coats, when worn, were fuller in cut and much longer than is normal by conservative standards, while all favoured brightly coloured shirts, pullovers or wind-breakers, and neckerchiefs.
>
> (Manning, 1958: 9)

Although Manning makes little reference to the leisure pursuits of the group, other sources indicate that as in Britain rock 'n' roll was the musical style the bodgies most strongly identified with: Buddy Holly, Gene Vincent and Eddie Cochran joining earlier heroes like Haley.

Manning's was an openly hostile study; it is subtitled 'A Study in Psychological Abnormality'. The New Zealand public and press largely shared his view of bodgies as juvenile delinquents who posed a social threat. The bodgie soon became a national bogey man, with alarmist newspaper reports about bodgie behaviour. During 1958, one Wellington paper reported that 'the parade of brutality' by bodgies and widgies had reached such a peak that many parents were 'fearful of allowing their children out at night'. Gender inscribed these discourses: the hysteria provoked by Devlin was a predominantly female phenomenon, which received little serious criticism; the male bodgie was a different matter:

> When they are not feeling in too violent a mood they confine their activities to pushing people off footpaths. When looking for thrills, they fight among themselves, often with knives and bicycle chains.
>
> (press reports)

Bodgies became identified with hooliganism or vandalism, and Parliament debated the problem. Young compulsory military trainees on leave harassed and beat up bodgies, forcibly taking over bodgie milk bars in central Auckland, while incoming trainees with bodgie haircuts were initially left unshorn, resulting in harassment.

The bodgie threat was clearly an exaggerated one. In conformist New Zealand of the late 1950s, bodgies and widgies stood out. The surprising fact was not that New Zealand had young delinquents, 'but that they are relatively such a small group' (NZ *Listener*, editorial, 18 April 1958).

ROCK, FREE SPEECH, AND THE NEW RIGHT

During the mid-1980s, a general trend towards censorship emerged in the United States:

> an attack on the right of free speech, spearheaded by well-organized and well-financed pressure groups from the New Right. This anti-rock, pro-censorship campaign represents a power play by the New Right, particularly the religious right, to impose censorship, via ratings and arrests, on musicians, filmmakers and writers whose points of view they do not agree with or approve of.
>
> (Sluka, 1991)

While the New Right is a complex network of political, secular and religious organizations rather than a unified grouping, it exerts considerable influence through its letter writing and petition campaigns, its television and radio programmes, and the publications of its ideological think-tanks. The various New Right groups recognised that shared public concerns with social issues can be successfully mobilized to achieve and maintain political support and solidarity.

Such conservative groups have historically targeted youth subcultures, most notably punk, and rock music as a threat to traditional 'family' values (Martin and Seagrave, 1988: Chapter 21). The music is perceived as embodying a range of negative influences, which need to be regulated and controlled. It is claimed that rock is:

> the single most powerful tool with which Satan communicates his evil message. MURDER MUSIC has led millions of young people into alcoholism, abortion, crime, drug addiction, incest, prostitution, sadomasochism, satanic worshipping, sexual promiscuity, suicide and much more. MURDER MUSIC has to be STOPPED NOW! The moral fiber of our country and young lives are at stake!
>
> ('Rock deprogrammer', Pastor Fletcher Brothers,
> abridged from Denselow, 1990: 264)

Initially the anti-rock campaign was spearheaded by fundamentalist Christian groups, aligned with powerful right-wing pressure groups sponsored by television evangelists, such as the Reverend Jerry Falwell's 'Moral Majority' and 'Clean Up America Crusade'. While pushing for stricter censorship legislation, such groups enjoyed more success through pressure on the music producers and distributors. Tele-evangelist Jimmy Swaggart, after equating rock with 'pornography and degenerative filth which denigrates all the values we hold sacred and is destructive to youth', met with company representatives of the Wal-Mart discount chain, whose 800 outlets subsequently stopped stocking rock and teen magazines and albums by a number of bands, including Ozzy Osbourne and Motley Crue, because of their alleged 'satanic' and 'pornographic' content (Kennedy, 1990: 135).

The PMRC

The New Right attack on rock and free speech was boosted by the formation, in 1985, of the Parent's Music Resource Center (PMRC). Headed by a group of 'Washington wives' – most were married to senators or congressmen – who were also 'born again' Christians, the PMRC dedicated themselves to 'cleaning up' rock music, which they saw as potentially harmful to young people, terming it 'secondary child abuse'. One of the founding members, Tipper Gore, became involved because she had bought her 8-year-old daughter a copy of Prince's album *Purple Rain* and found that one of its songs, 'Darling Nikki', referred to masturbation ('I met her in a hotel lobby, masturbating with a magazine').

The PMRC published a *Rock Music Report*, condemning what they claimed to be the five major themes in the music: rebellion, substance abuse, sexual promiscuity and perversion, violence-nihilism, and the occult. They started a highly organised letter-writing campaign, and began arguing for the implementation of a ratings system for records, similar to that used in the cinema. The PMRC also sent copies of lyrics of songs they saw as objectionable to programme directors at radio and television stations, to be screened for 'offensive material', and pressed record companies to reassess the contracts of artists who featured violence, substance abuse, or explicit sexuality in their recorded work or concerts.

All these measures were aimed at encouraging self-censorship in the music industry, and the group's tactics met with considerable success. The highpoint of their efforts was the 1985 US Senate Commerce Committee hearings on the influence of music (see Denselow, 1990: Chapter 10). No legislation came out of the hearings, but the Record Industry Association of America voluntarily responded by introducing a generic 'Parental Advisory Explicit Lyrics' label to appear on albums deemed to warrant it, a practice that became widespread during the 1990s. The next major focus for the PMRC was the Dead Kennedys obscenity trial during 1986–7.

'Penis Landscape'

In December 1985 a 13-year-old girl bought a copy of the Dead Kennedys' album *Frankenchrist* (Alternative Tentacles, 1985) from a record shop in the San Fernando Valley in California. The record contained a poster entitled 'Penis Landscape' by Swiss surrealist artist H.R. Giger, best known for his Oscar-winning work on the sets of the film *Alien*. The work was a detail from a larger painting, *Landscape #20, Where Are We Coming From?* and depicted male appendages arranged in neat rows. Jello Biafra, the

233

Dead Kennedys' lead singer, explained that he had included the print because 'The painting portrayed to me a vortex of exploitation and I realised that the same theme ran through the album'. The band put an 'alternative' warning sticker on the album: 'WARNING; the fold-out to this album contains a work of art by H.R. Giger that some people may find shocking, repulsive or offensive. Life can sometimes be that way'. The girl's parents saw it differently, and complained to the State Attorney-General's Office that it was 'pornographic'. In April 1986 police raided Jello Biafra's home and the office of Alternative Tentacles Records, the label founded by the Dead Kennedys, looking for obscene material. None was found, but, in June, Biafra was eventually charged with distributing harmful material to minors, and the case finally went to trial in August 1987.

The Dead Kennedys had been the subject of controversy and the target of New Right censorship before. Formed in San Francisco in 1978, the band played a form of punk thrash music with politically hard-edged lyrics. Their first single 'California Uber Alles' was a satirical attack on State Governor Jerry Brown, and included lines like 'Your kids will meditate in school' and 'You will jog for the master race'. Later work included 'Holiday in Cambodia' about the horrors of the Pol Pot regime, and the anti-alcohol warning 'Too Drunk To Fuck', which gained chart success despite its title and the subsequent lack of radio airplay. Shunned by the mainstream record companies, while their name alone practically ensured commercial failure in the US, the Dead Kennedys' records enjoyed considerable success in the European 'indie' charts. Albums such as *Bedtime for Democracy* tackled political subjects like Reagan's foreign policy and the US censorship lobby, satirized MTV, and attacked American business involvement in South Africa. While the group's punk thrash backing and Biafra's breakneck delivery often made the lyrics almost unintelligible, this was hardly work to endear the band to the establishment.

Jello's trial in Los Angeles in 1987 was seen as a major test case for the censorship of popular music. Support from Frank Zappa and Little Steven, and a series of benefit shows from European punk bands, helped raise the $70,000 needed for defence costs. Biafra defended himself, and was articulate in his opposition to censorship, and his support for free speech. He argued that there was a danger that the US was returning to the climate of the 1950s, when anti-communist witch hunts led to the banning of an earlier political songwriter, Pete Seeger. The case ran for two weeks. The jury deadlocked (7 to 5) in Jello's favour, but could make no further progress, and the judge finally declared a mistrial (Kennedy, 1990: 144).

Even if it was a victory for free speech, the case had finished the Dead Kennedys. Already having internal problems, with Biafra tied up in the litigation process, and prevented from performing, the group broke up in December 1986. Biafra went on to a career as a 'political performance artist', doing monologue style presentations such as 'Ollie North for President'; the PMRC remained active, and went on to new targets.

234

Rap

In the early 1990s, rap music became the main target of the 'anti-rock, pro-censorship' lobby. The new genre had already been attacked from the left for its sexism and homophobia, and was now criticised for its profanity and obscenity. A judge in Florida declared the rap group 2 Live Crew's album *As Nasty as They Want to Be* to be obscene, the first such ruling for a recorded work in United States history. Following this, a record store owner was arrested when he sold the album to an undercover police officer, and three members of the band were arrested for performing material from the album at a concert with an 'adults only' rating. The band members were eventually acquitted of the obscenity charge, but the conviction of the store owner was upheld (Gilmore, 1990: 14).

The anti-authority political attitudes and values in some rap music also attracted the attention of the New Right. The Los Angeles rap group Niggaz With Attitude (NWA) song 'Fuck the Police' and Ice-T's song 'Cop Killer' both caused considerable controversy and calls to ban their performers' concerts and records. In the United Kingdom, in October 1990, NWA released a single with a B-side 'She Swallowed It', dealing with oral sex. Many of the major department store chains, and some music retailers, refused to stock the record, conscious of the lack of clarity surrounding the 1959 Obscene Publications Act, and fearing prosecution. In June 1991, NWA released their second album, *Efil4zaggin* (Niggaz 4 life, backwards) in the UK, after it had already topped the American *Billboard* chart and sold nearly a million copies in its first week of release. The album contained a number of tracks featuring sexual degradation and extreme violence toward women, along with considerable swearing. The police raided the premises of Polygram, the record's UK distributor, and seized some 12,000 copies of the album, and shops withdrew the album from sale. A prosecution followed, using the Obscene Publications Act's definition of an 'obscene article' as one which 'tend(s) to deprave and corrupt'. The high profile court case revolved around free speech arguments versus claims that the record was obscene, especially in its portrayal of women. The magistrates who judged the case ruled that the album was not obscene under the terms of the Act; the seized stock was returned and the album went back on sale (see Cloonan, 1996, for a detailed treatment of this episode, and the associated issues).

Cop Killer

Ice-T's 'Cop Killer' (WB, 1992) is a revenge fantasy of the disempowered, in which the singer recounts getting ready to 'dust some cops off'. The warning sticker on the tape cassette version of the album *Body Count*, which includes 'Cop Killer', hardly appeased critics of the record: 'Warning: This tape contains material that may be offensive to someone out there!' It was claimed that the song glorified the murder of police, and both

235

President Bush and Vice-President Dan Quayle sided with law-enforcement groups in protesting Time Warner's release of the record. Several US national record-store chains stopped selling *Body Count*, and, in July 1992, Time Warner pulled the song at Ice-T's request after police groups picketed the media conglomerate's shareholders meeting in Beverley Hills. Anxious to avoid governmental regulation, in September, Warner Music Group executives met with several of the rappers on the label, including Ice-T, and warned them to change their lyrics on some songs or find another label for their work (*Los Angeles Times*, 10 December 1992). Time Warner's Sire Records delayed the release of Ice-T's *Home Invasion* album; the performer eventually changed labels, and the album was released on Rhyme Syndicate/Virgin in 1993.

In New Zealand, in July 1992, the Police Commissioner unsuccessfully attempted to prevent an Ice-T concert in Auckland, arguing that 'anyone who comes to this country preaching in obscene terms the killing of police, should not be welcome here'. Several record shop owners refused to stock the album containing the song. The local music industry, student radio stations, and several leading music journalists responded by defending the song as a piece of 'role play', linking it with the singer's recent performance in the film *New Jack City* and the right to free speech. Undeterred, the police took *Body Count* and the song's publishers and distributors, Warners, to the Indecent Publications Tribunal in an effort to get it banned under New Zealand's Indecent Publications Act. This was the first time in 20 years that a sound recording had come before this censorship body, and the first-ever case involving popular music (previous sound recording cases before the Tribunal were 'readings' from erotic novels or memoirs). As such, it created considerable interest, not least due to the appeal of rap among the country's Polynesian and Maori youth (see Chapter 11).

The case rehearsed familiar arguments around the influence of song lyrics. The police contended that:

> given the content of the songs, it is possible that people could be corrupted by hearing the sound recording, and in the case of the song 'Cop Killer' that some individuals may be exhorted to act with violence towards the Police. The course of conduct advocated in the song 'Cop Killer' is a direct threat to law enforcement personnel generally and causes grave concern to the police.
>
> (H. Woods, Senior Legal Adviser for the New Zealand Police; cited in Indecent Publications Tribunal Decision No.100/92)

Defence submissions argued that the album offered a powerful treatment of the:

> sense of disenfranchisement and hopelessness that a large segment of American youth are faced with, and the violence that is bred in such an environment. It is a social commentary that we would like to believe is far removed from our society

here in New Zealand. But whether this is so or not, the album has a validity and topicality as a reflection of the disenfranchised segment of our society.

(Karen Soich, Warner Brothers counsel, ibid.)

After reviewing the various submissions, and listening carefully to the album, the Tribunal concluded that 'the dominant effect of the album is complex'. While 'its lyrics are repugnant to most New Zealanders, it is a much bigger step to link those lyrics to subsequent anti-social behaviour' (ibid.). It found the song 'Cop Killer' to be 'not exhortatory', saw the album as displaying 'an honest purpose', and found *Body Count* not indecent.

These moral panics around popular music can be situated against the global emergence of a New Right, embracing free market politics and a moral cultural conservatism. Grossberg observes of this trend in the United States:

> The new conservatism is, in a certain sense, a matter of public language, of what can be said, of the limits of the allowable. This has made culture into a crucial terrain on which struggles over power, and the politics of the nation, are waged.
>
> (Grossberg, 1992: 162)

As he concludes, this struggle involves a new form of regulation: 'a variety of attacks become tokens of a broader attack, not so much on the freedom of expression as on the freedom of distribution and circulation' (ibid.: 163). The earlier debates were reprised through the 1990s, in the controversy surrounding the work of performers such as Eminem, Dr Dre, and Marilyn Manson.

In such a climate, the music industry moved further toward self-regulation. In 2000, white rapper Eminem's US chart-topping album, *The Marshall Mathers LP*, was heavily criticized for its homophobic and misogynist lyrics. In what has become routine industry practice, the record label (Interscope/Universal) excised entire tracks to create an alternative album that parents can buy for their children, while extensively editing the lyrics in the remaining songs to eliminate references to drugs, violence, profanity and hate (*The New York Times on the Web*, 1 August 2000).

Columbine and Marilyn Manson

The massacre at Columbine High School in Littleton, Colorado, on 29 April 1999, resulted in 15 deaths and 23 injuries, some severe. The two young men responsible were students at the school, and killed themselves at the end of their bloody rampage. News coverage of the shootings was intense. Speculation about its causes referred to the negative influence of violent media on youth, especially video games; neo-Nazi ideology; and rock music (see the special forum in *Popular Music and Society*, 23, 3,

237

Fall 1999). When it was revealed that the two boys who killed their classmates were Marilyn Manson fans, the band cancelled their American tour. (Ironically, at the same time, the National Rifle Association went ahead with their national meeting in Denver.) For some commentators, Marilyn Manson became the 'designated demon' for the Columbine massacre. Manson responded with an articulate statement in *Rolling Stone* ('Columbine: Whose Fault Is It?', 24 June 1999: 23–4), observing that such simplistic associations missed the deeper reasons for the tragedy, which lay in youth disenchantment and alienation.

The latest in a succession of entertainers whose career is based on confrontation and shock value, Marilyn Manson (formerly Brian Warner) was accustomed to controversy. He and his band members play under aliases combining a famous woman's name with the last name of a serial killer; in Warner's case the well-known star Marilyn Monroe, and Charles Manson. The self-appointed 'Antichrist Superstar' (the title of the band's second album), has been termed 'one of rock's biggest personalities and smartest social commentators' (*Q*, January 2000: 118). In songs such as 'The Dope Show' and 'Beautiful People', he examined the underbelly of American life and popular culture. Their highly theatrical act, reminiscent of Alice Cooper, was designed to shock audiences. Along with the songs, it gained the group a cult following in the mid-1990s, mainly among the goth subculture. During 1997–8 *Antichrist Superstar* pushed them into the commercial mainstream, while Manson hit the headlines with his proclamations against organized religion. Their third album, *Mechanical Animals* (1998), topped the charts in a number of countries, but caused outrage when Manson appeared as a naked, sexless android on the cover and in the video for the single 'The Dope Show' (D. Dalton, 'Pleased to Meet You', *MOJO*, September 1999, provides an insightful analysis of Marilyn Manson's career and persona up until that time).

Controversy over particular musical styles, their performers and fans, continues to surface sporadically, with extreme metal the most recent example (Kahn-Harris, 2006). The debates around their influence and the associated calls for the censorship of popular music and its performers are a reminder of the force of music as symbolic politics, operating in the cultural arena. In related fashion is the use of popular music to assert and support political views and causes, with considerable debate around the role of music in these initiatives. I turn to these in the following chapter.

NOTES

General studies of the regulation and censorship of popular music include:

Cloonan, M. and Garofalo, R. (2003) *Policing Pop*, Philadelphia, PA: Temple University Press.

Cloonan, M. (1996) *Banned! Censorship of Popular Music in Britain: 1967–92*, Aldershot: Arena.

Denselow, R. (1990) *When The Music's Over: The Story of Political Pop*, London: Faber & Faber.

Garofalo, R. (1992a) *Rockin' the Boat: Mass Music & Mass Movements*, Boston, MA: South End Press.

Freemuse documents international instances of, and campaigns against, music censorship: www.freemuse.org.

Chapter 14

'Revolution'

Social change, conscience rock and identities

In the general sense of the word, 'politics' permeates popular music studies. Practically every aspect of the production and consumption of popular music involves theoretical debates about the dynamics of economic, cultural, and political power and influence, and the reproduction of social structures and individual subjectivity. In addition to ongoing debates over the perceived negative 'effects' and influence of popular music, there have always been attempts to harness the music to social and political ends, and arguments around the validity of notions of music as an empowering and political force. My discussion here is on the role of popular music in creating social change, and its mobilization within social movements. I consider several examples of direct political activism and the phenomenon of 'conscience rock'. A major issue in each case is the influence of such cultural interventions and the role of music in bringing about social change. The second part of the chapter introduces gender identity and sexual politics, primarily with reference to the place of women in rock music.

MUSIC AND SOCIAL CHANGE

A central problem in social theory has been to explain how cultures change, and to identify the forms of social activity at work in processes of social transformation. While there is considerable theoretical debate over the relative importance of social structures and human agency, a key part of social change are changes in the cognitive identity ('head space') of the individuals involved. Popular music has played a prominent role in articulating this process, at both the individual and collective group level. At various historical points, popular music has translated political radicalism into a more accessible idiom, identifying social problems, alienation and oppression, and facilitating the sharing of a collective vision. Performers and songs contribute to forging a relationship between politics, cultural change and popular music. Popular music has frequently acted as a powerful means of raising both consciousness about, and funds for, political causes. At the same time, however, there is a tendency for such popular music forms to be co-opted, marketed, and watered down or neutralized by the music industry.

Examples of popular music playing an overt political role include campaigns and interventions at several levels. Internationally, the global phenomenon of Live Aid in 1985 addressed the issue of famine in Africa, and the Mil Foundation and the various Concerts for Tibet (since 1995), initiated by the Beastie Boys, raised issues of repressive Chinese government policies in that country. Examples at a national level include the Campaign for Nuclear Disarmament movement in the UK in the late 1950s; civil rights and the anti-Vietnam war movement in the US in the 1960s; Rock Against Racism (RAR) in the UK in the late 1970s and early 1980s, and Rock Against Bush in 2004–6. I shall have more to say about several of these later.

Further, many artists have individually used their music to make political statements on a variety of issues, including racism, class, gender politics, sexuality, and environmental concerns. These are frequently within the strong historical tradition of protest song, particularly in folk music, which has been carried on in genres such as reggae, punk, and alternative music. Even stars usually regarded as purely commercial and 'apolitical', use their music to raise concerns. Within its pop ballad format and catchy tune, country star Shania Twain's 'Black Eyes Blue Tears' alerts listeners to domestic violence (for the lyrics, see the discussion of her career in Chapter 4).

Rock is the popular music genre most commonly associated with political potential, but there is disagreement as to the cultural significance and force of rock musicians' political statements and their role in various campaigns. For Grossberg, 'on the one hand, so much activity is attempting to explicitly articulate rock to political activism; on the other hand, this activity seems to have little impact on the rock formation, its various audiences or its relations to larger social struggles' (Grossberg, 1992: 168). This argument rests on a perceived 'radical disassociation' of the political content of the music of bands such as Rage Against the Machine, NOFX, and Midnight Oil 'from their emotionally and affectively powerful appeals' (ibid.). It is clear that many listeners derive pleasure from such performers without either subscribing to their politics, or, indeed, even being aware of them.

On the other hand, a variety of examples can be adduced to illustrate that many listeners *do* have their ideological horizons both confirmed and extended by association with political rock (see Garofalo, 1992a; Street, 1986; Denselow, 1990). This can also have practical benefits – the Amnesty International tours of 1988 are estimated to have added some 200,000 new members to the organization in the USA alone. However,

242

Gracyk, in his survey of such successes, is not confident of the revolutionary potential of rock music:

> Rock, infused with the mythology of rebellion, would seem to attract an audience who could actually rebel and overthrow the system. We are to conclude that middle-class white teens are attracted to counterculture music ... because it openly speaks of an oppressive system that they dare not confront; the temporary release comes from the frank admission that contemporary life sucks.
>
> (Gracyk, 1996: 158)

This is to see rock's frequent oppositional stance as diluted into symbolic consumption.

It has been argued that the history of such attempts to use popular music to forge mass movements will always face two problems. First, the power of popular music is transitory by nature, novelty and shock value have a short life span, and routinization and disempowering follows. Second, there is the confused nature of musical power's 'collectivity':

> The power of mass music certainly comes from its mobilization of an audience; a series of individual choices (to buy this record, this concert ticket) becomes the means to a shared experience and identity. The question, though, is whether this identity has any political substance.
>
> (Frith and Street, 1992: 80)

A further dimension of this question, is the tendency of many commentators to incorrectly assume that 'youth' represent some sort of 'natural left' political constituency. Furthermore, popular music is hardly the preserve of the political left and broadly progressive politics. It can, and has been, used to support a broad range of political positions. President Bush's inaugural performances have included impressive line-ups of blues and soul artists; white supremacist organizations like the National Front in the UK and neo-Nazi groups in Germany have used punk rock and hardcore bands to attract new recruits; and US anti-abortion activists have co-opted 'We Shall Overcome' to maintain solidarity at sit-ins outside abortion clinics.

I want to situate this debate in relation to three brief examples of the politics of rock; each a particular historical moment in what is a broader history (see Denselow, 1990; Street, 1986).

The 1960s: 'Give Peace a Chance'

The 1960s were a benchmark for popular music and political activism. Music played a role in the US civil rights movement of the early 1960s, the student protests of 1968, especially in Europe, and in the anti-Vietnam war movement. Musicians wrote, performed, and recorded songs about these events, and their commercial success drew wider attention to the issues involved. There are numerous examples; a few must suffice here:

- Crosby, Stills and Nash, 'Chicago', on the harsh treatment by the police of demonstrators at the Democratic Convention in that city in 1968.
- John Lennon, 'Give Peace a Chance' and 'Power to the People', whose chanted lyrics provided anthems for peace marches and rallies internationally.
- Marvin Gaye, 'What's Goin' On?' arguably the most politically explicit number one record ever.
- The Byrds, 'Turn! Turn! Turn! (To Everything There is a Season)', while this is not on the surface a protest song, Roger McGuin added the line 'a time of peace, I swear its not too late', to Pete Seeger's bible-based song lyrics.

The music often spoke directly to the soldiers in Vietnam, as with The Fugs, 'Kill for Peace'; CCR's 'Run Through the Jungle' and 'Fortunate Son', on the ability of middle-class youth to avoid the draft; The Doors, 'The Unknown Soldier'; and Edwin Starr, 'War', which spent three weeks at Number 1 on *Billboard* in 1969. At Woodstock in 1969, Jimi Hendrix deconstructed the US national anthem, 'The Star-Spangled Banner', as a series of sirens, explosions, and shrieking feedback.

As the Vietnam War escalated, opposition to it grew. Events at Kent State University, in Ohio in 1970, were a defining moment. The National Guard fired on student demonstrators, four were killed, and many more injured, several seriously. Responding the same night the news was broadcast, Neil Young composed 'Ohio' (The lyrics can be found on the Neil Young fan site : hyperrust.org; the song is on Neil Young, *Greatest Hits*, Reprise, 2004). Neil Young continued to mix personal introspection and political issues of the day throughout his career (see Echard, 2005). Most recently, he released *Living With War* (2006), featuring lyrics condemning Bush and the war in Iraq.

Of course, the impact of these songs is difficult to judge, and the meaning and clarity of their lyrics are at times unclear. Yet their commercial exposure, and the widespread media and public interest in them, suggested they certainly had an impact. As Graham Nash, who wrote 'Chicago', later observed: 'people like us probably don't have any real answers, but at least we brought up the questions' (*Get Up*, 2004).

Rock Against Racism (RAR)

RAR is a further example of such associations between music and politics, conducting a partially successful mass campaign to confront the racism arising in the harsh urban landscapes of inner-city Britain in the 1970s. The 1950s and 1960s had seen increased immigration to Britain from former colonies in the Asian sub-continent and the West Indies, but the new immigrant communities were often targeted by racist organizations such as the National Front. In the three years under a Labour government between 1974 and 1977, unemployment had risen sharply, especially amongst youth; the National Front gained support, and racial tension increased. As a later retrospective observed: 'Power blackouts. Endless strikes. Police brutality. Race riots. Currency freefalls ... the mood of the country was bleak and growing bleaker' (*Uncut*, UK music magazine February 2003).

RAR was formed against this background, following a provocative remark by Eric Clapton, during a concert, that Britain would become 'a black colony within ten years' (Szatmary, 1991: 231). RAR used demonstrations, concerts, a magazine, and records to mobilize upwards of half a million people: 'black and white people, outside conventional politics, inspired by a mixture of socialism, punk rock and common humanity, got together and organized to change things' (Widgery, 1986: 8). In February 1981 *Rock Against Racism's Greatest Hits* (Virgin Records) was the first album to be done as a political gesture since those from The Concert for Bangla Desh (1971). Leading groups and artists (Tom Robinson Band, the Clash) contributed to mass concerts and carnivals, and anti-National Front rallies, which served to politicize while entertaining. While the campaign failed to stop racist attacks, far less racism, it was a factor in the sharp decline of the National Front's share of the vote in the general election of 1979, following the fascist organization's surge of support in the mid-1970s.

RAR strengthened the idea that popular music could be about more than entertainment, and in a sense provided the inspiration for similar campaigns in the 1980s. But as Street notes, the RAR campaign illustrates 'the delicacy of the relationship between a cause and its music', as the reliance on the music as the source of unity and strength threw into sharp relief differences of stylistic affiliations. Political strategies were 'played out and resolved in terms of musical choices', a process which indicated 'the limitations of a politics organized around music' (Street, 1986: 78). Similar difficulties were evident in attempts to harness rock to the cause of the striking British miners in 1984–5, and with Red Wedge, the opposition Labour party's attempt to use rock to win the youth vote in the 1987 UK general elections. In both cases, strongly held views about the correct relationship of political principle and musical style arguably seriously limited the impact of the efforts (see Denselow, 1990: Chapter 8; Frith and Street, 1992).

Rock against Bush, 2004

A more recent example of the engagement of popular music directly in politics is the 2004 American presidential campaign. In 2004, several organizations worked to get young people to register to vote (Rock The Vote: www.rockthevote.com; Punk Voter: www.punkvoter.com). Some, including Punk Voter, were explicitly against President George Bush, who was running for another term of office. Their activities included web sites (Rock the Vote was originally created through MTV in 1990); concerts, and, in the case of Punk Voter, compilation albums: *Rock Against Bush*, volumes 1 and 2. The proceeds from these were used to support the concerts staged during the election year.

A number of punk bands were very active in these campaigns, including NOFX, whose singer Fat Mike (Michael Burkett) helped found Punk Voter. 'Mainstream' stars, too, were part of the Presidential race. Bruce Springsteen endorsed Democratic candidate John Kerry's campaign against Bush, and the star's song 'No Surrender' became its unofficial theme song. Springsteen performed it, along with 'Promised Land', at campaign rallies, referring to how 'Senator Kerry honors these ideals'. International media coverage featured images of Springsteen and Kerry, arms around each other, with press captions asking 'Who Will Be the Boss?' (*Dominion Post*, 30 October 2004) neatly linking the election outcome to the title Springsteen fans have long accorded the rock star.

The hugely successful country crossover trio, The Dixie Chicks, endorsed Rock The Vote, but became more directly involved when singer Natalie Maines confided to British fans at a London concert: 'Just so you know, we're ashamed the President of the United States is from Texas' – the band's home state. Her comment was widely reported in the international media, and, as *MOJO* put it, 'the Dixie Chicks went from being country darlings to being enemies of the state' (*MOJO*, October 2003: 44). The remark touched off an extreme response, with a considerable public backlash: radio stations, mainly in the American south, banned the group's new release; and attempts were made to boycott their concerts. In June 2006, as the war in Iraq continued to escalate, and US casualties to mount, the earlier episode and Maine's remark were reprised when the Chicks launched a new album (*Taking The Long Way*) and tour. A media marketing blitz, and numerous interviews with the group, used the 2003 episode as a starting point: did Natalie regret saying it? Was she surprised at the backlash? Of course, not only did this draw attention to Bush and American policy in Iraq, it also gave the Dixie Chicks a good deal of useful publicity: the album went to the top of the charts. After Bush was re-elected, criticism continued of his policies, particularly the war in Iraq. Musicians remained part of this.

CONSCIENCE ROCK

In the 1980s, questions about the viability of music in the direct service of organized political movements were addressed by a different style of cultural politics: the 'mega-events' (Garofalo, 1992b), or what I term 'conscience rock'. This new phenomenon of political rock saw popular musician stars joining and reinforcing international concern at the grim effects of mass famine in Africa, and taking up anti-nuclear, environmental, and other international causes. The list of causes here is now a long one, and includes The Concert for Bangla Desh, Live Aid, Sun City, Farm Aid, the Nelson Mandela tribute concerts, several Amnesty International tours, numerous Greenpeace concerts, and Music for Tibet. Such efforts are not purely political: Rock Against AIDS has raised awareness about the epidemic, and funds to help combat it.

Here I want to consider Live Aid in the1980s as an example of 'conscience rock', opening up the question of the political potential of popular music to raise consciousness and money for social interventions. Band Aid's 'Do they know it's Christmas?' was the first of a number of singles to raise public consciousness and funds to aid famine relief in Africa, and established the pattern and format for those that followed. While the very name of the effort conceded its limitations, given the scale of the problem, Band Aid proved far more successful than any of those involved had anticipated. Recorded by 37 UK and Irish pop stars in London in late November 1984, the record was perfectly timed for the British Christmas market; it sold about 10 million copies and raised about £8 million (Rijven and Straw, 1989: 200; see also Denselow, 1990: 244ff).

The record cover contrasted the well-to-do children of the West and the poverty of their Ethiopian counterparts. The back of the cover sleeve constructed and celebrated a brotherhood of rock, in contrast to the music press's usual stressing of the individual image of performers. USA (United Support of Artists) for Africa followed with 'We are the World'. The song title neatly suggested global interdependence, while its lyrics reaffirmed nineteenth-century charity: 'Its time to lend a hand to life, so let's start giving', adding an echo of the Beatles' idealism with 'and the truth, you know, love is all we need'. The single became CBS's fastest seller ever. Together with an album, videos and the sales of posters and T-shirts, United Support of Artists grossed $50 million dollars; the bulk of this went to famine relief and longer-term aid in Africa, with 10 per cent going to the hungry and homeless in the USA. A number of similar regional and national Band Aid singles followed.

On 13 July 1985 Live Aid was broadcast worldwide via television, directly from Sydney, Australia, Wembley Stadium in London, and the JFK stadium in Philadelphia. The performers included David Bowie, Queen, U2, and Paul McCartney in London; Eric Clapton, Duran Duran, and Bob Dylan in Philadelphia. With the assistance of Concorde, Phil Collins performed at both shows. Seven telecommunications satellites beamed the event live to an estimated one billion viewers in some 150 countries, including the Soviet Union and China. Viewers were encouraged to phone in to their national contact and pledge their contribution. The records and concerts shared an air of patriotism; the notion of each nation doing its bit for the common cause – 'donationalism', and collectively they emphasized a sense of community and togetherness.

The Band Aid phenomenon raised a host of questions about the motives of the celebrities involved, marketing politics, and the reasons for the overwhelming public response to charity rock in the mid-1980s. Much analysis was critical, finding 'the various charity projects tasteless, self-serving for those involved, symptomatic of existing geo-political relations and politically inappropriate' (Rijven and Straw, 1989: 206). There was also criticism that the lineup of artists performing at the two main Live Aid concerts consisted primarily of white stars, and the majority of the recordings reflected 'the same muzak characteristics, transparent frameworks built on the conventions of pop song writing that only sell because of the Band Aid connotation' (ibid.: 203). Pragmatic rock politics, observed Straw, were now taking on the crasser aspects of the pop music industry.

Such criticism reflected a tendency on the part of the political left to claim the moral high ground, and was rooted in a 'rock ideology' preoccupied with notions of sincerity and authenticity. This rather misses the point that Band Aid was not about music, and popular music as a focal point for youth, but rather about raising money and consciousness. The critics' preoccupation with credibility and ideological purity is accordingly misplaced. As Rijven goes on to observe, somewhat cynically, the Band Aid projects showed 'a high media sensibility that feeds on itself – charity opens all doors' (ibid.). This is to acknowledge the multi-media nature of such high profile public events, which became a feature of them in the 1990s.

Rijven concludes by critiquing Band Aid for 'a naive political attitude combined with a moral superiority' (ibid.: 204). This was certainly evident, though to go beyond it was expecting too much of the musicians involved. After all, how many people are aware of the international dynamics of the international economy and their contribution to the Ethiopian situation? At least charity/aid is a first step, even if based intially on a simple apolitical humanitarianism. Political sophistication comes later, as Bob Geldof himself found when investigating the use of the funds the Live Aid concert generated: 'he was inevitably involved in a crash course in food-aid politics, the realities of the African scene, the problems of debt, and an understanding of the strings often attached to aid offers from West or East, and the amounts Africa spends, and is encouraged to spend, on armaments' (Denselow, 1990: 246; see also Geldof, 1986).

As Straw puts it, 'rock's discourse on politics is primarily concerned with nudging people rather than instances of political intervention'. He makes the point, usually overlooked, that the participation of artists in the various Ethiopia records is in many ways less significant than the involvement of the music industries: 'The waiving of record label, distributor and retail profits is much more unprecedented and spectacular than the gathering of artists for charity purposes' (Rijven and Straw, 1989: 208, 204). Since this industry concession provided the bulk of the money to the cause, it rendered irrelevant the debates over the credibility, motives and sincerity of the artists involved. The cultural significance of Live Aid's 'We are the World' lay in its commercial form as much as in its political focus.

MUSIC AND GENDER POLITICS

Writing in 1977, Chapple and Garofalo describe a situation that has been slow to change:

> The absence of women as creators in pop music can be called sexist. Sexism is the systematic discrimination against and degradation of women, and the denial of equal power to women in human affairs. Sexism is as pervasive in rock music as in any other form of music. It pervades the structure of the music industry along with the lyrics and instrumentation of the music itself.
>
> (Chapple and Garofalo, 1977: 269)

This volume, and a number of studies since, provide numerous examples of the difficult struggle experienced by women in all phases of the music business. Through the 1980s and into the 1990s, analyses of the treatment of girls and women in popular music and youth subcultures continued to see them as absent, 'invisible' or socially insignificant. In addition, critics could point to the male-dominated musical canon in musicology (McClary, 1991), and the manner in which girl fans and their musical tastes are often denigrated (see Chapter 10).

There remains a clear tendency to marginalize women performers, and associated genres in the history of popular music. Compare, for example, the status accorded contemporaries Jim Morrison (heroic, romantic 'rock icon') and Janis Joplin ('a sad figure'), despite her critical and commercial success, which more than matched his in the late 1960s. A recent *MOJO* Special Issue, *ICONS* (2004) is typical of the popular construction of a gender-based canon. Of the 100 featured performers, only fourteen are women; of these, Madonna is at number six, followed by Kate Bush at 29, with most women performers placed toward the bottom of the list. It could be argued, of course, that this simply 'reflects' some sort of musical reality, but the interesting question is what lies behind such relative standings.

A related issue is the perceived masculine or feminine nature of particular genres/ styles. Dance pop is generally seen as 'a girls' genre', while hard rock and heavy metal are regarded as primarily male-oriented genres (see under sexuality, below). Women performers predominate in *a cappella* and gospel music, and are prominent in folk and

249

country, and among singer-songwriters. Male DJs are the norm in the contemporary dance music scene. How 'natural' are such associations, and in what ways are they social constructs?

Gaar (1992) provides a revisionist account placing gender to the fore, correctly contending that popular culture analysts and rock journalists have continued to largely ignore the contributions of women to rock. She includes 'girl' groups, individual women artists, singer-songwriters, and women involved in the rock press and record companies (see also O'Brien, 2002). And there is now a body of work seeking to understand and explain how and why genres such as rock and heavy metal are 'actively produced as male' (Cohen, 1997; see also Gracyk, 2001: Chapter 10; Whiteley, 2005).

The term 'women in rock' emerged as a media concept in the early 1970s, and has persisted despite being criticized as a 'generic mushy lump' (L. O'Brien, 1995: 3), unrelated to the wide variation among female performers, even those within the rock genre. There are two main dimensions: women as performers, and women in the music industry, with women being marginalized and stereotyped in both. There is a lack of women in the male-dominated music industry, with the majority in stereotypically 'female' roles (mainly as press and office personnel); there are few women working in A&R, or as producers, managers, and sound mixers (see Dickerson, 1998, for some instructive exceptions). Several explanations can be provided for this situation.

Cohen found that, in the Liverpool music scene she studied in the 1980s, women were not simply absent, but were actively excluded. All-male bands tended to preserve the music as their domain, keeping the involvement of wives and girlfriends at a distance.

> On several occasions I was informed that two things split up a band: women and money. Many complained that women were a distraction at rehearsals because they created tension within the band and pressured the band's members to talk to them or take them home.
>
> (Cohen, 1991: 209)

Paradoxically, of course, the success of many bands depended upon their appeal to female consumers, and male band members appreciated the fact that band membership helped make them attractive to women.

This situation reflects the more restricted social position of women, with greater domestic commitments and less physical freedom; the lack of encouragement given to girls to learn rock instruments; and rock sexuality as predominantly masculine. Consequently, through the 1980s there were few women bands in rock, or women instrumentalists, and, most women rock performers were 'packaged as traditional, stereotyped, male images of women' (Cohen, 1991: 203). This situation continued, although women rock bands became more common, especially in the alternative and indie music scenes, after the impact of Riot Grrrl in the 1990s (Carson *et al.*, 2004; Whiteley, 2006).

Bayton's discussion of 'women and the electric guitar' is a good example of the social processes at work here (Bayton, 1997). Her Oxford (UK) study showed only between two and four per cent of instrumentalists in local bands were women, and 'the reasons for women's absence are entirely social'. Gender socialisation teaches girls how to be 'feminine' and not to engage in 'masculine' activities:

> Playing the flute, violin, and piano is traditionally 'feminine', playing electric guitar is 'masculine'. On TV and in magazines, young women are presented with repeated images of men playing electric guitar; there are few female role models to inspire them.
>
> (Bayton, 1997: 39)

Further, compared to boys, teenage women lack money, time, space, transport and access to equipment. Even if a girl does take up the electric guitar, they have difficulty gaining access to the informal friendship groups within rock-music making, which are crucial learning environments. Guitar shops are 'male terrain' and nearly all of Bayton's interviewees regarded them as alien territory. The technology associated with the electric guitar – leads, amplifiers, plug boards – is strongly categorized as 'masculine', and presents another hurdle to female performers . The association of guitar playing with masculine prowess, the 'axe' as an extension of the male body, and playing it a pseudo-masturbatory act, consolidate its status as an exclusively 'masculine' idiom.

Riot Grrrl

In the early 1990s this gendered soundscape was challenged by the Riot Grrrl movement. Initially based in Washington, DC and Olympia, Washington, Riot Grrrl quickly became the focus of considerable media attention. Through fanzines and sympathetic role models among female musicians, Riot Grrrl asserted the need to break down the masculine mateship of the alternative and hardcore music scenes, which marginalized girls and young women. They drew on feminism and punk DIY ideology to question conventional ideas of femininity; and rejected rockist ideas of cool and mystique, challenging the view that enhanced technical virtuosity is necessary to create music. Some writers referred to them as 'punk feminists' (see Leonard, 1997). Riot Grrrl aimed to create a cultural space for young women in which they could express themselves without being subject to male scrutiny. They played with conflicting images and stereotyped conventions; e.g. the appropriation of 'girl' and their assertive use of the term 'slut'. Musically, the performers linked to the Riot Grrrl movement (e.g. L7,

Bikini Kill) sounded very like traditional hardcore and late 1970s punk bands, but their emphasis was on the process rather than the product.

Inspired in part by Riot Grrrl, a number of prominent women-led bands emerged during the 1990s, including Hole, Veruca Salt, and Echobelly. Performers associated with the 'angry women in rock' media tag of the mid-1990s, notably Alanis Morissette and Fiona Apple, selectively appropriated key concepts from Riot Grrrl with considerable commercial successs. Schilt (2003) argues that this represented the incorporation of Riot Grrrl, and a dilution of its oppositional politics. Other performers, however, remained more closely aligned to the founding philosophy, including Sleater-Keater, formed in 1995 (they broke up in June 2006), and Le Tigre, formed in 1998 by Kathleen Hanna, after she had left Bikini Kill. Along with their predecessors, these performers have remained linked to locally based labels, and continue to assert a political feminism in their work. Many contemporary local indie scenes, including Wellington, New Zealand, include bands that identify themselves with the Riot Grrrl label.

Sexuality

Popular music is also a significant area of culture in which sexual politics are struggled over. Sexuality refers to the expression of sexual identity, through sexual activity, or the projection of sexual desire and attraction. Sexuality and desire are central human emotions, or drives, which have been an essential part of the appeal of the culture/ entertainment industries, including popular music, and the social processes whereby performers and their texts operate in the public arena.

Sexuality is central to discussions of how male and, more frequently, female performers are conceived of – socially constructed – as sex objects or symbols of desire. Here certain forms of subjectivity and identity are projected as 'normal', traditionally white, male heterosexuality. The operation of this process is a major focus in studies of music video and stardom, and in relation to particular genres of music. It involves considerations of the nature of spectatorship and the (gendered) gaze, utilizing conventions primarily developed in film studies (see the discussion of music videos in Chapter 5).

The debates here are most evident in the discourse surrounding Madonna's early career (see Schwichtenberg, 1993). Christina Aguilera utilizes similar modes of sexual expression to Madonna, and situates herself in the now-familiar debate. On the one hand, she is presenting her body as an object for the male gaze and voyeuristic desire, through provocative poses in CD sleeve booklets (*Stripped*, 2002) and magazine covers and stories. On the other, she is subverting dominant patriarchal attitudes and practices in her work. While Aguilera's songs follow the standard heterosexual romantic narrative (woman falls in love with/desires a man), she is also 'voicing compelling feminist notions of female independence, autonomy and sexual expression' (Smith, 2003: unpaginated), on songs such as 'Can't Hold Us Down' (on *Stripped*). Other women performers to use their careers to comment on female sexuality, vulnerability and power include Polly Harvey, Tori Amos, and Björk (Whiteley, 2005). At times, more 'mainstream' artists also grasp the opportunity to present assertive messages, as in Destiny Child's huge hit 'Independent Women' in 2001.

Sexual ambiguity is central to many forms of popular music, which has frequently subverted the dominant sexuality constructed around male–female binaries. Discussion has concentrated on exploring the relationship between sexual orientation, public personas, and a performer's music. Some performers openly represent or subvert and 'play with' a range of sexualities. Others constitute themselves, at times very self-consciously, as objects of heterosexual desire, or as icons for different ('deviant'?) sexualities and their constituencies. Several 1950s male stars were 'adored objects', catering to both homosexual desire and female consumption; e.g. Elvis Presley, Fabian. Later performers include representations of the homoerotic (e.g. Madonna, Morrissey); androgyny (Bowie during the Ziggy period), the effeminate (the Cure), and asexuality (Boy George); bi-sexuality (Morrisey again, Suede); and gay and lesbian (The Village People; Freddie Mercury; k.d. lang). The application of such labels, their connotations, and their relationship to actual gay communities have been at times strongly contested (see Geyrhalter, 1996; Hawkins, 2002; Whiteley *et al.*, 2004).

Some genres and performers are linked to particular sexualities/communities. Disco, for example, generally celebrates the pleasure of the body and physicality, and is linked to the gay community and specific club scenes; heavy metal has traditionally been associated with overt masculinity, as has hard rock – so dominated by male performers, it has even been referred to as 'cock rock' (Frith and McRobbie, 1990 [1978]). Walser argues that heavy metal has historically been actively *made* as male, and acts to 'reproduce and reflect patriarchal assumptions and ideologies' that underpin western society (1993: 111). He suggests that heavy metal bands promote male bonding and legitimate male power through a combination of misogyny (in song lyrics, videos) and exscription: the creation through the music, album covers, and videos of fantasy worlds without women, where male heroes battle against monsters and superhuman villains (ibid.:110). Arnett observes that even though some heavy metal fans are women, their involvement is often through a boyfriend, or due to the sexual attraction they feel toward the performers or fans; consequently they struggle 'to reconcile their enthusiasm for Heavy Metal with their sense of being not quite welcome in that world' (Arnett, 1996: 140).

As with political rock, there is considerable argument over how the lyrics and the associated cultural values in 'gendered' musical texts are understood and responded to by their listeners, audiences, and fans. Are the artists intended or preferred readings, embedded in the text, acknowledged, let alone assimilated into individual and social values and meanings?

253

CONCLUSION

The examples in this chapter show that the issue of the political role of popular music is hardly an 'either–or' argument. For every case of a performer, genre, text, or consumer constrained and regulated by gender expectations, capital, pressure groups, and the state, there are counter-examples of the successful use of the music to raise political consciousness, and finance political causes, and movements. In terms of cultural politics, popular music is a site of cultural struggle, with constant attempts to establish dominance, exploit cultural contradictions, and negotiate hegemony.

NOTES

General (see also the Notes to Chapter 13):
Gracyk, T. (2001) *I Wanna Be Me: Rock Music and the Politics of Identity*, Philadelphia, PA: Temple University Press.
Lipsitz, G. (1994) *Dangerous Crossroads: Popular Music, Postmodernism and the Poetics of Place*, London and New York: Verso.
Widgery, D. (1986) *Beating Time: Riot'n'Race'n'Rock'n'Roll*, London: Chatto & Windus.
Get Up, Stand Up. The Story of Pop and Politics, A Dora Production, 2004 (documentary series; also available on DVD).
The Dixie Chicks (2006) *Shut Up and Sing*, Directed by Barbara Kopple and Cecillia Peck. Cabin Creek Films, USA.
Web site: www.freemuse.org.

Gender and sexuality:
Key readings here include those collected in:
Frith, S. and Goodwin, A. (1990) *On Record*, London: Routledge.
Whiteley, S. (1997) *Sexing the Groove: Popular Music and Gender*, London and New York: Routledge.

See also:
Whiteley, S. (2000) *Women and Popular Music: Sexuality, Identity and Subjectivity*, London: Routledge.
Carson, M., Lewis, T. and Shaw, S.M. (2004) *Girls Rock! Fifty Years of Women Making Music*, Lexington, KY: The University Press of Kentucky.

Ethnicity (especially in relation to rap and hip-hop):
A related topic that I have not had space to explore here, is the relationship between music and ethnicity; see:
Forman, M. (2002) *The 'Hood Comes First. Race, Space, and Place in Rap and Hip-Hop*, Middletown, CT: Wesleyan University Press.

Gilroy, P. (1993) *The Black Atlantic: Modernity and Double Consciousness*, Cambridge, MA: Harvard University Press.

Hebdige, D. (1990) *Cut'N'Mix: Culture, Identity, and Caribbean Music*, London: Comedia/Routledge.

Ramsey, G.P. (2003) *Race Music: Black Cultures from Bebop to Hip-Hop*, Berkeley, CA: University of California Press.

Neal, M. (1999) *What the Music Said: Black Popular Music and Black Public Culture*, New York and London: Routledge.

Conclusion: 'Wrap it Up'
Popular music and cultural meaning

M y own location in pop culture, as a 'post-war baby boomer', illustrates the point that our response to popular music, and the various attempts to document and analyse it, is far from a purely intellectual one. Analysis and documentation cannot be divorced from the volatile and contested area of emotions and popular memory. My own emotional ties to the music and artists of the late 1960s, to subsequent styles and performers reminiscent of these, and to the notion of popular music as a politically significant cultural force, are clearly discernable in this account.

The core question I have addressed is: 'how is meaning produced within popular music culture?' Cultural interpretations and understandings are embedded in musical texts and performances: records, tapes, music videos, concerts, radio airplay, Internet downloads, film soundtracks, and so on. Such meanings are, in one sense, the creations of those engaged in making the music in these diverse forms, but they are also the result of how the consumers of these forms interact with the music. Further, music texts and performances are cultural commodities, produced largely by an international music industry ultimately concerned with maximizing profits. Meanings, or, rather, particular sets of cultural understandings, are produced by a complex set of interactions between these factors. Accordingly, the question of meaning in popular music cannot be 'read off' purely at one level, be it that of the industry, the aesthetic creators, the musical texts, or the audience. It can only be satisfactorily answered by considering the nature of the production context, including state cultural policy; the texts and their creators, and the consumers of the music and their spatial location. Most importantly, it is necessary to consider the interrelationship of these factors. Of course, to facilitate discussion, the very organization of this text has tended to perpetuate the notion

257

that these are indeed discrete aspects, although I have stressed throughout the links between them.

It is not possible to baldly state a model of the interrelationship between these aspects, or to claim primacy for any one of them in every case of the process whereby meaning is determined in popular music. I am convinced that an argument can be made for the overarching influence of political economy and the significance of the production context, including its technological aspects. While this is a persuasive perspective, it needs to be qualified. The commodity from which music takes, and the capitalist relations of mass industrial production under which commercial music is created, significantly affect the availability of particular texts and the meanings which they embody. However, such determination is never absolute: meanings are mediated, the dominant meanings of texts subverted, and 'alternatives' to 'mainstream', commercial music are always present. Accordingly, popular music must be seen as a site of symbolic struggle in the cultural sphere.

Appendix 1
The chapter song titles

Using US labels and release dates:

    Introduction: 'What's Goin' On?'. Marvin Gaye, Tamla, 1967. Produced by Marvin Gaye; written by Al Cleveland, Marvin Gaye, and Renaldo Benson.

1   'Every 1's a Winner'. Hot Chocolate, Infinity, 1978. Produced by Mickie Most; written by Errol Brown.

2   'Pump Up the Volume'. M/A/R/R/S, Fourth and Broadway, 1987. Produced by Martyn Young; written by Martyn and Steve Young.

3   'I'm Just a Singer (in a Rock'n'Roll Band)'. The Moody Blues, Threshold, 1973. Produced by Tony Clarke; written by Ray Thomas.

4   'So You Want to be a Rock 'n' Roll Star!'. The Byrds, Columbia, 1967. Produced by Gary Usher; written by Roger McGuinn and Chris Hillman.

5   'Message Understood'. Sandy Shaw, Pye, 1965. Produced by Eve Taylor, Chris Andrews and Sandy Shore; written by Chris Andrews.

6   'It's Still Rock and Roll to Me'. Billy Joel, Sony, 1977. Written by Billy Joel; producer uncredited.

7   'Shop Around'. The Miracles, Motown, 1960. Written and produced by Smokey Robinson and Berry Gordy.

8   'U Got the Look'. Prince, Paisley Park, 1987. Written and produced by Prince.

9   'On the Cover of *The Rolling Stone*'. Dr Hook and the Medicine Show, Columbia, 1972. Produced by Ben Affkine; written by Shel Silverstein.

10   'My Generation'. The Who, Decca, 1966. Produced by Shel Talmy; written by Pete Townshend.

11   'Sound of our Town'. The Del Fuegos, Slash, 1985. Produced by Mitchell Froom; written by Dan Zanes.

12   'We Are the World'. USA for Africa, Columbia, 1985. Produced by Quincy Jones; written by Michael Jackson and Lionel Richie.

13   'Pushin' Too Hard'. The Seeds, GNP Crescendo, 1966. Producer not credited; written by Sky Saxon.

14   'Revolution'. The Beatles, Apple, 1968. Produced by George Martin; written by John Lennon and Paul McCartney.
       Conclusion: 'Wrap it Up'. Sam and Dave, Stax, 1968. Written and produced by Isaac Hayes and David Porter.

Appendix 2
Musical analysis

The main sonic elements of music are rhythm (beat); melody; harmony; and, in songs, the voice. Also relevant to popular music are the related elements of riffs, hooks, and lyrics. These are considered briefly here in relation to their applicability in popular music. Fuller accounts of them, and other musical terms, can be found in the glossaries and accompanying discussions in Beard and Gloag, 2005; Charlton, 1994; Middleton, 1990; Moore, 1993; and, especially helpful, Tagg (Tagg, Philip: www.tagg.org).

Rhythm is the beat patterns underlying most forms of communication, pulses of varying lengths of time. Rhythms are often recurring or repetitive (as in a heartbeat) and follow a consistent pattern. In music, rhythm patterns generally indicate the emotional feel of different types of song; e.g. slow connotes emotional. A rhythm section is the group of musical instruments that maintain the beat pattern and the harmonic flow of a piece of music; these usually include drums, bass, and guitar/keyboards. The tempo is the pace of the beat. With popular music styles that include percussion, the rhythm is best followed by listening to the drums, and counting the beat aloud. The backbeat is beats two and four of a four-beat pattern, the accenting of which creates rock's basic rhythm.

Melody is an organized set of notes consisting of different pitches (high or low sounds). The melody of a song is what we would be singing if we substituted the syllable la for all the regular syllables. Melody is the variation in the lead singer's voice, without accompaniment. Various melodies are present in popular music forms: the main melody (sung by the lead singer). Background melodies (sung by other group members, or backup singers), and bass melodies.

261

Harmony is the simultaneous sounding of two or more different notes at the same time, e.g. guitar chords, blocks of notes on the piano, and the sounds of a chorus. The easiest place to hear harmonies is in the background melodies. Harmony varies from simple to complex, and often delineates one style from another. Harmony is important in popular music because it provides the texture of the total sound; it has been prominent in genres emphasizing vocals, such as *a cappella* and doo wop. Related to rhythm and harmony are riffs and hooks. The *hook* is the melodic or rhythmic pattern that is catchy and 'hooks' or attracts the listener to want to listen to the rest of the song, and, more importantly, want to hear it repeated. Hooks are central to commercially oriented popular music (see Burns, 1987). A *riff* is a short melodic or rhythmic pattern repeated over and over while changes take place in the music along with it. This 'sonic repetition' is a feature of number of 'classic' popular music records, most notably in The Rolling Stones 'Satisfaction'.

Voice: 'Popular music is overwhelmingly a "voice music". The pleasures of singing, of hearing singers, is central to it', and 'there is a strong tendency for vocals to act as a unifying focus within the song' (Middleton, 1990: 261, 264). Discussions of the role of the voice within popular music have focused on the relationship between lyrics, melodic types, and the singing styles characteristic of various genres and performers. Vocal timbre is part of this: tone quality as it relates to the characteristic differences among singing voices. A key concept is the 'grain' of the voice, very broadly its feeling, as opposed to the direct meaning of lyrics, and the way in which particular styles of voice convey certain sets of emotions, often irrespective of the words they are singing.

A number of authors have discussed how the voice is used in popular music, particularly with regard to rock. Three main aspects are evident. Firstly, attempts to distinguish between 'black' and 'white' voices, which tend to see the 'black' voice as demonstrative and communicating through a variety of vocal techniques, and the 'white' voice as more restrained and restricted. A second distinction is between 'trained' and 'untrained' voices, with the former found in a range of older popular musical styles rather than more contemporary forms. The 'untrained' voice is important in signifying authenticity in rock vocals, indicating effort, naturalness, and a lack of artifice. A third approach has been to associate specific genres with vocal styles, which are linked in turn to gender.

Moore argues that such distinctions are problematic because of their essentialist assumptions: 'they emphasise only one aspect of vocal production, and attempt to read meaning into the voice's presence on the basis of that single aspect', ignoring that a multitude of factors characterizes a vocal style (1993: 42). He suggests and elaborates four such factors: the register and range which any particular voice achieves; its degree of resonance; the singer's 'heard attitude' to pitch; and the singer's heard attitude to rhythm. Moore usefully illustrates these through a discussion of the vocal styles of Bill Haley, Little Richard, Fats Domino, and Elvis Presley. As Frith (1996) observes, it is the way in which singers sing, rather than what they sing, that is central to their appeal to listeners. Compare, for instance, the vocal styles of Elvis Presley, Björk, Margot Timmins (the Cowboy Junkies), Johnny Rotten (Sex Pistols), and Mick Jagger.

For most listeners, their response to popular music is 'a gut thing', at the level of the affective rather than the intellectual. While fans do intellectualize about the music, their attempts to do so are very much in terms of their physical and emotional response to it. Here students can be encouraged to interrogate the process of their listening: the foot-tapping or finger drumming response to the beat; the singing along with the chorus of well-known songs; the air guitar; and the abandonment of restraint through various modes of dance. Emotional associations, the links forged between people, places, moods, and particular songs means the experience of the song becomes polymorphous. Nor should the importance of the listening context be forgotten here. One of the major problems of classroom analysis of popular music, is that the relatively sterile environment and the anchoring of the physical body in place are far removed from the normal contexts in which the music is consumed – the pub, the club, the concert hall, and the home.

Appendix 3
The album canon

1985–99	Album	Musician(s)	Year
1	*Revolver*	The Beatles	1966
2	*Sgt. Pepper's Lonely HeartsClub Band*	The Beatles	1967
3	*Nevermind*	Nirvana	1991
4	*The Beatles*	The Beatles	1968
5	*Pet Sounds*	The Beach Boys	1966
6	*Abbey Road*	The Beatles	1969
7	*Dark Side Of The Moon*	Pink Floyd	1973
8	*The Velvet Underground & Nico*	The Velvet Underground	1967
9	*Blonde on Blonde*	Bob Dylan	1966
10	*OK Computer*	Radiohead	1997
11	*Astral Weeks*	Van Morrison	1968
12	*Exile On Main St.*	Rolling Stones	1972
13	*What's Going On*	Marvin Gaye	1971
14	*Never Mind The Bollocks…*	The Sex Pistols	1977
15	*Highway 61 Revisited*	Bob Dylan	1965
16	*The Joshua Tree*	U2	1987
17	*The Bends*	Radiohead	1995
18	*The Stone Roses*	The Stone Roses	1989
19	*London Calling*	The Clash	1979
20	*Blood On The Tracks*	Bob Dylan	1975
21	*Are You Experienced?*	Jimi Hendrix Experience	1967
22	*The Queen Is Dead*	The Smiths	1986
23	*Automatic For The People*	R.E.M.	1992
24	*Rumours*	Fleetwood Mac	1977
25	*Achtung Baby*	U2	1991
26	*Ten*	Pearl Jam	1992
27	*Born To Run*	Bruce Springsteen	1975
28	*Rubber Soul*	The Beatles	1965
29	*Let It Bleed*	Rolling Stones	1969
30	*(What's The Story) Morning Glory?*	Oasis	1995

Source: adapted from Von Appen and Doehring, 2006: 23

Appendix 4
Discography

For convenience, I have included only albums currently available on CD. The listing is obviously highly selective, and represents those artists/work I feel are representative of the popular music discussed in this volume; i.e. largely Anglo-American and since World War II. Following a common approach, presentation is primarily by 'decades'.

THE ANTECEDENTS OF ROCK 'N'ROLL

Blues

Robert Johnson, *The Complete Recordings*, Columbia, 1990.
Bessie Smith, *The Complete Recordings*, Columbia/Legacy, 1991.
Muddy Waters, *His Best 1947 to 1955*, Chess, Legendary Masters Series, 1997.
Howlin' Wolf, *Howlin' Wolf*, Chess/MCA, 1984.

R&B and gospel

Atlantic R&B 1947–1974, Atlantic, 1991.
Ruth Brown, *Rockin' in Rhythm: The Best of Ruth Brown*, Rhino, 1996.
Louis Jordan, *The Best of Louis Jordan*, MCA, 1989.
Big Joe Turner, *Big Bad and Blue*, Rhino, 1994.

Country and bluegrass

The Carter Family, *The Carter Family: Country Music Hall of Fame Series*, MCA, 1991.

Hank Williams, *40 Greatest Hits*, Polydor, 1988.

Rob Willis and his Texas Playboys, Anthology 1935–1973, Rhino, 1991.

THE 1950s

Chuck Berry, *The Great Twenty-eight*, Chess, 1984.

Johnny Cash, *The Sun Years*, Rhino, 1991.

Ray Charles, *The Birth of Soul*, Atlanta, 1991.

The Everly Brothers, *Cadence Classics*, Rhino, 1985.

Buddy Holly, *20 Golden Greats*, MCA, 1978.

Jerry Lee Lewis, *Anthology: All Killer No Filler*, Rhino, 1993.

Little Richard, *18 Greatest Hits*, Rhino, 1985.

Elvis Presley, *The Complete Sun Sessions*, RCA, 1987.

Elvis Golden Records, RCA, 1984.

Various Artists, *Loud, Fast & Out of Control: The Wild Sounds of '50s Rock*, Rhino, 1998 (4CD Boxed Set).

THE 1960s

The Animals, *The Best of the Animals*, MGM, 1966 (reissued on Abko).

The Band, *The Band*, Capitol, 1969.

The Beach Boys, *Pet Sounds*, Capitol, 1966.

The Beatles, *The Beatles/1962–1966*, Capitol, 1973.

The Beatles, *Sgt. Pepper's Lonely Hearts Club Band*, 1967.

James Brown, *20 All-Time Greatest Hits!*, Polydor, 1991.

The Byrds, *The Byrds Greatest Hits*, Columbia, 1967.

Cream, *Wheels of Fire*, Polydor, 1968.

Creedence Clearwater Revival, *Creedence Gold*, Fantasy, 1972.

The Doors, *The Best of the Doors*, Elektra, 1991.

Bob Dylan, *Highway 61 Revisited*, Columbia, 1965.

Aretha Franklin, *I Never Loved a Man the Way I Love You*, Atlanta, 1962.

The Grateful Dead, *American Beauty*, Warner Brothers, 1970.

The Jimi Hendrix Experience, *Electric Ladyland*, Reprise, 1968.

Led Zeppelin, *Led Zeppelin II*, Atlantic, 1969.

Otis Redding, *Otis: The Definitive Otis Redding*, Atlantic/Rhino, 1993.

The Rolling Stones, *Big Hits (High Tide and Green Grass)*, ABKO, 1966.

Phil Spector, *Back to Mono (1958–1969)*, ABKO, 1991.

Dusty Springfield, *Dusty in Memphis*, Rhino, 1969.
The Supremes, *Anthology*, Motown, 1974.
Various Artists, *The Best of the Girl Groups, Vol. 1&2*, Rhino, 1990.
The Who, *Meaty, Beaty, Big & Bouncy*, MCA, 1971.

THE 1970s

Aerosmith, *Rocks*, Columbia, 1976.
The Allman Brothers, *At Fillmore East*, Capricorn, 1971.
Black Sabbath, *Paranoid*, Warner Brothers, 1971.
Blondie, *Parallel Lines*, Chrysalis, 1978.
David Bowie, *Hunky Dory*, REC, 1971.
Jackson Browne, *Jackson Browne*, Asylum, 1972.
The Clash, *London Calling*, Epic, 1979.
The Eagles, *Hotel California*, Elektra/Asylum, 1976.
Fleetwood Mac, *Rumours*, Warner Brothers, 1977.
Marvin Gaye, *What's Goin' On*, Tamla, 1971.
Al Green, *Greatest Hits*, Hi, 1972.
The Harder They Come (Film Soundtrack), Mango/Island, 1972.
Elton John, *Greatest Hits*, MCA, 1974.
Carole King, *Tapestry*, ODE/CBS, 1971.
Kraftwerk, *Trans-Europe Express*, Capital, 1977.
Bob Marley and the Wailers, *Burnin'*, Tuff Gong/Island, 1973.
Van Morrison, *Moondance*, Warner Brothers, 1970.
Randy Newman, *12 Songs*, Reprise, 1970.
Ramones, *Ramones*, Sire, 1976.
The Rolling Stones, *Exile on Main Street*, Virgin, 1972.
Joni Mitchell, *Blue*, Reprise, 1971.
Pink Floyd, *Dark Side of the Moon*, Capitol, 1973.
Saturday Night Fever (Film Soundtrack), RSO/Polygram, 1977.
The Sex Pistols, *Never Mind the Bollocks Here's the Sex Pistols*, Warner Bros., 1977.
Rod Stewart, *Every Picture Tells a Story*, Mercury, 1971.
Stevie Wonder, *Innervisions*, Tamla/Motown, 1973.
Neil Young, *After the Gold Rush*, Reprise, 1970.

THE 1980s

Abba, *Abba Gold, Greatest Hits*, Polydor, 1992.
Afrika Bombaataa and the Soulsonic Force, *Planet Rock*, Tommy Boy, 1986.
Bon Jovi, *Slippery When Wet*, Mercury, 1986.

De La Soul, *Three Feet High and Rising*, Tommy Boy, 1989.

Eurythmics, *Greatest Hits*, Warner, 1991.

Guns 'N' Roses, *Appetite For Destruction*, Uzi Suicide/Geffen, 1987.

Michael Jackson, *Thriller*, Epic, 1982.

Joy Division, *Closer*, Factory, 1980 (reissued on Qwest).

Madonna, *Like a Prayer*, Sire, 1989.

Prince, *Purple Rain*, Warner Bros., 1984.

Public Enemy, *It Takes A Nation Of Millions to Hold Us Back*, Def Jam, 1989.

REM, *Document*, IRS, 1987.

The Smiths, *The Smiths*, Rough Trade/Sire, 1984.

Bruce Springsteen, *Born in the USA*, Columbia, 1984.

The Stone Roses, *Complete Stone Roses*, Geffen/Silverstone, 1995.

Talking Heads, *Stop Making Sense*, Sire, 1984.

U2, *The Joshua Tree*, Island, 1987.

THE 1990s

Beck, *Odelay*, Geffen/DCG, 1996.

Björk, *Post*, Polydor, 1995.

Garth Brooks, *No Fences*, Capital, 1990.

Jeff Buckley, *Grace*, Columbia, 1994.

Celine Dion, *Falling Into You*, Epic, 1996.

Bob Dylan, *Time Out of Mind*, Columbia, 1998.

The Fugees, *The Score*, Columbia, 1996.

Hole, *Live Through This*, DGC, 1994.

Madonna, *Ray of Light*, Maverick/Warner, 1998.

Massive Attack, *Blue Lines*, Virgin, 1991.

Sara McLachlan, *Fumbling Towards Ecstasy*, Arista, 1994.

Alanis Morissette, *Jagged Little Pill*, Maverick/Warner, 1995.

My Bloody Valentine, *Loveless*, Sire, 1991.

Nine Inch Nails, *Pretty Hate Machine*, TVT, 1989.

Nirvana, *Nevermind*, Sub Pop/DGC, 1991.

Oasis, *What's The Story Morning Glory?*, Creation/Epic, 1995.

Liz Phair, *Exile in Guyville*, Matador/Shock, 1993.

Pearl Jam, *VS*, Epic, 1993.

Rage Against The Machine, *Los Angeles*, 1999.

REM, *Automatic for the People*, Warner, 1992.

Roni Size/Reprazent, *New Forms*, Talkin Loud, 1998.

The Smashing Pumpkins, *Siamese Dream*, Virgin, 1993.

The Spice Girls, *Spice World*, Virgin, 1997.

Shania Twain, *Come On Over*, 1999.
U2, *Achtung Baby*, Island, 1991.

THE 2000s

Arcade Fire, *Funeral*, Rough Trade, 2006.
The Artic Monkees, *Whatever People Say I Am, That's What I'm Not*, Domino, 2006.
Christina Aguilera, *Stripped*, RCA, 2002.
Coldplay, *A Rush of Blood to the Head*, Parlophone, 2003.
Ry Cooder, *Chavez Ravine*, Nonesuch, 2005.
The Darkness, *Permission to Land*, Must Destroy/Atlantic, 2003.
Destiny's Child, *Survivor*, Sony, 2000.
Franz Ferdinand, *Franz Ferdinand*, Domino, 2004.
Goldfrapp, *Black Cherry*, Mute, 2003.
Outkast, *Speakerbox/The Love Below*, La Face/Arista, 2003.
The Shins, *Chutes Too Narrow*, Sub Pop, 2003.
Bruce Springsteen, *Devils and Dust*, Columbia, 2005.
Gwen Stefani, *Love Angel Music Baby*, Interscope, 2005.
Justin Timberlake, *Justified*, JIVE, 2003
Ali Farka Toure, *Savane,* One World Circuit, 2006.
Kanye West, *Late Registration*, Roc-A-Fella/Def Jam, 2005.
The White Stripes, *Elephant*, Third Man/XL, 2003

Further resources and bibliography

In addition to the books and articles listed here, I have made extensive use of music magazines and the Internet. These provide current and often extensive information on particular music scenes, genres, and performers, and the activities of record companies.

MUSIC MAGAZINES

Billboard
Guitar Player
ICE: The CD News Authority
Melody Maker
MOJO
Music Week
NME
Q
Record Collector
Rolling Stone (US and Australian editions; especially the annual yearbook)
UNCUT
Vibe

In addition to their print versions, several of these have websites, see below.

SELECTED WEBSITES

Note that these are subject to change; an enormous number of other sites can be accessed through these. More specialist websites have been indicated with their related chapters.

Labels

AOL Time Warner: www.timewarner.com
Bertelsmann A. G.: www.bertelsmann.com
EMI Group: www.emigroup.com
Island Records: www.islandrecords.com
Rhino Records: www.rhino.com
Sony Music: www.sonymusic.com
Warner Music Group: www.wmg.com

Periodicals, music press

UNCUT: www.uncut.net
NME: www.nme.com
Q: www.q4music.com
Vibe: www.vibe.com
Goldmine – The Collectors Record and Compact Disc Marketplace: www.krause.com/goldmine

General

ASCAP: www.ascap.com
APRA (Australia): www.apra.com.au
IASPM: www.iaspm.net
Internet Underground Music Archive, an excellent starting point: www.iuma.com
Music Resources on the Internet: www.music.indiana.edu
Performing Arts Reading Room, Library of Congress, which has excellent music resources and links: www.loc.gov/rr/perform/
Tagg, Philip: www.tagg.org
The online library of rock and roll: www.rocksbackpages.com

All Music Guide, a very comprehensive data base, constantly updating its print equivalent. You can search by artist, album, song titles, styles, and labels: www.allmusic.com

BIBLIOGRAPHY

Abrams, M. (1959) *The Teenage Consumer*, London Press Exchange Papers No. 5.

Adorno, T. with the assistance of Simpson, G. (1941) 'On Popular Music', in Frith, S. and Goodwin, A. (eds) *On Record: Rock, Pop, and The Written Word*, New York: Pantheon Books.

—— (1991) *The Culture Industry: Selected Essays on Mass Culture* (J. Bernstein, ed.), London: Routledge.

Agger, B. (1992) *Cultural Studies as Critical Theory*, London: Falmer Press.

Aizlewood, J. (ed.) (1994) *Love is the Drug*, London: Penguin.

Amber, J. (2005) 'Dirty Dancing', *Essence*, 35, 11 (March): 163–5.

AMG (1995) *All Music Guide to Rock* (M. Erlewine, V. Bogdanov, and C. Woodstra, eds), San Francisco, CA: Miller Freeman.

Arnett, J. (1996) *Metalheads: Heavy Metal Music and Adolescent Alienation*, Boulder, CO: Westview Press.

Arnold, M. (1986 [1869]) *Culture and Anarchy*, Cambridge: Cambridge University Press.

Atton, C. (2001) '"Living in the Past?" Value Discourses in Progressive Rock Fanzines', *Popular Music*, 20, 1: 29–46.

Azerrad, M. (2001) *Our Band Could Be Your Life: Scenes from the American Indie Underground 1981–1991*, Boston, MA: Little, Brown and Company.

Bagdikian, B.H. (1997) *The Media Monopoly*, Boston, MA: Beacon Press.

Baker, S. (2002) 'Bardot, Britney, Bodies and Breasts: Pre-teen Girls' Negotiations of the Corporeal in Relation of Pop Stars and their Music', *Perfect Beat*, 6, 1: 3–17.

Bangs, L. (1990) *Psychotic Reactions and Carburretor Dung* (G. Marcus, ed.), London: Minerva.

—— (1992) 'Heavy Metal', in DeCurtis, A. and Henke, J. (eds) *The Rolling Stone Illustrated History of Rock 'n' Roll* (3rd edn), New York: Random House.

Banks, J. (1996) *Monopoly Television. MTV's Quest to Control the Music*, Boulder, CO: Westview Press.

Barfe, L. (2004) *Where Have All the Good Times Gone? The Rise and Fall of the Record Industry*, London: Atlantic Books.

Barker, C. (2002) *Making Sense of Cultural Studies: Central Problems and Critical Debates*, London: Sage Publications.

Barlow, W. (1989) *Looking Up At Down: The Emergence of Blues Culture*, Philadelphia, PA: Temple University Press.

Barnard, S. (1989) *On the Radio: Music Radio in Britain*, Milton Keynes: Open University Press.

Barnes, K. (1988) 'Top 40 Radio: A Fragment of the Imagination', in Frith, S. (ed.) *Facing the Music*, New York: Pantheon.

275

Barnes, R. (1979) *Mods*, London: Eel Pie Publishing.

Barnett, R.J. and Cavanagh, J. (1994) *Global Dreams: Imperial Corporations and the New World Order*, New York: Simon & Schuster.

Barrow, S. and Dalton, P. (1997) *Reggae: The Rough Guide* (J. Buckley, ed.), London: The Rough Guides.

Bayton, M. (1997) 'Women and the Electric Guitar', in Whiteley, S. (ed.) *Sexing the Groove: Popular Music and Gender*, London and New York: Routledge.

Beadle, J. (1993) *Will Pop Eat Itself?: Pop Music in the Soundbite Era*, London: Faber & Faber.

Beard, D. and Gloag, K. (2005) *Musicology: The Key Concepts*, New York, Routledge.

Beattie, K. (2004) *Documentary Screens: Non-Fiction Film and Television*, London: Palgrave.

—— (2005) 'It's Not Only Rock and Roll: Rockumentary, Direct Cinema, and the Documentary Mode', *Australasian Journal of American Studies*, December: 18–26.

Becker, H. (1997 [1963]) 'The Culture of a Deviant Group: The "Jazz" Musician', in Gelder, K. and Thornton, S. (eds) *The Subcultures Reader*, London and New York: Routledge.

Beebe, R., Fulbrook, D. and Saunders, B. (eds) (2002) *Rock Over the Edge: Transformations in Popular Music Culture*, Durham, NC: Duke University Press.

Beer, D. (ed.) (2005) 'Special issue; Music and the Internet', *first monday*, 10, 7.

Belk, R.W. (2001) *Collecting in a Consumer Society* (2nd edn), London: Routledge.

Bego, M. (1992) *Madonna: Blonde Ambition*, Melbourne: Bookman Press.

Bennett, A. (2000) *Popular Music and Youth Culture: Music, Identity and Place*, London: Macmillan.

Bennett, A. and Kahn-Harris, K. (eds) (2004) *After Subcultures*, London: Ashgate.

Bennett, A., Shank, B. and Toynbee, J. (eds) (2006) *The Popular Music Studies Reader*, London: Routledge.

Bennett, H.S. (1990) 'The Realities of Practice', in Frith, S. and Goodwin, A. (eds) *On Record: Rock, Pop, and the Written Word*, New York: Pantheon Books.

Bennett, T., Frith, S., Grossberg, L., Shepherd, J. and Turner, G. (1993) *Rock and Popular Music: Politics, Policies, Institutions*, London: Routledge.

Berkenstadt, J. and Cross, C.R. (1998) *Nevermind: Nirvana*, New York: Schirmer Books.

Berland, J. (1988) 'Locating Listening: Technological Space, Popular Music, Canadian Mediations', *Cultural Studies*, 2, 3: 343–58.

—— (1991) 'Free Trade and Canadian Music: Level Playing Field or Scorched Earth?', *Cultural Studies*, 5, 3: 317–25.

Bertsch, C. (1993) 'Making Sense of Seattle', *Bad Subjects*, 5 (March/ April), unpaginated.

Bishop, J. (2005) 'Building International Empires of Sound: Concentrations of Power and Property in the "Global" Music Market', *Popular Music and Society*, 28, 4: 443–72.

Bishton, D. (1986) *Black Heart Man*, London: Chatto & Windus.

Bliss, K. (1999) 'Canada: Busting Out All Over', in *Billboard*, 16 January: 50.

Bloom, A. (1987) *The Closing of the American Mind*, New York: Simon & Schuster.

Bloustien, G. (ed.) (1999) *Musical Visions*, Sydney: Wakefield Press.

Bollinger, N. (2004) 'Dread, marimba and blood', *New Zealand Listener*, 26 June.

Bordo, S. (1993) 'Material Girl: The Effacements of Modern Culture', in Schwichtenberg, C. (ed.) *The Madonna Connection: Representational Politics, Subcultural Identities, and Cultural Theory*, St Leonards, NSW: Allen & Unwin.

Bordowitz, H. (2004) *Turning Points in Rock and Roll: The Key Events That Affected Popular Music in the Latter Half of the 20th Century*, New York: Citadel Press.

Borthwick, S. and Moy, R. (2004) *Popular Music Genres: An Introduction*, Edinburgh: Edinburgh University Press.

Bourdieu, P. (1984) *Distinction: A Social Critique of the Judgement of Taste*, London: Routledge and Kegan Paul.

Bowman, R. (2003) 'Session Musicians', in Shepherd, J., Horn, D., Laing, D., Oliver, P. and Wicke, P. (eds) *The Continuum Encyclopedia of Popular Music, Volume Two: Performance and Production*, London and New York: Continuum.

Boyd, J. (2006) *White Bicycles: Making Music in the 1960s*, London: Serpent's Tail.

Boyd, T. (1994) 'Check Yo Self, Before You Wreck Yo Self: Variations on a Political Theme in Rap Music and Popular Culture', *Public Culture*, 7: 289–312.

Brackett, D. (1995) *Interpreting Popular Music*, Cambridge: Cambridge University Press.

—— (2005) *The Pop, Rock, and Soul Reader: Histories and Debates*, New York and Oxford: Oxford University Press.

Bradley, D. (1992) *Understanding Rock'n'Roll: Popular Music in Britain 1955–1964*, Buckingham: Open University Press.

Brake, M. (1985) *Comparative Youth Culture*, London: Routledge and Kegan Paul.

Brantlinger, P. (1990) *Crusoe's Footprints: Cultural Studies in Britain and America*, New York: Routledge.

Breen, M. (1991) 'A Stairway To Heaven Or A Highway To Hell?: Heavy Metal Rock Music In The 1990s', *Cultural Studies*, 5, 2 (May): 191–203.

—— (1995) 'The End of the World as We Know it: Popular Music's Cultural Mobility', *Cultural Studies*, 9, 3 (October): 486–504.

—— (1999) *Rock Dogs*, London: Pluto Press.

Brennan, M. (2006) 'This Rough Guide to Critics: Musicians Discuss the Role of the Music Press', *Popular Music*, 25, 2: 221–34.

Broughton, S., Ellingham, M., Muddyman, D. and Trillo, R. (eds) (1994) *World Music: The Rough Guide*, London: The Rough Guides.

Brown, C.T. (1994) *The Art of Rock and Roll* (3rd edn), Englewood Cliffs, NJ: Prentice Hall.

Brown, J. and Schulze, L. (1990) 'The Effects of Race, Gender and Fandom on Audiences: Interpretations of Madonna's Music Videos', *Journal of Communication*, 40, 2: 88–102.

Brown, M.E. (ed.) (1990) *Television and Women's Culture*, London: Sage.

Buckley, P. and Clark, D. (2005) *The Rough Guide to iPods, iTunes & Music Online* (updated edn), London: The Rough Guides.

Bull, M. (2000) *Sounding out the City: Personal Stereos and the Management of Everyday Life*, Oxford and New York: Berg.

Burnett, R. (1990) 'From a Whisper to a Scream: Music Video and Cultural Form', in Roe, K. and Carlsson, V. (eds) *Popular Music Research, an anthology from NORDICOM-Sweden*, Goteborg: NORDICOM, University of Goteborg.

—— (1996) *The Global Jukebox: The International Music Industry*, London: Routledge.

Burns, G. (1987) 'A Typology of Hooks in Popular Records', *Popular Music and Society*, 6, 1: 1–20.

Butler, M. (2003) 'Taking it Seriously: Intertextuality and Authenticity in Two Covers by the Pet Shop Boys', *Popular Music*, 22, 1: 1–20.

Cantin, P. (1997) *Alanis Morissette Jagged*, London: Bloomsbury.

Carnoy, G. (1990) 'Geography of Music: Inventory and Prospect', *Journal of Cultural Geography*, 10, 2: 35–48.

—— (ed.) (2003) *The Sounds of People and Places. A Geography of American Music from Country to Classical and Blues to Bop* (4th edn), Lanham, MD: Rowman & Littlefield.

Carson, M., Lewis, T. and Shaw, S.M. (2004) *Girls Rock! Fifty Years of Women Making Music*, Lexington, KY: The University Press of Kentucky.

Casey, B., Casey, N., Calver, B., French., L. and Lewis, J. (2002) *Television Studies: The Key Concepts*, London and New York: Routledge.

Cavicchi, D. (1998) *Tramps Like Us: Music and Meaning Among Springsteen Fans*, New York: Oxford University Press.

Cawelti, J. (1971) 'Notes Toward an Aesthetic of Popular Culture', *Journal of Popular Culture*, 5, 2 (Fall): 255–68.

Chambers, I. (1985) *Urban Rhythms: Pop Music and Popular Culture*, London: Macmillan.

—— (1986) *Popular Culture: The Metropolitan Experience*, London: Methuen.

Chanan, M. (1995) *Repeated Takes: A Short History of Recording and its Effects on Music*, London: Verso.

278

Chapman, R. (1992) *Selling the Sixties: The Pirates and Pop Music Radio*, London and New York: Routledge.

Chapple, S. and Garofalo, R. (1977) *Rock 'n' Roll Is Here To Pay*, Chicago, IL: Nelson-Hall.

Charlton, K. (1994) *Rock Music Styles: A History* (2nd edn), Madison, WI: Brown & Benchmark.

Chauncey, S. (1999) 'The Artists', *Canadian Musician*, 20th Anniversary Issue, 21, 2 (March/April): 48–58.

Chevigny, P. (1991) *Gigs: Jazz and the Cabaret Laws in New York City*, Routledge.

Christe, I. (2003) *Sound of the Beast: The Complete Headbanging History of Heavy Metal*, New York: HarperEntertainment.

Christenson, P.G. and Roberts, D.F. (1998) *It's Not Only Rock & Roll: Popular Music in the Lives of Adolescents*, Cresskill, NJ: Hampton Press, Inc.

Christgau, R. (1982) *Christgau's Guide: Rock Albums of the '70s*, London: Vermilion.

—— (1990) *Christgau's Record Guide: The '80s*, London: Vermilion.

—— (1998) *Grown Up All Wrong: 75 Great Rock and Pop Artists from Vaudeville to Techno*, Cambridge, MA and London: Harvard University Press.

Christianen, M. (1995) 'Cycles of Symbolic Production? A New Model to Explain Concentration, Diversity and Innovation in the Music Industry', *Popular Music*, 14, 1: 55–93.

Citron, M. (1993) *Gender and the Musical Canon*, Cambridge: Cambridge University Press.

Clarke, D. (ed.) (1990) *Penguin Encyclopedia of Popular Music*, London and New York: Penguin.

—— (1995) *The Rise and Fall of Popular Music*, London: Viking/The Penguin Group.

Clayton, M., Herbert T. and Middleton, R. (eds) (2003) *The Cultural Study of Music. A Critical Introduction*, New York and London: Routledge.

Cline, C. (1992) 'Essays from Bitch: The Women's Rock Newsletter with Bite', in Lewis, L. (ed.) *The Adoring Audience: Fan Culture and the Popular Media*, London: Routledge.

Cloonan, M. (1996) *Banned! Censorship of Popular Music in Britain: 1967–92*, Aldershot: Arena.

Cloonan, M. and Garofalo, R. (eds) (2003) *Policing Pop*, Philadelphia, PA: Temple University Press.

Cloonan, M., Williamson, J. and Firth, S. (2004) 'What is Music Worth? Some Reflections on the Scottish experience', *Popular Music*, 23, 2: 205–12.

Cohen, Sara (1991) *Rock Culture in Liverpool: Popular Music in the Making*, Oxford: Clarendon Press.

—— (1997) 'Men Making a Scene: Rock Music and the Production of Gender', in Whiteley, S. (ed.) *Sexing the Groove: Popular Music and Gender*, London and New York: Routledge.

—— (1998) 'Sounding Out the City: Music and the Sensuous Production of Place', in Leyshon, A., Matless, D. and Revill, G. (eds) *The Place of Music*, New York: The Guilford Press.

—— (1999) 'Scenes', in Horner, B. and Swiss, T. (eds) *Key Terms in Popular Music and Culture*, Oxford: Blackwell.

Cohen, Stanley (1980) *Folk Devils and Moral Panics*, Oxford: Robertson.

Cohn, N. (1970) *Awopbopaloobop Alopbamboom: Pop From the Beginning*, St Albans: Paladin, Granada.

—— (1992) 'Phil Spector', in DeCurtis, A. and Henke, J. (eds), *The Rolling Stone Illustrated History of Rock 'n' Roll* (3rd edn), New York: Random House.

Coleman, J. (1961) *The Adolescent Society*, New York: Free Press.

Cogan, J. and Clark, W. (2003) *Temples of Sound: Inside the Great Recording Studios*, San Francisco, CA: Chronicle Books.

Cook, P. (ed.) (1989) *The Film Book*, London: British Film Institute.

Cooper, B.L. (1990) *Popular Music Perspectives: Ideas, Themes, and Patterns in Contemporary Lyrics*, Bowling Green, OH: Bowling Green State University Press.

—— (1992) 'A Review Essay and Bibliography of Studies on Rock 'n' Roll Movies, 1955–1963', *Popular Music and Society*, 16, 1: 85–92.

Cope, N. (1990) 'Walkmen's Global Stride', *Business*, March: 52–9.

Covach, J. and Boone, G.M. (eds) (1997) *Understanding Rock. Essays in Musical Analysis*, New York: Oxford University Press.

Crafts, S.D., Cavicchi, D. and Keil, C. and the Music in Daily Life Project (1993) *My Music*, Hanover, NH and London: Wesleyan University Press.

Crisell, A. (1994) *Understanding Radio* (2nd edn), London and New York: Routledge.

Critcher, C. (2003) *Moral Panics and the Media*, Buckingham: Open University Press.

Cross, B. (1993) *It's Not About a Salary: Rap, Race and Resistance in Los Angeles*, New York: Verso.

Cross, C. (2005) *Room Full Of Mirrors. A Biography of Jimi Hendrix*, London: Sceptre.

Crowley, M. (2005) 'Washington Diarist', *Washington Post*, 24 August, unpaginated.

Crowthers, L. (2007) *Globalisation and American Popular Culture*, Plymouth: Rowman & Littlefield.

Cubitt, S. (1991) *Timeshift: On Video Culture*, London: Routledge.

Cunningham, M. (1996) *Good Vibrations: A History of Record Production*, Chessington: Castle Communications.

Curran, J., Morley, D. and Walkerdine, V. (eds) (1996) *Cultural Studies and Communications*, London and New York: Arnold.

Curtis, J. (1987) *Rock Eras: Interpretations of Music and Society 1954–1984*, Bowling Green, OH: Bowling Green State University Press.

Cusic, D. (1996) *Music in the Market*, Bowling Green, OH: Bowling Green State University Press.

Cyrus, C. (2003) 'Selling an Image: Girl Groups of the 1960s', *Popular Music*, 22, 2: 173–94.

Daley, M. (1997) 'Patti Smith's "Gloria": Intertextual Play in a Rock Vocal Performance', *Popular Music*, 16,3: 235–253.

Dannen, F. (1991) *Hit Men: Power Brokers and Fast Money Inside the Music Business*, New York: Vintage Books.

Davis, A. (1997) 'Spice Invaders!', *Record Collector*, 213 (May): 34–9.

Dean, E. (2001) 'Desperate Man Blues' in Guralnick, P. and Wolk, D. (eds) *Da Capo Best Music Writing 2000*, printed and published in the USA.

DeCurtis, A. (ed.) (1991) 'Rock and Roll Culture', *South Atlantic Quarterly*, Special Issue, 90, 4 (Fall).

—— (1992) 'Bruce Springsteen', in DeCurtis, A. and Henke, K. (eds) *The Rolling Stone Illustrated History of Rock and Roll* (3rd edn), New York: Random House.

DeCurtis, A. and Henke, J. (1992) *The Rolling Stone Illustrated History of Rock and Roll* (3rd edn), New York: Random House.

Denisoff, R.S. (1986) *Tarnished Gold: The Record Industry Revisited*, Edison, NJ: Transaction.

Denselow, R. (1990) *When The Music's Over: The Story of Political Pop*, London: Faber.

DeRogatis, J. (1996) *Kaleidoscope Eyes: Psychedelic Rock from the '60s to the '90s*, Secausus, NJ: Citadel Press.

Dettmar, K.J.H. (2006) *Is Rock Dead?*, New York and London: Routledge.

Dettmar, K. and Richey, W. (eds) (1999) *Reading Rock and Roll: Authenticity Appropriation, Aesthetics*, New York: Columbia University Press.

DFSP (1999) 'The Canadian Recording Industry', Presentation prepared by DFSP, Ottawa: Department of Canadian Heritage.

Dickerson, J. (1998) *Women On Top: The Quiet Revolution That's Rocking the American Music Industry*, New York: Billboard Books.

Dimery, R. (General editor) (2005) *1001 Albums You Must Hear Before You Die*, London: Quintet Publishing.

Dixon, W. with Snowden, D. (1989) *I Am The Blues: The Willie Dixon Story*, London: Quartet Books.

Doggett, P. (1997) 'Rock Books', *Record Collector*, 212 (April): 35–57.

Doherty, T. (1988) *Teenagers & Teenpics: The Juvenilization of American Movies in the 1950s*, Boston, MA: Unwin Hyman.

Donnelly, K.J. (1998) 'The Classical Film Forever: Batman, Batman Returns and Post Classical Film Music', in Neale, S. and Smith, M. (eds) *Contemporary Hollywood*, London: Routledge.

281

Dorland, M. (ed.) (1996) *The Cultural Industries in Canada: Problems, Policies and Prospects*, Toronto: James Lorimer & Company.

Doss, E. (1999) *Elvis Culture: Fans, Faith and Image*, Lawrence, KS: University Press of Kansas.

Draper, R. (1990) *Rolling Stone Magazine: The Uncensored History*, New York: Doubleday.

Duffett, M. (2003) 'False Faith or False Comparison: A Critique of the Religious Interpretation of Elvis Fan Culture', *Popular Music and Society*, 26, 4: 513–22.

Dunaway, D. (2000) 'Digital Radio Production: Towards and Aesthetic', *New Media & Society*, 2, 1: 29–50.

Dychtwald, K. (1989) *Age Wave*, Los Angeles, CA: Tarcher.

Dyer, R. (1990) 'In Defence of Disco', in Frith, S. and Goodwin, A. (eds) *On Record: Rock, Pop, and the Written Word*, New York: Pantheon Books.

Echard, W. (2005) *Neil Young and the Poetics of Energy*, Bloomington, IN: Indiana University Press.

Edgar, A. and Sedgwick, P. (eds) (1999) *Key Concepts in Cultural Theory*, London and New York: Routledge.

Ehrlich, D. (1997) *Inside the Music: Conversations with Contemporary Musicians About Spirituality, Creativity, and Consciousness*, Boston, MA and London: Shambhala.

Eisenberg, E. (1988) *The Recording Angel: Music, Records and Culture From Aristotle to Zappa*, London: Pan Books.

Eliot, M. (1989) *Rockonomics: The Money Behind the Music*, New York and Toronto: Franklin Watts.

Ennis, P.H. (1992) *The Seventh Stream: The Emergence of Rock' n' Roll in American Popular Music*, Hanover, NH and London: Wesleyan University Press.

Epstein, J.S. (ed.) (1994) *Adolescents and Their Music. If It's Too Loud, You're Too Old*, New York and London: Garland Publishing.

Escott, C. with Hawkins, M. (1991) *Good Rockin' Tonight: Sun Records and the Birth of Rock 'n' Roll*, New York: St Martins Press.

Evans, L. (1994) *Women, Sex and Rock 'n' Roll: In Their Own Words*, London: Pandora/HarperCollins.

Evans, M. (1998) 'Quality Criticism – Music Reviewing in Australian Rock Magazines', *Perfect Beat*, 3, 4 (January): 38–50.

Ewbank, A.J. and Papageorgiou, F.T. (eds) (1997) *Whose Master's Voice? The Development of Popular Music in Thirteen Cultures*, Westport, CT: Greenwood Press.

Ewen, S. (1988) *All Consuming Images: The Politics of Style in Contemporary Culture*, New York: Basic Books.

Eyerman, R. and Jamison, A. (1995) 'Social Movements and Cultural Transformation: Popular Music in the 1960s', *Media, Culture & Society*, 17, 3: 449–68.

Fabbri, F. (1999) 'Browsing Music Spaces: Categories and the Musical Mind', paper delivered at IASPM (UK) conference. Available online at: www.tagg.org/others/ffabbri9907.html

Fairchild, C. (1995) '"Alternative" Music and the Politics of Cultural Autonomy: The Case of Fugazi and the D.C. Scene', *Popular Music and Society*, 19, 1: 17–36.

Farrell, G. (1998) 'The Early Days of the Gramophone Industry in India: Historical, Social, and Musical Perspectives', in Leyshon, A., Matless, D. and Revill, G. (eds) *The Place of Music*, New York: The Guilford Press.

Feigenbaum, A. (2005) '"Some Guy Designed This Room I'm Standing In": Making Gender in Press Coverage of Ani DiFranco', *Popular Music*, 24, 1 (January): 37–56.

Fenster, M. (1995) 'Two Stories: Where Exactly is the Local?', in Straw, W., Johnson,, S., Sullivan, R. and Friedlander, P. (eds) *Popular Music – Style and Identity*, Montreal: Centre for Research on Canadian Cultural Industries and Institutions.

Finnegan, R. (1989) *The Hidden Musicians: Music-Making in an English Town*, Cambridge: Cambridge University Press.

Fiske, J. (1989) *Understanding Popular Culture*, Boston, MA: Unwin Hyman.

—— (1992) 'The Cultural Economy of Fandom', in Lewis, L. (ed.) *The Adoring Audience: Fan Culture and the Popular Media*, London: Routledge.

Flanaghan, B. (1987) *Written in my Soul: Rock's Great Songwriters Talk about Creating their Music*, Chicago, IL: Contemporary Books.

Flohel, R. (1990) 'The Canadian Music Industry: A Quick Guide', in Baskerville, D. (ed.) *Music Business Handbook and Career Guide*, New York: Sherwood.

Fonarow, W. (2006) *Empire of Dirt: The Aesthetics and Rituals of British Indie Music*, Middletown, CT: Wesleyan University Press.

Forman, M. (2002) *The Hood Comes First: Race, Space, and Place in Rap and Hip-Hop*, Middletown, CT: Wesleyan University Press.

Friedlander, P. (1996) *Rock And Roll: A Social History*, Boulder, CO: Westview Press.

Frith, S. (1978) *The Sociology of Rock*, London: Constable.

—— (1983) *Sound Effects: Youth, Leisure and the Politics of Rock 'n' Roll*, London: Constable.

—— (1987) 'Towards an Aesthetic of Popular Music', in Leppert, R. and McClary, S. (eds) *Music and Society*, Cambridge: Cambridge University Press.

—— (ed.) (1988a) *Facing the Music*, New York: Pantheon.

—— (1988b) *Music for Pleasure: Essays in the Sociology of Pop*, Cambridge: Polity Press.

—— (1988c) 'Video Pop: Picking Up The Pieces', in Frith, S. (ed.) *Facing the Music*, New York: Pantheon Books.

—— (ed.) (1989) *World Music, Politics and Social Change*, Manchester: Manchester University Press.

—— (ed.) (1993) *Music and Copyright*, Edinburgh: Edinburgh University Press.

—— (1996) *Performing Rites: On the Value of Popular Music*, Cambridge, MA: Harvard University Press.

—— (2001) 'Pop Music', in Frith, S., Straw, W. and Street, J. (eds) *The Cambridge Companion to Pop and Rock*, Cambridge: Cambridge University Press.

—— (2002) 'Look! Hear! The Uneasy Relationship of Music and Television', *Popular Music*, 21, 3: 277–90.

Frith, S. and Goodwin, A. (eds) (1990) *On Record: Rock, Pop, and The Written Word*, New York: Pantheon Books.

Frith, S. and Horne, H. (1987) *Art Into Pop*, London: Methuen.

Frith, S. and Marshall, L. (eds) (2004) *Music and Copyright* (2nd edn), Edinburgh: Edinburgh University Press.

Frith, S. and McRobbie, A. (1990 [1978]) 'Rock and Sexuality', in Frith, S. and Goodwin, A. (eds) *On Record: Rock, Pop, and the Written Word*, New York: Pantheon Books.

Frith, S. and Street, J. (1992) 'Rock Against Racism and Red Wedge', in Garofalo, R. (ed.) *Rockin' the Boat: Mass Music and Mass Movements*, Boston, MA: South End Press.

Frith, S., Straw, W. and Street, J. (eds) (2001) *The Cambridge Companion to Pop and Rock*, Cambridge: Cambridge University Press.

Gaar, G. (1992) *She's A Rebel: The History of Women in Rock and Roll*, Seattle, WA: Seal Press.

Gaines, D. (1991) *Teenage Wasteland. Suburbia's Dead End Kids*, New York: HarperCollins.

Gambaccini, P., Rice, T. and Rice, J. (1987) *British Hit Singles. Edition 6: Every Hit Single Since 1952*, Enfield: Guinness Superlatives.

Gamman, L. and Marshment, M. (1988) *The Female Gaze: Women As Viewers of Popular Culture*, London: The Women's Press.

Gammond, P. (ed.) (1991) *The Oxford Companion to Popular Music*, Oxford: Oxford University Press.

Garnham, N. (1987) 'Concepts of Culture: Public Policy and the Cultural Industries', in *Cultural Studies*, 1, 1 (January): 23–7.

Garofalo, R. (1987) 'How Autonomous is Relative: Popular Music, the Social Formation and Cultural Struggle', *Popular Music*, 6, 1 (January): 77–92.

—— (1991) 'The Internationalization of the US Music Industry and its Impact on Canada', *Cultural Studies*, 5, 3: 326–31.

—— (ed.) (1992a) *Rockin' the Boat. Mass Music and Mass Movements*, Boston, MA: South End Press.

—— (1992b) 'Understanding Mega-Events', in Garofalo, R. (ed.) *Rockin' the Boat: Mass Music and Mass Movements*, Boston, MA: South End Press.

—— (1993) 'Whose World, What Beat: The Transnational Music Industry, Identity, and Cultural Imperialism', *The World of Music*, 35, 2: 16–32.

—— (1994) 'Culture versus Commerce: The Marketing of Black Popular Music', *Public Culture*, 7: 275–87.

—— (1997) *Rockin' Out: Popular Music in the USA*, Boston, MA: Allyn & Bacon.

—— (2003) 'I Want My MP3: Who Owns Internet Music?', in Cloonan, M. and Garofalo, R. (eds) *Policing Pop*, Philadelphia, PA: Temple University Press.

Garon, P. (1975) *Blues and the Poetic Spirit*, London: Eddison.

Garratt, S. (1999) *Adventures in Wonderland: A Decade of Club Culture*, London: Headline.

Gatten, J. (1995) *Rock Music Scholarship An Interdisciplinary Bibliography*, Westport, CT: Greenwood Press.

Gay, P. du and Negus, K. (1994) 'The Changing Sites of Sound: Music Retailing and the Composition of Consumers', *Media, Culture & Society*, 16, 3: 395–413.

Gay, P. du, Hall, S., Jones, L, Mackay, H. and Negus, K. (1997) *Doing Cultural Studies: The Story of the Sony Walkman*, London and Thousand Oaks, CA: Sage, in association with The Open University Press.

Gelatt, R. (1977) *The Fabulous Phonograph, 1877–1977*, New York: Macmillan.

Gelder, K. and Thornton, S. (eds) (1997) *The Subcultures Reader*, London and New York: Routledge.

Geldof, B. (1986) *Is That It?*, London: Penguin Books.

Gendron, B. (1986) 'Theodor Adorno Meets the Cadillacs', in Modleski, T. (ed.) *Studies in Entertainment*, Bloomington, IN: Indiana University Press.

George, N. (1989) *The Death of Rhythm & Blues*, New York: Pantheon.

—— (1999) *Hip Hop America*, New York: Penguin Books.

Geyrhalter, T. (1996) 'Effeminacy, Camp and Sexual Subversion in Rock: The Cure and Suede', *Popular Music*, 15, 2: 217–24.

Gilbert, J. (1986) *A Cycle of Outrage: America's Reaction to the Juvenile Delinquent in the 1950s*, New York: Oxford University Press.

Gilbert, J. and Pearson, E. (1999) *Discographies: Dance Music, Culture and the Politics of Sound*, London and New York: Routledge.

Gilbert, P. and Taylor, S. (1991) *Fashioning The Feminine: Girls, Popular Culture and Schooling*, Sydney: Allen & Unwin.

Gillet, C. (1983) *The Sound of the City: The Rise of Rock and Roll* (rev. edn), London: Souvenir Press.

Gilmore, M. (1990) 'The Season of the Witch Hunt', in *Rolling Stone, 1990 Yearbook*, Surrey Hills, NSW: Rolling Stone Australia.

Gilroy, P. (1993) *The Black Atlantic: Modernity and Double Consciousness*, Cambridge, MA: Harvard University Press.

—— (1997) 'Diaspora, Utopia, and the Critique of Capitalism', in Gelder, K. and Thornton, S. (eds) *The Subcultures Reader*, London and New York: Routledge.

Golden, A.L. (1997) *The Spice Girls: The Uncensored Story Behind Pop's Biggest Phenomenon*, New York: Ballantine Books.

Goldstein, R. (1969) *The Poetry of Rock*, New York: Bantam Books.

Goodman, F. (1997) *The Mansion on the Hill: Dylan, Young, Geffen, Springsteen, and the Head-On Collision of Rock and Commerce*, New York: Time Books/Random House.

Goodwin, A. (1987) 'Music Video in the (Post) Modern World', *Screen*, 28, 3: 36–55.

—— (1990) 'Sample and Hold: Pop Music in the Digital Age of Reproduction', in Frith, S. and Goodwin, A. (eds) *On Record: Rock, Pop, and the Written Word*, New York: Pantheon Books.

—— (1991) 'Popular Music and Postmodern Theory', *Cultural Studies*, 5, 2 (May): 174–90.

—— (1993) *Dancing in the Distraction Factory: Music, Television and Popular Culture*, Oxford, MN: University of Minnesota Press.

—— (1998) 'Drumming and Memory: Scholarship, Technology, and Music-Making', in Swiss, T., Sloop, J. and Herman, A. (eds) *Mapping the Beat: Popular Music and Contemporary Theory*, Malden, MA and Oxford: Blackwell.

Gorman, P. (2001) *In Their Own Write: Adventures in the Music Press*, London: Sanctuary.

Gracyk, T. (1996) *Rhythm and Noise: An Aesthetics of Rock*, Durham, NC and London: Duke University Press.

—— (2001) *I Wanna Be Me: Rock Music and the Politics of Identity*, Philadelphia, PA: Temple University Press.

Grant, B. (1986) 'The Classic Hollywood Musical and the "Problem" of Rock 'n' Roll', *Journal of Popular Film and Television*, 13, 4 (Winter): 195–205.

Gratten, J.N. (1995) *Rock Music Scholarship: An Interdisciplinary Bibliography*, Westport, CT: Greenwood Press.

Gray, M. (1995) *Last Gang in Town: The Story and Myth of the Clash*, New York: Henry Golt.

Greco, A.N. (ed.) (2000) *The Media and Entertainment Industries. Readings in Mass Communications*, Boston, MA: Allyn & Bacon.

Green, L. (2001) *How Popular Musicians Learn: A Way Ahead for Music Education*, Aldershot: Ashgate.

Grenier, L. (1993) 'Policing French-Language Music on Canadian Radio', in Bennett, T., Frith, S., Grossberg, L., Shepherd, J. and Turner, G. (eds) *Rock and Popular Music*, London: Routledge.

Grossberg, L. (1992) *We Gotta Get Out of This Place: Popular Conservatism and Postmodern Culture*, New York: Routledge.

Grossberg, L., Nelson, C. and Treichler, P. (eds) (1992) *Cultural Studies*, New York and London: Routledge.

Guilbault, J. (1993) *Zouk: World Music in the West Indies*, Chicago, IL: University of Chicago Press.

Guralnick, P. (1989) *Feel Like Going Home*, London: Omnibus Press.

—— (1991) *Sweet Soul Music: Rhythm and Blues and the Southern Dream of Freedom*, London: Penguin.

Hager, B. (1998) *On Her Way: The Life and Music of Shania Twain*, New York: Berkley Boulevard Books.

Haggerty. G. (1995) *A Guide to Popular Music Reference Books: An Annotated Bibliography*, Westport, CT: Greenwood Press.

Halfacree, K. and Kitchin, R. (1996) '"Madchester Rave On": Placing the Fragments of Popular Music', *Area*, 28, 1: 47–55.

Hall, S. (1980) 'Cultural Studies: Two Paradigms', *Media, Culture & Society*, 2, 1: 57–72.

—— (1981) 'Notes on Deconstructing "the Popular"', in Samuel, R. (ed.) *People's History and Socialist Theory*, London: Routledge and Kegan Paul.

Hall, S., Critcher, C., Jefferson, T., Clarke, J. and Roberts, R. (1978) *Policing the Crisis*, London: Macmillan.

Hall, S. and Jefferson, T. (eds) (1976) *Resistance Through Rituals: Youth Subcultures in Post-War Britain*, London: Hutchinson.

Hall, S. and Whannell, P. (1964) *The Popular Arts*, London: Hutchinson.

Hamm, C. (1995) *Putting Popular Music in Its Place*, Cambridge: Cambridge University Press.

Hanke, R. (1998) '"Yo Quiero Mi MTV!": Making Music Television for Latin America', in Swiss, T., Sloop, J. and Herman, A. (eds) *Mapping the Beat: Popular Music and Contemporary Theory*, Malden, MA and Oxford: Blackwell.

Hansen, B. (1992) 'Doo-Wop', in DeCurtis, A. and Henke, J. (eds) *The Rolling Stone Illustrated History of Rock and Roll* (3rd edn), New York: Random House.

Hardy, P. and Laing, D. (eds) (1990) *The Faber Companion to Twentieth Century Popular Music*, London: Faber & Faber.

Harker, D. (1980) *One For The Money: Politics and Popular Song*, London: Hutchinson.

—— (1997) 'The Wonderful World of IFPI: Music Industry Rhetoric, the Critics and the Classical Marxist Critique', *Popular Music*, 16, 1 (January): 45–79.

Harris, J. (2004) *The Last Party: Britpop, Blair and the Demise of English Rock*, London: Harper Perennial.

Haslam, D. (2001) *Adventures on the Wheels of Steel: The Rise of the Superstar DJ*, London: Fourth Estate.

Hatch, D. and Millward, S. (1987) *From Blues to Rock: An Analytical History of Rock Music*, Manchester: Manchester University Press.

Hawkins, S. (2002) *Settling the Pop Score: Pop Texts and Identify Politics*, Aldershot: Ashgate.

Hayward, P. (ed.) (1992) *From Pop to Punk to Postmodernism: Popular Music and Australian Culture from the 1960s to the 1990s*, Sydney: Allen & Unwin.

—— (1995) 'Enterprise on the New Frontier: Music, Industry and the Internet', *Convergence*, 1, 2: 29–44.

—— (ed.) (2004) *Off The Planet: Music, Sound and Science Fiction Cinema*, London: John Libbey Perfect Beat Publications.

Hayward, P., Mitchell, T. and Shuker, R. (eds) (1994) *North Meets South: Popular Music in Aotearoa/New Zealand*, Sydney: Perfect Beat Publications.

Hayward, S. (2000) *Key Concepts in Cinema Studies*, London and New York: Routledge.

Headlam, D. (1997) 'Blues Transformation in the Music of Cream', in Covach, J. and Boone, G.M. (eds) *Understanding Rock: Essays in Musical Analysis*, New York: Oxford University Press, pp.59–89.

Hebdige, D. (1979) *Subculture: The Meaning of Style*, London: Methuen.

—— (1988) *Hiding In The Light: On Images and Things*, London: Comedia/Routledge.

——(1990) *Cut'N'Mix: Culture, Identify, and Caribbean Music*, London: Comedia/Routledge.

Henderson, L. (1993) 'Justify Our Love: Madonna and the Politics of Queer Sex', in Schwichtenberg, C. (ed.) *The Madonna Connection: Representational Politics, Subcultural Identities, and Cultural Theory*, St Leonards, NSW: Allen & Unwin.

Hendy, D. (2003) *Radio in the Global Age*, London: Polity Press.

Herbert, T. (1998) 'Victorian Brass Bands: Class, Taste, and Space', in Leyshon, A., Matless, D. and Revill, G. (eds) *The Place of Music*, New York: The Guilford Press.

Herman, E. and McChesney, R. (1997) *The Global Media: The New Missionaries of Global Capitalism*, London: Cassell.

Herman, G. (1971) *The Who*, London: November Books.

Herman, G. and Hoare, I. (1979) 'The Struggle for Song: A Reply to Leon Rosselson', in Gardner, C. (ed.) *Media, Politics and Culture*, London: Macmillan.

Hesmondhalgh, D. (1997) 'Post-Punk's Attempt to Democratise the Music Industry: the Success and Failure of Rough Trade', *Popular Music*, 16, 3 (October): 255–92.

—— (2002) *The Cultural Industries*, London: Sage.

Hesmondhalgh, D. and Negus, K. (eds) (2004) *Popular Music Studies*, London: Arnold.

Heylin, C. (ed.) (1992) *The Penguin Book of Rock and Roll Writing*, London: Penguin.

—— (1993) *From the Velvets to the Voidoids: A Pre-Punk History for a Post-Punk World*, London: Penguin.

—— (1998) *Never Mind the Bollocks, Here's the Sex Pistols: The Sex Pistols*, New York: Schirmer Books.

Hill, D. (1986) *Designer Boys and Material Girls: Manufacturing the 80's Pop Dream*, Poole: Blandford Press.

Hill, T. (1992) 'The Enemy Within: Censorship in Rock Music in the 1950s', in DeCurtis, A. (ed.) *Present Tense Rock & Roll Culture*, Durham, NC and London: Duke University Press, 39–72.

Hills, M. (2002) *Fan Cultures*, London and New York: Routledge.

Hoggart, R. (1957) *The Uses of Literacy*, London: Penguin.

Hollows, J. and Milestone, K. (1998) 'Welcome to Dreamsville: A History and Geography of Northern Soul', in Leyshon, A., Matless, D. and Revill, G. (eds) *The Place of Music*, New York: The Guilford Press.

Homan, S. (2003) *The Mayor's a Square: Live Music and Law and Order in Sydney*, Newtown, NSW: LCP.

—— (ed.) (2006) *Access All Eras: Tribute Bands and Global Pop*, Milton Keynes: Open University Press.

Hornby, N. (1995) *High Fidelity*, London: Random House.

Horner, B. and Swiss, T. (eds) (1999) *Key Terms in Popular Music and Culture*, Malden, MA: Blackwell.

Hoskyns, B. (ed.) (2003) *The Sound and the Fury: A Rock's Back Pages Reader – 40 Years of Classic Rock Journalism*, London: Bloomsbury.

Hull, G.P. (2004) *The Recording Industry* (2nd edn), New York and London: Routledge.

IFPI (1990) *World Record Sales 1969–1990: A Statistical History of the Recording Industry* (M. Hung and E.G. Morencos eds and compilers), London: International Federation of the Phonographic Industry.

—— (2006a) 'Global Digital Music Sales Triple to US $1.1 Billion in 2005 as a New Market takes Shape', 19 January, Press Release. Available http://www.ifpi.org;site-content/press/20060119.htm (accessed 18 August 2005).

—— (2006b) 'Recorded Music – Driver of a US $100 Billion Economic Sector', 22 June. Press Release. Available http: http://www.ifpi.org;site-content/press/20060622.htm (accessed 18 August 2005).

Inglis, I. (2001) '"Nothing You Can See That Isn't Shown": The Album Covers of the Beatles', *Popular Music*, 20, 1: 83–98.

Irvin, J. (ed.) (2003) *The MOJO Collection: The Ultimate Music Companion*, Edinburgh: Canongate.

James, M. (2002) *Fatboy Slim: Funk Soul Brother*, London: Sanctuary.

Jameson, F. (1984) 'Postmodernism, or the Cultural Logic of Late Capitalism', *New Left Review*, 146 (July/August): 53–93.

Jenkins, H. (1997) 'Television Fans, Poachers, Nomads', in Gelder, K. and Thornton, S. (eds) *The Subcultures Reader*, London and New York: Routledge.

Jipson, A. (1994) 'Why Athens?', *Popular Music & Society*, 18, 3: 19–31.

Johnson, B. (2000) *The Inaudible Music: Jazz, Gender and Australian Modernity*, Sydney: Currency Press.

Johnson, P. (1996) *Straight Outa Bristol: Massive Attack, Portishead, Tricky and the Roots of Hip Hop*, London: Sceptre.

Jones, A. and Kantonen, J. (1999) *Saturday Night Forever: The Story of Disco*, Edinburgh and London: Mainstream Publishing.

Jones, D. (2005) *iPod, Therefore I Am*, London: Phoenix.

Jones, Simon (1988) *Black Culture, White Youth: The Reggae Tradition from JA to UK*, London: Macmillan.

Jones, Simon and Schumacher, T. (1992) 'Muzak: On Functional Music and Power', *Critical Studies in Mass Communications*, 9: 156–69.

Jones, Steve (1992) *Rock Formation: Music, Technology, and Mass Communication*, Newbury Park, CA: Sage.

—— (2000) 'Music and the Internet', *Popular Music*, 19, 2: 217–30.

—— (ed.) (2002) *Pop Music and the Press*, Philadelphia, PA: Temple University Press.

Jones, Steve and Lenhart, A. (2004) 'Music Downloading and Listening: Finding from the Pew Internet and American Life Project', *Popular Music*, 27, 2: 221–40.

Kahn-Harris, K. (2003) 'Death Metal and the Limits of Musical Expression', in Cloonan, M. and Garofalo, R. (eds) *Policing Pop*, Philadelphia, PA: Temple University Press.

—— (2006) *Extreme Metal: Music and Culture on the Edge*, Oxford: Berg.

Kalinak, K. (1992) *Setting the Score: Music and the Classical Hollywood Film*, Madison, WI: University of Wisconsin Press.

Kaplan, E.A. (1987) *Rocking Around the Clock. Music Television, Postmodernism, and Consumer Culture*, New York: Methuen.

Kärjä, A.-V. (2006) 'A Prescribed Alternative Mainstream: Popular Music and Canon Formation', *Popular Music*, 25, 1 (January): 3–20.

Karlen, N. (1994) *Babes in Toyland: The Making and Selling of a Rock and Roll Band*, New York: Avon Books.

Kassabian, A. (1999) 'Popular', in Horner, B. and Swiss, T. (eds) *Key Terms in Popular Music and Culture*, Oxford: Blackwell.

Katz, M. (2004) *Capturing Sound: How Technology has Changed Music*, Berkeley, CA: University of California Press.

Kealy, E. (1979 [1978]) 'From Craft to Art: The Case of Sound Mixers and Popular Music', in Frith, S. and Goodwin, A. (eds) *On Record: Rock, Pop, and the Written Word*, New York: Pantheon.

Keightley, K. (2003) 'Album; Album Cover; Concept Album; Cover Version', in Shepherd, J., Horn, D., Laing, D., Oliver, P. and Wicke, P. (eds) *The Continuum Encyclopedia of Popular Music, Volume One: Media, Industry and Society*, London and New York: Continuum.

Keil, C. (1966) *Urban Blues*, Chicago, IL: University of Chicago Press.

Keil, C. and Field, S. (1994) *Music Grooves*, Chicago, IL: University of Chicago Press.

Kellner, D. (1995) *Media Culture: Cultural Studies, Identity and Politics Between the Modern and the Postmodern*, London: Routledge.

Kelly, K. and McDonnell, E. (1999) *Stars Don't Stand Still in the Sky*, London: Routledge.

Kennedy, D. (1990) 'Frankenchrist Versus the State: The New Right, Rock Music and the Case of Jello Biafra', *Journal of Popular Culture*, 24, 1: 131–48.

Kennedy, R. and McNutt, R. (1999) *Little Labels – Big Sound: Small Record Companies and the Rise of American Music*, Bloomington, IN: Indiana University Press.

Kenney, W. (1993) *Chicago Jazz: A Cultural History, 1904–1930*, New York: Oxford University Press.

Kibby, M.D. (2000) 'Home on the Page: A Virtual Place of Music Community', *Popular Music*, 19, 1 (January): 91–100.

Kiedis, A. with Sloman, L. (2004) *Scar Tissue*, London: Time Warner Books.

Kirschner, T. (1994) 'The Lalapalooziation of American Youth', *Popular Music and Society*, 18, 1: 69–89.

—— (1998) 'Studying Rock: Towards a Materialist Ethnography', in Swiss, T., Sloop, J. and Herman, A. (eds) *Mapping the Beat: Popular Music and Contemporary Theory*, Malden, MA and Oxford: Blackwell.

Klosterman, C. (2002) *Fargo Rock City: A Heavy Metal Odyssey in Rural North Dakota*, London: Simon & Schuster.

Kong, L. (1995) 'Popular Music in Singapore: Exploring Local Culture, Global Resources, and Regional Identities', *Environment and Planning D: Society and Space*, 14, 3 (June): 273–92.

Kotarba, J. (1994) 'The Postmodernization of Rock and Roll Music: The Case of Metallica', in Epstein, J. (ed.) *Adolescents and their Music*, New York and London: Garland Publishing.

Krims, A. (2000) *Rap Music and the Poetics of Identity*, Cambridge: Cambridge University Press.

Kruse, H. (1993) 'Subcultural Identity in Alternative Music Culture', *Popular Music*, 12, 1: 33–41.

Laing, D. (1985) 'Music Video: Industrial Product, Cultural Form', *Screen*, 26, 2: 78–83.

—— (1986) 'The Music Industry and the "Cultural Imperialism" Thesis', *Media, Culture & Society*, 8: 331–41.

—— (1988) 'The Grain of Punk: An Analysis of the Lyrics', in McRobbie, A. (ed.) *Zoot Suits and Second Hand Dresses: An Anthology of Fashion and Music*, Boston, MA: Unwin Hyman.

Lanza, J. (1995) *Elevator Music: A Surreal History of Muzak, Easy-Listening, and Other Moodsong*, New York: Picador.

Larkin, C. (ed.) (1993) *The Guinness Encyclopedia of Popular Music* (concise edn), London: Guinness Press.

—— (ed.) (1995) *The Guinness Who's Who of Indie New Wave* (2nd edn), London: Guinness Press.

Lawrence, T. (2003) *Love Saves the Day: A History of American Dance Music Culture, 1970–1979*, Durham, NC: Duke University Press.

LeBlanc, L. (1999) 'CANADA: They're Never Home Anymore!', *Billboard*, 16 January: 49, 58.

Lee, S. (1995) 'An Examination of Industrial Practice: The Case of Wax Trax! Records', in Straw, W., Johnson,, S., Sullivan, R. and Friedlander, P. (eds) *Popular Music – Style and Identify*, Montreal: Centre for Research on Canadian Cultural Industries and Institutions.

Lemish, D. (2003) 'Spice World: Constructing Femininity the Popular Way', *Popular Music and Society*, 26, 1: 17–29.

Lentini, P. (2003) 'Punk's Origins: Anglo-American Syncreticism', *Journal of Intercultural Studies*, 24, 2: 153–74.

Leonard, M. (1997) 'Rebel Girl, You are the Queen of My World: Feminism, "Subculture" and Grrrl Power', in Whiteley, S. (ed.) *Sexing the Groove. Popular Music and Gender*, London and New York: Routledge.

Leonard, M. and Strachan, R. (2003) 'Music Press' (pp. 38–42); 'Journalistic Practices' (pp. 253–7), entries in Shepherd, J., Horn, D., Laing, D., Oliver, P. and Wicke, P. (eds) *The Encyclopedia of Popular Music of the World, Volume 1: The Industry, Contexts and Musical Practices*, London: Cassell.

Levy, S. (2003) *Ready, Steady, Go! Swinging London and the Invention of Cool*, London and New York: Fourth Estate.

Lewis, G.H. (ed.) (1993) *All That Glitters: Country Music in America*, Bowling Green, OH: Bowling Green State University Press.

Lewis, L.A. (1990) *Gender Politics and MTV: Voicing the Difference*, Philadelphia, PA: Temple University Press.

292

—— (ed.) (1992) *The Adoring Audience: Fan Culture and the Popular Media*, London: Routledge.

Leyser, B. (1994) *Rock Stars/Pop Stars. A Comprehensive Bibliography 1955–1994*, Westport, CT: Greenwood Press.

Leyshon, A., Matless, D. and Revill, G. (eds) (1998) *The Place of Music*, New York and London: The Guilford Press.

Linbergh, U., Guomundsson, G., Michelson, M. and Weisethaunet, H. (2000) *Rock Criticism from the Beginning. Amusers, Bruisers and Cool-Headed Cruisers: The Fields of Anglo-Saxon and Nordic Rock Criticism*, Arhus: Peter Lang Publishing,

Lipsitz, G.(1994) *Dangerous Crossroads: Popular Music, Postmodernism and the Poetics of Place*, London and New York: Verso.

Longhurst, B. (1995) *Popular Music and Society*, Cambridge: Polity Press.

Lopes, P. (1992) 'Aspects of Production and Consumption in the Music Industry, 1967–1990', *American Sociological Review*, 57, 1: 46–71.

McClary, S. (1991) *Feminine Endings: Music, Gender, and Sexuality*, Minnesota, MN: University of Minnesota Press.

McClary, S. and Walser, R. (1990) 'Start Making Sense! Musicology Wrestles with Rock', in Frith, S. and Goodwin, A. (eds) *On Record: Rock, Pop, and the Written Word*, New York: Pantheon.

McCourt, T. (2005) 'Collecting Music in the Digital Realm', *Popular Music and Society*, 28, 2 (May): 249–52.

McIntyre, P. (2006) 'Paul McCartney and the Creation of "Yesterday": The Systems Model in Operation', *Popular Music*, 25, 2 (May): 201–20.

McIver, J. (2000) *Extreme Metal*, London: Omnibus Books.

McLeay, C. (1994) 'The "Dunedin Sound" – New Zealand Rock and Cultural Geography', in *Perfect Beat*, 2, 1 (July): 38–50.

—— (1998) 'The Circuit of Popular Music', unpublished Ph.D. thesis, Human Geography, School of Earth Sciences, Macquarie University.

McLeod, K. (2001) '*1/2: A Critique of Rock Criticism in North America', *Popular Music*, 20, 1: 29–46.

—— (2005) 'MP3s are Killing Home Taping: The Rise of Internet Distribution and Its Challenge to the Major Label Music Monopoly, *Popular Music and Society*, 28, 4 (October): 521–32.

McNeil, L. and McCain, G. (1996) *Please Kill Me: The Uncensored Oral History of Punk*, New York: Grove Press.

McRobbie, A. (ed.) (1988) *Zoot Suits and Second Hand Dresses: An Anthology of Fashion and Music*, Boston, MA: Unwin/Hyman.

—— (1991) *Feminism and Youth Culture: From 'Jackie' to 'Just Seventeen'*, Basingstoke: Macmillan.

293

McRobbie, A. and Garber, J. (1976) 'Girls and Subcultures: An Exploration', in Hall, S. and Jefferson, T. (eds) *Resistance Through Rituals*, London: Hutchinson/ BCCCS.

Malone, B.C. (1985) *Country Music USA*, Austin, TX: University of Texas Press.

Mann, B. (2000) *I Want My MP3! How to Download, Rip, & Play Digital Music*, New York: McGraw-Hill.

Manning, A.E. (1958) *The Bodgie: A Study in Psychological Abnormality*, Sydney: Angus & Robertson.

Marcus, G. (1991a [1977]) *Mystery Train* (4th edn), New York: Penguin.

—— (1991b) *Dead Elvis: A Chronicle of a Cultural Obsession*, New York: Penguin.

—— (1992) 'Anarchy in the UK', in DeCurtis, A. and Henke, J. (eds) *The Rolling Stone Illustrated History of Rock and Roll* (3rd edn), New York: Random House.

Marsh, D. (1983) *Before I Get Old: The Story of the Who*, New York: St Martin's Press.

—— (1989) *The Heart of Rock and Soul: The 1001 Greatest Singles Ever Made*, New York: Plume/Penguin.

—— (1992) 'The Who', in DeCurtis, A. and Henke, J. (eds) *The Rolling Stone Illustrated History of Rock 'n' Roll* (3rd edn), New York: Random House.

Marsh, D. with Swenson, J. (eds) (1984) *The Rolling Stone Record Guide*, New York: Random House/Rolling Stone Press.

Marsh, G. and Callingham, G. (eds) (2003) *Blue Note Album Cover Art: The Ultimate Collection*, San Francisco, CA: Chronicle Books.

Marshall, P.D. (1997) *Celebrity and Power: Fame in Contemporary Culture*, Minneapolis, MN: University of Minnesota Press.

Martin, L. and Seagrave, K. (1988) *Anti-Rock: The Opposition to Rock 'n' Roll*, Hamden, CT: Archon Books.

Melhuish, M. (1999) 'The Business', *Canadian Musician*, 20th anniversary issue, 21, 2 (March/April): 67–80.

Mellers, W. (1974) *Twilight of the Gods: The Beatles in Retrospect*, New York: The Viking Press.

—— (1986) *Angels of the Night: Popular Female Singers of Our Time*, Oxford: Blackwell.

Melly, G. (1970) *Revolt Into Style*, London: Penguin.

Middleton, R. (1990) *Studying Popular Music*, Milton Keynes: Open University Press.

Miklitsch, R. (2006) *Roll Over Adorno: Critical Theory, Popular Culture, Audiovisual Media*, New York: State University of New York Press.

Milano, B. (2003) *Vinyl Junkies: Adventures in Record Collecting*, New York: St Martin's Press.

Miles, B. (1997) *Paul McCartney: Many Years From Now*, London: Vintage.

Millard, A.J. (1995) *America on Record: A History of Recorded Sound*, Cambridge: Cambridge University Press.

Miller, J. (ed.) (1980) *The Rolling Stone Illustrated History of Rock 'n' Roll*, New York: Random House.

—— (1999) *Flowers in the Dustbin: The Rise of Rock and Roll, 1947–1977*, New York: Simon & Schuster.

Mitchell, T. (1996) *Popular Music and Local Identity*, London and New York: Leicester University Press.

—— (ed.) (2001) *Global Noise: Rap and Hip-Hop Outside the USA*, Middletown, CT: Wesleyan University Press.

Moore, A. (2002) 'Authenticity as Authentication', *Popular Music*, 21, 2: 225–36.

—— (1993) *Rock: The Primary Text. Developing a Musicology of Rock*, Buckingham: Open University Press.

—— (2001) *Rock: The Primary Text – Developing a Musicology of Rock* (2nd edn), Buckingham: Open University Press.

—— (ed.) (2003) *Analyzing Popular Music*, Cambridge: Cambridge University Press.

Moorefield, V. (2005) *The Producer as Composer: Shaping the Sounds of Popular Music*, Cambridge, MA: The MIT Press.

Morris, K. (1992) 'Sometimes It's Hard to be a Woman: Reinterpreting a Country Music Classic', *Popular Music and Society*, 16, 1 (Spring): 1–12.

Muesterberger, W. (1994) *Collecting: An Unruly Passion: Psychological Perspectives*, Princeton, NJ: Princeton University Press.

Muggleton, D. (2000) *Inside Subculture: The Postmodern Meaning of Style*, Oxford and New York: Berg.

Muggleton, D. and Weinzierl, R. (eds) (2003) *The Post-subcultures Reader*, Oxford and New York: Berg.

Mundy, J. (1999) *Popular Music on Screen: From the Hollywood Musical to Music Video*, Manchester: Manchester University Press.

Murray, C.S. (1989) *Crosstown Traffic: Jimi Hendrix and Post-War Pop*, London: Faber & Faber.

—— (1991) *Shots From The Hip*, London: Penguin.

Neal, M. (1999) *What the Music Said: Black Popular Music and Black Public Culture*, New York and London: Routledge.

Negus, K. (1992) *Producing Pop: Culture and Conflict in the Popular Music Industry*, London: Edward Arnold.

—— (1996) *Popular Music in Theory*, Cambridge: Polity Press.

—— (1999) *Music Genres and Corporate Cultures*, London and New York: Routledge.

Negus, K. and Pickering, M. (2004) *Creativity, Communication and Cultural Value*, London: Sage Publications.

Neill, K. and Shanahan, M.W. (eds) (2005) *The Great New Zealand Radio Experiment*, Palmerston North: Thomson/Dunmore Press.

O'Brien, K. (1995) *Hymn To Her Women Musicians Talk*, London: Virago Press.

295

O'Brien, L. (1995) *She Bop: The Definitive History of Women in Rock, Pop and Soul*, London: Penguin.

—— (2002) *She Bop II: The Definitive History of Women in Rock, Pop, and Soul*, London and New York: Continuum.

O'Connor, A. (2002) 'Local-Scenes and Dangerous Crossroads: Punk and Theories of Cultural Hybridity', *Popular Music*, 21, 2: 225–36.

O'Sullivan, T., Hartley, J., Saunders, D., Montgomery, M. and Fiske, J. (1994) *Key Concepts in Communications*, London: Methuen.

Ochs, M. (1996) *1000 Rock Covers*, Cologne: Taschen.

Oliver, P. (ed.) (1990) *Black Music in Britain*, Buckingham: Open University Press.

Olson, M.J.V. (1998) '"Everybody Loves Our Town": Scenes, Spatiality, Migrancy', in Swiss, T., Sloop, J. and Herman, A. (eds) *Mapping the Beat: Popular Music and Contemporary Theory*, Malden, MA and Oxford: Blackwell.

Palmer, T. (1970) *Born Under a Bad Sign*, London: William Kimber.

Parker, M. (1991) Reading the Charts: Making Sense of the Hit Parade', *Popular Music*, 10, 2: 205–17.

Pattison, R. (1987) *The Triumph of Vulgarity. Rock Music in the Mirror of Romanticism*, New York and Oxford: Oxford University Press.

Pearce, S.M. (1995) *On Collecting*, London: Routledge.

—— (1998) *Collecting in Contemporary Practice*, London: Sage.

Pearson, B.L. and McCulloch, B. (2003) *Robert Johnson: Lost and Found*, Urbana, IL: University of Illinois Press.

Pease, E. and Dennis, E. (eds) (1995) *Radio: The Forgotten Medium*, New Brunswick, NJ and London: Transaction Publishers.

Perry, J. (1998) *Meaty, Beaty, Big & Bouncy: The Who*, New York: Schirmer Books.

Peterson, R.A. (1990) 'Why 1955? Explaining the Advent of Rock Music', *Popular Music*, 9, 1: 97–116.

Peterson, R.A. and Berger, D.G. (1975) 'Cycles in Symbolic Production: The Case of Popular Music', *American Sociological Review*, 40; republished in Frith, S. and Goodwin, A. (eds) *On Record: Rock, Pop, and the Written Word*, New York: Pantheon.

Pinch, T.J. and Bijsterveld, K. (2003) '"Should One Applaud?" Breaches and Boundaries in the Reception of New Technology in Music', *Technology and Culture*, 44, 3: 536–59.

Plasketes, G. (1992) 'Romancing the Record: The Vinyl De-Evolution and Subcultural Evolution', *Journal of Popular Culture*, 26, 1: 109–22.

Pollock, B. (2002) *Working Musicians. Defining Moments from the Road, the Studio, and the Stage*, New York: HarperCollins.

Potter, R. (1995) *Spectacular Vernaculars: Hip-Hop and the Politics of Postmodernism*, Albany, NY: SUNY Press.

Pratt, R. (1990) *Rhythm and Resistance: Explorations in the Political Use of Popular Music*, New York: Praeger.

Prendergast, M.J. (2003) *The Ambient Century: From Mahler to Moby: The Evolution of Sound in the Electronic Age*, London: Bloomsbury.

Ramsey, G.P., Jr. (2003) *Race Music. Black Cultures from Bebop to Hip-Hop*, Berkeley, CA and London: University of California Press.

Read, O. and Welch, W.L. (1976) *From Tin Foil to Stereo: The Evolution of the Phonograph*, Indianapolis, IN: Howard Sams.

Reader, A. and Baxter, J. (1999) *Listen to This: Leading Musicians Recommend Their Favorite Recordings*, New York: Hyperion.

Redhead, S. (1990) *The End-Of-The-Century Party: Youth and Pop Towards 2000*, Manchester: Manchester University Press.

—— (1997) *Subculture to Club cultures: An Introduction to Popular Cultural Studies*, Oxford: Blackwell.

Reich, C. (1967) *The Greening of America*, New York: Penguin.

Regev, M. (1994) 'Producing Artistic Value: The Case of Rock Music', *Sociological Quarterly*, 35: 85–102.

—— (2004) 'The "Pop-rockization" of Popular Music', in Hesmondhalgh, D. and Negus, K. (eds) *Popular Music Studies*, London: Arnold.

—— (2006) 'Introduction', *Popular Music*, 25, 1: 1–2.

Rex, I. (1992) 'Kylie: The Making of a Star', in Hayward, P. (ed.) *From Pop to Punk to Postmodernism: Popular Music and Australian Culture from the 1960s to the 1990s*, Sydney: Allen & Unwin.

Reynolds, S. (1990) 'Return of the Inkies', *New Statesman and Society*, August: 26–7.

—— (1998) *Energy Flash*, London: Picador.

Reynolds, S. and Press, J. (1995) *The Sex Revolts, Gender, Rebellion and Rock 'n' Roll*, London: Serpents Tail.

Ribowtsky, M. (1989) *He's A Rebel*, New York: E. P. Dutton.

Riesman, D. (1950) 'Listening to Popular Music', *American Quarterly*, 2; republished in Frith, S. and Goodwin, A. (eds) *On Record: Rock, Pop, and the Written Word*, New York: Pantheon Books.

Rijven, S. and Straw, W. (1989) 'Rock for Ethiopia (1985)', in Frith, S. (ed.) *World Music, Politics and Social Change*, Manchester: Manchester University Press.

Rimmer, D. (1985) *Like Punk Never Happened: Culture Club and the New Pop*, London: Faber.

Riordan, J. (1991) *Making It In The New Music Business*, Cincinnati, OH: Writer's Digest Books.

Roach, C. (1997) 'Cultural Imperialism and Resistance in Media Theory and Literary Theory', *Media, Culture & and Society*, 19: 47–66.

Roberts, R. (1996) *Ladies First: Women in Music Videos*, Jackson, MI: University of Mississippi.

Robinson, D., Buck, E., Cuthbert, M. *et al.* (1991) *Music at the Margins: Popular Music and Global Diversity*, Newbury Park, CA: Sage.

Rogers, D. (1982) *Rock 'n' Roll*, London: Routledge and Kegan Paul.

Romanowski, W.D. and Denisoff, R.S. (1987) 'Money for Nothin' and the Charts for Free: Rock and the Movies', *Journal of Popular Culture*, 21, 3 (Winter): 63–78.

Romney, J. and Wootton, A. (1995) *Celluloid Jukebox: Popular Music and the Movies Since the 50s*, London: British Film Institute.

Rose, Tricia (1994) *Black Noise*, Hanover, NH: Wesleyan University Press.

Ross, A. and Rose, T. (eds) (1995) *Microphone Fiends*, London and New York: Routledge.

Ross, K. and Nightingale, V. (2003) *Media and Audiences*, Buckingham: Open University Press.

Ross, P. (2005) 'Cycles in Symbolic Production Research: Foundations, Applications, and Future Directions', *Popular Music and Society*, 28, 4: 473–88.

Rosselson, L. (1979) 'Pop Music: Mobiliser or Opiate?', in Gardner, C. (ed.) *Media, Politics and Culture*, London: Macmillan.

Rothenbuhler, E. (2006 [1985]) 'Commercial Radio as Communication', in Bennett, A., Shank, B. and Toynbee, J. (eds) *The Popular Music Studies Reader*, London and New York: Routledge.

Rothenbuhler, E. and Dimmick, J. (1982) 'Popular Music: Concentration and Diversity in the Industry, 1974–1980', *Journal of Communications*, 32 (Winter): 143–9.

Rubey, D. (1991) 'Voguing at the Carnival: Desire and Pleasure on MTV', *South Atlantic Quarterly*, 90, 4: 871–906.

Rutten, P. (1991) 'Local Popular Music on the National and International Markets', *Cultural Studies*, 5, 3 (October): 294–305.

Ryan, B. (1992) *Making Capital from Culture: The Corporate Form of Capitalist Production*, Berlin and New York: Walter de Gruyter.

Sabin, R. (ed.) (1999) *Punk Rock: So What? The Cultural Legacy of Punk*, London and New York: Routledge.

Samuels, S. (1983) *Midnight Movies*, New York: Collier/Macmillan.

Sanjek, R. (1988) *American Popular Music and Its Business. The First Four Hundred Years. Volume III: From 1900 to 1984*, New York: Oxford University Press.

Santelli, R. (1993) *The Big Book of the Blues: A Biographical Encyclopedia*, New York: Penguin.

—— (1999) 'The Rock and Roll Hall of Fame and Museum: Myth, Memory, and History', in Kelly, K. and McDonnell, E. (eds) *Stars Don't Stand Still in the Sky*, New York: New York University Press.

Sardiello, R. (1994) 'Secular Rituals in Popular Culture: A Case for Grateful Dead Concerts and Dead Head Identity', in Epstein, J.S. (ed.) *Adolescents and Their Music: If It's Too Loud, You're Too Old*, New York and London: Garland Publishing.

Savage, J. (1988) 'The Enemy Within: Sex, Rock and Identity', in Frith, S. (ed.) *Facing the Music*, New York: Pantheon Books.

—— (1991) *England's Dreaming: Sex Pistols and Punk Rock*, London: Faber & Faber.

Schiller, D. (1999) *Digital Capitalism: Networking the Global Market System*, Cambridge, MA: MIT Press.

Schilt, K. (2003) '"A Little Too Ironic": The Appropriation and Packaging of Riot Grrrl Politics by Mainstream Female Musicians', *Popular Music*, 26, 1: 5–16.

Schloss, J.G. (2004) *Making Beats: The Art of Sample-Based Hip-Hop*, Middletown, CT: Wesleyan University Press.

Schroeder, P.R. (2004) *Robert Johnson, Mythmaking, and Contemporary American Culture*, Urbana, IL: University of Illinois Press.

Schwichtenberg, C. (ed.) (1993) *The Madonna Connection. Representational Politics, Subcultural Identities, and Cultural Theory*, St Leonards, NSW: Allen & Unwin.

Sernoe, J. (1998) '"Here You Come Again": Country Music's Performance on the Pop Singles Charts from 1955 to 1966', *Popular Music and Society*, 22, 1 (Spring): 17–40.

Shank, B. (1994) *Dissonant Identities: The Rock 'n' Roll Scene in Austin, Texas*, Hanover, NH: Wesleyan University Press.

Shapiro, B. (1991) *Rock and Roll Review: A Guide to Good Rock on CD*, Kansas City, MO: Andrews and McMeel.

Shapiro, H. (1992) *Eric Clapton: Lost In The Blues*, London: Guinness Publishing.

Shaw, G. (1992) 'Brill Building Pop', in DeCurtis, A. and Henke, J. (eds) *The Rolling Stone Illustrated History of Rock and Roll* (3rd edn), New York: Random House.

Shepherd, J. (1991) *Music as Social Text*, Cambridge: Polity Press.

Shepherd, J., Horn, D., Laing, D., Oliver, P. and Wicke, P. (eds) (2003) *The Continuum Encyclopedia of Popular Music, Volume One: Media, Industry and Society*, London and New York: Continuum.

—— (eds) (2003) *The Continuum Encyclopedia of Popular Music, Volume Two: Performance and Production*, London and New York: Continuum.

Shepherd, J., Horn, D., Laing, D., Oliver, P., Wicke, P., Tagg, P. and Wilson, J. (eds) (1997) *Popular Music Studies: A Select International Bibliography*, London: Mansell.

Shepherd, J., Virden, P., Vulliamy, G. and Wishart, T. (1977) *Whose Music?*, London: Latimer.

Shevory, T. (1995) 'Bleached Resistance: The Politics of Grunge', *Popular Music and Society*, 19, 2: 23–48.

Shore, M. (1985) *The Rolling Stone Book of Rock Video*, London: Sidgwick & Jackson.

Shuker, R. (1994) *Understanding Popular Music*, London and New York: Routledge.

—— (2001) *Understanding Popular Music* (2nd edn), London and New York: Routledge.

—— (2003/4) 'New Zealand Popular Music and Cultural Identity', *British Review of New Zealand Studies*, 14: 105–18.

—— (2004) 'Beyond the "High Fidelity" Stereotype: Defining the (Contemporary) Record Collector', *Popular Music*, 23, 3: 311–30.

—— (2005) *Popular Music. The Key Concepts* (2nd edn), London and New York: Routledge.

Shuker, R. and Openshaw, R. with Soler, J. (1991) *Youth, Media and Moral Panic in New Zealand*, Delta Monograph, Palmerston North: Department of Education, Massey University.

Shuker, R. and Pickering, M. (1994) 'We Want the Airwaves: The NZ Music Quota Debate', in Hayward, P., Mitchell, T. and Shuker, R. (eds) *North Meets South: Popular Music in Aotearoa/New Zealand*, Sydney: Perfect Beat Publications.

Shute, G. (2005) *Making Music in New Zealand*, Auckland: Random House.

Sinclair, D. (1992) *Rock on CD: The Essential Guide*, London: Kyle Cathie.

Sluka, J. (1991) 'Censorship and the Politics of Rock', unpublished paper, Department of Social Anthropology, Massey University, Palmerston North, New Zealand.

Small, C. (1987) 'Performance as Ritual', in White, A. (ed.) *Lost in Music: Culture, Style and the Musical Event*, London: Routledge.

—— (1994 [1987]) *Music of the Common Tongue*, London: Calder.

Smith, G. (1995) *Lost in Music*, London: Picador.

Smith, L. (2003) 'Christina Aguilera – Can't Hold Us Down', *The F Word: Contemporary UK Feminism*. At www.thefword.org.uk/review/.

Smith, P. (2001) *Cultural Theory: An Introduction*, Oxford: Blackwell.

Smithies, G. (2004) 'Staying true to their roots', *Sunday Star Times: Supplement*, 8 June: 26.

Stahl, G. (2003) 'Tastefully Renovating Subcultural Theory: Making Space for a New Model', in Muggleton, D. and Weinzierl, R. (eds) *The Post-subcultures Reader*, Oxford and New York: Berg.

—— (2004) '"It's Like Canada Reduced": Setting the Scene in Montreal', in Bennett, A. and Kahn-Harris, K. (eds) *After Subcultures*, London: Ashgate.

Stahl, M. (2002) 'Authentic Boy Bands on TV? Performers and Impresarios in The Monkees and Making the Band', *Popular Music*, 21, 3: 307–29.

Stambler, I. (1989) *The Encyclopedia of Pop, Rock and Soul* (revised edn), London: Macmillan.

Stanford, C. (1996) *Kurt Cobain*, New York: Random House.

Starr, L. and Waterman, C. (2003) *American Popular Music*, New York and Oxford: Oxford University Press.

Steffen, D. (2005) *From Edison to Marconi. The First Thirty Years of Recorded Music*, Jefferson, NC: McFarland.

Stephens, M.A. (1998) 'Babylon's "Natural Mystic": The North American Music Industry, the Legend of Bob Marley, and the Incorporation of Transnationalism', *Cultural Studies*, 12, 2 (April): 139–67.

Stevenson, N. (2002) *Understanding Media Cultures: Social Theory and Mass Communication* (2nd edn), London: Sage Publications.

Steward, S. and Garratt, S. (1984) *Signed, Sealed, and Delivered: True Life Stories of Women in Pop*, Boston, MA: South End Press.

Stock, M. (2004) *The Hit Factory:The Stock Aitken Waterman Story*, London: New Holland Publishers.

Stockbridge, S.(1992) 'From Bandstand and Six O'clock Rock to MTV and Rage: Rock Music on Australian Television', in Hayward, P. (ed.) *From Pop to Punk to Postmodernism: Popular Music and Australian Culture from the 1960s to the 1990s*, Sydney: Allen & Unwin.

Stokes, M. (ed.) (1994) *Ethnicity, Identity and Music: The Musical Construction of Place*, Oxford: Berg.

Stratton, J. (1982) 'Between Two Worlds: Art and Commercialism in the Record Industry', *Sociological Review*, 30, 2: 267–85.

—— (1983) 'What is Popular Music?', in *Sociological Review*, 31, 2: 293–309.

Strausbaugh, J. (2001) *Rock Til You Drop: The Decline from Rebellion to Nostalgia*, New York: Verso.

Straw, W. (1990) 'Characterizing Rock Music Culture: The Case of Heavy Metal', in Frith, S. and Goodwin, A. (eds) *On Record: Rock, Pop, and the Written Word*, New York: Pantheon Books.

—— (1992) 'Systems of Articulation, Logics of Change: Communities and Scenes in Popular Music', in Nelson, C., Grossberg, L. and Treichler, P. (eds) *Cultural Studies*, London and New York: Routledge.

—— (1993) 'The English-Canadian Recording Industry since 1970', in Bennett, T., Frith, S., Grossberg, L., Shepherd, J. and Turner, G. (eds) *Rock and Popular Music: Politics, Policies, Institutions*, London: Routledge.

—— (1996) 'Sound Recording', in Dorland, M. (ed.), *The Cultural Industries in Canada: Problems, Policies and Prospects*, Toronto: Lorimer.

—— (1997) 'Sizing Up Record Collections: Gender and Connoisseurship in Rock Music Culture', in Whiteley, S. (ed.) *Sexing the Groove: Popular Music and Gender*, London: Routledge.

—— (1999) 'Authorship', in Horner, B. and Swiss, T. (eds) *Key Terms in Popular Music and Culture*, Oxford: Blackwell.

—— (2001) 'Dance Music', in Frith, S., Straw, W. and Street, J. (eds) *The Cambridge Companion to Pop and Rock*, Cambridge: Cambridge University Press.

Straw, W., Johnson, S., Sullivan, R. and Friedlander, P. (eds) (1995) *Popular Music: Style and Identity*, Montreal: The Centre for Research on Canadian Cultural Industries and Institutions.

Street , J. (1986) *Rebel Rock: The Politics of Popular Music*, Oxford: Blackwell.

—— (1997) *Politics and Popular Culture*, Cambridge: Polity Press.

Strong, M.C. (1998) *The Wee Rock Discography*, Edinburgh: Canongate.

Swingewood, A. (1977) *The Myth of Mass Culture*, London: Macmillan.

Swiss, T., Herman, A. and Sloop, J.M. (1998) *Mapping the Beat: Popular Music and Contemporary Theory*, Malden, MA and Oxford: Blackwell Publishers.

Szatmary, D.P. (1991) *Rockin' in Time: A Social History of Rock and Roll* (2nd edn), Upper Saddle River, NJ: Prentice Hall.

Tagg, P. (1982) 'Analysing Popular Music', *Popular Music*, 2: 37–67.

—— (1994) 'From Refrain to Rave', *Popular Music*, 14, 3: 209–22.

Tagg, P. and Clarida, B. (2003) *Ten Little Title Tunes: Towards a Musicology of the Mass Media*, New York and Montreal: The Mass Media Musicologists' Press.

Takasugi, F. (2003) 'The Development of Underground Musicians in a Honolulu Scene, 1995–1997', *Popular Music*, 26, 1: 73–94.

Task Force on the Future of the Canadian Music Industry (1996) *A Time for Action: Report of the Task Force on the Future of the Canadian Music Industry*, Ottawa: Department of Heritage, March.

Taylor, P. (1985) *Popular Music Since 1955: A Critical Guide to the Literature*, London: G.K. Hall.

Taylor, T. (2001) *Strange Sounds: Music, Technology and Culture*, New York: Routledge.

Théberge, P. (1991) '"Musicians" Magazines in the 1980s: The Creation of a Community and a Consumer Market', *Cultural Studies*, 5, 3: 270–93.

—— (1993) 'Technology, Economy and Copyright Reform in Canada', in Frith, S. (ed.) *Music and Copyright*, Edinburgh: Edinburgh University Press.

—— (1997) *Any Sound You Can Imagine: Making Music/Consuming Technology*, Hanover, NH: Wesleyan University Press.

—— (1999) 'Technology', in Horner, B. and Swiss, T. (eds) *Key Terms in Popular Music and Culture*, Oxford: Blackwell.

Thomas, B. (1991) *The Big Wheel*, London: Penguin.

Thornton, S. (1994) 'Moral Panic, the Media and British Rave Culture', in Ross, A. and Rose, T. (eds) *Microphone Fiends*, London and New York: Routledge.

—— (1995) *Club Cultures: Music, Media and Subcultural Capital*, London: Polity Press.

Toop, D. (1991) *Rap Attack 2*, London: Serpent's Tail.

Tosches, N. (1984) *Unsung Heroes of Rock 'n' Roll*, New York: Scribners.

Treagus, M. (1999) 'Gazing at the Spice Girls: Audience, Power and Visual Representation', in Bloustien, G. (ed.) *Musical Visions*, Sydney: Wakefield Press.

Trondman, M. (1990) 'Rock Taste – on Rock as Symbolic Capital: A Study of Young People's Tastes and Music Making', in Roe, K. and Carlsson, V. (eds) *Popular Music Research, an anthology from NORDICOM-Sweden*, Goteborg: NORDICOM, University of Goteborg.

Tsitsos, W. (1999) 'Rules of Rebellion: Slamdancing, Moshing, and the American Alternative Scene', in *Popular Music*, 18, 8: 397–414.

Tunstall, J. (1977) *The Media are American*, London: Constable.

Turner, G. (1992) 'Australian Popular Music and its Contexts', in Hayward, P. (ed.) *From Pop to Punk to Postmodernism: Popular Music and Australian Culture from the 1960s to the 1990s*, Sydney: Allen & Unwin.

—— (1994) *British Cultural Studies: An Introduction* (revised edn), Boston, MA: Unwin Hyman.

Toynbee, J. (2000) *Making Popular Music: Musicians, Creativity and Institutions*, London: Arnold.

Vermorel, F. and Vermorel, J. (1985) *Starlust. The Secret Fantasies of Fans*, London: W.H. Allen.

Vernallis, C. (2004) *Experiencing Music Video: Aesthetics and Cultural Context*, Columbia, OH: Columbia University Press.

The Virgin Encyclopedia of Rock (1993), London: Virgin Press.

Vogel, H.L. (1994) *Entertainment Industry Economics: A Guide to Financial Analysis* (3rd edn), New York: Cambridge University Press.

Von Appen, R. and Doehring, A. (2006) 'Nevermind The Beatles, Here's Exile 61 and Nico: "The Top 100 Records of all Time" – A Canon of Pop and Rock Albums from a Sociological and an Aesthetic Perspective', *Popular Music*, 25, 1 (January): 21–40.

Waksman, S. (1996) *Instrument of Desire: The Electric Guitar and the Shaping of Musical Experience*, Cambridge, MA: Harvard University Press.

—— (2003) 'Reading the Instrument: An Introduction', *Popular Music and Society*, 26, 1 (October): Special Issue: 'Reading the Instrument'.

Wall, T. (2003) *Studying Popular Music Culture: Studying the Media*, London: Arnold.

—— (2006) 'Out on the Floor: The Politics of Dancing on the Northern Soul Scene', *Popular Music*, 25, 3 (October): 431–46.

Wallis, R. and Malm, K. (1984) *Big Sounds from Small Countries*, London: Constable.

—— (eds) (1992) *Media Policy and Music Activity*, London: Routledge.

Walser, R. (1993) *Running With the Devil, Power, Gender and Madness in Heavy Metal Music*, Middletown, CT: Wesleyan University Press.

Ward, E., Stokes, G. and Tucker, K. (1986) *Rock of Ages: The Rolling Stone History of Rock and Roll*, New York: Rolling Stone Press/Summit Books.

Warner, T. (2003) *Pop Music – Technology and Creativity: Trevor Horn and the Digital Revolution*, Aldershot: Ashgate.

Weinstein, D. (1991) *Heavy Metal: A Cultural Sociology*, New York: Lexington.

—— (2000) *Heavy Metal: The Music and its Culture*, Boulder, CO: Da Capo Press.

—— (2004) 'Creativity and Band Dynamics', in Weisbard, E., *This Is Pop: In Search of the Elusive at Experience Music Project*, Cambridge, MA: Harvard University Press.

Weisbard, E. (2004) *This Is Pop: In Search of the Elusive at Experience Music Project*, Cambridge, MA: Harvard University Press.

Weisbard, E. with Marks, C. (1995) *SPIN Alternative Record Guide*, New York: Vintage/ Random House.

Weissman, D. (2005) *Blues: The Basics*, New York and London: Routledge.

Welsh, R. (1990) 'Rock 'n' Roll and Social Change', *History Today* (February): 32–9.

Wertham, F. (1955) *Seduction of the Innocent*, London: Museum Press.

Whitburn, J. (1988) *Billboard: Top 1000 Singles 1955–1987*, Milwaukee, WI: Hal Leonard Books.

Whitcomb, I. (1972) *After the Ball*, Harmondsworth: Penguin.

White, A. (ed.) (1987) *Lost in Music: Culture Style and the Musical Event*, London: Routledge and Kegan Paul.

White, T. (1989) *Catch A Fire: The Life of Bob Marley* (revised edn), New York: Holt, Rinehart & Winston.

Whiteley, S. (1992) *The Space Between the Notes: Rock and the Counter-Culture*, London: Routledge.

—— (ed.) (1997) *Sexing the Groove: Popular Music and Gender*, London and New York: Routledge.

—— (2000) *Women and Popular Music: Sexuality, Identify ad Subjectivity*, London: Routledge.

—— (2005) *Too Much Too Young: Popular Music, Age and Gender*, London and New York: Routledge.

Whiteley, S., Bennett, A. and Hawkins, S. (eds) (2004) *Music, Space and Place. Popular Music and Cultural Identity*, Aldershot: Ashgate.

Wicke, P. (2003) 'Musicians', in Shepherd, J., Horn, D., Laing, D., Oliver, P. and Wicke, P. (eds) *The Continuum Encyclopedia of Popular Music, Volume Two: Performance and Production*, London and New York: Continuum.

Widgery, D. (1986) *Beating Time: Riot 'n' Race 'n' Rock 'n' Roll*, London: Chatto & Windus.

Wiener, J. (1984) *Come Together: John Lennon in his Time*, New York: Random House.

Williams, R. (1981) *Culture*, London: Fontana.

—— (1983) *Keywords*, London: Fontana.

Willis, E. (1981) *Beginning to See the Light: Pieces of a Decade*, New York: Knopf.

Willis, P. (1978) *Profane Culture*, London: Routledge.

Willis, P., Jones, S., Canaan, J. and Hurd, G. (1990) *Common Culture: Symbolic Work at Play in the Everyday Cultures of the Young*, Milton Keynes: Open University Press.

Winfield, B.H. and Davidson, S. (eds) (1999) *Bleep! Censoring Rock and Rap Music*, Westport, CT: Greenwood Press.

Wynette, T. with Drew, J. (1980) *Stand By Your Man: An Autobiography*, London: Hutchinson.

York, N. (ed.) (1991) *The Rock File: Making it in the Music Business*, Oxford: Oxford University Press.

Zak III, A.J. (2001) *The Poetics of Rock: Cutting Tracks, Making Records*, Berkeley, CA: University of California Press.

Zappa, F. with Occhiogrosso, P. (1990) *The Real Frank Zappa Book*, London: Pan Books.

Zemke-White, K. (2000) 'Rap Music in Aotearoa: A Sociological and Musicological Analysis', PhD thesis, University of Auckland, New Zealand.

Zollo, P. (1997) *Songwriters on Songwriting*, New York: Da Capo Press.

Index

307

Related titles from Routledge

Introduction to the Theories of Popular Culture
Second Edition
Dominic Strinati

Praise for the first edition:

> 'An excellent introduction to popular culture. Complex theories are presented in a clear and concise manner'
>
> Stephen Dawkins, *Park Lane College*

An Introduction to Theories of Popular Culture is a clear and comprehensive guide to the major theories of popular culture. Dominic Strinati provides a critical assessment of the ways in which these theories have tried to understand and evaluate popular culture in modern societies.

Among the theories and ideas the book introduces are mass culture, the Frankfurt School and the culture industry, semiology and structuralism, Marxism, feminism, postmodernism and cultural populism. Strinati explains how theorists such as Adorno, Barthes, Althusser and Hebdige have grappled with the many forms of popular culture, from jazz to the Americanization of British popular culture, from Hollywood cinema to popular television series, and from teen magazines to the spy novel. Each chapter includes a guide to key texts for further reading and there is also a comprehensive bibliography. This new edition has been fully revised and updated.

ISBN 13: 978-0-415-23499-3 (hbk)
ISBN 13: 978-0-415-23500-6 (pbk)

Available at all good bookshops
For ordering and further information please visit:
www.routledge.com

Related titles from Routledge

Framing Celebrity
Su Holmes and Sean Redmond

> 'This important new book stakes out the breadth of current work on the attractions and obsessions of celebrity culture. Fame, power, adoration, idolization, gossip, madness, and death are all here. *Framing Celebrity* poses significant questions about the mediation of public identities and the popular figures who undeniably exert such influence in our lives.'
>
> Dr Paul McDonald, Reader in Film Studies & Director of the Centre for Research in Film and Audiovisual Cultures, *Roehampton University*

Celebrity culture has a pervasive presence in our everyday lives – perhaps more so than ever before. It shapes not simply the production and consumption of media content but also the social values through which we experience the world. This collection analyses this phenomenon, bringing together essays which explore celebrity across a range of media, cultural and political contexts.

The authors investigate topics such as the intimacy of fame, political celebrity, stardom in American 'quality' television (Sarah Jessica Parker), celebrity 'reality' TV (*I'm a Celebrity ... Get Me Out of Here!*), the circulation of the porn star, the gallery film (*David*/David Beckham), the concept of cartoon celebrity (*The Simpsons*), fandom and celebrity (k.d. lang, *NSYNC), celebrity in the tabloid press, celebrity magazines (*heat*, *Celebrity Skins*), the fame of the serial killer and narratives of mental illness in celebrity culture.

The collection is organized into four themed sections:

- Fame Now broadly examines the contemporary contours of fame as they course through new media sites (such as 'reality' TV and the internet) and different social, cultural and political spaces.
- Fame Body attempts to situate the star or celebrity body at the centre of the production, circulation and consumption of contemporary fame.
- Fame Simulation considers the increasingly strained relationship between celebrity and artifice and 'authenticity'.
- Fame Damage looks at the way the representation of fame is bound up with auto-destructive tendencies or dissolution.

ISBN 13: 978-0-415-37709-6 (hbk)
ISBN 13: 978-0-415-37710-2 (pbk)

Available at all good bookshops
For ordering and further information please visit:
www.routledge.com